High School Journalism

High School Journalism

by
Homer L. Hall

THE ROSEN PUBLISHING GROUP, INC.
NEW YORK

*I dedicate this revision to my wife (Lea Ann), my two daughters (Lynlea and Ashley)
and my four grandchildren (Briana Hall Keightley, Ashlyn Keightley, Evanne Louise Dill,
and Watson Malone Dill).*

Acknowledgments

Without the cooperation of my wife, Lea Ann, and my daughters, Lynlea and
Ashley, this book would not have been possible. My family often took second
place while the research was being done.

Special thanks to the following students or former students of journalism at
Kirkwood High School, who also contributed immeasurably to the book: Ashley
Hall, Sharon Karohl, David Keiser, Diane Mittler, and Betsy Perabo.

Published in 1985, 1993, 1998, 2003 by The Rosen Publishing Group, Inc.
29 East 21st Street, New York, NY 10010

Copyright 1985, 1993, 1998, 2003 by Homer L. Hall

Revised Edition, 2003

Library of Congress Cataloging in Publication Data

Hall, Homer L.
    High school journalism.

    Summary: Includes a brief history of American
journalism and discusses the duties of a journalist,
styles of writing, the parts of a newspaper,
newspaper and yearbook design, photography, and careers
in journalism.
    Includes index.
    1. Journalism, High School–United States.
[1. Journalism] I. Title.
LB3621.5.H35 1985 373.18′97′0973 85-1899
ISBN 0-8239-3926-X

Book design by Olga M. Vega

Manufactured in the United States of America

Table of Contents

TABLE OF CONTENTS

About the Author

Homer L. Hall, former yearbook and newspaper sponsor at Kirkwood High School, Kirkwood, Missouri, taught journalism classes at the secondary level for thirty-six years. He retired in 1999 and moved to Tennessee to enjoy his four grandchildren. His publications at Kirkwood consistently won high awards from the Columbia Scholastic Press Association, the National Scholastic Press Association, and Quill and Scroll. The yearbook, *Pioneer*, and the newspaper, *The Kirkwood Call*, were cited as Pacemaker publications by NSPA. Both publications were charter members of NSPA's Hall of Fame. The CSPA presented its Trendsetter and Gold Crown Awards to the *Pioneer* and the *Call,* and the *Call* received Quill and Scroll's George H. Gallup Award all twenty-three years in which Hall advised the publication.

Growing up on a farm near Avilla, MO, Hall spent his early school years in a one-room schoolhouse. He attended high school at Carthage and won a curator's scholarship to the University of Missouri. There he earned a BS degree in education, and he later received an MS from the University of Kansas.

His interest in journalism was furthered by two years in military service during which he served as public information officer and editor of the *Hercules Herald* for the 1st Missile Battalion, 62nd Artillery, while he was a lieutenant at Scott Air Force Base, Illinois. In 1965 he was awarded a fellowship by the *Wall Street Journal* to attend a Newspaper Fund Seminar at the University of Minnesota. For two years (1966-67) he received $150 awards from the Newspaper Fund for his work as a junior high journalism teacher. In 1968 he was named one of the Distinguished Advisers by the Newspaper Fund and received a $500 award, the highest ever given a junior high teacher. That same year Richards Rosen Press published his textbook *Junior High Journalism*. He again received recognition from the Fund when in 1981 he was named a Distinguished Adviser and in 1982, National Journalism Teacher of the Year. In 1991 he received the Carl Towley Award, the highest award

JEA gives to journalism teachers for their contributions to scholastic journalism.

Hall is a former member of the editorial board of *Communication: Journalism Education Today*, a publication of the Journalism Education Association. He has frequently served as contributing editor to that publication. He has held offices in the Missouri Journalism Education Association and the Sponsors of School Publications of Greater St. Louis, and he has served as JEA state director. He has also served on and chaired local, state, and national journalism committees. He served six years as JEA's secretary, and he served two years as chairman of JEA's Certification Commission. In 1993 he was elected vice-president of JEA, and in 1995 JEA named him the first national yearbook adviser of the year. In 1996 he was elected president of JEA, and in 1998 he was reelected to that position.

He is a frequent speaker at journalism workshops and conventions around the country, having spoken in thirty-three states. He has served as coordinator for the Ball State Yearbook and Newspaper Summer Workshops. In 1982 he wrote *Yearbook Guidebook* for NSPA.

In 1973 he was named Missouri Journalism Teacher of the Year, and in 1979, Missouri Teacher of the Year. He has also received the Gold Key from CSPA, the Pioneer Award from NSPA, the Medal of Merit from JEA, and the Horace Mann Award from the Missouri-National Education Association.

In 1992 the Oklahoma Interscholastic Press Association inducted him into the Scholastic Journalism Hall of Fame, and in 1993 the Ball State Journalism Department presented him with its Scholastic Journalism Award. He was also inducted into the Missouri Interscholastic Press Association's Hall of Fame in 1997. JEA presented him with a Lifetime Achievement Award in 1999.

In 2000 the Southern Interscholastic Press Association and the Michigan Interscholastic Press Association presented Hall with their Distinguished Service Awards. In 2002 the Interscholastic League Press Conference chose him as one of 75 Legends in Texas Scholastic Journalism.

Preface

No one ever said that journalism was easy. At least, this author has never heard it said. Journalism covers a wide range of written and broadcast materials. *Webster's New Collegiate Dictionary* defines journalism as "the collection and editing of material of current interest for presentation through news media." To learn how to collect, edit, and disseminate news is no easy task. Nor is it easy to tell someone how to perform those tasks well. Of the several types of news media, this book will zero in on newspaper and yearbook production and broadcast journalism at the secondary school level. Because the intent is to give an overview of production techniques, no attempt has been made to explain all facets of the process. The emphasis is on writing.

In the space available it has been impossible to discuss all components of the writing process, but this book should give the reader a grasp of the elements of secondary school journalism. It is hoped that it will help the student become an effective disseminator of facts through the written word.

CHAPTER
one

A Brief History of American Journalism

It was published only once, but it was a beginning. On September 25, 1690, in Boston, Benjamin Harris issued *Publick Occurrences, Both Foreign and Domestick*. That was the first American newspaper. Four days after its publication, the political officials, having found its content objectionable, issued an order forbidding its further publication and requiring any similar publications to obtain a license prior to printing.

Publick Occurrences was a three-page paper, 6 x 9½ inches in size. The fourth page was left blank, presumably so Boston readers could add their own news before sending the paper to friends in other areas.

It was fourteen years later, in 1704, that John Campbell founded the *Boston News-Letter*. The first continuously published American newspaper, it was a two-page weekly, although on occasion it went to four pages.

Another paper, the *Boston Gazette*, was begun in 1719. William Brooker, the town postmaster, edited it as a weekly. James Franklin was the first printer of the *Gazette*, and his thirteen-year-old brother, Benjamin, served as his apprentice. James eventually started his own paper, the *New England Courant*, in 1721. The *Courant* provided more entertainment than its predecessors, but it also was the first crusading paper; it was outspoken against inoculation for smallpox. James also started the *Rhode-Island Gazette*, the first paper in Rhode Island, in 1732. He and Benjamin founded the *Newport Mercury* in 1758.

The first newspaper outside Boston was the *American Weekly Mercury*, which Andrew Bradford founded in Philadelphia in 1719. The *Mercury* was somewhat outspoken, and Bradford was often at odds with authorities. A rival paper appeared in 1728 when Samuel Keimer started publishing the *Pennsylvania Gazette*. Benjamin Franklin purchased the *Gazette* in 1729. The paper quickly became noted for its superior news coverage and sharp appearance.

Franklin also started the first foreign-language paper, the *Philadelphia Zeitung*, in 1732, but it was short-lived. It was also Franklin who began one of the first American magazines, the *General Magazine*, which went on sale three days after Andrew Bradford's *American Magazine* in January 1741. Although neither lasted a full year, the magazine concept was born.

Journalists were also experimenting with newspapers in New York. William Bradford founded the *New York Gazette* in 1725. The best-known figure in New York journalism, however, was probably John Peter Zenger, who founded the *Weekly Journal* in 1733. The paper carried articles asserting that freedoms were in danger and that the governor of New York had tampered with the right of trial by jury. Zenger was arrested and spent nine months in jail before being brought to trial. Alexander Hamilton served as Zenger's lawyer. Hamilton appealed to the jury to accept Zenger's statements as the truth, and he won the case— a victory for freedom of the press. As problems with Great Britain continued, more and more papers began speaking out against tyranny and the loss of freedoms.

Mary Katherine Goddard learned her trade as a printer from her father, and she assisted her mother in publishing the weekly *Providence Gazette* from 1765 to 1768. In 1768, she joined her brother, William, in Philadelphia to help publish the *Pennsylvania Chronicle*. In 1774, the Goddards closed their shop in Baltimore, and Mary Katherine again joined her brother and published the *Maryland Journal*. She officially became its publisher in 1775. In January 1777, she printed the first copy of the Declaration of Independence, including the names of the signers. She became postmaster of Baltimore in 1775 and held that position until 1789.

Isaiah Thomas started *The Massachusetts Spy* in 1770. He intended *The Spy* to be a nonpartisan paper, but it quickly became a voice for the Patriot cause. Tory threats against

> ➢ *Early Printing*
> *Printing existed in the colonies for more than half a century before the appearance of a newspaper. Printers knew they faced loss of business and even more severe punishments if they offended the government in any way. Besides, the reading public they served at that time was not highly literate.*
>
> *After the disappearance of* Publick Occurrences, Both Foreign and Domestick, *it was 14 years before the next paper appeared. John Campbell founded the Boston News-Letter in 1704. The paper was "Published by Authority," which meant the governor or someone in his office approved the contents of each issue.*

Thomas and his printers forced him to move the paper from Boston to Worcester. Thomas established papers elsewhere. He later founded the American Antiquarian Society and wrote the first historical account of American newspapers.

The Spy and other Revolutionary War papers signaled the beginning of partisan politics in the press. Following the war, papers were divided between support for the Federalists (advocates of a federal union and the adoption of a U.S. constitution) and their opponents, the Republicans. This increased an interest in the press, which also increased readership. Thus in 1783 Benjamin Towne turned his *Pennsylvania Evening Post* into a daily paper, the first in America.

Magazines were also experiencing growth at this time. Noah Webster started the *American Magazine* in New York in 1787. It lasted only one year, but others had more success. Boston, New York, and Philadelphia were the leaders in magazine publishing, as they had been in newspapers, but as the population shifted westward newspapers sprang up everywhere. There were approximately 200 papers in the United States in 1800, nearly 1,200 papers thirty-three years later, and nearly 3,000 by 1860. By that year more than 1,000 magazines were also being published.

Part of the increase in available newspapers can be attributed to the penny press. Before the advent of the penny press, most daily newspapers were sold by annual subscription, and many publishers would not sell single copies. Dr. H. S. Shepard tried selling his *New York Morning Post* for one cent in 1833. The venture was unsuccessful; however, he had planted an idea in the minds of other publishers. In September 1833, Benjamin Day started the daily *New York Sun* and sold it for one cent. Its emphasis on human interest stories and on sensationalism put its circulation above all other New York papers within four months.

Other papers soon followed the *Sun's* example. In 1835 James Gordon Bennett founded the *New York Herald*. By the 1850s it had overtaken the *Sun* in circulation. The cheaper papers made it possible for people at all economic levels to read the news daily.

Newspapers continued to be divided along party lines.

➢ New Yorker
  Harold Ross launched New Yorker magazine Feb. 21, 1925. Its 75th anniversary issue in 2000 included articles by Woody Allen and Steve Martin. Conde Nast purchased the magazine in 1999.

➢ **Web Networking**
  One way to get information about professional and scholastic journalism organizations is to check their Web sites on the Internet.
    National Scholastic Press Assoc. (http://studentpress. journ.umn.edu)
    Journalism Education Assoc. (http://www.jea.org)
    Columbia Scholastic Press Assoc. (http://www.columbia. edu/cu/cspa)
    Dow Jones Newspaper Fund (http://www.dowjones. com/newsfund)
    Quill and Scroll (http://www. uiowa.edu/~ quill-sc)
    Society of Professional Journalists (http://spj.org)
    Student Press Law Center (http://www.splc.org)
    Freedom Forum (http:// www.freedomforum.org)
    Poynter Institute (http://www.poynter.org)
    Newseum (http://www.newseum.org)
    Society for News Design (http://www.snd.org)
    The Reporters Committee for Freedom of the Press (http://www.rcfp.org)

William Cullen Bryant made the *New York Evening Post* an advocate for the Democratic party, and the major advocate for the Whig party in New York was James Watson Webb's *Courier and Enquirer.* In 1841 Horace Greeley founded the *New York Tribune,* which was also a Whig supporter. The *Tribune* was enterprising in news gathering, and it remained ethical in all its reporting. It soon earned the nickname "The Great Moral Organ." The paper crusaded for labor unions, for prohibition of the sale of liquor, and for the abolition of slavery.

When Frederick Douglass escaped slavery, he met William Lloyd Garrison, the most prominent white abolitionist at the time. Douglass was influenced by Garrison's emancipation movement, and in 1847 he moved to Rochester, New York, and began publication of the *North Star.* The new paper said its object was "to attack slavery in all its forms and aspects; advocate Universal Emancipation; promote the moral and intellectual improvement of the colored people; and to hasten the day of freedom to our three million enslaved fellow-countrymen." Douglass claimed he was not affiliated with any party. He was simply advocating the slave's cause. He had to mortgage his house to keep the paper going. He needed the help of Julia Griffiths, an Englishwoman, in 1848 to help put the paper's finances in order. The *North Star* merged with the *Liberty Party Paper* in 1851, and it became known as *Frederick Douglass' Paper.* The paper continued to founder, and in 1860 it became a monthly. It eventually ceased publication in 1863. During its day, it was probably the most important vehicle for black writers and reformers, and it was considered to be well written and edited.

Amelia Jenks married Dexter Bloomer in 1840. Dexter was coeditor of the *Senaca County Courier* in New York. After their marriage, Amelia wrote articles for her husband's newspaper on social, moral, and political issues. She also contributed articles to the *Water Bucket,* a local temperance journal. Eventually, in 1849, she began publishing *Lily,* a temperance paper. The *Lily* started printing articles on women's rights as well. Mrs. Bloomer's views on temperance were uncompromising. She also used *Lily* to promote the wearing of pantalettes—eventually to become known as bloomers. Women operators of *Lily*'s presses wore pantalettes since long skirts and dresses could easily be caught in the machinery. In 1853 the Bloomers moved to Mount Vernon, Ohio, and Dexter purchased an interest in the *Western Home Visitor*. Amelia Bloomer became an assistant editor of the new paper, and she continued to edit *Lily*, which had a circulation of more than 6,000 by this time. She eventually moved to Iowa and sold the *Lily*, but she continued to speak on behalf of woman's suffrage.

Magazines also continued to experience growth. Robert Bonner's New York *Ledger* had a circulation of 400,000 by 1860. In 1850 *Harper's Monthly* of New York was started. It was an instant success, partly because of its illustrations.

Magazines spread across the country, as did newspapers. In 1878 Joseph Pulitzer bought the St. Louis *Dispatch*, which had been founded in 1864, and combined it with the St. Louis *Post*. The *Post-Dispatch*, like the *Tribune* in New York, became a crusading newspaper. In 1883 Pulitzer bought the New York *World* and added crusading journalism to its sensationalism.

Other newspapers that began in the late 1800s were Henry Grady's Atlanta *Constitution*, Henry Watterson's Louisville *Courier-Journal*, Melville Stone's Chicago *Daily News*, and William Rockhill Nelson's Kansas City *Evening Star*.

The Hearst family became involved in journalism when George Hearst bought the San Francisco *Evening Examiner* in 1880. His son, William Randolph Hearst, brought sensationalism to the *Examiner*, just as Pulitzer had done with the New York *World*. In 1895 William Randolph Hearst purchased the New York *Morning Journal*, and the *Journal* and *World* quickly became rivals. Thus began a phase of American newspaper publishing known as yellow journalism. The two papers sought to outdo each other, often using scare headlines and fake interviews.

In 1897 Hearst bought the *Vamoose*, a yacht, and sent Richard Harding Davis, a fiction writer, and Frederic Remington, an illustrator, on the yacht to Cuba to report on the Cuban insurrection, which had begun in 1895. Remington supposedly sent a telegram to Hearst saying everything was quiet and that there would be no war. Hearst supposedly told

> ➢ *Photojournalists*
> One of the most noted photojournalists in the 20th century was Ed Clark, who died Jan. 22, 2000. Clark was noted for his pictures of former presidents Franklin Roosevelt and John F. Kennedy, as well as his photographs of Marilyn Monroe. Clark's photos became well-known when he worked for Life magazine. He also at one time worked for the Nashville Tennessean. Some readers thought his most famous photograph was one of a tearful musician in Warm Springs, GA, as he played his accordion while a train carrying President Franklin Roosevelt's body was moving out. Clark dropped out of Hume-Foog High School in Nashville to pursue a career in photojournalism.

Katherine Graham, publisher of the Washington Post, *died July 17, 2001, following a fall while attending a business conference in Sun Valley, ID. Graham took control of the* Post *in 1963 following her husband's death. She was probably best known for her leadership at the* Post *during the Watergate scandal of 1972–74 when reporters Bob Woodward and Carl Bernstein won a Pulitzer Prize for their stories that eventually led to Richard Nixon resigning as president of the United States. Graham supported the two reporters despite pressure from the government. Graham also received a Pulitzer Prize in 1998 for her autobiography,* Personal History. *Under her leadership, the* Post *had $2.4 billion in revenue in 2000. She helped make the* Post *one of the world's great newspapers.*

Remington to remain, writing "You furnish the pictures, and I'll furnish the war." There is apparently no proof that Hearst ever said that, but he did publish articles to indicate a war was imminent. In April 1898, the Spanish-American War began and U.S. troops were sent to Cuba.

It was partially because of yellow journalism that the American Society of Newspaper Editors in 1923 adopted rules of ethics to be followed by its members. Nevertheless, the American public continued to remain skeptical of what they read in newspapers and magazines. That same skepticism remains today, in part because the ethics of some journalists, particularly tabloid reporters, have become suspect. The *Washington Post* gained recognition in the 1970s when it uncovered the Watergate incident that eventually led to the resignation of President Richard M. Nixon; but it was the same paper that lost prestige in 1981 when reporter Janet Cooke returned a Pulitzer Prize she had won for a story on an eight-year-old heroin addict. Cooke returned the prize after she admitted to her editors that the story was a composite, that quotes attributed to the child were fabricated, and that several main events described as having been witnessed never happened. James Michener, a Pulitzer Prize winner himself, told *U.S. News & World Report* that the "incident was one of the saddest weeks in the history of American journalism."

It is because of such incidents that readers continue to question what they read in professional publications. Readers blamed the media, especially the *Miami Herald*, for Gary Hart's failure to win the Democratic presidential nomination in 1988. People also blamed the press for the controversy surrounding the nomination of Clarence Thomas for U.S. Supreme Court justice in 1991. The media overanalyzed accusations of sexual harassment made by law professor Anita Hill at the hearings. Questions were raised about what the public has a right to know.

Following all of these incidents, newspapers and magazines took a fresh look at their ethical policies that dated to the 1920s.

It was also in the 1920s that Briton Hadden and Henry Luce founded Time, Inc. Their magazine was originally called

Fact, but they soon renamed it *Time*. A sample issue came out in December 1922, but the first issue was dated March 3, 1923. Although it was a struggle to keep the magazine afloat at first, the publishers turned a profit by 1926. Hadden died in 1927, but Luce started *Fortune* magazine in that year, and in 1936 he established *Life*. In 1954 the company bought *Sports Illustrated*. Time-Life, Inc. continues to be one of the major magazine publishers in the United States.

Another magazine that had its beginnings in the 1920s was *Reader's Digest*. DeWitt Wallace founded the publication in 1922. Its original formula was condensing articles from other publications. Today it originates much of its own material but still publishes condensed articles from other sources.

Time and *Reader's Digest* continue to be among the top selling magazines in the United States today. Others with large circulations include *TV Guide, Newsweek, Sports Illustrated, Better Homes and Gardens, U.S. News & World Report, Good Housekeeping, McCall's, Family Circle,* and *Ladies' Home Journal.*

Several thousand magazines are published in the United States. Most of them are consumer magazines—those sold at newsstands and aimed at the general public. Other categories are business magazines, association magazines, public relations magazines, religious magazines, and one-shot magazines. A one-shot magazine is issued to capitalize on a hot topic, phenomenon, or idea. Such magazines have been published on well-known personalities such as Elvis Presley and the Beatles, or on catastrophic news events such as the assassination of President John F. Kennedy or the death of Princess Diana. A yearbook could also be considered a one-shot magazine.

It was in the 1920s that radio burst upon the scene. Station KDKA in Pittsburgh is usually credited with the first regularly scheduled broadcasting, beginning with the Harding-Cox presidential election returns on November 2, 1920. Station WWJ in Detroit claims to have been the first to broadcast, on August 20, 1920, but the first station to be issued a license was WBZ in Springfield, Massachusetts, on September 15, 1921. Radio grew rapidly thereafter, and governmental regulation began. The Federal Communications

> ➤ *Obtaining Diversity*
> The American Society of Newspaper Editors in 1978 set as a goal for 2000 for newspaper publishers to hire people of color equal to the same percentage as the national minority population (approximately 25%). In 1998, ASNE realized it would not meet its goal, so it replaced it with a new challenge urging American newspapers to "reflect the diversity of American society" by no later than 2025. By that time, the minority population in the United States could be as large as 40%. By 2050, at the current growth trend, Hispanics will make up nearly 25% of the United States's population and will be the largest ethnic minority population. These trends show why diversity in the newsroom is more important than ever.

Commission (FCC) was established as a permanent regulatory agency in 1934. Its major areas of control have been the issuance and renewal of licenses. The FCC established FM radio in 1940.

By 1950 television was beginning to create competition for radio. Some 2,000 AM radio stations and 700 FM stations were operating in 1950, compared to 100 television stations. But by 1954 television revenues had outpaced those of radio. Competition among the three major networks (ABC, NBC, and CBS) was evident in both radio and television. Today these networks are being challenged by additional networks, such as Fox and UPN, and by cable TV and by Internet services.

Mass media is a term used today to refer to both the print and the broadcast media.

Today's mass media vary considerably in size and function. Newspapers range from the large metropolitan dailies of sixty or more pages to the small-town dailies of eight pages or less. Some newspapers are owned by chains such as Gannett, which owns more than eighty papers across the United States, and Knight-Ridder, which owns more than twenty.

Besides the approximately 1,500 dailies in the United States, there are nearly 8,000 weekly newspapers. Many are located in small towns, but some are printed in large metropolitan areas, such as the Journal newspapers in St. Louis. The Journal newspapers print several editions to capitalize on local news. The *West County Journal*, for example, reports primarily the news happenings in the western portion of the city and county of St. Louis, while the *South County Journal* reports primarily on the southern portion. The suburban weeklies highlight local happenings much more than the dailies. For the reader who is interested in local news rather than national or international news, suburban weekly newspapers will meet his or her needs.

Each newspaper has its own editorial policy, just as a high school newspaper should have. Many professional newspapers include statements about accuracy and ethics, with an emphasis on remaining free of obligation to any special-interest group. To be professional means to be fair and accurate, so editorial poli-

➢ *The Role of Radio and TV*

By 1950, the average American listened to a radio for more than four hours per day. By 1960, approximately 96% of all Americans had at least one radio set, and more than 90% of all programming was music.

Television began to draw away some of radio's audience in the 1950s, and by the 1960s rapid changes were made in radio programming—as comedy, drama, and variety shows began disappearing. The Amos and Andy show was discontinued in 1960 after 32 years on the air. By 1960, the number of homes with television sets exceeded 50 million, about 87% of all homes in the United States.

cies normally emphasize respect for the rights of others and the need for accuracy in stories, headlines, and pictures.

Most publishers agree that a newspaper should operate in the public's interest, but readers need to be aware that a paper's policy may lean toward the beliefs of one political party over another, or one race over another. Others may lean toward the beliefs of one particular religion, as the *Christian Science Monitor* does.

Good newspapers will not editorialize in news stories, will not present just one side of a story, will not omit a story due to advertising or political pressure to keep information from the public, and will not publish only the part of a story that favors its viewpoint. An editorial policy will emphasize that a paper will print all the facts necessary for complete understanding of a story.

In general, today's newspapers are somewhat conservative in nature. Few support only one political party as some have in the past, but they may still lean toward one political viewpoint. In towns that still have two daily papers, the two may adopt different editorial viewpoints on some topics in an attempt to gain more readers.

Large metropolitan dailies have been struggling to maintain readership in recent years, and afternoon dailies in particular have been folding. For example, the Philadelphia *Bulletin* closed in 1982, and the St. Louis *Post-Dispatch* switched from an afternoon to a morning paper in 1984. This switch intensified its competition with the St. Louis *Globe-Democrat*, a morning newspaper. Both started running contests to lure readers. Winners of the contests, which required readers to match headlines and/or numbers, received prizes of cars or money.

Both newspapers reported an increase in circulation at the time of their contests, an indication that readers will buy a paper when they have a chance for financial gain. The *Globe-Democrat* eventually folded in 1985. The *Post* picked up some of the *Globe's* readers, but the *Post-Dispatch* continued to run contests to gain additional readership. In 1991, it ran a contest involving birthdates: If a person's initials and birthdate appeared in an issue of the *Post*, the person received $50.

➢ *Influence of Magazines*

By the 1950s, magazines were playing a prominent role in American journalism. By 1960, 11 magazines had a circulation of more than five million. These included Ladies' Home Journal, Life, Look, McCall's, Reader's Digest, *the* Saturday Evening Post, *and* TV Guide.

TV Guide *began in 1953, and by 1960 its circulation had topped seven million.*

By the late 1990s, Sports Illustrated *was printing editorial supplements that went to fans of NBA and NCAA basketball, and it introduced a sports news cable channel with CNNSI.*

African American on Wheels *was published for the first time in 1995 to show the popularity of cars in the African American community.*

Most newspapers aim their content toward a general audience in order to attract as many readers as possible. This is why papers include a variety of features, sports, news, and editorials. Many readers would complain if their favorite comic strip were dropped. Papers periodically survey their readers to find out which comic strips are most liked. Reader-interest surveys usually indicate that the entertainment content of a paper is more popular than other content.

Other print media include association, trade, and professional papers published by organized groups such as industries, clubs, and labor unions. These papers center their content around the specific interest group. Other newspapers are printed in the languages of various ethnic groups.

Several magazines also aim their content toward a specific audience. *TV Guide*, for example, appeals to those who watch television or who are interested in articles about TV personalities. *Sports Illustrated* appeals to sports fans. *U.S. News & World Report, Time*, and *Newsweek* all appeal to readers who want a more in-depth look at news stories than their newspaper provides. Many magazines are aimed at the average consumer, but some, such as *Arizona Highways*, are primarily public relations organs.

General-interest magazines include publications such as *Reader's Digest* and *Life*. Magazines of interest to women include *Good Housekeeping, Better Homes and Gardens, Redbook, Woman's Day,* and *Ladies' Home Journal. GQ, Details,* and *Sports Illustrated* are magazines aimed at male readers.

Special magazines are aimed at business professionals: *Fortune, Forbes,* and *Business Week*; and at religious readers: *Upper Room, Catholic Digest,* and *Christianity Today.*

Several newspapers carry magazine supplements in the Sunday edition. Usually aimed at the general audience, these include *Parade* and *Family Weekly.* Regardless of a magazine's audience, each probably has some influence on its readers, just as radio and TV stations have some influence on their listeners and viewers.

Surveys have indicated that many adults obtain most of their news from radio and television. By the late 1990s and into the 21st century, individuals were also obtaining their news via the Internet as newspapers and magazines throughout the world were posting their publications on Web sites. Drive time (time needed to drive to and from work) is important for radio, as most car commuters listen to their favorite station during that time.

Music is probably the largest part of today's radio programming. Large metropolitan areas usually have a variety of music stations ranging from country and western to alternative rock to rap to classical. Most of these stations also carry five-minute newscasts at least once each hour.

Talk shows also do well in some areas. KMOX-AM in St. Louis, for example, has become famous for its "At Your Service" programming, which enables listeners to call in to ask questions or to make comments. Topics range from sports to politics to marital problems. National Public Radio (NPR) is extremely popular, broadcasting "All Things Considered," which covers a variety of newsworthy and human interest stories. Some talk shows become popular based on a certain radio personality, such as Don Imus, Howard Stern, and Rush Limbaugh. These shows are often broadcast in syndication and heard all across the country.

Whereas drive time is an important part of the broadcast day for radio, prime time (7 to 11 p.m.) is an important part of the broadcast day for television. The first hour of prime time is often devoted to news reports or other local programming, and the next three hours are network programming. The local stations and the networks (ABC, CBS, FOX, NBC, UPN, and The WB) rely heavily on commercials to support their programming. In recent years the networks have had stiff competition from cable television. Cable TV companies charge a monthly fee for the viewer to receive cable programming. Cable programs (as well as network programs) carry warnings to the viewer that content may not be suitable for children. The content of many network and cable movies and other programs has come under fire from some viewers, but the courts have generally held that each viewer has control over what to watch and may either change channels or turn off the television.

➢ *Peanuts*
One of the most popular newspaper cartoonists, Charles Schulz, the creator of "Peanuts," decided to stop drawing the "Peanuts" characters in 2000. Schulz drew more than 18,000 strips in 50 years before stopping the daily ones on Jan. 3, 2000 and the Sunday ones on Feb. 13. Schulz suffered a heart attack Feb. 12 and died shortly before the final "Peanuts" strip ran off the presses. "Peanuts" appeared in 2,600 newspapers in 75 countries, and it was printed in 21 languages. Readers fell in love with Charlie Brown, Lucy, Linus, Snoopy, and all the gang. Schulz's strip carried lessons in faith, hope and charity.

When Schulz was in high school, a teacher urged him to submit some of his drawings to the yearbook staff, but the yearbook never ran them. Schulz posthumously received the National Cartoonists Society's Lifetime Achievement Award, May 27, 2000.

➢ Technology

By the beginning of the 21st century, start-up Internet companies, including iCraveTV.com, were threatening to change the television industry. Live network TV and cable stations were put on the Internet by iCraveTV for the first time.

CBS, Fox, Walt Disney, and others filed a lawsuit against iCraveTV to prevent them from carrying network programs. The founder of iCraveTV, Bill Craig, operated outside Toronto, Canada. He was using a loophole in Canadian law to pull in broadcast signals and turn them into digital streaming video before pumping the channels out to the Internet at iCraveTV's Web site.

The plaintiffs in the case claimed iCraveTV was stealing. A U.S. district court judge agreed with the plaintiffs and issued an injunction against iCraveTV. After the lawsuit was filed, iCraveTV stopped its rebroadcasting service.

More recent developments, such as video cassette recorders and video discs, mean that viewers are not bound to regular programming; these devices enable viewers who aren't at home during a showing to tape the program to watch later.

"Via satellite" has also become a familiar term in TV programming. Early Bird, launched in 1965, made possible transatlantic satellite communication between Europe and North America. Newspapers also use satellites. The *Wall Street Journal* and *USA Today* are newspapers published in various regions of the country that rely heavily upon satellites in order to make the news content the same in all editions.

Other developments have also influenced the print media. The Associated Press introduced the Laserphoto in the late 1970s, to replace its wirephoto machines. A laser beam scans the original photo at its transmission point. A transmitter then converts the information into electronic impulses and sends it over telephone lines to laser receivers in newspaper offices around the country. The receiver uses its own laser beam to expose a special photographic paper, and a heat processor inside the receiver automatically develops the picture.

The Laserphoto system speeds the delivery of photos, just as the AP's DataStream, introduced in 1974, made possible the high-speed delivery of the written word. It can transmit 1,200 words per minute.

Computerized typesetting has also sped up the production process for newspapers and magazines. The most common process is one using a video display terminal (VDT), which has an input keyboard and a phototypesetter. The VDT looks like a TV screen with a typewriter keyboard. The writer may read on the screen what he has typed on the keyboard and edit the copy by correcting, adding, or deleting.

Similarly, offset printing has sped up the printing process. In offset printing, the printing plate is made from a photographic negative. Any kind of typewritten material may be reproduced. Photographs, however, require screening to break up the surface for the ink and water treatment. The offset process enables even school publication staffs to make their material camera-ready by doing their own pasteups of copy and photos.

In the 1980s laptop computers and satellites were responsible for the biggest change in the way newspapers provided information. The technology boom has provided better quality and faster production. It has also provided ways to improve news reporting, changed the design of newspapers, and brought those pages to readers across the nation. *USA Today,* a nationally distributed newspaper, began in the 1980s because of the availability of satellite distribution.

The new technology eliminated (for most staffs) cut-out acetate sheets that had been available since the mid-1970s to aid a staff with design and to speed the pasteup process. Formatt and Chartpak are two examples of acetate cutouts available today. The acetate sheets include a wide range of typefaces, rule lines, dot screens, and other shading media. Using an Exacto knife, a staff member may cut out letters, for example, and place them directly on the layout sheet. Use of acetate sheets gives a staff a variety of options in typefaces at a relatively low cost.

In the mid-1980s, however, most staffs turned to desktop publishing for producing yearbooks, newspapers, and literary magazines, and acetate sheets became a thing of the past. Many schools use Macintosh computers for desktop publishing, but IBM computers are also popular. Using software programs like PageMaker, Quark Express, and Ready, Set, Go, staffs design their pages on the computer screen. The software programs also provide a variety of fonts, rule lines, and screens. Desktop publishing has given staffs much more control over design. Using numerous programs like Aldus Freehand and Adobe Illustrator, staffs have been able to keep graphics simple but sophisticated. Yearbook companies have also developed programs that enable staffs to produce better-quality books. Many yearbook staffs are using disk submission programs. Pasteups have almost disappeared, and staffs are submitting completed pages on disks to the companies. The companies then use Linotronic printers to create the finished product. These printers provide a much sharper reproduction

> ➢ *Digital Video*
>
> CD-ROM yearbooks gained popularity in the 1990s. Sound bites and virtual tours of a school's campus, as well as features about key events of the year, were common on CDs. By the turn of the century, Digital Video Discs were becoming part of the communications industry. Yearbook staffs, who had been creating CD-ROM yearbooks in the late 1990s, were not out of date as the new DVDs were backward compatible—meaning yearbook CDs created in the immediate years prior to 2000 could still be viewed. A DVD interactive yearbook and even a DVD interactive newspaper will probably be the wave of the 21st century. "Digital video is the major catalyst to most of major changes in publications today."—Kenny Irby, visual journalism leader, Poynter Institute

Computer Terms

RAM: Random access memory. A computer has two ways of storing data: the hard drive and internal memory (RAM). A computer takes data and sends the information into RAM for temporary storage. More RAM means quicker processing. It operates faster than taking data directly from a hard drive. Many software programs require 16MB of RAM to run smoothly. Because of new developments, computer buyers should look for computers that allow for installing additional RAM later.

Hard drive: Also referred to as a hard disk. The hard disk stores the computer's operating system, programs, files, and documents.

Modem: An acronym for modulator/demodulator. It connects a computer to a phone line so that information can be sent from one computer to another or so the user can gain access to an online service or the Internet.

Baud or kbps (kilobits per second): A measure of the speed at which the modem can send and receive information over phone lines. The faster the better.

MHz: Megahertz. The clock speed of the microprocessor. The higher the number, the faster the information is processed.

than LaserWriter printers—the type that most schools use. Yearbook companies have also created indexing programs and design templates to assist staffs.

By the late 1990s, new technology was continuing to change the way schools produced their publications. Digital cameras meant some schools began closing their darkrooms. Digital cameras allow a staff to transfer pictures from the camera directly to the computer. Then a staff can print the image directly or crop it to the area desired. You can also copy a picture and place it in another application, and you can change the image's bit depth. Staffs, however, did not rely on digital cameras alone for their photography. They still used other cameras to stop action. For some staffs, however, this still meant bypassing the darkroom and using a scanner to scan the photographic images into their computers. By using programs like Adobe Photoshop, they could enhance the quality of a picture before final production. Most yearbook staffs, however, were still sending their photos to the yearbook companies for scanning because of the time factor involved and because yearbook companies had more sophisticated scanners.

Zip drives also became prominent in the late 1990s. By attaching a zip drive to a computer, a staff added significant memory. Printing companies placed proofs on zip drives so they could include all photos on a page. When a staff called up the page proofs, they could see the actual pictures, and they could even manipulate them by changing position or recropping.

Other programs, like Timbuktu, allowed schools to communicate directly with a printing company. The school and the company could look at the same page simultaneously to discuss problems and how they might be solved.

The largest computer network that evolved in the 1990s, however, was the Internet, a large network of computers connected via telephone cables. To get on the Internet, it was necessary to have the proper software, a computer, a modem, and a phone line. By the 21st century, the Internet was taking publishing to new heights as schools sent pages via their modem connections to printing plants. The Internet also provided

> *Internet Terms*
> *Chat: Talk online.*
> *Chat room: An assigned room for private conversations.*
> *Dot: Period.*
> *E-mail: Electronic mail.*
> *Lurking: Joining a discussion group and reading others' messages.*
> *Newbie: Newcomer on the Net.*
> *Screen name: The name a user is known by online.*
> *URL: Web site address.*

publication staffs with a large avenue of research—to gain information for articles. An Internet user can literally communicate with people throughout the world. A whole new glossary of terms has cropped up because of the Internet, also known as the Information Superhighway or Cyberspace. Other nicknames for the Internet are the World Wide Web, the Web, or the Net.

Because the Internet provided a plethora of information for those using it for research, most users found it easier to use a search engine, such as Webcrawler or Yahoo! A search engine allows the user to enter a term, and then the engine searches its database to find sites that have information relating to the topic. Even with the best search engine, however, the Internet has so much information that it is impossible to find exactly what one wants all the time.

Some users have developed Web sites or home pages, which means they created one or more pages around a single topic. Some high school papers created their own Web sites, which they updated regularly with each issue of the paper. The Internet changes daily as new Web sites are added, deleted or modified.

Any Web site contains links to other sites on the Internet. All Web sites have their own addresses called URLs. A link contains an address, and when it is selected on the computer, the user is sent to the new address. When a user goes from page to page, this is called surfing the Net or browsing the Web. To surf the Net, the user needs a Web browsing software, such as Netscape.

To find information on the Web, a user simply needs to know the address of a site that has the type of information sought. URLs start with http://, which stands for hypertext transfer protocol. Web pages are written in hypertext markup language (html). Html is text with special characters that tell the Web browser what to display. The http:// is often followed by www, which stands for World Wide Web. For example, the address of the Journalism Education Association is http://www.jea.org and the address of the *New York Times* is http://www.nytimes.com. The address for the Webcrawler search engine is http://www.webcrawler.com, and the address

➢ *Internet Abbreviations Used with E-Mail*

BFN: Bye for now

BTSOOM: Beats the stuffing out of me

BTW: By the way

FWIW: For what it's worth

FAQ: Frequently asked questions

FYI: For your information

IMHO: In my humble opinion

IOW: In other words

JFTR: Just for the record

NRN: No reply necessary

OIC: Oh, I see

OTOH: On the other hand

RR: Reply requested

RSN: Real soon now

TIA: Thanks in advance

TIC: Tongue in cheek

URR: Urgent reply requested

WYSIWYG: What you see is what you get

for Yahoo! is http://www.yahoo.com. However, if the user does not know a specific URL, he or she can usually find addresses by typing in a keyword, such as "Writing." All sites where "Writing" topics occur will show up. These sites are the links that the user needs. All he or she has to do then is click on the name of one of the sites, and the browsing has begun. The Internet in the 21st century will be taking publication staffs in directions never encountered before.

The printing industry has been revolutionized since offset printing was introduced, and new developments in computer technology in the 21st century will probably continue that revolution.

EXERCISES

1. Select one of the persons mentioned in this chapter and write a report on his or her life and contributions to American journalism.

2. Write a report on the growth of cable television in the United States. Show how its development in some communities has created controversy.

3. Select a major magazine and write a report on its history.

4. Newspapers, magazines, radio stations, and television stations are being criticized today for irresponsible reporting. Interview a professional journalist and get his or her ideas about how the various media are trying to overcome this charge. Write a paper on your findings.

5. Compare one week's issues of *U.S. News & World Report, Time,* and *Newsweek* and write a summary of their coverage for that week. Are their cover stories different? Do they cover different topics or all the same topics? Does their reporting seem to be biased? Have they taken an editorial stand on anything? How much real news is covered compared to the amount of space devoted to sensational stories?

> Position Statement

In 1999, the Journalism Education Association adopted the following position statement concerning speech on the Internet:

"JEA strongly opposes any restriction on legally protected speech on scholastic journalism Web sites and specifically endorses the use of student names and/or photos. The Supreme Court's decision in the Communication Decency Act in 1996 said, 'As the most participatory form of mass speech yet developed, the Internet deserves the highest form of protection from government intrusion.' Since commercial print publications have no restrictions on use of names and/or photos, and since JEA believes scholastic publications should also experience similar freedoms, we see no difference in the way the scholastic publications using the Internet should be treated."

➢ Online Publishing

Yearbooks or newspapers that publish online should include, but not be limited to, the following:

- *A design that is graphically related to the print publication.*
- *A means of interactivity such as letters to the editor, surveys, or message boards where readers can give feedback.*
- *Repetitive elements that carry throughout the pages.*
- *Text, images, animation, sound, and video.*
- *Text big enough to read.*
- *Columns of text narrower than a book to make reading easier.*
- *Paragraphs in normal type—not bold or italic.*
- *Buttons and bars that are easy to understand and use.*
- *Consistent navigation.*
- *Page titles that explain what the page is about.*
- *Clear links.*
- *Matching text links to graphic links.*
- *Articles written specifically for the online publication.*
- *Writing with correct journalistic style.*
- *Headlines that convey the emotion, tone, and flavor of the copy.*
- *Captions of two or more sentences for each photograph.*
- *Photographs that tell stories and enhance coverage.*
- *A staff page with list of staff members and e-mail addresses.*
- *An online publication policy.*

6.   Write a history of a newspaper in your hometown or state.

7.   Write an account of the media's role in the election of George W. Bush in 2000.

8.   Write an account of how the media covered the anthrax scare in 2001.

9.   Write an account of the *Washington Post*'s Watergate investigation.

10. Write an account of Janet Cooke's story about Jimmy, an eight-year-old heroin addict. Do a follow-up to the story to show how professional publications changed their editing procedures.

11. By using the Internet, complete a research paper on First Amendment rights. The Broadcast Media Online File Room (http://fileroom.aaup.uic.edu/Fileroom/documents/Mbroadcastmedia.html), the Media Watchdog (http://theory.lcs.mit.edu/~mernst/media), and U.S. First Amendment Law Online (http://fatty.law.cornell.edu/topics/firstamendment.html) are good sources for information. The first two sites provide information about censorship, and the last one provides information about how the First Amendment applies to present-day issues.

12.   Contact schools which you exchange newspapers with to determine how many of those are publishing there papers online. Interview the editors to determine problems they have encountered with their online publications. Make an oral presentation to class to report your findings.

13.   A high school newspaper in Indiana dropped its print newspaper at the turn of the century and went to strictly an online publication. What advantages and disadvantages can you see in doing that?

14.   What is your district's policy concerning online publishing? Compare your district's policy to a neighboring district. Which one do you think is the best and why?

15.   Select a well-known cartoonist or comic strip creator, such as Charles Schulz, and write a history of his/her life or describe the messages presented in his/her work.

CHAPTER
t w o

Rights and Responsibilities of Journalists

The case of *Tinker v. Des Moines* (393 U.S. 503) culminated in 1969 in a U.S. Supreme Court decision that was to have a historic effect on the future of high school publications, but the case of *Hazelwood School District v. Cathy Kuhlmeier* (86-836) in 1988 had even greater impact.

The *Tinker* case developed because secondary students in Des Moines had been wearing black armbands to protest American involvement in the Vietnam War. The administration ordered them to stop because it considered the action disruptive and a violation of a school regulation. The students refused and were suspended. The case eventually reached the Supreme Court.

The Court decided against the administration, ruling that neither students nor teachers "shed their constitutional rights to freedom of speech or expression at the schoolhouse gate."

The majority opinion went on to say that "undifferentiated fear or apprehension of disturbance [in schools] is not enough to overcome the right of freedom of expression," and it suggested that censorship might be allowable only if student expression (written or verbal) materially disrupted classwork or if it involved "substantial disorder or invasion of the rights of others."

Since the *Tinker* decision, numerous court cases have clarified the rights of school publications in regard to freedom of the press. It should be emphasized that those decisions pertain primarily to public schools and not to private schools.

Bethel School District No. 403 v. Fraser, handed down in 1986, was also important. In a 7-to-2 decision, the Supreme Court

➢ Tinker v. Des Moines

• "It can hardly be argued that either students or teachers shed their constitutional rights to freedom of speech or expression at the schoolhouse gate." —Tinker v. Des Moines Independent Community School District

• Under Tinker, student expression is constitutionally protected unless it materially and substantially disrupts normal school activities or invades the rights of others.

said that administrators at Bethel High School in Washington did not violate the First Amendment rights of Matt Fraser when they suspended him in 1983 for giving a speech in a school assembly that contained sexually suggestive language.

In 1983, Fraser had endorsed a candidate for student government with the following speech:

"I know a man who is firm—he's firm in his pants, he's firm in his shirt, his character is firm—but most of all, his belief in you, the students of Bethel, is firm. Jeff Kuhlman is a man who takes his point and pounds it in. He doesn't attack things in spurts—he drives hard, pushing and pushing until finally he succeeds. Jeff is a man who will go to the very end—even the climax, for each and every one of you. So vote for Jeff for ASB vice-president—he'll never come between you and the best our high school can be."

Teachers complained to school administrators about the speech, and the administration suspended Fraser for three days for using vulgar and indecent language, and it dropped his name from the graduation speaker ballot. The administration said it had the right to control such speech because its policies prohibited conduct that materially and substantially interfered with the education process, including the use of obscene, profane language and gestures. Fraser filed suit, and the U.S. District Court in Washington held that the school's suspension violated Fraser's right to freedom of speech. It also said that the school's disruptive-conduct rule was vague and that the removal of Fraser's name from the graduation speaker's list violated the Fourteenth Amendment's due process clause.

Fraser did give his graduation speech. However, the school district appealed to the Ninth Circuit Court of Appeals. That court upheld the lower court's decision rejecting Bethel's argument that the speech was disruptive to the educational process. Even though the school district had lost twice, it appealed to the U.S. Supreme Court, asking it to decide if school officials have the authority to control indecent speech that is not legally obscene. The Court decided that "determination of what manner of speech in the classroom or in school assembly is inappropriate properly rests with the school board." Thus the appeals court decision was overturned.

Although the Fraser case was not one that directly involved school publications, it did involve freedom of speech. The Hazelwood case, however, pertained directly to high school publications.

The January 13, 1988, decision in the Hazelwood case upheld the right of public high school administrators at Hazelwood East High School in Missouri to censor stories concerning teen pregnancy and the effects of divorce on children, written by members of the Hazelwood East *Spectrum* staff. The 5-3 vote reversed the decision of the U.S. Court of Appeals for the Eighth Circuit in St. Louis. That court had upheld the rights of the students to print the articles.

The U.S. Supreme Court said that the rights of public school students are not necessarily the same as those of adults in other settings. The *Spectrum*, it said, was not a "forum for public expression" by students, and thus the students were not entitled to First Amendment protection of freedom of speech. The Court said that when a school's decision to censor is "reasonably related to legitimate pedagogical concerns," it is permissible. In other words, if administrators can present a reasonable justification for censorship, that censorship will be allowed. The Court said that the Hazelwood East principal had acted reasonably in removing the stories in question. Even though the Court's decision dramatically cut back the First Amendment protections the *Tinker* case presented to students, the decision did not say that administrators had to censor. It said they had the right to. The decision does not apply to all high school publications. It applies only to those school-sponsored ones that are not public forums for expression by students, whether produced in a class or as an extracurricular activity. Underground publications have stronger First Amendment rights. The Court mentioned three criteria it would use to determine if a publication is school-sponsored: (1) Is it supervised by a faculty member? (2) Was the publication designed to impart particular knowledge or skills to student participants or audiences; and (3) Does the publication use the school's name or resources?

"If high school teachers would read the decision [Hazelwood] carefully they would know that the censorship authority provided goes far beyond a school-sponsored student newspaper. The Supreme Court included all student expression in its censorship maw. And that maw is big enough to swallow the teaching materials used by teachers for their students. Many teachers probably do not realize that the censorship sweep can include student written and produced newspapers, news magazines, books, yearbooks, handbooks and calendars."—Dr. Louis Ingelhart, former journalism department chair at Ball State University

Impact of *Hazelwood*

• *The decision applies to those school-sponsored publications that are not public forums for expression by students, whether produced in a class or as an extracurricular activity.*

• *The Supreme Court listed three criteria it might look for in determining if a publication is school-sponsored: (1) Is it supervised by a faculty member? (2) Was the publication designed to impart particular knowledge or skills to student participants or audiences? and (3) Does the publication use the school's name or resources?*

• *Student publications that could be considered "school-sponsored" could still be entitled to strong First Amendment protection if they are "public forums for student expression."*

• *A public forum occurs when school officials "by policy or practice" have opened a publication for unrestricted use by students. Where student editors have clearly been given final authority over content decisions or where the school has specifically designated a student publication as a forum, the* Hazelwood *decision does not apply. However, the court said a forum did not exist in* Hazelwood.

Even those publications that could be considered "school-sponsored" could still be entitled to First Amendment protection if they are "public forums of expression." A publication becomes a public forum if administrators have "by policy or practice" opened a publication for unrestricted use by students. A forum may not exist if the adviser is the final authority in controlling a publication's content.

The Court gave several examples of what administrators might censor, including material that is "ungrammatical, poorly written, inadequately researched, biased or prejudiced, vulgar or profane, or unsuitable for immature audiences." It also said that potentially sensitive topics could be censored, and that administrators could censor materials that would "associate the school with anything other than neutrality on matters of political controversy." In other words, administrators may censor a great number of things just because they disapprove of them. In fact, the Court said that administrators can demand that their student publications have standards "higher than those demanded by some newspaper publishers. . .in the real world."

Even though the *Hazelwood* case gave administrators more control, the Court still said that it was reaffirming the *Tinker* case and the notion that neither students nor teachers lose their constitutional rights at the schoolhouse gate. For all the school-sponsored publications that are forums for student expression, the *Tinker* standard is still the law. School officials can censor those publications only when they can demonstrate a material and substantive disruption of school activities or an invasion of the rights of others.

The *Hazelwood* case affects more than just student publications. The Court specifically mentions theatrical productions; presumably art shows, science fairs, debates, research projects, and cheerleading squads could also be censored.

The U.S. Supreme Court's decision dealt only with the protections of the First Amendment to the U.S. Constitution. This means that state laws or constitutions might override the decision. By the mid-1990s, Arkansas, Colorado, Iowa, Kansas, and Massachusetts had passed legislation guaranteeing student

➢ **Kincaid v. Gibson**
    In the late 1990s, the sixth circuit court's three-judge panel applied the Hazelwood *case in its decision in* Kincaid v. Gibson. *This was the first time the* Hazelwood *decision had been used in determining a case involving a college publication. The case began in 1995, when Kentucky State students Charles Kincaid and Capri Coffer sued the university. Coffer, editor of the yearbook, and Kincaid, a student who had paid the mandatory student activity fee entitling him to a yearbook, sued Betty Gibson, vice president of student affairs. They argued she had violated their First Amendment rights when she seized all 2,000 copies of the yearbook and refused to distribute them. Gibson said she objected to the color of the yearbook's cover (purple), its theme ("Destination: Unknown,"), the inclusion of a current events section, and a lack of captions for some photos. The sixth circuit by a 2-1 vote ruled in favor of Gibson saying the* Hazelwood *case justified censorship of the college press*

    (Continued)

because the yearbook at Kentucky State was not a public forum and, therefore, did not enjoy the full protection of the First Amendment. Kincaid's lawyers asked the sixth circuit to rehear the case in front of a full panel of judges, and the sixth circuit agreed to do so. The full panel overturned the earlier decision in 2001.

➤ **Establishing Freedom of Expression**

The Student Press Law Center suggests student journalists can do the following in order to protect student freedom of expression:

• Become informed about any case involving student freedom of expression and make sure other students are familiar with the cases as well.

• Ask school administrators to support a statement establishing student publications as public forums.

• Ask administrators to express their support for student free expression in writing and inform your readers about those expressions.

freedom of expression. California had a state law before the U.S. Supreme Court's decision that protected the free expression rights of students.

The Student Press Law Center in Washington, D.C., has written a suggested freedom of expression bill for students. Journalism teachers in several states are using those guidelines for writing their own bills.

Even if your state has its own bill, other Court decisions have emphasized that school publications may not print obscenities, libelous statements, statements that will disrupt the educational process, or statements that tend to be an invasion of privacy.

In a 1973 U.S. Supreme Court case (*Miller v. California*), the justices ruled that the local community must define obscenity. The majority opinion indicated three basic guidelines to determine what is obscene: (1) "the average person, applying community standards," would find that the article in question appealed to prurient interests; (2) the article described in a patently offensive way sexual conduct specifically defined in state law; and (3) the article lacked serious artistic, political, or scientific value. Therefore, it is impossible to give a definition of obscenity that would fit every community in the United States.

Libel is easier to define than obscenity, but it is still difficult because there are fifty-one legal jurisdictions (fifty states and the District of Columbia), and each jurisdiction has its own laws regarding libel.

Libel, however, can be thought of as any false statement, written or broadcast, that causes a person to be hated, shunned, avoided, or to suffer financial loss. For libel to occur, four elements must be present: *defamation* (also known as harm), *identification, publication* and *fault*. A plaintiff must show these four elements to prove he has been libeled.

Defamation means that the printed or broadcast word has damaged someone's reputation. *Identification* means that someone in the reading audience not connected with the publication or broadcast station is able to identify the person who has been defamed. Even though someone isn't named specifically, his or her identity may be obvious to some read-

24

Taking Precautions

• In 1996, the advice columnist "Dear Abby" changed her policy and started asking all letter writers to include a phone number so she could verify the authenticity of the letters. She had printed a letter that had caused the person discussed in the letter to suffer humiliation. The letter writer had, as a joke, made up the information in the letter.

• A columnist at a high school in Wisconsin wrote a column in which he fantasized about having sex with the female assistant principal at his school. The principal censored the article because it allegedly "offended the community sense of decency." The question was raised whether a publication should print any article that it knows would offend some readers.

• Before deciding to print any article, a staff should ask the following questions: (1) Will it offend any readers? (2) Is it in good taste? (3) Does the reader have the right to know? (4) What is the purpose of the article? Is it for shock value? (5) Is it accurate? (6) Is it balanced? Does it present all sides? (7) Is it objective? (8) Does it eliminate the writer's opinion, unless it is an opinion piece? (9) Why are we running this article? (10) What end will be served? (11) Should we consult someone of another race/ethnicity? Do we have enough expertise on other races/cultures to be sure we have covered their viewpoint sufficiently? (12) Have we explained the significance of the story? (13) Does anyone mentioned in the story need protection? Was this person involved in the story by choice or by chance? (14) Will the reporter cause considerable harm to someone just by asking questions? (15) What alternative approaches might the reporter take to minimize the harm of privacy invasion?

➤ Ethical Issues

Besides legal issues, high school journalists must also face ethical issues. Publication staffs should urge collaborative decision-making as there is value in having multiple voices solve problems.

"We must develop the individual ability and the organizational culture that produce excellence. We must be at our best on the most difficult of assignments. Anything less is unacceptable."—Bob Steele, ethics program director, Poynter Institute

er. For example, if a writer refers to the principal of a high school without using his or her name, readers will know who is meant. If the writer gives name, age, address, and occupation of a person, complete identification has occurred. *Publication* means that someone not connected with the publication has seen the printed material. Conceivably, if a newspaper reaches a newsstand, publication has occurred. *Fault* means that before the plaintiff can win money, he or she must prove that the publication did something it was not supposed to do. Examples of fault range from printing a statement believed to be false to using unreliable sources to trying to defame someone deliberately.

Even if a libelous statement appears in a publication, courts generally will not hold a publication accountable for the libel unless it can be proved that the publication was at fault (sloppy, careless in reporting) in printing the statement. In many instances, malice (reckless disregard for the truth/intent to cause harm) also has to be proven.

Libel is of two types: *libel per se* and *libel per quod. Libel per se* can occur when a reporter uses a word or phrase that, taken at face value, appears to be libelous. For example, if a reporter calls someone a crook, the word "crook" is potentially libelous since it implies wrongdoing. Even the word *chicken* has been construed as libelous. In 1979 Dan Williams, a former wide receiver for the San Diego Chargers, was awarded $300,000 because he was called "chicken" in a book, *The Nightmare Season*, by Dr. Arnold Mandell.

Libel per quod, on the other hand, does not include words that, taken at face value, appear to be libelous. For example, a reporter might write that Joe Smith attended a football game on Sunday. Taken at face value, that statement appears to be devoid of libel. However, if Joe's religion does not permit him to attend games on Sunday, and if in fact he did not attend one, the reporter may have damaged Joe's reputation. Libel per quod is probably more frightening to the average journalist and requires more alertness than libel per se.

There are several defenses that a publication or broadcast station may use if a libel suit is brought against it. The best

➢ Hazelwood Stories

The stories that appeared in the Hazelwood East Spectrum were on the following topics:
• Teenage pregnancy.
• Divorce.
• Runaways.
• Delinquents.

Student rights have long been a topic of debate. Tinker v. Des Moines Independent Community School District *and* Hazelwood v. Kuhlmeier *affect student rights, as indicated by the above article from the* Lion, Lyons Township High School, La Grange and Western Springs, IL.

defense against libel, however, is good reporting. Reporters should always check facts. If they are absolutely certain that a story contains no false statements, it is doubtful that a libel suit would be brought even if someone's reputation were somewhat damaged. If a suit is filed, however, the best defense is truth. Truth alone is a complete defense in some jurisdictions, but in other jurisdictions it must be accompanied by good motives.

When motives enter into the picture, the question of malice usually arises. *Malice* is the intent, without good cause, to commit an act that will result in harm to some person or group. The key word in that definition is *intent*. It is often difficult to prove what someone intended to do unless there are witnesses who can testify about the reporter's behavior. Obviously, a school publication or broadcast station is not the place for a student reporter to vent his or her wrath against anyone.

Red Flags

• *Statements that accuse or suggest that a person has been involved in serious sexual misconduct or is sexually promiscuous.*

• *Statements that associate a person with a loathsome or socially stigmatizing disease.*

• *Statements that accuse another of committing a crime, or of being arrested, jailed, or otherwise involved in criminal activity.*

• *Negative statements that affect a person's ability to engage in his livelihood, business, trade, profession, or office.*

• *Statements that attack a person's honesty or integrity.*

• *Negative statements about grades or academic ability.*

• *Statements that allege racial, ethnic, or religious bigotry.*

• *Statements that accuse a person of associating with criminals, "shady characters," or publicly disfavored groups.*

• *Statements that question a person's creditworthiness, financial stability, or economic status.*

• *Any negative statement about a lawyer.*

—Taken from Law of the Press *by the Student Press Law Center*

our policy

THE FEATHERDUSTER, THE NEWS-magazine of Westlake High School, attempts to inform and entertain its audience in a broad, fair and accurate manner on subjects which concern the readers. This publication also seeks to provide a forum of ideas and opinions between the staff of the newsmagazine, the students, the faculty and the local community about issues presented. Content decisions rest in the hands of the staff, despite the Supreme Court's ruling in Hazelwood v. Kuhlmeier.

Opinions expressed in the columns that appear in the FEATHERDUSTER do not necessarily reflect the opinions and views of the entire FEATHERDUSTER staff, the school administration or the advertisers.

The staff encourages letters to the editor as an avenue for expressing the opinions of the readers. However, all letters must be signed to be considered for publication. Due to frequent space limitations, not all letters will be published and the editorial board reserves the right to edit them for placement purposes.

No material, opinionated or otherwise, will be printed that is libelous, advocates an illegal activity or which the editorial board deems in poor taste. This restriction includes letters to the staff, advertising, guest columns and anything else the board feels presents an inappropriate message.

All material produced or published by the FEATHERDUSTER staff is copyright 1996 FEATHERDUSTER. No part of this work may be reproduced in any form without written consent of the editorial board.

Submit letters in room 128, call 432-0041 ext. 227 or mail letters to 4100 Westbank Drive, Austin, Texas 78746 and let your voice be heard.

The above editorial policy is from the Featherduster, *Westlake High School, Austin, TX. Note the statement that no part of the paper can be reproduced in any form without written permission. Written permission was obtained to reproduce the above.*

➤ *Defamation of Character*

If a plaintiff can prove that the following statements were published inaccurately, that person can usually satisfy the harm or defamation element of libel.

• *Statements that attack a person's integrity.*

• *Statements that allege racial, ethnic, or religious bias.*

• *Statements that accuse a person of committing a crime.*

• *Statements that accuse someone of being in jail.*

• *Statements that indicate a person has a socially stigmatizing disease.*

• *Statements that suggest a person has been involved in sexual misconduct or is sexually promiscuous.*

• *Statements that affect a person's ability to hold a job.*

➤ *Intent of* Hazelwood

The Court in the Hazelwood *case ruled that "a school official could impose reasonable restrictions on the speech of students, teachers and other members of the school community for legitimate pedagogical reasons." It did not describe those reasons, but it suggested the following as examples of what could be censored:*

• *Poorly written copy.*

• *Inadequately researched copy.*

• *Biased or prejudiced copy.*

• *Vulgar or profane copy.*

• *Ungrammatical copy.*

• *Copy that is unsuitable for immature audiences.*

➤ *Public Figure Rule*

• *The Supreme Court has ruled that public officials and public figures must prove actual malice. That means the publishers knew the material was false and/or were reckless in verifying accuracy.*

• *In most states, courts have ruled that school principals are public officials, but Georgia, Illinois, and Ohio have ruled they are not.*

• *Most states have not ruled that teachers are public officials.*

• *It is probably best to always assume that the people you are writing about are private individuals—not public officials.*

Another primary defense in libel cases is *fair comment and criticism.* Courts have held that publications have the right to criticize someone fairly who relies on the public for support. That means that the publication may criticize the person's public role, not his private life. Included are sports figures, movie stars, politicians, and other performers. Without that protection, it would be nearly impossible to write an unfavorable review of anything or to comment on political affairs.

The third primary defense is *privilege.* There are two types of privilege—*qualified* and *absolute.* Members of Congress and other federal and state government officials have *absolute privilege* when they are speaking during official proceedings. That immunity does not necessarily apply to city government; the decisions are not clear. Others who enjoy absolute privilege are witnesses in court trials, jurors, and trial lawyers, as long as their comments are made in court. The U.S. Supreme Court ruled in 1979 that congressional immunity does not protect members of Congress from libel suits for statements they make in news releases or newsletters.

Journalists enjoy *qualified privilege.* They have the right to report on official proceedings without fear of being sued for libel. A person tried for a crime and found not guilty can't sue reporters or publications for stories about testimony against him during the trial. The news stories should always make it clear, however, that the individual is accused and should never imply that a person is guilty until there is a conviction.

There are several secondary defenses against libel. They probably would not win a libel suit, but they might lessen the amount of damages awarded. These secondary defenses are: (1) *retraction and apology;* (2) *settlement;* (3) *reply;* (4) *proof of previous bad reputation;* and (5) *reliance on a usually reliable source.*

If a publication realizes it has defamed someone, it should print a *retraction* and an *apology* immediately and, if possible, on the same page on which the libel occurred or in a more prominent place. If a libel occurs in a school publication, it is difficult to print a retraction immediately because of the infrequency of the publication. Staffs might consider apologizing over the intercom if the person libeled wants immediate

SPJ updates its code of ethics

Editor's note: The Society of Professional Journalists has struggled with updating its code of ethics for two years. One of the main problems was that the membership couldn't decide whether there should be an enforcement provision in the code. It was finally decided to bypass the problem. The following code was released last month.

Preamble

Members of the Society of Professional Journalists believe that public enlightenment is the forerunner of justice and the foundation of democracy. The duty of the journalist is to further those ends by seeking truth and providing a fair and comprehensive account of events and issues. Conscientious journalists from all media and specialties strive to serve the public with thoroughness and honesty. Professional integrity is the cornerstone of a journalist's credibility.

Members of the Society share a dedication to ethical behavior and adopt this code to declare the Society's principles and standards of practice.

Seek truth and report it

Journalists should be honest, fair and courageous in gathering, reporting and interpreting information. Journalists should:

• Test the accuracy of information from all sources and exercise care to avoid inadvertent error. Deliberate distortion is never permissible.
• Diligently seek out subjects of news stories to give them the opportunity to respond to allegations of wrongdoing.
• Identify sources whenever feasible.

The public is entitled to as much information as possible on sources' reliability.
• Always question sources' motives before promising anonymity. Clarify conditions attached to any promise made in exchange for information. Keep promises.
• Make certain that headlines, news teasers and promotional material, photos, video, audio, graphics, sound bites and quotations do not misrepresent. They should not oversimplify or highlight incidents out of context.
• Never distort the content of news photos or video. Image enhancement for technical clarity is always permissible. Label montages and photo illustrations.
• Avoid misleading re-enactments of staged news events. If re-enactment is necessary to tell a story, label it.
• Avoid undercover or other surreptitious methods of gathering information except when traditional open methods will not yield information vital to the public. Use of such methods should be explained as part of the story.
• Never plagiarize.
• Tell the story of the diversity and magnitude of the human experience boldly, even when it is unpopular to do so.
• Examine their own cultural values and avoid imposing those values on others.
• Avoid stereotyping by race, gender, age, religion, ethnicity, geography, sexual orientation, disability, physical appearance or social status.
• Support the open exchange of views, even views they find repugnant.
• Give voice to the voiceless; official and unofficial sources of information can be equally valid.
• Distinguish news from advertising and shun hybrids that blur the lines between the two.
• Recognize a special obligation to ensure that the public's business is conducted in the open and that government records are open to inspection.

Minimize harm

Ethical journalists treat sources, subjects and colleagues as human beings deserving of respect. Journalists should:

• Show compassion for those who may be affected adversely by news coverage. Use special sensitivity when dealing with children and inexperienced sources or subjects.
• Be sensitive when seeking or using interviews or photographs of those affected by tragedy or grief.
• Recognize that gathering and reporting information may cause harm or discomfort. Pursuit of the news is not a license for arrogance.
• Recognize that private people have a greater right to control information about themselves than do public officials and others who seek power, influence or attention. Only an overriding public need can justify intrusion into anyone's privacy.
• Show good taste. Avoid pandering to lurid curiosity.
• Be cautious about identifying juvenile suspects or victims of sex crimes.
• Be judicious about naming criminal suspects before the formal filing of charges.
• Balance a criminal suspect's fair trial rights with the public's right to be informed.

Act independently

Journalists should be free of obligation to any interest other than the public's right to know. Journalists should:

• Avoid conflicts of interest, real or perceived.
• Remain free of associations and activities that may compromise integrity or damage credibility.
• Refuse gifts, favors, fees, free travel and special treatment, and shun secondary employment, political involvement, public office and service in community organizations if they compromise journalistic integrity.
• Disclose unavoidable conflicts.
• Be vigilant and courageous about holding those with power accountable.
• Deny favored treatment to advertisers and special interests and resist their pressure to influence news coverage.
• Be wary of sources offering information for favors or money; avoid bidding for news.

Be accountable

Journalists are accountable to their readers, listeners, viewers and each other. Journalists should:

• Clarify and explain news coverage and invite dialogue with the public over journalistic conduct.
• Encourage the public to voice grievances against the news media.
• Admit mistakes and correct them promptly.
• Expose unethical practices of journalists and the news media.
• Abide by the same high standards to which they hold others. ∎

The Society of Professional Journalists adopted the above Code of Ethics, which appeared in the St. Louis Journalism Review *in 1996. Publication staffs might consider including some of these in their editorial policies.*

➢ Fraser v. Tinker

The Supreme Court distinguished Fraser from Tinker on the following grounds:

• Fraser's speech was lewd and indecent and expressed no particular political viewpoint, whereas the Tinkers were not lewd and indecent and did express a political viewpoint.

• Permitting lewd speech undermines the school's basic educational mission. The Tinkers' action did not do that.

• Attendance at the assembly where Fraser spoke was mandatory and therefore gave the impression that the school sanctioned his remarks. No one was forced to follow the Tinkers in their demonstration.

• Fraser's speech did cause disruption among the students during and after the assembly, but the court ruled the Tinkers' action was not disruptive.

action. A yearbook staff can retract and apologize in an issue of the school paper; it certainly would not want to wait a year until the next book was published.

Settlement is a secondary defense only in that it will probably keep the publication out of court. As the word implies, however, some financial settlement has probably been reached, usually involving a substantial sum of money and suggesting that the publication has admitted guilt. A settlement can sometimes be a retraction and apology. A settlement should be put in writing and witnessed.

Reply may be used as a defense in dealing with controversial news. The defendant must show that the defamatory statement was printed in reply to some other statement, and that the reply was not made maliciously.

Proof of *previous bad reputation* can sometimes be used as a secondary defense, but the publication must be sure that the plaintiff's bad reputation is current. A person fifty-five years

➤ **Public Forum**

In the Hazelwood *case, the Supreme Court ruled that the* Spectrum *was not a forum for public discussion. It said a school was a public forum only if administrators had by practice or by written policy opened its facilities for indiscriminate use by the public or by some segment of the public. Since there was no public forum at Hazelwood, the administrators had the right to place reasonable restrictions on students' speech. The Supreme Court established the public forum theory in 1939 in* Hague v. the Committee for Industrial Organizations, *and it reinforced it in 1983 in the case of* Perry Education Association v. Perry Local Educator's Association. *The Perry case dealt with who had the right to place items in teachers' mailboxes. The court ruled that the school district could dictate that the mailboxes were for school-related business. Thus, the mailboxes were not a public forum open for all individuals to use.*

old who had been involved in shoplifting at eighteen may not be considered to have a previous bad reputation because his offense is not current; he may have led an exemplary life since he was eighteen. The defendant must show that the plaintiff's reputation is so bad that any further defamatory statement will not further mar his name.

Reliance on a *usually reliable source* may also be a secondary defense. If the publication can prove that its source has always been right in the past and that it had no reason to think that the source was wrong this time, the jury might be more lenient in awarding damages.

Juries may award three types of damages: *general damages* compensate the plaintiff for damage to his reputation; *special damages* compensate him for financial loss; and *punitive damages* compensate him for malice.

School publications obviously want to avoid getting involved in any type of lawsuit. However, they should not shy away from covering controversial issues. School administrators cannot restrict schools from publishing controversial stories. In 1972 the U.S. Supreme Court ruled against prior restraint *(Shanley v. Northeast Independent School District)*, and in 1973 a New Hampshire court ruled that prior restraint could be used only if the material in question were libelous, obscene, or disruptive *(Vail v. Board of Education)*. In such cases the burden of proof rests upon the administration. To clarify further the right of school publications to cover controversial issues, a U.S. Circuit Court in 1975 upheld the right of a newspaper staff to publish a sex-education supplement *(Bayer v. Kinzler)*, and in 1976 another decision *(Gambino v. Fairfax)* held that the "school newspaper is not in reality a part of the curriculum of the school"; therefore it "is entitled to First Amendment protection." In the *Gambino* case, Virginia school administrators had prevented the school newspaper from publishing information about birth control because school rules prohibited teaching contraception in sex-education classes. The court rejected the defendants' argument that high school students are a "captive audience."

Merely because the courts have granted school publica-

Using Names of Minors

• *According to the Student Press Law Center, it is up to a publication to decide whether to use a juvenile's name in a story.*

• *In 1979, the U.S. Supreme Court ruled that the First Amendment protects the right of journalists to use the names of minors in newsworthy stories as long as the information is "lawfully obtained" and "truthfully" reported. In this case in particular, the court overturned a West Virginia law that prohibited the publication of names of juvenile offenders.*

• *Access to information about juveniles may be difficult to obtain from official government sources, but this does not mean that the media are prohibited from using such information if they are able to obtain it some other way.*

• *Relying on unofficial sources, however, can be risky, but once the information has been verified, there is no legal barrier to publishing it.*

• *Many news organizations do not, as a rule, publish the names of minors accused of criminal activity, but this is an editorial or ethical decision, not one compelled by law.*

> New York Times v. Sullivan

The Supreme Court's ruling in this case set the standard for libel lawsuits. The court said: "The Constitution requires, we think, a federal rule that prohibits a public official from recovering damages for a defamatory falsehood relating to his official conduct unless he proves that the statement was made 'with actual malice,' that is, with the knowledge that it was false or with reckless disregard of whether it was false or not."

Scroll Editorial Policy

To best serve the public, the *Scroll* staff will strive to maintain an effective and consistent editorial policy.

1. The *Scroll* is a forum for student expression. Letters to the Editor must be signed and the submission of essays and other works is encouraged. The *Scroll*, however, reserves the right not to print articles which contain libelous or obscene statements or those found to be in poor taste by the editorial board, and to edit those which exceed space available.

2. Unsigned editorials represent the opinion of the editorial board. Signed editorials express the writer's opinion and do not necessarily reflect the opinion of the *Scroll*.

3. Any criticism will be printed on the opinion page and must be supported with fact and a logical solution.

4. The *Scroll* will print a correction or retraction for any factual error or libelous statement brought to the attention of the staff.

5. Every effort will be made by the *Scroll* to cover both sides of any controversial story printed in the paper.

6. Current and future events will be concentrated upon for all sports stories.

7. The staff reserves the right to refuse advertisements deemed illegal or inappropriate for a high school newspaper.

8. The staff will strive to work with the administration in all matters regarding censorship in accordance with the Hazelwood decision.

The above editorial policy is from the Scroll, Gladstone High School, Gladstone, OR. Note that statement one indicates the paper is a "forum for student expression." Such a statement is important according to Hazelwood guidelines if the administration is not to control the contents.

tions First Amendment protection does not mean that staffs have a right to print whatever they wish. A reporter should ask himself/herself: Is the story in good taste? Does the public have a right to know? What end will be served? It is essential for the student reporter to remember that every right carries the duty of responsibility. For that reason most school newspapers have eliminated the gossip column and the April Fool's Day issue. Creating items of gossip about people and poking fun at them can often result in a negative viewpoint on the part of readers. There is nothing journalistically sound about invented articles. School publications, like professional publications, should deal with facts.

Be careful not to offend unnecessarily. A yearbook in Texas in 1981 dedicated its publication to Jesus Christ. Several people were offended, others were outraged, and some questioned its constitutionality in regard to separation of church and state. A college newspaper editor at the University of Louisville was discharged in 1979 for refusing to recant an April Fool story that falsely reported that the football team had been arrested on sex charges. The coach and team members threatened to sue.

Offending persons unnecessarily or failing to stick to the facts could be considered irresponsible reporting. Lack of responsibility could lead to publication of something that would disrupt the educational process. Careful scrutiny of all copy to insure accuracy should prevent this. However, if a staff knows it is dealing with a "hot" issue, it should approach the topic with extreme care. A staff should never print anything that it knows will create a disruption, such as calling for a student revolt or protest.

Be careful also of word choice. The word *if* does not mean the same as *since*. *If* implies that the writer is questioning some position.

Finally, school publications, like all other publications, should be aware that courts have ruled that publications may not indulge in an invasion of privacy. The right to privacy means that a person has the right to live his or her private life without it being exposed to the public for comment, criticism, or ridicule.

➢ *The Buckley Amendment*

• *The Buckley Amendment was passed by Congress in 1974. The law required that students be allowed access to their education records to ensure that the information contained therein was accurate. The law also prohibited schools from releasing a student's education records without that student's permission.*

• *Some schools interpreted "education records" to mean all records regardless of whether they were related to a student's academic performance. This meant journalists could not have access to campus police records.*

• *Congress amended the Buckley Amendment in 1992 to exclude police records from its coverage.*

35

High School Journalism

Privacy is not well defined in law, and at the high school level it is sometimes difficult to determine which of a student's actions at school are private. Generally, however, if a student is involved in school activities, his performances are considered to be public. That does not mean, however, that his grades or any disciplinary action taken against him are public information; those have generally been considered private. The law is clear in most states when it comes to advertisements. Publications may not use a person's name or photograph in an ad without his/her approval. If the person is a minor, parental permission is necessary.

Members of the high school press also have a responsibility of being aware of copyright laws. Copyright protects an author against unauthorized use of his or her work. This includes cartoon characters, photos, song lyrics, news stories, and books, but it does not protect titles, short phrases, slogans, or facts. In other words, a newspaper may copyright a news story, but the facts that support the story are not copyrighted. Most works are owned by the person who created them. However, the "works for hire" description gives an employer the right to work created by an employee while on the job. To avoid a conflict, both the employer and employee might sign an agreement as to who owns the work. This would be true for student publications as well.

Anything copyrighted before Jan. 1, 1978 has a copyright term of 28 years and may be renewed for another 28 years. Beginning Jan. 1, 1978, copyrights became renewable for a second term of 47 years. After Jan. 1, 1978 the copyright for works not made for hire lasts for 50 years after the death of the last surviving creator, and for works of hire, a copyright lasts for 75 years from the first publication or for 100 years from the time of creation, whichever comes first.

Student journalists should be aware of their rights and their responsibilities. Anyone who works on a school publication should become familiar with the publication's editorial policy, which should clearly define those rights and responsibilities. Every school publication should have a written editorial policy to guarantee that all administrators, school board

➢ *First Amendment Message Adopted in 1990*

• High school students should have the same rights of freedom of speech and freedom of press as adults, and it is up to us—journalists, educators, parents, and others—to ensure those freedoms are maintained.

• School officials should resist censorship pressures and encourage student expression as a form of citizenship training.

• State legislatures should enact laws that strengthen or enhance these local provisions for student freedom.

• School boards and school administrators should employ qualified journalism teachers and adopt clear policies that ensure free speech and a free press in school.

members, advisers, and staff writers know exactly what it may or may not do. An editorial policy should be based on applicable court decisions.

School publications are no different from the professional media. All print and broadcast media have the same concern for rights and responsibilities. Most professional publications have a written editorial policy that covers such things as libel and invasion of privacy.

A sample editorial policy for a scholastic publication follows:

SAMPLE GUIDELINES FOR SCHOOL NEWSPAPERS AND YEARBOOKS

I. INTRODUCTION:

The school newspaper and yearbook, like other publications, have the right, as well as the responsibility, to inform and entertain their readers and to serve as media of interpretation of and commentary on events affecting their readers. At the same time, however, it should be noted that both publications are regular classes and, as such, function as learning experiences for their staff members. Therefore, they come under the jurisdiction of the educational code, which requires the publications to practice only objective, responsible journalism.

II. LEGAL STATUS OF PUBLICATIONS:

A. Both the school newspaper and the yearbook have the right of freedom of the press as granted under the First Amendment (*Tinker v. Des Moines Independent Community School District*, 393 U.S. 503; 1969).

B. Neither the administration nor the board of education has the right of prior restraint (*Shanley v. Northeast Independent School District*, 462 F. 2d 960 5th Cir., 1972). Prior restraint may be used only if the material in question is libelous, obscene, or disruptive (*Vail v. Board of Education*, 354 F. Supp.

> *Constitutional Guarantee*
> • *Congress shall make no law respecting an establishment of religion, or prohibiting the free exercise thereof; or abridging the freedom of speech, or of the press; or the right of the people peaceably to assemble, and to petition the government for a redress of grievances.* —The First Amendment of the U.S. Constitution

➢ New York Times v. Sullivan

•*The New York Times ran an ad on April 5, 1960, asking for contributions to the Committee to Defend Rev. Martin Luther King, Jr.*

• *The ad said students at Alabama State College had been expelled after singing "My Country 'Tis of Thee" on the state-house steps in Montgomery. When the students protested, the dorms were padlocked to "starve them into sub-mission."*

In actuality, the students were expelled for seeking service at a lunch counter, the dorm wasn't padlocked, and the students sang "The Star-Spangled Banner."

L.B. Sullivan, city commissioner, argued that the ad charged him with "grave misconduct," and he sued for libel, winning a $500,000 judgment.

592; D. N.H., 1973). In cases where prior restraint is exercised, the burden of proof rests upon the administrators involved (*New York Times Co. v. United States*, 403 U.S. 713; 1971). Prior restraint may be exercised if copy is:

1. *Obscene; i.e.,* meets the following three tests:
   a. it must appeal to the average reader's prurient interest in sex;
   b. it must portray, in a patently offensive manner, sexual conduct specifically defined in the applicable state law;
   c. it must lack serious literary, political, or scientific value. (*Miller v. California*, 413 U.S. 15; 1973).

2. *Libelous; i.e.,* according to the Student Press Law Center the information in question must:
   a. be communicated to a third party;
   b. be false, or be printed with a reckless disregard of whether it was false or not (*New York Times Co. [I] v. Sullivan*, 376 U.S. 254; 1964), (*Gertz v. Robert Welch, Inc.*, 94 S. Ct. 2997, 1974);
   c. be regarded as referring to and reflecting on a specific individual, business, or product. This criterion is not at issue if the allegedly libelous communication specifically mentions the plaintiff (*New York Times Co. [I]*);
   d. be defamatory; i.e., destroy or harm the plaintiff's good reputation either in the eyes of the general reader or, if his professional reputation is involved, in the eyes of the fellow members of his profession;
   e. be published with actual malice when referring to a public official (*New York Times Co. [I]*).

3. *Disruptive; i.e.,* administrators can show that it would cause material and substantial interference with school operations (*Quarterman v. Byrd*, 453 F. 2d 54 4th Cir. 1971).

4. Administrators may regulate the time and place of distribution of the publication, as long as such regulation does not concern content (*Fujishima v. Board of Education*, 460 F. 2d 697 7th Cir., 1972).

III. RESPONSIBILITIES:

It is the responsibility of both publications not to incite questions of legality of content mentioned in Section I. Toward this end the school newspaper and yearbook will:

A. not print material that is obscene, libelous, or disruptive (see definitions in II, B);
B. not print material that would constitute invasion of privacy through:
    1. publication of private (not open to public record), although truthful, information about an individual;
    2. publication of false material;
    3. use of a person's name or picture in an advertisement without the permission of the person;
    4. unethical methods of obtaining quotes; i.e., through unauthorized use of recording equipment or quoting without the subject's permission;
C. not incorporate fictionalized material into a story unless it is clearly labeled as such;
D. strive for accuracy in reporting and writing;
E. print retractions for errors when discovered and present a prompt apology to all of those concerned. The yearbook staff will print apologies in the newspaper if time allows;
F. print only criticism that the staff deems constructive; i.e., when the desire is both reasonable and attainable. The newspaper will not print repeated criticisms that would constitute harassment of any responsible individual or group;
G. present fairly, openly, and clearly views on contro-

➢ *More on Hazelwood*
• *Some lower courts have suggested that extracurricular student publications might be exempt from Hazelwood's limitations. Other courts, however, have disagreed with this idea.*
• *Policy and practice determine whether or not a school publication has "forum status." Policy refers to the school's statements in school board policies, in student handbooks, and in memos from school officials. Practice refers to the way the publication has operated in the past.*
• *Although editorial policies printed in a student publication are not necessarily school district policies, such printed statements might be used to show that the publication had been operating as a public forum for student expression.*
• *Decisions since* Hazelwood *make clear that school policy outweighs publication policy if a conflict*

(Continued)

versial issues;

H. comment on and recognize persons or groups when the adviser or staff or both deem that credit is due;

I. run each publication as a business as nearly as possible;

J. publish no profanity except when it makes no scatological or sexual references and its deletion would alter considerably the forcefulness or meaning of the quote (e.g., "The idea was damn stupid," he said.).

IV. GENERAL EDITORIAL POLICY

A. Both the newspaper and yearbook staffs will make every reasonable effort to verify quotations in final approved copy with the individual(s) quoted, in the interest of accuracy.

B. Copy in both the newspaper and the yearbook will bear bylines when, in the opinion of the adviser with the editor's approval, the writer has earned recognition and running the byline is acceptable journalistically.

C. If newspaper editorial doesn't bear a byline, it reflects the opinion of the entire staff. A bylined editorial reflects only the opinion of the writer. In either case, viewpoints expressed in newspaper editorials are not necessarily shared by any members of the faculty (including the adviser), administration, or board of education. (This policy will be stated in abbreviated form in some issues of the newspaper.)

D. All letters to the editor of the newspaper or yearbook must be signed, but the staffs may withhold names upon request. Because of space limitations, letters of 300 words in length will receive preference, and longer letters will be subject to condensation with the cooperation of the writer. The final decision of whether to print a letter rests solely with the staff. (This policy will be stated, in abbreviated form, in some issues of the newspaper.)

E. Both the newspaper and the yearbook have the right to accept or reject any advertisement, including political advertisements. The staffs will obtain written permission from the persons involved if a photograph is included with the ad.

EXERCISES

1. Make a detailed study of one or more of the court cases cited in the sample editorial policy. Report your findings to the class.

2. Analyze the daily paper in your town for one week. Did you find anything in headlines, captions, photographs, or articles that might border on obscenity, libel, or invasion of privacy? Discuss your findings in class.

3. Some professional publications have a Reader's Advocate column in which the advocate responds to readers' criticisms. If your hometown paper has one, read the column in a recent issue and discuss in class whether you agree or disagree with the reader.

4. Look through issues of your school newspaper and yearbook and list items that could be considered embarrassing to the persons involved. Determine if the items were printed intentionally or if the embarrassing item is a mistake like a typographical error. This could be a good start toward compiling a list of bloopers that have appeared in your school's publications.

5. Read the following editorial. Discuss its possible consequences. Is it likely that a libel suit might be filed? Why or why not? What should the newspaper's defense be?

> **Zero Tolerance**
> Following the shootings at Columbine High School in Colorado in April 1999, school districts across the country started adopting zero tolerance polices toward student speech. In Texas, a seventh grader spent six days in a juvenile detention center after he was arrested for writing a Halloween horror story in which he described accidentally shooting two classmates and a teacher. A North Carolina student was arrested for a speech he made. A jury convicted him of communicating threats by leaving a message on a school computer screen that said, "The end is near." He received a 45-day suspended sentence with 18 months of probation, and he had to complete 48 hours of community service for the message. School administrators also expelled him for one year. These incidents indicate that freedom of expression carries a freedom of responsibility.

For the third consecutive year the instrumental music department at Belleview has failed to live up to its abilities.

It seems astounding that students who received A's or higher at music festivals for their individual performances when they were in junior high have slipped to B's and in some cases even C's.

Is this because they are losing their abilities? According to the music students themselves, that is not the case. The students have simply lost interest in music and, therefore, are not trying to perform to the best of their abilities.

Why this loss of interest? Perhaps the band instructor can answer that question. He is probably the only one who can. Not only have students lost interest in their individual performances, but there also seems to be a lack of interest in music groups.

Four years ago more than 250 students were enrolled in some type of instrumental music class. This year total enrollment has dropped to 109.

Who is responsible? We feel there is only one answer. Isn't it time the administration decided to change instructors?

6. Create a courtroom drama by reenacting one of the cases mentioned in the sample editorial policy, or write your own fictitious case and create a trial scene.

7. Obtain copies of the *Student Press Law Center Report* and give an oral presentation on censorship cases affecting secondary schools since the Hazelwood case.

8. Read through your school's exchange yearbooks and exchange newspapers and see if you can find examples of reporting that might embarrass someone needlessly or that might border on damaging someone's reputation. Make an oral report to the class of your findings.

9. Read one of the chapters in *Law of the Student Press* by the Student Press Law Center and make an

oral presentation to the class on your findings.

10. Do a report on the *Kincaid vs. Gibson* case where the Circuit Court applied the Hazelwood case to a college publication. Do you think Hazelwood should be applied to college publications. Why or why not?

11. Accuracy should be an important part of any editorial policy. Look through several issues of your school paper and look through last year's yearbook and list the number of times you found a misspelled word, including student names.

12. Editorial policies should include a statement about articles providing balance. Analyze your school's publications to determine if there is diversity in student quotes--compare quotes from various ethnic backgrounds, male vs. female, and freshmen vs. seniors. Also, in controversial stories, has the number of quotes on both sides been equalized? In looking at racially balanced quotes, determine what percentage of your population falls into each ethnic background. For example, if 25% of your student body are Hispanic, then at least 25% of your quotes should come from Hispanics.

13. Use the Internet and contact various national organizations like the Poynter Institute in Florida, the Freedom Forum in Washington, D.C. and the First Amendment Center in Tennessee to find out their policies concerning diversity and ethics. Prepare an oral or a written report for class.

14. Analyze the last issue of your school paper and/or the last issue of the school yearbook to determine what additional steps you might have taken to have made each story more complete and more balanced.

15. Does your publication include guidelines for covering crises like the shootings which occurred at Columbine High School in Colorado in 1999? If not, write guidelines to cover such crises situations. Check with other high school publications to see what their guidelines are.

CHAPTER
three

Style and Editing

To enable reporters to be consistent and brief in their writing styles, publications develop a stylebook outlining rules of writing. Professional publications have stylebooks, and school publications should have their own. The *Associated Press Stylebook* can provide suggestions for high school journalists.

Each publication should develop its own style rules based on correct grammar. Correct spelling is also part of style.

Most publications use the first spelling given in the dictionary; however, a second spelling may be preferred, such as using "advisor" instead of "adviser." Preferred second spellings should be included in the stylebook.

Copy preparation is also part of style. A suggested method is as follows: Have all copy written in ink or typed double-spaced on 8 1/2" x 11" paper. In the upper left corner of each page, the writer places his or her name, the name of the story (slug or guideline), and his or her class. For example, if the story is about the school play, the guideline might be "Play." In the upper right corner of the first page of copy, the writer notes the number of words in the story. This serves to determine the number of inches the story will cover in print. For example, it is possible to get about 40 words to a vertical inch in a column of type two inches wide set in 8-point type. Therefore, at 40 words per inch it would take about 400 words to fill a two-inch-wide column of 8-point type, 10 inches long. There are 72 points to a vertical inch, so 8-point type is approximately 1/9 of an inch high.

The writer begins the story halfway down the first page to leave room for a headline and for lead revisions, if necessary.

If the story is more than one page in length, the word "more" should be written at the bottom of each page but the last one. Include "30" or the symbol "#" at the bottom of the last page to indicate the end of the story.

"More," "30," and "#" are used to help the writer or the editors make corrections in the copy faster. Many publications now use electronic editing, having their own word processors and video display terminals. That makes copyediting symbols unnecessary because corrections can be made at the machine as a story is being typeset. Copyreading symbols, however, are still used with handwritten or typewritten copy. The symbols are given at the end of the proposed stylebook in this chapter. All reporters should memorize them and use them with handwritten or typewritten copy. They are standard worldwide.

Proofreading symbols are also standard worldwide and even with computers are still used in correcting copy by hand. Students should not rely on computer spellcheckers or grammar programs to catch all mistakes. A computer may know if a word is spelled correctly, but it does not know if it is the correct word. For example, a computer does not know the difference between *their* and *there*, or between *effect* and *affect*. Spellcheckers skip over words that are spelled correctly. It is essential, therefore, that even if a story is set on a computer, a copy be printed to be proofread by hand.

Reporters must also learn style rules. One rule that most journalists follow is to write copy in the active voice, not the passive.

To understand active and passive voice, the writer must be able to recognize the subject and the predicate (verb) of a sentence. A verb is in the active voice when its subject performs the action. A verb is in the passive voice when its subject receives the action.

> All the students failed the exam. (Active)
> The exam was failed by all the students. (Passive)
> Jack Jobe led the team to victory. (Active)
> The team was led to victory by Jack Jobe.
> (Passive)

> ➢ *Coaching Vs. Fixing*
>
> One role of a copy editor is to work with writers on ways to improve writing. The editor, however, should coach the writer, not fix the writing.
> • Fixing corrects errors, coaching corrects tendencies to write improperly.
> • Fixing is quickly done, coaching takes more time.
> • Fixing improves copy, coaching improves writing.
> • Fixing means finding fault, coaching means finding things to praise.
> • Fixing means correcting problems, coaching means focusing on ways to correct them.

Faculty members voted to donate $500 toward a scholarship. (Active)

It was decided by the faculty to donate $500 toward a scholarship. (Passive)

Note that in the passive voice some form of the verb *be (am, is, are, was, were, been)* is used with another verb.

It is possible, however, to have passive voice in a sentence without using a *be* verb.

"Varsity Valor," played by the band, entertained the crowd.

The verb *played* is in the passive voice, even though *entertained* is in the active voice. Therefore, the dependent clause is passive. The word *by* can sometimes be an indicator of the passive voice, but not always.

The book was read by several students. (Passive)

Jack Jobe walked by the room. (Active)

Many writers confuse the passive voice with the past tense; they are not the same. Passive voice may occur in any tense. Journalists normally write in the active voice because it is more direct and generally shorter.

Persons who edit copy must have an excellent command of English, must know all style rules, and must be knowledgeable about any topic. That means that a copy editor must be familiar with many areas of life—social, political, and economic—that are pertinent to a school community as they are pertinent to any community.

Copy editors should be able to prevent inaccuracies from appearing in a publication, and they should be able to distinguish editorializing (the writer's opinion) from fact. Copy editors should improve an article in any way possible, providing the reporter has already had a chance to rewrite. Sometimes deadlines do not allow a reporter to rewrite. If the copy edi-

➢ *Verbs*

• *A verb expresses action or state of being.*

• *A transitive verb is usually accompanied by a direct object.* The boy threw a ball across the street. Ball *is the direct object of* threw.

• *An intransitive verb requires no object.* The runners flew along the course.

• *A linking verb shows the relationship of the subject to the predicate noun.* Her favorite color is blue.

• *Tense indicates the time of action or state expressed by a verb. The principal parts of a verb are the present, past, and past participle. For example:* walk, walked, walked. *A fourth principal part is the present participle, which is formed by adding "ing" to the present tense form of a verb.*

tor cannot make necessary corrections, or if she is unsure of all the facts, the story should not run. The copy editor should take nothing for granted. She should be skeptical of every fact, search for libelous or obscene statements, and be aware of invasion of privacy or statements that might cause disruption.

Obviously, each reporter should edit his own copy before turning it in, but others should read it also. The more staff members who read a piece of copy, the more likely that mistakes will be avoided.

Three common errors that occur in high school publications are errors in noun-pronoun agreement, in subject-verb agreement, and in modification.

If nouns are singular, they must have singular pronouns.

> Wrong: The band played their music for the entire school.
> Right: The band played its music for the entire school.
> Wrong: The team lost their game, 24-0.
> Right: The team lost its game, 24-0.

It is common for many writers to use *their* in place of its. However, *team* and *band* are singular nouns and take the singular pronoun *it*. Subjects and verbs must agree in person and number.

> Wrong: Each of the girls plan to attend the meeting.
> Right: Each of the girls plans to attend the meeting.
> Wrong: Everyone at school were planning to attend.
> Right: Everyone at school was planning to attend.

Each and *everyone* are singular nouns and take singular verbs.

Be careful of starting sentences with participial phrases. Most participles end in *ing* or *ed*. Some past participles, however, change the *ed* form. Starting a sentence with a participle

➢ *Nouns*
• *A noun is the name of a person, place or thing.*
• *A common noun is the name of any one of a class of persons, places, or things. It is not capitalized:* toy, dog, door, screen.
• *A proper noun is the name of a particular person, place, or thing:* U.S. House of Representatives, Lea Ann Hall, Evanne Dill, Watson Dill, Briana Keightley, Ashlyn Keightley.
• *A collective noun names a group of persons or objects:* faculty, family, crowd.
• *Nouns may be singular or plural, and they have four genders (masculine, feminine, neuter, and common). Nouns have common gender when they may be either masculine or feminine (person, player, pal).*

can often lead to a misplaced or dangling modifier and cause the writer to say something other than what was intended.

> Wrong: Entering the room, the smell of hot dogs overwhelmed him.
>
> Right: Entering the room, he smelled hot dogs.
>
> Wrong: Awarded the first prize, it was fun for Joan to enjoy her achievements.
>
> Right: Awarded the first prize, Joan enjoyed her achievements.

In the first wrong sentence, the subject of the sentence is *smell*, but the smell did not enter the room. In the second wrong sentence it sounds as if *it* was awarded first prize instead of Joan.

The copy editor also needs to be aware of sound-alikes such as: *a lot* and *allot; to, too, two; their, there, they're;* and *then, than.* Careful, unhurried editing will help assure that the correct word is used.

A skilled copyreader must check many other things. Are names spelled correctly? Are titles correct? Are dates correct? Do statistical figures add up? Do quotes make sense? Is there proper transition? Have unnecessary words been eliminated? The key is to take nothing for granted. Double-check and perhaps even triple-check all facts.

After type has been set, a publication must have proofreaders with the same high level of skill as the copyreaders. Proofreading is the final insurance against mistakes appearing in print. Whereas copyediting marks are usually made in the lines of copy, proofreaders make a mark where the error occurs and show in the margin what correction should be made.

Proofreader's symbols are not the same as copyreader's symbols. All editors should familiarize themselves with both sets of symbols and use them properly.

Following is a sample stylebook, but each publication should adopt rules pertinent to its own situation.

➤ *Pronouns*

• *A pronoun is a word used in place of a noun.*

• *A personal pronoun is a direct substitute for a noun. Like a noun, it has number, gender, and case. Person is shown in pronouns by a change of form to indicate the person speaking (first person), the person spoken to (second person), or a person or thing other than the speaker and the one spoken to (third person).*

• *A relative pronoun relates or connects a clause to its antecedent—the noun to which it refers. The most often used relative pronouns are* who, which, *and* that.

• *A demonstrative pronoun points out and identifies. It has number but no gender or case. The demonstrative pronouns are* this, that, these, *and* those.

SUGGESTED STYLEBOOK

Capitalization

1. Capital letters distinguish proper nouns from common nouns. Proper nouns refer to specific people, places, and things and are capitalized. Common nouns refer to general or nonspecific people, places, and things and are not capitalized.

2. The principal of the school is a specific person. His or her name is capitalized.

3. The word *nations* is general, as opposed to a specific nation. Write: *The nations violated the agreement.*

4. Trademarks are specific and therefore are capitalized. Unless a trademark name is essential to the story, use the generic word. Write *tissue*, instead of *Kleenex*.

5. General directions are lowercase, but terms designating specific regions are capitalized. *He was a native of the Middle West* indicates a region. *Turn west at the intersection* indicates direction.

6. Capitalize awards: *All-American Award, George H. Gallup Award, Richard MacKenzie Award.*

7. The word *Capitol* is uppercase when referring to the building in Washington, D.C., or to a specific state capitol. The word *capital* is lowercase when it refers to the capital city of the United States or of a state.

8. Names of races, nationalities, and religions are proper nouns and capitalized. Reference to skin color is a common noun and therefore is not capitalized.

9. Capitalize specific government bodies such as *Congress, Senate, House of Representatives.*

10. Academic rank such as *freshman* and *sophomore* is lowercase except when it is part of a proper noun, such as *Sophomore Week.*

> **Courtesy Titles**
>
> The Associated Press decided to drop courtesy titles in most of its articles in February 2000. The AP style is to identify women and men on first reference by first and last name and by last name on second reference. Previously, the AP's style was to use no courtesy titles for men, but it did use courtesy titles for women on second and subsequent references unless a woman asked that none be used. Under the new guidelines, AP will use courtesy titles if a woman requests one. The AP eliminated courtesy titles several years ago in sports stories. Even though the AP has opted not to use courtesy titles, each school publication's staff needs to make its own decision. The key is consistency.

• *An adjective modifies a noun or a pronoun.*

• *Adjectives tell what kind of, how many, which one. Adjectives are of two general kinds—descriptive and limiting. Descriptive adjectives might be a* red *bottle or a* smashed *car. Limiting adjectives might be a* former *employee or* cloudy *days.*

• *Adjectives include the articles* a, an, *and* the.

11. Seasons of the year are lowercase except when they are part of a proper noun, such as *Winter Formal.*

12. Honorary or earned degrees—academic, fraternal, and all others—are lowercase when written out. They are capitalized and punctuated when abbreviated; *bachelor of journalism,* B.J.

13. The words *government, federal,* and *state* are lowercase unless they are part of a proper noun. *It's a federal project,* but *Consult the Federal Register.*

14. Do not capitalize the words *varsity* or *junior varsity.*

15. Do not capitalize offices such as *principal's office, nurse's office, attendance office.*

16. Capitalize names of buildings: *North Building, Science Building, East Building, Denver Miller Gymnasium.*

17. Capitalize special days: *Red and White Day, Turkey Day.*

18. Capitalize words that are derived from a proper noun and still depend on it for meaning: *English, Spanish, Shakespearean, Christianity, French, American.*

19. Lowercase words that are derived from a proper noun but no longer depend on it for meaning: *french fries, venetian blind.*

20. Capitalize the primary words in titles (books, movies, poems, songs, radio and television programs, poems, etc.) Do not capitalize articles or prepositions of four letters or less unless they begin the title: *The Natural,* but *Gone with the Wind.*

21. Capitalize course titles, but not subject areas: World History I, world history.

22. Capitalize a class with its years of graduation, but not names of classes in the school: Class of 2005, the freshman class.

Titles, Identifications

1. Titles may be capitalized or lowercase, depending on their function. Capitalize formal titles. A formal title denotes specific authority or professional or academic achievement. It precedes the name and acts as individual identification: *The speaker is Principal Franklin McCallie.* Occupational descriptions follow the name and are lowercase and set off by commas: *The principal, the head of the school.*

2. Formal titles are used in first mention only: *Dr. Robert Jones,* but in subsequent mentions, *Jones.* Generally, formal titles are used only with the full name.

3. The formal title always accompanies names of presidents of the United States, heads of state, and other world figures.

4. Courtesy titles of Miss, Ms., and Mrs. are rarely used in first mention and subsequent mention of adult women. (See rule 3 at top of page 55) Mr. is used in first mention of adult men. You might define an adult as anyone who is a high school graduate. Do not use the courtesy title in subsequent mentions of a person's name; use last name only. Do not use courtesy titles for students. (See marginalia on page 49.)

5. Titles standing alone (without a person's name) are lowercase. If the title is used before the name (two words or less), it is capitalized: *The president spoke last night,* but *President George W. Bush spoke last night.*

6. Titles of two words or less precede names and are capitalized. They are not set off by commas. Titles of three words or more follow names, are lowercase, and are set off by commas: *Associate Principal Joyce West* but *Dr. Robert Jones, superintendent of schools, will speak tonight.*

7. Titles without names follow the same rule as

➢ Adverbs
• An adverb modifies a verb, an adjective, or another adverb by describing, limiting, or in some other way making the meaning more exact.
• An adverb tells how, when, where, why, to what extent. The boy walked slowly down *the street. He enjoyed the parade* recently, *and he* certainly liked *the band's music.*

titles following names; as identifications, they are lowercase: *The mayor spoke.*

8. Identify people in stories and captions the first time they are mentioned.

9. Choose the most appropriate identification for an individual. For example, identify sports figures by their position on the team—quarterback, center, left half. Generally, the grade a student is in will serve as proper identification.

Organizations

1. The word *organization* refers to any group—civic, political, school, governmental. The name of any organization, regardless of the number of words it contains, is a proper noun and is written out on first mention: *Student Council meets tonight.* If you know the organization will be mentioned again, give the abbreviation: *Student Council (SC) meets tonight.* Note that no periods are used in the abbreviation.

2. Subsequent mentions are abbreviated, without periods, when the abbreviation will be clear to the reader: *SC, NEA, GPC.*

3. When the reader is not likely to recognize the abbreviation, a shortened form of the name may be used: *Missouri Interscholastic Press Association, the association.*

4. All words in an organization name are capitalized except articles *a, an,* and *the* and prepositions under five letters. Such articles and prepositions are capitalized if they begin the name.

5. Capitalize the common noun *party* when it is part of a proper noun: *Democratic Party, Republican Party.* Do not capitalize when *party* is used as an adjective: *Democratic and Republican parties.* When the political entity is a form of government or an ideology, it is lowercase: *The communist goal is world domination.*

> **Prepositions**
>
> • A preposition is a linking word used to show the relationship of a noun or pronoun to some other word in the sentence. It is usually followed by an object. *The plane flew over the cloud.*
>
> • The following is a good way to remember what a preposition is: a preposition is basically anything a plane can do with a cloud. *It can fly* over, under, through, by, between, at, beside, along, around, above, on, toward, with, from, in, near, about, across, after, against, among, behind, below, beneath, beyond, *and* upon. *Some prepositions, like* except, concerning, *and* during, *don't fit the above definition.*

Dates

1. Months without dates are written out.

2. Months of five letters or more are abbreviated when written with dates: *Jan. 15, Feb. 27, April 4.* Note that the date immediately following the month is a bare (cardinal) number: *Jan. 15,* not *Jan. 15th.* Do not use *rd, th, st, nd* after dates.

3. Adding the year makes no difference in whether the months are written out or abbreviated: *February 1998,* and *Feb. 4, 1998.*

4. Keep the date of publication in mind when writing for newspapers. Use *today* if the story happens on the date of publication, use *tomorrow* if it is on the day after publication and *yesterday* if it is on the day before publication.

5. Use *last Monday* or this *Thursday* if the event falls within the week of publication.

6. If the event does not fall within the week of publication, use the specific date: *March 25.* Do not use the year if the event falls within the year of publication.

7. Do not use the word "on" before a date. It is not necessary.

8. Do not abbreviate days of the week.

Places

1. All state names are written out when standing alone.

2. If a state name is accompanied by a city name, abbreviate the state name if it has six or more letters: *Kirkwood, MO.*

3. In two cases a city name does not require the state: a city mentioned in a story published in the home state, and a widely known city such as New York City or Los Angeles.

4. In three cases the city name requires the state name in the first mention. When a city lies in

➢ *Conjunctions*
 • *A conjunction is a linking word used to connect words or groups of words in sentences.*
 • *Coordinating conjunctions (and, but, for, or, nor) join words or groups of words of equal rank.*
 • *Subordinating conjunctions (if, as, since, because, although, while, so that, when) join dependent clauses to main clauses.*

➢ *Clauses*

• *A clause is a group of words that has both a subject and a predicate.*

• *An independent (main, principal) clause makes a complete statement and may stand alone. It makes sense if the rest of the sentence is omitted. Although she should have been studying, she watched the ballgame instead. The part of the sentence after the comma is the independent clause.*

• *A dependent clause cannot stand alone. It depends upon the rest of the sentence to complete its meaning. In the above example, the first part of the sentence is the dependent clause.*

two states, the state name is needed for clarification. The state name is also needed when the story is published outside the state and when the city has the same name as another city.

5. Use ZIP (Zone Improvement Program) code abbreviations for states when accompanied by a specific city: *Kirkwood, MO; Springfield, IL; Fort Hays, KS; Murray, KY; Glendale, CA.* If the state name is used in the middle of a sentence, set it off with commas: *Students will visit Kirkwood, MO, tomorrow.* You will seldom use the ZIP code number, but if you do, the five digits are run together without a comma: *Kirkwood, MO 63122.* Nine-digit code numbers are also used: *Chapel Hill, NC 27599-2200.*

6. When used with a specific address, abbreviate *drive, road, boulevard, place,* and *avenue;* otherwise, spell them out: *18 Park Pl., 600 Northern Blvd.*

7. Abbreviate *street* when used in a specific address: *801 Essex St.* Otherwise, capitalize and spell it out: *Seventh Street.* Always spell out *circle* and *alley.*

8. Capitalization of *street* or a synonym depends on whether it is a proper or common noun. *Main Street* is a proper noun. In *Main* and *First streets, streets* is a common noun.

9. Compass directions do not alter the abbreviation or capitalization status of *street* or its synonyms. Write: *East Argonne Street, 1422 W. Northlin St., Manchester Boulevard NW, 1422 Manchester Blvd. NW.* Note the absence of punctuation in compound directions such as *southwest (SW).*

Names, Titles

1. The first mention of a person's name is written in full, including given name or initials:

Harry L. Hall, H. L. Hall, Harry Hall.

2. Subsequent mention requires only the surname.

3. In only four cases are courtesy titles *(Mr., Mrs., Miss, Ms.)* used in copy. They are used the first time an adult is mentioned. They are used if a husband and wife are mentioned together *(Mr. and Mrs. Hall)*. They are used if a name is part of a direct quote and if the story is an obituary.

4. Other abbreviated and capitalized titles used before the full name are: *Dr., Gov., Lt. Gov., Rep., Sen., the Rev.*

5. Formal titles that are never abbreviated are: *Attorney General, President, Professor,* and *Superintendent.*

6. Formal titles, whether abbreviated or written out, accompany only the full name.

Periods in Abbreviations

1. The general rule for punctuation of two-word or longer abbreviations is to use periods if the abbreviation spells an unrelated word: *c.o.d.* Use no periods in an abbreviation that does not spell a word; *GPC (Girls' Pep Club).*

2. *Ante meridiem* is abbreviated *a.m.,* and *post meridiem, p.m.* Note that they are not capitalized: *6 a.m.; 7 p.m.*

3. Degrees, earned and honorary, in academic, religious, and fraternal fields are lowercase when written out but capitalized and punctuated when abbreviated.

4. Write out United States and United Nations when they are nouns; abbreviate them when they are adjectives: *In the United States,* but *in U.S. history.*

Symbols

1. Symbols are used as abbreviations. The symbol $ can substitute for the word *dollar: $10.*

2. Note that round sums of money and clock hours carry no zeros or punctuation: *$5, $50, $14, 2 p.m.*

3. Any sum of money less than $1 uses the ¢ symbol: *10¢.*

4. In casual or general use, sums of money—whether dollars or cents—are written out: *The dollar amount was low.*

5. The ampersand (&) is used only when it is part of a name: *Dow Jones & Co., Inc.*

6. The % symbol is used for any specific percent: *27%, 9%.* Spell out *percent* if no specific figure accompanies it: *A small percent of the student body cheats.* For amounts of less than 1%, precede the decimal with a zero: *0.7%.* Always use decimals, not fractions. The word *percent* takes a singular verb when standing alone or in a singular construction: *The principal said 70% was a failing grade. He said 90% of the membership was there.* It takes a plural verb in a plural construction: *The principal said 60% of the boys were there.*

Period

1. The reporter saves space and perhaps promotes reader understanding by omitting periods in some abbreviations.

2. Periods are omitted in abbreviations of organizations: *Girls' Pep Club, GPC; University of Missouri, UM.*

3. Periods are omitted in abbreviations of time zones: *Central Standard Time, CST.*

4. Abbreviations that take periods include titles of persons, academic degrees, months, and places (streets, states, etc.): *Dr., B.A., Jan. 15, 21 St., James Rd.*

5. The period is always placed inside quotation marks.

6. The period is placed inside or outside paren-

➢ **Attributions**

• *Bury attributions in the middle or at the end of a quote.* "I really love journalism," he said," because I enjoy the power of words," *or* "I really love journalism because I enjoy the power of words," he said. *It is best to bury the attribution in the middle of a sentence when there is a logical break in thought.*

• *The best attribution for most quotes is* said. *Avoid using words like* commented *or* remarked, *which are longer than* said. *Avoid using* went on *and* concluded. *Both are obvious to the reader. Unless a person* shouted *or* yelled *to show emotion, there is no better word for* said *than* said.

• *Avoid using* when asked *someone* replied. *To begin with,* when asked *is passive voice, and in addition, it is obvious to the reader no one would have replied if they had not been asked.*

• *Be sure to attribute correctly information obtained from the Internet. Just as you would attribute a news-*

(Continued)

56

theses, depending on the parenthetical material. When the parenthetical material is part of the sentence proper, the period is placed outside the parenthesis: *He wrote all the stories (except the football article)*. When the parenthetical material is a sentence, the period is placed inside the parenthesis: *She wrote all the stories. (She wanted a good grade.)*

7. A series of three periods forms the punctuation mark called an ellipsis, which indicates the omission of a word or words within a sentence: *Joan said . . . more than enough . . ..* Note that an ellipsis is treated as a three-letter word and takes spaces on both sides.

8. A series of four periods indicates word omission at the end of a sentence: *That was enough....* The last period is the punctuation mark to end the sentence.

Comma

1. A parenthetical element is set off by commas. A parenthetical element is a word or group of words that has no grammatical bearing on the rest of the sentence: *Our dog, blast him, chewed up the newspaper.*

2. In a complex sentence that begins with a dependent clause, a comma is used to separate the dependent from the independent clause: *If he were the editor, he would have all stories rewritten.*

3. An appositive is set off by commas. An appositive is a word or group of words having the function of identifying or pointing out: *St. Louis, a city on the Mississippi River, plans to celebrate its founding.*

4. A comma is used before a coordinating conjunction if there are two complete thoughts. The coordinating conjunctions are *and, but, for,*

paper or a magazine as a source, you would also attribute the Internet as a source. Give credit where credit is due.

• It is always best to use primary sources (personal interviews) for information rather than secondary sources newspapers, magazines, Internet). Do your own interviewing. Use the secondary sources for background information to give you ideas for questions to ask the primary sources.

• Place the name of the person giving the quote before the attribution. You say he said, *or* she said, *so you should say* Mr. David Dill said, *or* Mr. John Keightley said *rather than* said Mr. David Dill *or* said Mr. John Keightley.

➢ *Editorializing*

• *Avoid including writer's opinion in copy except for editorials and columns.*

• *Words like diligently, intently, and enjoy are opinionated. They should not be used in body copy or in captions.*

• *Let the facts speak for themselves without writer interpretation.*

• *Use direct quotes for opinion. Let the subjects tell the story in their own words.*

• *Don't forget balance. Improper balance is also a type of opinion.*

• *Do not take quotes out of context. That can also be a type of opinion.*

• *Half-truths are not enough. Outright lies, ignorance, and misinformation should not be tolerated.*

• *Separate rumor from fact.*

or, nor. A compound sentence has at least two independent clauses, which are usually joined by a coordinating conjunction. To determine whether a sentence is compound, read what comes before the conjunction and see if the thought is complete. If there are not two complete thoughts, no comma is needed: *The students toured the facility, and they ate lunch,* but *The students toured the facility and asked questions.*

5. Commas are used to separate words, phrases, or clauses in a series of three or more words, phrases, or clauses in the same construction: *The sophomores, juniors, and seniors enjoyed the presentation.*

6. Commas are used to separate two or more adjectives when they are coordinate modifiers of the same noun: *Long, skinny, slimy worms crawled through the window.*

7. A comma is placed inside quotation marks.

8. Commas separate digits of three in numbers of 1,000 and above. Exceptions: year, zip code, phone number, social security number.

9. The source of a quotation is set off by a comma if the source comes within the sentence: *"Kirkwood," he said, "is a nice place to live."* Always bury attributions (sources) in the middle or at the end of the quote. What a person says is usually more important than who said it. If the attribution is in the middle of a quote, set it off by commas, as above. If at the end of the quote: *"Kirkwood is a nice place to live,"* he said.

Colon, Semicolon

1. Colons replace commas in separating long direct quotes, formal statements, or listings from the source.

2. Semicolons set off a series of groupings that contain internal commas: *Jack Jay, president; Jill Street, vice-president; Bill Thomas, secretary; and Jerry Moye, treasurer.*

Dash

1. Dashes—two strokes of the hyphen key—indicate a break in sentence thought to set off information.

Hyphen

1. The hyphen joins two or more words functioning as a single adjective: *40-yard line.*
2. The hyphen sometimes joins a prefix and a word: *ex-student.*
3. The hyphen is used by sports writers in expressing scores: *Missouri defeated Notre Dame, 51-0.*

Quotation Marks

1. Quotation marks are used with titles of paintings, songs, poems, and other compositions.
2. Nicknames are placed in quotation marks.
3. Names of books, newspapers, magazines, movies, pamphlets, and bulletins are underlined to indicate italic type.
4. Periods and commas are placed inside quotation marks.
5. Colons and semicolons are placed outside quotation marks.
6. Whether question marks and exclamation points are placed inside or outside quotation marks depends on syntax . If the entire sentence is a question or an exclamation, the punctuation is placed outside the quotation marks: *"Who wrote* <u>*Misery*</u>*"*? If only part of the sentence is in quotation marks, the punctuation is placed inside the quotation marks: *"How many hours will it take?" he asked.*

➤ *Apostrophes*

Debate continues as to whether or not to use an apostrophe after girls *and* boys *when referring to a sport. For example, should it be* girls' varsity basketball team *or* girls varsity basketball team? *The Associated Press is unclear on the issue. It says not to add an apostrophe to a word ending in s when it is used primarily in a descriptive sense:* citizens band radio, *a* teachers college. *However, if you say* men's basketball team *or* women's basketball team, *an apostrophe is needed since those words do not end in s. They require the* 's *for possessive. At the high school level, however, it is best to refer to the teams as* girls' *or as* boys' *teams, since the Associated Press says a girl becomes a woman at her 18th birthday and a boy becomes a man at his 18th birthday. As always, the key is to be consistent. If you think the team belongs to the boys or the girls, then use an apostrophe after the '*s.'

7. Capitalize the first word in a quotation if it is a sentence, if it is set off from the source by a comma or a colon, and if it is a direct quotation: *"The principal said: 'We do not agree with you.'"*

8. Quotation marks are placed at the beginning of each paragraph in a quotation of several paragraphs and only at the end of the last paragraph of the series.

9. Use quotation marks around slang words.

Apostrophe

1. The apostrophe usually indicates possession. If the word ends in s, simply add the apostrophe. If the word does not end in s, add *'s*.

2. The apostrophe pluralizes single letters: *too many A's.*

3. The apostrophe may be used for years: *He is a '95 graduate.*

4. Use the apostrophe for singular and plural possessives: *The boy's book was lost. The girls' basketball team won state.*

5. Use apostrophes for possessives ending in s: *Doris' dress.*

Cardinal Numbers

1. Numbers that are always written in figures are: addresses, ages, aircraft numbers, dates, highways, monetary units, No., percentages, speeds, sport scores, temperatures, times (clock). For example: *801 W. Essex, 7-year-old boy, Boeing 707, Feb. 28, U.S. Highway 40, $7, 6¢, No. 1 player, 9%, 7 miles per hour, the score was 53-40, 7 degrees, 2:30 a.m.*

2. Avoid repetition in times, such as *5 a.m., Thursday morning.* Use *noon* or *midnight*, not *12 noon* or *12 midnight.*

3. Spell out a number that begins a sentence.

4. In all other cases spell out numbers one through nine and use figures for numbers 10 and over.

Ordinal Numbers

1. Ordinal numbers are figures with a suffix of *st, nd, rd, th.*
2. Political designations such as district, ward, or precinct are expressed in ordinal numbers: *1st Congressional District, 33rd District.*
3. Numbered streets are written in ordinal numbers, if they are of two or more digits: *15th Street, Second Street.*
4. In other circumstances, spell out *first* through *ninth* and use suffixes for *10.*

Roman Numerals

1. Some sequential numbers are always expressed in Roman numerals: *H. L. Hall IV, World War II, Pope John XXII.*
2. Roman numerals are not separated by punctuation from the noun they follow.

Word Usage

1. *Arbitration* is the process of hearing evidence from all persons concerned and handing down a decision. *Mediation* is the process of trying by the exercise of reason or persuasion to bring two parties to an agreement.
2. A person is not guilty until found so in a trial of law. He may be *accused of* killing his neighbor, or he has *allegedly* killed his neighbor.
3. *Affect* as a verb means *to influence.* As a noun, it has only a psychological meaning. *Effect* as a verb means *to bring about;* as a noun it means *the result: The game will affect the team's standing. The full effect of the win will not be known until the end of the season. The coach may then effect some changes in the lineup.*

> *Is Good Grammar Disappearing?*
>
> *Ann Landers often receives letters from readers about the poor grammar apparent in print publications and elsewhere. One writer asked Ann to tell her readers that a plural word does not use the apostrophe. The apostrophe is reserved for the possessive case or for contractions. The reader said she had seen a store sign advertising* Banana's. *The reader wondered if the store belonged to Mr. Banana. The reader also said the worst abuse was with the word* it's, *the contraction for it is. The possessive uses NO apostrophe, and is spelled its. A good way to remember the correct form is to substitute it is. If it makes sense, use the apostrophe. If it doesn't, don't use it. Ann told the writer she shared his/her pain. She went on to say that when people see a word misused or misspelled time after time, they become accustomed*

(Continued)

to it. She mentioned she had seen the word grateful misspelled so many times that even she wasn't sure what was right anymore. She also said she often reads her mail with pen in hand, and when she sees mistakes she has a compulsion to correct them. She said the letter writers did not know she was doing that, but it made her feel better.

➤ *Things to Avoid*
• *Avoid unnecessary changes in tense.* Courtney walked to school and slides into the classroom.
• *Avoid careless shifts in voice.* The trash is collected, and then the custodians throw it out.
• *Avoid nonparallel construction.* He is tall, muscular, and a man of handsome stature. *It would be better to say:* He is tall, muscular, and handsome. She likes swimming and to dive *should be* She likes swimming and diving.
• *Avoid writing sentences all the same length.*

Spelling

1. Always use first dictionary spellings—*adviser* instead of *advisor*, for example.
2. Know how to spell these commonly misspelled words: a cappella, accommodate, all right, a lot, already, baby-sit, baby-sitting, baby sitter, baccalaureate, benefit, benefited, benefiting, bookkeeper, buses, bused, commitment, council, counsel, counselor, curriculum, doughnut, exaggerate, extracurricular, freshman, independent, intramural, judgment, junior, kindergarten, liaison, libel, license, occur, occurred, occurring, permissible, personal, personnel, picnic, picnicked, picnicking, principal, principle, refer, referee, referred, sizable, sophomore, stationary, stationery, superintendent, zero, zeros.

Other General Rules

1. Use the indefinite article "a" before consonant sounds and the indefinite article "an" before vowel sounds: *a Christmas gathering, an open lunch policy.*
2. Use *allege* or *allegedly* if a person has been arrested for a crime but not yet found guilty.
3. Use *alumna* to refer to an individual female graduate and *alumnae* for female graduates. Use *alumnus* to refer to an individual male graduate and *alumni* for male graduates.
4. Use *among* with more than two and *between* with two. *The ten students argued among themselves. Two of them decided between the two groups.*
5. Avoid using clichés like "it goes without saying."
6. Use *everybody* and *everyone* with singular pronouns and verbs. *Everybody wants her right to speak.*
7. Do not use hopefully to mean "I hope" or

"Let's hope," as in "Hopefully it will be passed." *Hopefully* is an adverb that means "in a hopeful manner": *The boy looked hopefully at the coach in hopes he would be put into the game.*

8. Keep paragraphs short to enhance readability —normally no more than 40 words.

9. Write *vs.* instead of *versus* in sports references: *Kirkwood vs. Webster.* However, use *v.* when citing legal cases: *Hazelwood v. Kuhlmeier.*

10. Use *girl* for any female still in high school. Use *woman* for anyone over eighteen and out of high school.

COPYREADING SYMBOLS

1. Delete letters, words, or phrases not needed and close up space.

2. Delete a letter in the middle of a word and close up space.

3. Delete a one-unit symbol—a letter at the beginning or end of a word or a punctuation mark.

4. Insert a letter or word.

5. Insert a comma.

6. Insert quotation marks.

7. Separate run-together words.

8. Lowercase—do not capitalize.

9. Uppercase—capitalize.

10. Spell out an abbreviated word, abbreviate a spelled-out word, write a spelled-out number in figures, change figures to a spelled word.

11. Transpose letters or words.

12. Insert a period.

13. Begin a paragraph.

14. Insert a hyphen.

15. Boldface type.

> *Transitions*
> • *Use transitions within a sentence, between sentences, and between paragraphs.*
> • *To add some ideas, use* in addition, another way, a second method, moreover, besides, also.
> • *To contrast ideas, use* but, yet, nevertheless, however, still, in contrast, otherwise, on the other hand.
> • *To compare ideas, use* like, similar.
> • *To show purpose, use* in order to, for this reason.
> • *To show result, use* therefore, as a result, consequently, thus.
> • *To show time, use* then, a little later, immediately, in the meantime, afterward, in those days, earlier.

63

16. Center copy. ⨆⨅ or ⟩⟨
17. Continue copy on next page. move or 2
18. Disregard corrections—leave copy as original-ly written. stet
19. Italicize copy. ———
20. End of story. 30 cr #
21. Run together—no paragraph. ⌒
22. No paragraph. no ⅋
23. Close up space entirely. ◯
24. Close up partially. ⌢
25. Insert apostrophe. ⌄

PROOFREADING SYMBOLS

1. Flush left copy. ⌐ or ⟨
2. Flush right copy. ⌐ or ⟩
3. Center copy. ⨆⨅ or ⟩⟨
4. Wrong font—wrong typeface. wf
5. Blurred or broken type. ✕
6. Italicize copy. ital
7. Boldface copy. bf
8. Set in roman type. rom
9. Do not capitalize—lowercase. lc
10. Invert letter. 9
11. New paragraph. ⅋
12. No paragraph. no ⅋
13. Lower to the point indicated. ⊔
14. Raise to the point indicated. ⊓
15. Leave less space. ⌣
16. Indent 1 em (an em is the width of the letter m in the size of type being used). ▯
17. Indent 2 ems. ▭▭
18. Equalize spacing. eq #
19. Delete letters or words indicated. ℯ
20. Insert extra space. #
21. Transpose letters or words. tr
22. Insert quotation marks. ⌄⌄ ⌄⌄
23. Insert comma. ⌃
24. Insert period. ⊙

25. Insert question mark. ?/
26. Insert hyphen. /=/
27. Insert em dash. /$\frac{1}{em}$/
28. Insert en dash (an en is 1/2 the width of an em). /$\frac{1}{en}$
29. Disregard corrections—leave copy as originally written. Stet
30. Close up space entirely. ◯
31. Insert letter or word where indicated. ∧
32. Spell out. ◯
33. Straighten. =
34. Push down space. ⊥

EXERCISES

1. Use copyreading symbols to correct the following sentences:

A. For example, coming back from Niagra Falls to our hotel was really a mess.
B. And I'll come to a conclusion about what I should do, then I'll put it together and won't do anything.
C. But mostly try to understand things which is hard sometimes but I'll find a way to think it out, even though it is hard after I did it long enough, it seems easy, just give it a try and it all will seem easy.
D. Not far from Help Valley layed a small village called Cleanville.
E. This sign appealed to me in every way, because I as myself am a great skier.

F.   I've skied everything from the "Alps" in Switzerland to the long and trecherous mountains of Colorado.

G.   So I walked up to the desk where the young travel agent was standing and asked to see some pamphlets on skiing in Michigan

H   Sitting next to me on the plane was a pretty and very exciting young women.

I.   Though others may wish to help, give to, or take from that life, they cannot do so with out consent from the owner.

2.   Every good copyreader should know certain information automatically, without having to consult any source. That information varies according to the publication. Assuming you are a reporter for your high school yearbook or newspaper, you should know the answers to the following questions. You should also know how to spell each person's name.

A.   Who is the school principal?

B.   Who are the assistant principals?

C.   Who are the teachers on the faculty, and what subjects do they teach?

D.   Who is the head custodian?

E.   How many faculty members are there?

F.   Who is the president of the Student Council?

G.   Who is the president of each school club or organization?

H.   Who is the head coach of each athletic team?

I.   Who is the superintendent of schools?

J.   Who are the school board members?

K.   What is the school enrollment? How many students are in each grade?

L.   When are the vacation periods for the

school year?

M. When is the last day of school? When is graduation?

N. Who is the athletic director?

O. Who are the department heads?

P. Who is the school nurse?

Q. Who is the sponsor of each club or organization?

R. How many subscribers are there to the school newspaper and the yearbook?

S. What are the school's graduation requirements?

3. Correct the following sentences according to style rules.

A. Mr. and Mrs. Spider visited Kirkwood senior high school on Thurs. Mr. Spider was stepped on by Mr. Fast so Mrs. Spider became a black widow.

B. It was recently announced by F. McCallie that the Kirkwod call is being closed down. This week's call will be the last issue.

The announcement came after a series of discussions with the staff and administration. The reason given for the closing was the lack of student interest. The faculty voted ninety nine to nothing to close down the paper.

According to Frank Jones, Haed custodian, 3 out of 5 fires in the restrooms have resulted from past issues of the call being burned in protest.

The faculty and Administration are currently debating on whether to close the parking lots due to the mounds of old Calls that are covering the Lots. The

Kirkwood police department says that by not later than Apr. 2003, the Parking Lot will be clear enough for all motorcycles and teacher's Edsels.

As a result of the close-down N150 will become a sex education room beginning Next Mon.

C. People may be wondering why the chicked crossed Man. Road at Geyer Road, but if you ask us, if he crossed Manchester Road at Geyer Road, he's no chicken. Dumb! But no chicken.

D. People are so up tight about the Drug situation nowadays, that at Kirkwood senior high school they arrested the Heronie of the school play. As a result the school cafeteria is no longer serving Hash.

E. Let's hope that Feb. 22nd is a sunny day, so George can get his Washing done.

F. Coach Meyer and Coach Diaz have reported- on plans to carpet the Gymnasium this year so that we will have a rugged basketball team.

G. Polls show that President Reagan is a favoirte among junoirs and sophmores at Kirkwood high school. This ss probably a result of his stand on the "forgoentt middle classes."

H. One student at Kirkwood found himself in an embarrasing position when he refered to Mrs., Librarian, as a bookie.

I. The favoirite food of some students is reportedly flower kraut.

J. Spies behind the lines have reported that Webster's Track Team is putting butter in their shoes before meets so they can win by a better margarine.

K. Mrs. Conkins' home ec ins truction in

Clothin is guaranteed to keep the students in sittches.

L.   Mr. Bush announced that all burning candle experiments should be dconucted on Fri. This is because they must be lit at the end of the wick.

M.   In a recent survey taken in sophmore Homerooms, twenty-eight & said they could recite their locker combinations, 32% said they didn't know their locker combinations but give the chance, they could find their lockers, and the remaining 39 percent were in the wrong Homeroom.

N.   Mr. Hall ahs announced that his teaching planns this year will continue to be carried out in the Hall Way.

4.   Correct spelling and word usage are part of style. Learn to spell the words below as well as the correct usage of each. Be prepared for a quiz. Some definitions are given; look up in a dictionary those you do not know. Always use first spellings listed in the dictionary.

accept: to receive; to consider proper.
except: to exclude.
accused (takes the preposition *of*: accused of a crime).
acknowledgment
ad-lib (v. or adj.).
admissible
adviser (not *advisor*).
advisory
aesthetic
afterward (not *afterwards*).
aid: assistance.
aide: person who serves as an assistant.

à la carte

à la king

à la mode

allot: to distribute as if by lot.

a lot: a quantity; a great many.

all right (not *alright*).

allude: to speak of something without specifically mentioning it.

refer: to mention something directly.

allusion: an indirect reference.

illusion: an unreal or false impression.

alma mater

altar: tablelike platform used in church services.

alter: to change.

any body/any one (singling out one element of a group: *Any one of them can do the job*).

anybody/anyone (indefinite reference: *Anyone can do that*).

assistant

backward (not *backwards*).

biannual: twice a year.

biennial: every two years.

blond (noun for males; adjective for all applications).

blonde (noun for females).

boyfriend

broadcast (both present and past tenses).

bus (conveyance), buses

buss (slang for *kiss*), busses

carat: unit of weight for precious stones.

caret: insertion mark in writing and printing.

chauffeur

clientele

compose: to form by putting together; to create.

comprise: to contain; to include; to be made up of or embrace.

continual: taking place in rapid succession.

continuous: uninterrupted in space or time.

council: a deliberative body.

counsel: one who advises.

cut off (v.): to bring to an abrupt end.

cutoff (n.): the act of cutting off.

demolish: to destroy completely (cannot be partial).

disinterested: impartial.

uninterested: lacking any interest whatever.

doughnut

farther: physically more distant: *New York is farther from my home.*

further: to a greater degree of extent: *I don't wish to pursue the conversation further.*

fiancé: man engaged to be married.

fiancée: woman engaged to be married.

filibuster: to block legislative action by means of lengthy speeches.

flair: conspicuous talent.

flare: to blaze with sudden light; to burst out in anger.

freshman; sophomore, junior; senior.

gamut: a scale of notes; any complete range or extent.

girlfriend

good (adj.): of average or better than average quality.

well (adj.): suitable, proper, healthy; (adv.): skillfully, in a satisfactory manner.

grammar

harassment

heroin: illegal drug.

heroine: woman of bravery; principal female character in a literary work.

impostor

incredible: unbelievable.

incredulous: skeptical.

lay: to place; to put or set down; past tense,

laid; present participle, *laying*; past participle, *laid. Please lay the book on the table. He laid the book on the table. Laying the book on the table, he departed. The book was laid on the table.*

lie: to be in a horizontal position; past tense, *lay*; present participle, *lying*; past participle, *lain. Please lie down. The child lay on the couch. Lying on the couch, the child watched cartoons. Having lain down for a while, the child felt better.*

lie: to tell a falsehood; past tense, *lied*; present participle, *lying*; past participle, *lied. Do not lie to me. You lied to me yesterday. Lying about the incident, he said she had done it. Having lied before, you have little credibility.*

nowadays

organization

percent

picnic, picknicked, picknicking, picknicker.

planning

poinsettia

premier: prime minister.

premiere (n.): first performance; (adj.) first in importance.

privilege, privileged

principal (n.): person of first importance; (adj.) most important or influential.

principle: fundamental truth, law, doctrine, or motivating force.

pupil: child in kindergarten through grade 12.

student: acceptable for grade 9 through higher education.

racquet (also racket): lightweight implement used in tennis and other games.

racket: unseemly noise.

receive

shake up (v.): to shock or jar mentally or

physically.

shake-up (n.): act of shaking up; reorganization.

shut off (v.): to cut off; stop.

shutoff (n.): something (such as a valve) that stops or interrupts.

shut out (v.): to exclude.

shutout (n.) game in which one team fails to score.

superintendent

teammate

their: (personal pronoun).

there (adv.): at or into that place.

they're (contraction): they are.

toward (not *towards*).

upward (not *upwards*).

CHAPTER
four

News Writing

The American Heritage Dictionary defines news as "a recent event or happening, especially one that is unusual or notable; information about recent events of general interest, especially as reported by newspapers; new information."

For high school newspapers the word "recent" in that definition sometimes causes problems that it does not cause for the professional media. Because many high school papers publish only once a week or even once a month, it is difficult for them to publish recent news if "recent" means something that has occurred within the last 24 hours.

Therefore, high school papers should strive to fulfill the last part of the definition—to provide new information about an event. By doing this, the newspaper staff can still see that the news it is reporting is "recent." This is particularly true for past events. Generally future events are more important than past events for high school papers. Old news tends to be stale.

Being recent or timely is just one element that high school newspaper staffs should keep in mind when deciding whether to publish a story. Other news elements that the professional media consider and that the high school media also need to consider are:

1. *Proximity.* Write on topics dealing with your high school's community or at least on topics of concern to teenage readers. A national topic such as a proposal to reduce the minimum wage for teenagers would be of vital interest

to readers at any school. However, be sure to localize a national or state topic by quoting readers or local community experts.

2. *Consequence.* Always be aware of any effect the story will have on the readers. A story dealing with increased graduation requirements will affect more readers than one naming new members of the National Honor Society, for example.

3. *Names.* Names make news, and the names of well-known persons involved in an event are more newsworthy than those of unknowns. For example, a story on the principal of your school involved in a lawsuit would be more newsworthy than a story on an unknown freshman similarly involved.

4. *Conflict.* Readers like controversial events. A conflict between groups about the number of religious songs to sing at a choral concert would be more newsworthy than the naming of the new cheerleaders, unless there were a controversy about the method of cheerleader selection.

5. *Emotions.* Stories that play on the emotions— that make the reader laugh, cry, or become upset—are more newsworthy than ones that evoke no reaction. For example, a story on a study reporting that girls are smarter than boys might impel boys to write letters to the editor. A topic such as differences in abilities between sexes often touches the reader's emotions. Possible stories might be a comparison of how many girls and how many boys have been named National Merit Finalists in the past 10 years, or how many of each sex have been selected to the National Honor Society, or how many of each sex have received athletic scholarships, or how many of

➢ *The Question*
• *Be sure you phrase all questions to get a good response. Once, a reporter on* Headline News *asked an eyewitness to an airplane crash to describe what she had seen. After the eyewitness concluded her comments, the reporter asked, "Were you able to see anything more than what you saw?" Obviously the eyewitness had no idea how to respond to this question, so she proceeded to repeat everything she had just said.*

Remediation programs continue to have success in reteaching basic skills

Competency results indicate 'probable' future scores

by Suzanne Chung Bin

Slightly more students failed the minimal competency test this year than last year in all three categories. However, remediation of students who failed the tests continues successfully, according to the teachers who head the review classes.

This year, nearly 28 percent of all freshmen failed the math test. In the Sophomore Class, about 21 percent failed the language usage test and almost 9 percent failed the reading.

THESE FIGURES are about a one percent increase from last year's. Last year, 27 percent failed math, 20 percent failed language usage, and almost 8 percent failed reading.

Mr. Richard Deptuch, head of the Math Department, believes that the increases are not too important.

He had been concerned, though, with what this year's testing results would be. This year was the third year the tests were given. The differences in the percentages of failure between the first and second year of testing had been "dramatic." "There was a seven percent increase in math, an eight percent increase in language usage, and a three percent increase in reading. Deptuch had wondered whether there would be another dramatic increase, whether they would be back down to what they were the first year,

or whether they would level out.

SINCE THIS YEAR'S results are so similar to last year's he now believes that the school has "an indication of the probable range of scores."

Students who did not pass last fall's tests must take a six-week review course sometime this semester in the area in which they failed.

In the math program, students work on their own to correct individual weaknesses pinpointed by the competency test. If there is a general weakness that most of the students have, teachers Lucia Valentino or Pat Prentice, may give a general lecture to the whole class.

As soon as the teachers are confident that any student's weaknesses have been corrected, that student may retake the test. If he passes, the student does not have to attend review sessions any longer.

DEPTUCH BELIEVES that this set-up gives students an incentive to do well and get

the course over with.

A student only has one chance to pass the retake, but, if he doesn't pass, he must take the review course again in the next six weeks.

Valentino said that success had been "tremendous." She said that around 90 percent of the students taking the retake have passed. So far this semester, 100 percent of the students have passed the retake.

"Scores have been very high (on the retest)," Valentino said. "These students didn't just get by. Students often get perfect papers or just one wrong."

THE READING review course has had similar success, according to Mr. Peter Mahonchak, teacher of the class. He estimates that 95 percent pass the retake.

The reading course consists of 25 lessons which cover practical skills, such as reading ads in a newspaper and understanding train schedules. Unlike math, the whole class works at the same pace. There is a series of

questions at the end of each lesson which the students answer and grade on their own.

Mahonchak checks each of the student's work daily. If a student has particular problems with a certain lesson, he supplies additional work.

At the moment, Mahonchak does not see any problems with the way the reading system is running. However, he believes that the school should conduct a "periodic re-examination of questions and courses" to find out "how effective (the minimal competency program) is and to see if the test continues to examine skills we deem desirable."

THE LANGUAGE usage class taught by either Mr. Pat McGinty or Mrs. Lola McIntosh has a format similar to the reading one.

The course, according to Pat McGinty, is a series of lessons, each dependent on each other. Some topics covered are language usage, paragraph development, and punctuation.

McGinty said that the success rate on the retake is around 75 percent. Attendance is the major difficulty.

He believes this is so because no grade or credit is given and passing the test is not required to graduate. "A student has no reason to go (to the class)," he said.

McGinty believes that passing the test should be required for graduation.

Looking at the pass(★) fail(☆) breakdown

Reading	72%
Language Usage	79%
Math	91%
	28%
	21%

★ = approximately 39 test takers

The use of a chart adds impact to a news story from the Trapeze, Oak Park River Forest High School, Oak Park, IL. A strong summary lead gives the reader the important facts first.

each sex have won special honors of any kind.

6. *Unusualness.* The more uncommon the event, the more likely it is to be newsworthy. Any event that is likely to make the reader sit up and say "Wow" provides a human-interest angle that appeals.

7. *Human Interest.* The human interest angle emphasizes the "people perspective" of a story. If possible, the reporter should provide insight into the personal side of the event. If she can do that, the human interest aspect might be reason enough to write the story.

The reporter should keep all the news elements in mind when writing the story, but the key thing to remember is that he must find facts that will interest most of the readers. Not every story can interest every reader, but the reporter must try to write about events that will interest many readers. That is why he must remember the last part of the dictionary definition of news: new information. By providing new information, the reporter should be able to find facts that interest readers.

To provide new information, the reporter must research her topic. That includes talking to as many people as possible who have any information pertinent to the event being covered. If it is a controversial event, the reporter must be sure that her story is balanced, giving both sides of the controversy equal coverage, and that it is objective, leaving out the reporter's opinion. Above all, the reporter must be accurate; deal with fact, not rumor.

Investigative news stories are probably of greater interest to more readers than stories covered merely because of the "new information." A straight coverage story might be the naming of the new members of the Pom Pom squad. An investigative story might reveal that there were no African American judges and that no African American girls made the squad. Further investigation might uncover a system that had been established in 1985 for selecting judges that required

> *A Different Look*
> • *"Let's do something new. It's time to take a radical look at all high-school publications and student newspapers in particular. I want you to forget everything that you think you know about newspapers. Forget the inverted pyramid. Forget objectivity. Forget the 5Ws and H."*
> —Bobby Hawthorne, The Radical Write
>
> • *Look for the "why" and the "how" of every story. Dig deeper than the surface. Observe the action take place, and then ask yourself "why" it happened. Don't just describe the action. Is it possible the story could be told through the eyes of a participant or an observer?*

that one fourth of the judges be African American. Still further investigation might show that 15 of the 18 new members are sisters of present or former squad members. The reporter should investigate these findings to discover why they occurred.

All reporters should develop a questioning attitude. That does not mean that they should seek to find wrong; it simply means that they should seek to tell the complete story behind an event. If they are always looking for "new information," it is likely that they will find it. Being content with reporting only what everyone already knows will not result in any "new information" and will guarantee a boring newspaper.

One way to compile information is through interviews. Because interviews are probably the main source of information, one needs to find the right people to interview. Obviously, it is best to talk to the primary sources: the persons who are directly involved in the event.

Before conducting an interview, the reporter should prepare a list of questions that require more than a "yes" or "no" response. Questions should allow the interviewee to do most of the talking. In preparing a list of questions, the reporter should first research the topic. One of the most important things to remember when conducting an interview is to listen to the responses. The responses should trigger new questions that the reporter had not considered previously. In fact, a good interviewer seldom refers to his list of questions once the interview has started. It is essential to be on time for the interview, and it is wise to let the interviewee know in advance how long the interview will probably take. At the high school level, the principal is often a primary source of news stories. Her time is valuable; keep her as a friendly source by using her time wisely.

In the interview, use of a tape recorder is acceptable only if the interviewee agrees. If a tape recorder is not used, the reporter should make every effort to verify all quotes. High school reporters, in particular, usually have time to verify. It is considered journalistic courtesy to do so and can prevent the problems created when someone is misquoted. When the

➤ *The Response*
• *"A writer can only hope, when his words reach someone on the other end, that that person will like what he or she is reading. The writer won't be there for the interaction; the writer will never know whether or not his words pleased someone he has never met."—Bob Greene, syndicated columnist*
• *It is the writer's job—in all stories—to play on the reader's emotions. Make the reader grimace, or cry, or grin, or laugh. According to Bob Greene, that is the reason writers should write—to get a reaction from the reader. If there is no reaction, there is no connection to the writing.*

CAMPUS CLIPBOARD

DECA members in slammer

Seniors Brent Connelly, Jennifer Reynolds, Kim Bro, Adam Langdon and Amanda Bullock took part in the KMTV 3 Muscular Dystrophy Association (MDA) Telethon.

The program was aired Monday, Sept. 2 from 3-4 p.m. The five DECA representatives were "put in jail" for the duration of this hour in order to raise money for MDA, a national DECA sponsor.

DECA sponsor Don Gilpin was pleased with the outcome. The students helped to raise $762.

This type of activity is called civic consciousness.

"Civic consciousness is in order to realize the need to give back to the community," Gilpin said.

Outdoor Ed gets underway

A few Westside students have been chosen to be counselors in the Outdoor Education program.

Sixth grade students participating in Outdoor Ed spend three days and two nights at Platte River State Park and are supervised by the counselors. During this time, participants learn basic outdoor skills such as archery, fishing and many others.

There are four sessions for Outdoor Ed. Oakdale, Rockbrook and Sunset Hills are attending the first session of Outdoor Ed Wednesday, Sept. 25 through Friday, Sept. 27. Loveland, Prairie Lane and Underwood Hills have the second session Monday, Sept. 30 through Wednesday, Oct. 2. Paddock Road and Westgate have the third session Wednesday, Oct. 2 through Friday, Oct 4. Swanson and Hillside have the last session from Monday, Oct. 7 through Wednesday, Oct. 9. Westside is providing counselors for all sessions.

Key Club holds lake cleanup

Key Club held their annual lake cleanup Saturday, Sept. 14, at Lake Zorinsky. Forty-five Key Club members participated in this activity. After the cleanup they gathered for a picnic. Each student earned two hours of service learning for the activity.

Effective packaging of the above news brief column adds to reader appeal. The Lance, Westside High School, Omaha, NE, uses a Campus Clipboard to group its news briefs.

➢ *Briefly Speaking*

News briefs are a good way to present information that does not need in-depth treatment. The Round Up, *Andrews High School, Andrews, TX, captured three events in a brief space. To be considered briefs, they should not be much longer than 100 words.*

---

8 ___ shortstuff ___

Madrigal carols

●During the week before Christmas, the Madrigal Singers will sing French and Spanish holiday carols on a local radio station. According to Alan Orsini, one of the twenty Madrigals, "The carols will be recorded and played on WMAL (630 AM) throughout the holiday season. The songs will be recorded at WS on November 24.

The elite singers have several holiday season concerts scheduled. They will perform at Burke Town Plaza December 4, at Woodward and Lothrop in Landmark Shopping Center on December 11. They will perform for WS students on December 14.

These concerts include traditional carols, a medieval procession, French and Spanish carols and spoofs like "Good King Kong" and "Twelve Days After Christmas."

Yearbook deadline

● The color selections of the 1982-83 Olympian yearbook are being put together by the Olympian staff, in order to meet a November 28 deadline. The cost of this section is approximately $4000.

Approximately 1800 yearbooks are sold each year, however, Spartans who had an opportunity to purchase a yearbook last month, will not be able to purchase the set this spring. Only new and transfer students will be able to purchase the book at that time.

The last Olympian copy deadline is February 15. All events taking place after this date, such as spring sports, graduation, the senior prom, Sweetheart Week, and the senior class play, will be included in a Spring Supplement which was included in the $23 cost of the yearbook.

DECA trip

●Members of WS' chapter of the Distributive Education Clubs of America will travel to Reading, Pennsylvania this month. Approximately 70 students went on a similiar trip last year, and visited factory outlets and did comparative shopping.

Next month, according to club sponsor Bill Gibson, DECA will sell jewelry to earn funds for a trip to New York in March. Club members have sold M&M's for two months to raise money for the Reading trip.

According to Gibson, another purpose of the trip is to study the many different types of fashions.

the oracle ___

Members of the marching band practice during fourth period last month. Symphonic and concert band members are now rehearsing for the December 16 concert (photo by Tom Giallorenzi).

Spaghetti dinner

●Seniors are cooking up the annual Spaghetti Dinner, Saturday December 4. This annual fund raising event will be held in the cafeteria from 7:00 p.m. to 11:00 p.m.

For a fee of $3 ($1.50 for children under 12) a dinner consisting of spaghetti, Italian bread, salad dessert, and dinner mints.

In addition, WS students will sing, dance, tell jokes and perform in a band for entertainment. Other students will help serve, or work in the kitchen, or wait tables.

This Saturday, the senior class is participating in the Cystic Fibrosis Bowl-a-thon. Later next month, the class will sponsor a bloodmobile visit.

G/T internship

●The Gifted and Talented Internship program, the only one of its kind in Virginia, is entering its sixth year at WS, according to program sponsor, Dr. Elizabeth Moores.

This novel program for above average students allows 40 juniors and seniors to obtain part time jobs with professionals in the community. They earn two credits for working a total of at least 360 hours per school year.

A seminar is given by sponsor Moores until all participants in the program have jobs. An Employer Appreciation Luncheon is held each May so that the parents of the 40 students have the opportunity to meet with their child's employer.

The students receive recognition from their employers. Last year, G/T senior Kennen Thompson was the recipient of an outstanding service and monetary award of $100 along with a plaque from the Naval Research Lab for his work throughout the school year. Also, Anne Birn was presented a $100 savings bond donated by her employer, attorneys Mason, Wheatley, & Baumann.

Keyettes

●With the holiday season arriving soon, so will the chance for WS' service clubs to reach out to their community.

The Keyettes, an all girl club, will start their community service by making food baskets for needy families during Thanksgiving week.

Later in November, the girls will visit Leewood Nursing Home and entertain the elderly residents of this facility. According to Keyette President Mary Conlon, doing things to make people happier is what Keyettes are all about.

Honors Choir

●Two senior girls from the Spartan Choir, Kim Krenzke and Donna Carey, will perform in Richmond today as part of the Virginia Honors Chorus. They were selected earlier this year to join the 100 senior singers that make up this choir.

Orchestra concert

●The WS Orchestra, along with orchestras from Washington Irving Intermediate and other area schools, will present a concert in the WS auditorium on December 15. The program starts at 7:30 p.m., with the WS Orchestra taking the stage at 8:30 p.m.

The Oracle, *West Springfield High School, Springfield, VA, groups its news briefs in a column entitled "Shortstuff." Note that a partial cutout photograph and close registration around the photograph add visual appeal.*

reporter verifies quotes, the interviewee is apt to grant further interviews because she knows that what she says will be accurately reported.

The reporter, however, must not take a quote out of context. Even if the quote is accurate, when taken out of the context of the entire interview it can change the meaning of what the interviewee said.

Be sure to dig for meaningful, unusual quotes. A good rule

is: If anyone else can say it, it is not a good quote. For example, if you ask for an opinion of the school rule that forbids boys to wear hats in school, most anyone could say, "I think it stinks." Instead, dig for an unusual quote, such as, "I don't know why there is such a rule. I have a collection of more than 100 hats, and now I can't wear them to school. I've tried to get a hat from every college campus I've visited. They've cost me a lot of money, and now they have to stay in my closet. I plan to start a petition against the rule. Let's hear it for hats!"

Generally, a one-sentence quote is too short to provide much depth to the situation. The key rule in interviewing is to dig, dig, dig!

The wording of each question should result from the specifics gathered in background research. Know your subject before asking questions. The reporter should ask interpretive questions that call for the interviewee to draw conclusions and state opinions about the activity, event, or issue.

Questions should be planned well in advance so that each can be posed in a way that helps the reporter keep control of the interview.

When beginning the interview, the reporter should take a conversational approach to make the interviewee feel comfortable. The reporter should clearly define the reason for the interview. Be sure the setting is quiet and comfortable, and be sure to allow enough time.

The reporter should refuse "off-the-record" comments. Before asking the first question, the reporter should tell the interviewee not to make off-the-record statements. That will avoid any conflict between commitment to the readers and to the confidentiality of the source.

As you conduct the interview, take notes as inconspicuously as possible, but guarantee that completeness and accuracy prevail. Develop a system that allows eye contact at the same time you are taking notes.

When concluding the interview, be sure to thank the interviewee for his or her time and for the information supplied.

After all the information has been compiled, it is time to

> ➢ *Creating a*
> *Good Short Story*
> • *Write your article like you were writing a short story.*
> • *Most good short stories are based on conflict. The lead of your news story should establish the conflict.*
> • *Conflict usually falls into one of four major categories— character v. character, characters v. society, character v. nature, or character v. self.*
> • *The structure of the story should help the writer present the conflict to readers.*
> • *The structure should include background information about the characters, the setting, the dramatic situation.*
> • *Part of the story structure should include situations that increase the tension of the conflict.*
> • *The highest point of the conflict should be the climax—the showdown.*

District to achieve six 'America 2000' goals

Omaha, Baltimore top the nation in Education

Kelly McGlynn
— asst. copy editor

George Bush wants to be known as the "education president." In order to achieve this, he has proposed a program known as America 2000.

This program consists of a set of eduction goals the Bush Administration has developed that is hoped to be reached by the year 2000.

These goals include: (1) All kids will start school ready to learn; (2) The high school graduation rate will rise to 90%; (3) American students in grades fourth, eighth, and 12 will exhibit competencies; (4) Students will be first in the world in math and science; (5) All adults in the US will be literate; and (6) Every school will be free of drugs and violence.

As part of this America 2000 program, Bush has singled out two cities for their exemplary achievements in education. These cities are Baltimore and Omaha.

These cities were chosen as example America 2000 cities due to the excellent level of education that can

be found there, according to Shari Hofschire, District 66 School Board member.

All facets of the community, including businesses in these cities is committed to placing an emphasis on education, Hofschire said.

The entire community is involved in the education of the people in the Omaha area, which is one reason the city was chosen as an example America 2000 city. It is on its way to completing the six goals adopted by the President.

"The entire city is considered for America 2000. The program includes excellence in education from the preschool education offered in a city through elementary school, high school, colleges and universities, and graduate school," Hofschire said. "All levels of education are considered."

This program is necessary to help schools in America realize they have fallen behind nationally in the area of education, Liz Karnes, District 66 School Board president, said.

"The program is wonderful, but

we [in District 66] still have a long way to go," Karnes said.

Cities in the Midwest generally stress the importance of education more than other cities across the country, according to Hofschire.

"Everybody here [in the Midwest] really values the importance of education and has a genuine concern for the kids," Hofschire said.

Because of the emphasis placed on education, Omaha was selected as an example city.

"I think it's really appropriate [that Omaha was chosen]. I am concerned when national reports say education in the United States is failing," Hofschire said. "Especially in Westside I can see the national goals are being accomplished. This

> **Everybody here really values the Importance of education and has a genuine concern for the kids.**
> — board member Shari Hofschire

doesn't mean, however, we can't keep improving."

Students agreed with Hofschire that it is an honor for Omaha to be chosen.

"It feels good to know that I attend a school in a city recognized for its excellent education programs," junior Penny Waskow said.

"It is very nice to know that the school systems here in Omaha can be compared to a larger city such as Baltimore," junior Scott Foral said.

Day-to-day activities of the students will not be affected by the fact that Westside, a is a part of the Omaha school system, has been selected as a representative school for the America 2000 program, Hofschire said.

District 66 will continue to strive

to reach the national goals, Karnes said.

"The main goal of ours, as a district, is to make sure the six goals are achieved," Karnes said.

In order to oversee the accomplishment of these goals, a committee, known as Omaha 2000, was set up. Members of this committee include various community leaders.

Karnes represents District 66 as a member of this organization.

The America 2000 program will greatly attract national attention to the Omaha schools, according to Hofschire.

"More people will start asking, 'What are you [Omaha] doing that's right? And how can we emulate your programs?'" Hofschire said.

Westside Community Schools will continue their quest for excellence. According to the two board members, Hofschire and Karnes, District 66 schools are still not perfect; they are, however, well on their way to completing Bush's goals for the year 2000.

Notice how the Lance, *Westside High School, Omaha, NE, finds a local angle to the tie-in to a national story. International, national, and state stories can often be localized to tie into a school situation.*

(Continued)

➤ *Thinking Through a Story*

• *Before you start writing, always ask yourself what your story is about. What is its focus? What is its purpose?*

• *Apply critical thinking skills to your story.*

• *Force yourself to dig deeper for those meaningful, unusual quotes.*

• *Ask yourself what you can say in one sentence that tells the reader the meaning of the story.*

• *Decide on the images that stick in your mind that will help you convey the subject to the reader.*

• *What statistics should be included?*

• *Perhaps you might try writing the ending before the lead to give you an indication of the direction you want your story to go.*

• *Look at the story from different points of view—from the points of view each person in your story might have.*

write the story. Be sure to attribute all direct quotes to the sources of the information. Bury attributions in the middle or at the end of the quotes. Do not start the sentence with an attribution. Wrong: He said, "Since the Minnesota Twins have never lost a World Series game in the Metrodome, I think their stadium should be torn down. They beat the St. Louis Cardinals in 1987 four times in the dome, and they repeated that feat against the Atlanta Braves in 1991." Right: "Since the Minnesota Twins have never lost a World Series game in the Metrodome," he said, "I think their stadium should be torn down. They beat the St. Louis Cardinals in 1987 four times in the dome, and they repeated that feat against the Atlanta Braves in 1991."

Each quote should be a separate paragraph. Attribute paraphrases in the same way as direct quotes: Bury the attributions in the middle or at the end of the paraphrase.

Reporters use three types of quotations: direct, partial, and indirect. Direct and partial quotations both use a source's words, but a partial quotation uses phrases rather than complete sentences. Indirect quotations paraphrase a source's comments. For example:

Direct Quotation: "Because reporters fail to verify their information," Principal John Johnson said, "they often fail to quote a source accurately."

Partial Quotation: Principal John Johnson said that because reporters fail to check facts, they often "fail to quote a source accurately."

Indirect Quotation: Reporters often fail to quote accurately because they do not verify their facts, according to Principal John Johnson.

Do not use a paraphrase and then repeat the same information in a direct quote. For example:

Principal John Johnson plans to resign.
"I plan to resign," said Principal John Johnson.

A beginning reporter often commits that writing sin.

Quotations that include several sentences need to be attributed only once. Try to place the attribution at a logical thought break in the first sentence or at the end of the first sentence. If the quote is more than 40 words in length, you should divide it into two or more paragraphs. Put quote marks at the beginning of each paragraph and at the end of the last paragraph. Do not use quote marks at the end of any paragraph except the last one.

It is possible for reporters to change a direct quote if they are deleting unnecessary words, correcting grammatical errors, or eliminating profanities. Be sure not to change the meaning of the quote if you eliminate unnecessary words.

Several unnecessary words have been eliminated from the following example:

"Look, you know I think recycling is absolutely necessary," she said.
"I think recycling is necessary," she said.

It is also proper to add ellipses to inform readers of deletions from quotes. An ellipsis consists of three periods unless the deletions occur at the end of a sentence, in which case four periods are necessary (one for the sentence punctuation). For example:

- *What facts did you discover that were the most surprising?*
- *What facts absolutely must be included? Which ones can be left out?*
- *Did you learn anything that you didn't expect to learn?*
- *Remember, you are a gatekeeper of the news. What you include in the story will open some gates. What you leave out will close others. The tone and style of your story will make a difference.*
- *Try writing the first draft of your story without using notes. Then refer to your notes to check for accuracy.*
- *Tell someone else your story. Then write the story as you told it.*

➢ *Ten Commandments for Reporters*
- *Observe! Observe! Observe!*
- *React to everything you observe to determine its newsworthiness.*
- *Stretch your mind by thinking what news angles there are based on your observations.*
- *Become well acquainted with a large number of sources.*
- *Read! Read! Read!*
- *Take the initiative.*
- *Be patient.*
- *Use imagination, but don't be a "pipe" reporter. (See page 92.)*
- *Be accurate.*
- *Be balanced and objective.*

"I think recycling is necessary, because it will lead to a cleaner environment and it will help us have a cleaner campus," she said.

"I think recycling is necessary, because ... it will help us have a cleaner campus," she said.

Reporters should also consider the following guidelines for the use of quotations and attribution:

1. Do not attribute quotes to inanimate objects such as organizations. Attribute to a person who is a member of that organization. Wrong: "He dropped out when he was 17, according to the school." Right: "He dropped out when he was 17, Principal Joan Jarvis said."

2. Do not place quotation marks around a single word or two. These are called orphan quotes and usually are meaningless. Quotation marks around single words are sometimes used to indicate an oddity.

3. Reporters can clarify a quotation by placing an explanation in parentheses. However, parenthetical matter should be brief and should be used as seldom as possible—rarely more than twice in a single story. For example: "He (Mayor Paul Meyer) wants to place a curfew on teenagers," said Principal Martha Matthews.

4. Indirect quotations require more attribution than direct quotations. A single attribution placed at the beginning of an indirect quotation may be inadequate. Each new idea or statement of opinion in an indirect quotation must be attributed.

The most important part of the story is the lead, which is basically the topic sentence of the story. The lead needs to grab readers immediately, to keep them reading.

Most news stories use the summary lead. In writing a

Auditorium closure due to safety concerns

By Kitty Fung
Reporter

Because of poor maintenance and resulting safety concerns, the auditorium has been temporarily shut down.

Performing Arts Department Chair Leonard Narumi has filed a concern with Principal Terrance Devney and the Montebello Unified School District Office regarding the condition of the auditorium. Narumi asked that the auditorium be temporarily shut down to all non-performing arts department groups and clubs until it can be made safer.

"I would like to see the refurbishing issues addressed so we can have a better facility and school," said Narumi

"It's definitely a safety hazard and part of the district's responsibility is to keep the facilities safe" said Assistant Principal Bill Peirce.

Some concerns from faculty and students are that potentially hazardous equipment, such as curtains, needs to be replaced because of vandalism and an installation error. Also, many seats are broken and unusable.

No fire extinguishers are in the auditorium, but the stage has a fire hose. The boy's dressing room door has been vandalized and can no longer be locked. In addition, the house sound system and intercom are not in good working condition.

According to Narumi, the lighting system is old and needs to be replaced with new technology, like dimmers and floods that are similar to the light boards and controls for dimmers and floods that have been upgraded at Montebello High and Bell Gardens High Schools within the last few years. These improvements have not been made at Schurr.

The stage's built-out platform should be replaced with more stable risers. With a firm platform, entertainers can perform without tripping or falling over uneven risers.

"Last year, one guy fell off the built-out stage because one of the risers fell over," said sound crew member Anthony Gallego.

According to Narumi, other things to consider include installing air conditioning and fixing the coating on the aisles. If the auditorium is not in working condition by December, the Performing Arts Department may be forced to find an alternative performance hall for rehearsals and programs.

> *"It's definitely a safety hazard and part of the district's responsibility is to keep the facility safe."*
> **Bill Peirce**
> *Assistant Principal*

Use of a pulled quote draws the reader to this news story from the Spartan Scroll, *Schurr High School, Montebello, CA. The article does a good job of describing the safety problems in the auditorium, including making comparisons to what has happened in other high schools.*

> ➢ *The 5 W's of Journalism from a Diverse Perspective*
>
> *Who: Who's missing from the story?*
>
> *What: What's the context for the story?*
>
> *Where: Where can we go for more information?*
>
> *When: When do we use racial or ethnic identification?*
>
> *Why: Why are we including or excluding certain information?*
>
> *—Compiled by Aly Colón, Ethics & Diversity Faculty, Poynter Institute*

summary lead, the writer first needs to decide which of the five W's (who, what, when, where, why) and the H (how) is the most important part of the story. It is not necessary to include all five W's and the H in the lead, but most leads include at least two or three.

The writer should choose words carefully, so that he or she can get to the point quickly and avoid long or confusing sentences. A good rule of thumb is to avoid sentences of more than 30 syllables. That obviously cannot be done in all instances, but keeping it in mind does help the reporter keep sentences short and concise, and therefore clearer to the reader.

The lead must have impact, but it must not waste words. Its purpose is to persuade the reader to continue.

Most news stories begin with the "what" element, because readers are generally more interested in what happened than in when or where it happened. The second most widely used W is the "who," because readers find prominent people interesting. The "who" lead is used when the person is well known or when there would not be a story without it; be careful not to overuse the "who" lead.

"When" and "where" are generally part of the lead but included toward the end. "When" or "where" might begin a lead if there had been a time or place change for an event and the paper was the first to report it. That is unlikely to happen at the high school level because of the absence of timeliness for most stories.

If "when" or "where" is not the lead, the writer should avoid such openings as "At a meeting," "Tonight," "Tomorrow," "At 10 a.m.," "Recently" or "On Sept. 19." "Recently" is a poor word to use anywhere in a story because of its vagueness; to some readers it might mean within the past week, and to others, within the past year or even five years.

Other poor opening words are "a," "an," "the" and "there are" or "there is." The first four or five words should have visual appeal to the reader. They are the most important. "A," "an," "the, "there are" and "there is" provide no visual impact.

Usually a lead is only one paragraph in length, but it may be longer if necessary to summarize the event.

Some reporters are relegating the 5W's and H lead to the second paragraph in stories and using one that is more interesting. Be careful, however. A news story is not a feature story. The reader still needs the most important information first. Following are examples of other interesting leads for news stories:

> ***Personal-level lead.*** *Everything costs more these days, but few items have gone up as much for students as the cost of lunch in the cafeteria. The price of lunch has increased from $1 to $1.75 this year because of higher food costs, according to Rosalie Kinder, cafeteria manager.* Note that the second sentence contains the summary of the story. If you use a personal-level lead (one that ties the story directly to the reader), be sure you have a second sentence for summary.
>
> ***Anecdote lead.*** A story can be personalized even more by showing how it affects one individual

---

➤ *Possible Leads*

• *Past Participle:* Shocked by the destruction that Hurricane Fran had caused, Principal Jack Jules formed a committee to come up with ideas for rebuilding the school.

• *Gerund phrase (using the "ing" form of a verb as a noun):* Typing 70 words a minute is the requirement for passing keyboarding class.

• *Prepositional Phrase:* After reading the editorial in the school newspaper, Principal Jack Jules decided to read all content in the future before publication.

•*Conditional phrase (begins with* if, unless *or* provided): If the football team can avoid injuries, Coach Billy Blue thinks it can win the conference.

(real or imaginary). *When James Overholt received his Preliminary Scholastic Aptitude Test scores, he was amazed to see a statement that said, "Scores arrived too late to be part of the scholarship competition." Overholt gasped when he saw that he had scores higher than those needed to be a National Merit Semifinalist, but then he grew angry when he realized he could not compete for any financial rewards. He complained to the administration, but to no avail.*

Principal Franklin McCallie said that someone had misplaced Overholt's exam. "It was an honest mistake," McCallie said, "and we regret the error. Someone locked Overholt's test in the safe, and it was not discovered until three weeks after the test should have been sent to the National Merit Corporation for scoring."

Note that the anecdote lead also requires additional paragraphs to help summarize the story.

When the reporter has finished the leads, he writes the rest of the story in inverted pyramid style. That means he arranges the facts from most important to least important.

The inverted pyramid style allows the hurried reader to get the important facts if he doesn't have time to read the entire story. It also gives the editor an easy way to shorten a story, if necessary, by merely trimming paragraphs from the end.

Part of the art of writing is making the story flow smoothly and logically from sentence to sentence. That means mastering the art of transition. Transition can be achieved by repetition of key words or phrases or by use of words such as "however," "therefore," "furthermore," "although," "then," "in addition," "nevertheless," "still," "also," "otherwise," "consequently," "meanwhile," "for example," "earlier," "before," "after," "as a result," "since," "thus," or "similarly." Be constantly aware of transitional devices in order to guide the reader easily through the story.

Some guidelines the writer should keep in mind when

> ➢ *The Interview*
> • *Before the interview, be sure you have enough paper to take notes and be sure you have at least two writing utensils. Also, be sure you have done all the necessary background research so you are prepared.*
> • *During the interview, position yourself so you can write comfortably. Create your own personal shorthand so you can take notes rapidly. Take down information word-for-word only when it is an important quote.*
> • *Immediately after the interview, read your notes for clarity and understanding. Underline all key ideas as well as any good quotes. Follow up on references and other examples cited during the interview.*

developing the story include the following:

➤ **Finding an Idea**
• There should never be a problem with having enough stories to fill a paper. Ideas are every-where. Read exchange papers, read professional papers, read maga-zines, use a beat sys-tem, and observe everywhere you go. Story ideas are all around you.
• There should never be enough space to get in all the news. Always plan for more stories than you can possibly run.
• Remember that news is new informa-tion about any-thing—information that was previously unknown. News is also people who merit special atten-tion for something they have done.

1. Write short sentences and short paragraphs (about 20 words maximum to a sentence and 40 words maximum to a paragraph).
2. Alternate long and short paragraphs to avoid monotony.
3. Vary word usage.
4. Vary paragraph openers.
5. Use active voice verbs.
6. Write in the third person.
7. Be specific and thorough. Don't say that several hundred dollars were raised by the Pep Club; say that the Pep Club raised $700.
8. Check all facts. Verify spelling of names.
9. Do not editorialize. Keep your opinion out of the copy.
10. Avoid vague words such as "many," "various," "numerous," "nice," "enjoyable," "several," "a lot," "few," "some," and "interesting." Be cau-tious in the use of adjectives and adverbs. When you use them, make them specific. "Tall" means nothing; to describe a basketball player as 6'11" is specific and visual for the reader.
11. Attribute all direct quotes and indirect quotes.
12. Avoid the phrase "when asked." It is obvious that if someone responded, he was asked.
13. Identify all persons the first time mentioned. Use class (freshman, sophomore, junior, senior) for students, unless it is a sports story; then position on the team will suffice for iden-tification.
14. Follow the stylebook.
15. Don't be content with the obvious facts; probe for the "why" and "how."
16. Rewrite and then rewrite again. There is always room for improvement.
17. Read a professional newspaper daily. Reading good writing improves one's own writing.

18. Read your story aloud. The ear is more practiced than the eye at picking up weaknesses in structure and style.

19. Avoid writing in chronological order. It is rare that a news event occurs in chronological order of importance.

20. Check publication date. When you write the story, the event may not have occurred, but when the paper comes out the event may be in the past.

21. Reread your article and cut out every unnecessary "a" and "the." Also eliminate the words "very" and "that" when possible.

22. When covering an event, go with an open mind.

23. Talk to people on both sides of an issue.

24. Don't try to draw conclusions, evaluate an event, or preach.

25. Skip the jargon. Do not write: "In case of. . ."

26. Use everyday language. Do not write over the reader's head.

27. Be wary of too much punctuation. Keep it simple.

28. Keep your language conversational.

29. Remember that the first five words are most important. Keep them interesting.

30. Avoid adjectives and adverbs.

31. Use vivid verbs. Avoid *to be* verbs *(is, was, are, were,* etc.) as much as possible.

32. Make sure paragraphs flow from one to another by repeating words from the previous paragraph, by finding synonyms for words in the previous paragraph, by referring back to an idea from the previous paragraph, and by using transitional words to tie them together.

33. Avoid opening with a direct quote. This type of lead often turns off the reader.

The preceding guidelines pertain to all four types of news

➢ *Using the Reader*

• *Let the interviewee tell most of the story in his or her own words by using direct or indirect quotes.*

• *Direct quotes allow readers to learn what people had to say rather than what the reporter says they have said. Quotes can be used to add credibility to the facts.*

• *Use indirect quotes to summarize long statements. They can also serve as transitions from one set of facts to another set of facts.*

stories—single feature, multiple feature, action, and quote.

A *single feature story*, as its name implies, features only one fact. An example of a single feature lead:

> Twenty-one credits are needed to graduate from high school beginning next fall, as a result of a decision made by the school board last night.

Each succeeding paragraph gives more details of the school board's decision, with the least important details last.

A *multiple feature story* emphasizes more than one fact in the lead. For example:

> Twenty-one credits are needed to graduate from high school next fall, and the varsity football team will play all of its games on Saturday afternoons, according to decisions made by the school board last night.

The next paragraphs give the most important details about the graduation requirements. Those are followed by the most important details of the football decision. Then the writer gives the least important details about graduation and then the least important details about football. Obviously, by placing the graduation requirements first in the lead, the reporter is saying that they are more important than the football decision. That is one of the difficult tasks a reporter has in the news selection process, but he should select the feature that has the most impact on the greatest number of readers. Multiple feature stories often occur in coverage of meetings. A school board, the Student Council, or the Pep Club usually makes more than one decision per meeting. If more than one important decision is made, all should be included in the lead.

A third type of news story is the *action story*: a description of an event that involved a lot of motion, such as a battle to put out a fire or an active classroom project. The most common action story at the high school level is the sports story; sports writing is covered in Chapter 5.

The *quote story* is one in which the information is presented primarily through quotes. This type of story is based almost entirely on an interview or a speech. The lead of a quote story usually is a quotation or an indirect quotation of what the person said. When using a quote, be sure that it is unusual enough to shock, intrigue, or excite the reader. It may be a quote that summarizes the story, but it is rare that a speaker or an interviewee summarizes his or her comments for the reporter.

A speech story is a typical quote story. Report what the speaker said, not just the fact that he or she spoke.

Before covering a speech story, be sure to get background information on the speaker. Why is he/she an expert on the subject? Use a tape recorder, if possible. Be sure to observe audience reaction; sometimes that is more important than what the speaker says. Obtain a copy of the speech if one is available. If not, be sure to get several direct quotations. As in interview stories, be careful not to take the speaker's comments out of context. Always try to talk to the speaker if you wish additional information. Sometimes you can get clarification during a question-answer session.

Be sure to write the story immediately after the speech, while it is still fresh in your mind. Organize your notes in inverted pyramid order.

The lead of the story should emphasize what the speaker said, not the fact that he or she spoke. A paraphrase or indirect quote may work better for the lead than a direct quote.

After the lead, tell where the speech was presented and when. A brief biography of the speaker should also be included.

Intersperse paragraphs of paraphrase with direct quotations. Don't bunch paragraphs of each type together.

One of the most difficult tasks for high school reporters is finding news stories. The following list suggests possible sources:

1. *Beats.* Each staff should establish a beat system under which reporters check regularly with teachers, administrators, sponsors, and coach-

The Piped Story

• Reporters today supposedly do not use "piped" stories because they are unethical. The term "piped story" probably is of New York origin because of the proximity of Manhattan police headquarters to Chinatown, where people have been known to smoke opium. Thus, reporters who embellish their news stories are said to have been "smoking the pipe." In the past, many of these reporters did not write. They phoned their stories to rewrite men, but they often filled in their own facts to embellish the story.

• One "pipe" reporter was Frank Bastable of the New York American. He reported that escaping robbers had presented a raspberry sucker to a little girl as she skipped rope on the sidewalk in front of the candy store they had robbed of $40. The robbery had occurred, but he had invented the little girl. However, other papers chided their reporters for missing the "little girl" angle.

• H. L. Mencken's story in the New York Evening Mail in 1917 was totally fake. He wrote that the country had ignored the 75th anniversary of the introduction of the bathtub in the United States. He reported that Millard Fillmore took the first presidential bath in 1851. None of the story was true, but everyone believed it, and it still lives today in reference books.

es for news tips. This alerts source people to recognize noteworthy items and be prepared for the reporter's regular contact. Although a beat source may tell a reporter there is nothing new, a good technique is to "chew the fat" for a few minutes anyway; the source may say something significant while chatting, without realizing it is newsworthy.

2. *Alumni.* Former students can often provide information on graduates that might be newsworthy.

3. *Professional newspapers.* Look for stories that can be localized for the high school reader, such as drunk-driving laws or teenage marriages.

4. *Exchange newspapers.* Find out what other schools are covering. Some of their topics may be pertinent to your readers.

5. *Community bulletins.* Local fairs and other community events may involve students. Report their participation.

6. *Colleges.* Report on activities pertinent to high school seniors especially, such as the proposed construction of a branch campus or changes in entrance requirements.

7. *Brochures on special events.* Special days such as National Ice Cream Day or the Great American Smokeout Day may be newsworthy if you have students participating.

EXERCISES

1. Make a list of all news stories appearing in 10 exchange papers. Indicate which ones you think your school should cover and why.

2. Clip from professional newspapers or magazines five stories of interest to teenagers. Indicate how your school paper could

➢ *The Speech Story*
• *Speech story leads usually include who said what, when and where, and to whom (in that order).*
• *The body of a speech story usually starts with a direct quote supporting the theme of the lead. This will be followed by a paragraph giving the background of the theme and the purpose of the speech.*
• *Additional paragraphs will elaborate the main theme, which will be followed by any additional points the speaker might have made.*
• *Include significant mannerisms or gestures of the speaker, the audience reaction, and material from the question and answer period or a post-speech interview.*

➤ *Featuring News Leads*

Because most high school papers lack timeliness, it is impossible to report news as it happens. Therefore, writers should featurize their leads by finding a unique way to present information. Good feature stories are built on strong quotes. Good news stories should also be built on strong quotes. A good source of information for those interested in avoiding the basic summary lead would be Bobby Hawthorne's book The Radical Write.

localize these articles.

3. Select one of the ideas you found in an exchange paper and one you found in a professional publication and write a news story on each one that might be published in your school's paper.

4. Make a list of all news stories appearing in the last issue of your school paper and identify each by type of story. Discuss their strengths and weaknesses. Look for information that should have been included but wasn't. Was each story written in inverted pyramid style? Was each lead effective? Why or why not?

5. Write *leads only* for the following sets of facts. Add facts as necessary, but do not change those given. Vary your openings. Use varying grammatical forms, such as conditional clause *(If all home football games must be played on Saturday afternoons, many working students will not be able to attend.)*; temporal clause *(When the football team begins playing all of its home games on Saturday afternoons, the crowd might be smaller because working students cannot attend.)*; infinitive phrase *(To allow parents to participate in other community events on Friday nights, the school board has decided to have all varsity football games on Saturday afternoons.)*; participial phrase *(Led by Bob Morris, school board president, members of the community have persuaded the administration to switch football games to Saturday afternoons.)*; prepositional phrase *(Over the objection of Superintendent Rae Morris, the school board still decided to switch varsity football games from Friday nights to Saturday afternoons.)*. Regardless of the grammatical form used, remember to get the most important fact in the first four or five words and to summarize the entire event.

A. Teachers get new assignments for next year. Seven teachers switched to other departments. Declining enrollment part of the reason. Five of the teachers do not like their new assignments. The other two are pleased. In addition to the switches, four new teachers will be hired to replace the eight who are retiring. Declining enrollment is the reason for not replacing all eight.

B. Beautification of the smoking area behind schedule. Smokers to do the work. Financial concerns and apathy seem to be the major problems. Kelly Jeffress, committee chairperson in charge of beautification, blames the principal for not providing money. The principal blames the committee for being lazy and uninterested. Main project is to paint a mural of school life on the gymnasium wall (the south side of the area). Jeffress says the committee has not received approval for the mural from the principal. The principal says no plan has been presented to him.

C. Principal's award given to most outstanding senior. This year's award presented to Billie Allison. Award given on May 22. Controversy surrounds the award, which, according to the criteria, should   go to the person who is most outstanding in scholarship, athletics, music, extracurricular activities. Some students think that the recipient, who has a 2.5 grade point average on a 4.0 scale, does not meet the criteria.

D. Club to participate in city parade. Parade to be on Jan. 30. Pep Club will decorate cars, and those members who can play instruments will form a band. Purpose of the parade is to welcome home an astronaut—local boy becomes hero. All 200 members of the club are

➢ *Interviewing*
Rules
• *Gather back-ground information about the person you are interviewing before the interview.*
• *Prepare a list of questions based on the background information.*
• *Be on time for the interview. Make a good first impression.*
• *Pause after an interviewee answers a question before pro-ceeding with the next question. He/she might have more to say.*
• *Change your line of questioning if the interviewee takes you in a another direction.*
• *Let the inter-viewee tell the story.*
• *Avoid "off the record" questions.*
• *Get specific details to add emotion to the story. Quotes should relate the feelings of the interviewee.*
• *Seek the unusual. The readers may already know that the auditorium stage col-lapsed as student actors were practicing for a play, but they won't know what the actors were thinking*

(Continued)

expected to participate in some way.

E. New Student Council officers. Jessica Goodall, president. Paula Hall, vice-presi-dent; Steve Hardester, secretary; Jim Goodall, treasurer. Jim is Jessica's broth-er, and both Paula and Steve are cousins of Jim and Jessica. Election held last Thursday. New officers to begin duties at next week's meeting. Jessica has said her first priority is to persuade the administration to start an Open Lunch program for seniors, allowing them to leave campus for lunch.

F. Homecoming Queen candidates select-ed. Seven girls chosen in all-school vote. The girl with most votes will be named queen at the dance, to be held Nov. 17. 2,000 students in school, but only 131 voted in the election. Some students think such competitions are sexist. The new queen will be crowned by last year's queen, Leigh Simmons. Theme for the dance is "One More Time." "Treat," a five-member band, will provide the music. Dance will be from 8 to 11 p.m. Tickets will be $8 per couple. The seven girls chosen were Libby Fantroy, Angie Ehrhardt, Kristine Powell, Ann Hopkins, Julie Hall, Joy Sears, and Karen Angel.

G. Sixteen families host 21 city transfer stu-dents. Students involved in extracurricu-lar activities stay with the host families after school on game days so the stu-dents will find it easier to participate in events. Most students ride the bus for 10 to 15 miles daily. If it weren't for the host families, they would get home only in time to turn around and come back for the night event. Host families are all volunteers. There are still 16 city transfer students who need host families. The administration hopes to have host families for all students by Dec. 1.

H.   Two music students receive honor. Amy Jones and Maurice Powell, both seniors. Named to all-state choir. Will perform at state capitol in March. Your school is the only one with more than one student selected. Fifty students from around the state on the all-state choir. Three other students—John Cook, Mark Clouse, and Tammy Hall—named to all-district choir. John and Mark are juniors and Tammy is a senior.

I.   Dr. Ken Hope. Received Outstanding Science Educator Award from state department of education. Will accept the award during an all-school assembly to be held in his honor, Jan. 5. His award is for "38 years of outstanding work in the field of science." Hope has written a high school science textbook and published more than 50 magazine articles on various science topics. In 1983 he was selected District Teacher of the Year by his fellow teachers.

J.   District to close two elementary schools. Declining enrollment is the reason. This will reduce the elementary schools to five. Will also move the ninth grade to the high school and will move all sixth grades to the two present junior high schools, creating two sixth-eighth grade middle schools. Many parents upset about the closing of their neighborhood schools.

when the incident occurred. Dig for the specifics.

• Ask the subject to repeat what he/she said for clarification.

• Besides taking notes about what the interviewee says, also take notes about the interviewee's facial expressions and gestures. Facial expressions and gestures add emotion to copy.

• Thank the interviewee for his/her time and ask permission to make further contact for clarification or additional information.

➢ Featurizing
News Leads

• "With the commercial success of ABC's hit game show Who Wants to Be a Millionaire, a yet unidentified individual has apparently misinterpreted the show's rules and begun his or her own quest for the seven-digit mark by stealing an estimated $17,000 from the WHS safe sometime in early November of last year." —The Spokesman, Wheeling High School, Wheeling, IL

By using a comparison and contrast lead and by alluding to a TV program most readers are familiar with, the Spokesman reporter has provided a feature to a theft story—a theft that most readers had probably already heard about. Because of a lack of timeliness for most stories in high school papers, it is often a good idea to featurize the news.

• "English teacher Mrs. Elizabeth

(Continued)

K. City police crack down on teenage parties. Several teenagers holding alcoholic parties when parents are out of town. Most parties are open to anyone whether the teenager knows them or not. One student, Craig Wall, a senior, said more than 300 people showed up at one of his parties. There was lots of damage. Police are patrolling neighborhoods more frequently and are checking ID's. Chief of police also wrote a letter to parents asking to have their sons/daughters supervised when they leave town.

L. For any reason except illness, students will receive a zero if they miss any day of school prior to a vacation period. This is a new decision announced by the principal. The principal says that absenteeism is high, especially one or two days before a vacation. "I see no reason why some students should be allowed to have an extended vacation," the principal said. The new rule will be published in the student handbook. Many students upset with the ruling, especially since it was made just seven days before spring break and many had plans to leave for Florida early.

6. Write complete news stories for all the exercises in number 5. Add facts as necessary, including names and quotes, but do not change any of the facts given. Be sure to use inverted pyramid style.

7. Select an event that is occurring at your school and write a complete news story. Be sure to interview to get all the facts.

8. One of the jobs of a reporter is to gain an understanding of which facts should be included in a

story and which should be left out. Write a news story based on the following facts, but include only those facts essential to reader understanding. You may add facts, if necessary.

18 members in Backscratching Club.

13 members attended annual Halloween Party.

Party held Oct. 30 from 8 to 10:30 p.m.

Parents also attended.

It was the third annual Halloween Party.

It was held in 118 W (room at your school).

Sponsor, Paul Ivy, age 46.

Mr. Ivy is the dramatics teacher.

Small fire broke out in an electrical switchbox at 8:59 p.m.

Everyone forced to evacuate.

Half hour later party resumed in 122 W.

Genuine walnut backscratcher awarded by Mr. Ivy to Susie Smythe.

Susie won it for raising the most money, $23, by selling desk calendars.

Club sold $200 worth of desk calendars.

Fire damage: two electric typewriters in 118 W were destroyed—damage to electrical switchbox—probably be three weeks before it is repaired—means that typing classes will have to use manual typewriters for next three weeks.

Money raised was used for party and the award; any left over will be used to buy a backscratcher for each club member.

Fire also caused smoke damage to 118 W, 119 W, and 120 W; the smoke and water damage will force classes to meet in other rooms for one week.

Fire department was called; put out fire in 23 minutes.

Next meeting of club will be its annual Christmas party—to be in 118 W.

Hope to have all backscratchers bought by

(Continued)

then, perhaps even buy for parents and principal.

Officers of club are Jack Roberts, president; Jill Stone, vice-president; and Skinny Slippery, secretary-treasurer.

9. Rewrite the leads of five news stories from recent issues of your school paper. Be prepared to discuss why you made the changes you did.

10. Invite a local journalist to speak to your class. Write a speech story based on the reporter's comments.

11. Invite the principal to class to speak on his or her dreams for your school. Write a speech story based on the comments.

12. Create a role-playing situation on a controversial topic at your school. Let one student play the role of the principal and another play the role of a person on the opposite side. Interview both and write a story. If a controversial topic already exists at your school, the role-playing can be based on a real situation.

13. Have each student in class clip five or six stories of no more than 10 paragraphs from a daily newspaper. Cut the articles apart by paragraphs after numbering them on the back. Give the stories to other students to try to put them back in the original inverted pyramid order.

14. Clip from a daily newspaper what you consider to be an outstanding news story. Discuss its attributes in class. Does the lead summarize the entire story? Does it lead the reader to the next paragraph? Were good transitions used between sentences and paragraphs? Is the story written in inverted pyramid order? Is it correct in grammar and spelling?

15. Make a list of synonyms for the word said that could be used to attribute quotes. Remember, however, that there is no better word for said than said. It is short, and all journalistic writing must be brief. Many

high school writers use commented; however, it is much longer than said and offers no visual appeal. If someone shouted, use shouted because it indicates something about the statement. Avoid using stated unless the source being quoted is an official source. More than 100 words could be used at appropriate times as synonyms of said. Make a list of at least 100 words.

16. Attend a meeting of your school board and write a news story on decisions made. Select a meeting at which the members are scheduled to discuss items of interest to high school students.

17. Attend a meeting of one of your school's organizations and write a news story on it. Remember to avoid chronological order unless the events occur in order of importance chronologically.

18. Find a news story in a daily paper and edit it by eliminating all unnecessary words such as "very" and "the."

19. Find a news story in your school paper and edit all quotes to eliminate unnecessary words. Be careful not to change the meaning of any quote.

20. Attend a meeting of your school board and write a news story about its agenda. Remember not to write in chronological order.

21. Write a news story based on the following set of facts. You may make up additional facts as necessary to make your story complete. Do not change any facts given. (Obviously, if you were writing the story from your own personal observations, you could not make up facts. However, when you are writing stories from a fact sheet, there may not be enough facts to make your story complete—you might have to do additional research.)

SITUATION: The school board at its meeting last Monday night voted to abolish the student smoking area in one month and to eliminate smoking everywhere on campus, including sports events, in one year. The school board had created the smoking area in 1971. You covered the school board meeting for an issue of the paper to be published tomorrow. All quotes were made at the meeting.

QUOTES: "The smoking policy looked fine on the blackboard, but it was by no means successful. We had hoped that setting up a specialized smoking area would alleviate the problem of smoking in restrooms around campus. Unfortunately, the problem seemed to grow. I'm afraid that our only alternative is to prohibit tobacco everywhere on campus."

—Jerry Winter, superintendent.

"By and large, parents are against the smoking area. The Parent/Teacher Association overwhelmingly voted against smoking on campus. I'm sure that there will be a slight outcry from the kids, but it's in their general interest."

—Juanita Morales, school board president.

"As you'll remember, I was opposed to the original plan, and I'm even more adamant now than I was then. There is the students' health to consider. In addition, we're avoiding littered school grounds, messy drinking fountains, and smoke-filled restrooms. We're also avoiding the physical damage caused by the use of cigarettes and chewing tobacco. In short, we're protecting the students' health as well as our own tax dollars."

—Derrick Skinner, school board member.

"We can't stop the kids from smoking, but we can make it difficult for them. That's what I favor. It's time we detected the sweet smell of success at our school, rather than the foul stench of burning tobacco."

—Jessie Mangan, principal.

"I don't smoke, but I'm going to speak up for those who do. We should have one clear set of values prevailing. Teachers have a smoking lounge. If you're going to eliminate the student smoking area, then you have to eliminate the teacher one as well. You should eliminate both of them immediately— not just the student one. Why are you waiting a year to eliminate the teachers' smokers lounge? Don't have two sets of rules for the next year. Eliminate all smoking on campus now."

—Yolanda Miller, junior.

"By closing the smoking area, you are not going to eliminate smoking. You'll see even more smoking in the bathrooms. Are you going to hire patrols to police the campus. I have no intention of stopping. I have smoked for years, and nothing you will do can stop me. I suppose you could expel me, but you're going to have to expel about 500 students. Don't infringe on our rights. Smokers do have rights."

—Bill Underwood, freshman.

ADDITIONAL INFORMATION: Under the guidelines unanimously approved by the board, the elimination of the students' smoking area will occur in 30 days, and the no-smoking-everywhere - on-campus edict will occur in 12 months. Students caught smoking or carrying any form of tobacco on campus will be suspended. Because of the school board action, yours will be the only school in the state to have a completely smoke-free campus. Chris McDaniel, student council president, said she plans to lead a petition effort against the board's action. "Without a smoking area, we'll have even more smoke in the restrooms," she said. "There is no way the faculty can police every restroom every hour of the day. The problem will actually make things worse for the nonsmokers. I hope to get at least 75% of the student body to sign a petition protesting the board's action."

22. Compose a question based on a news event that is currently happening at your school. Have each student ask five people the question. Dig for good quotes. Bring your quotes back to the class and have a discussion to select the best ones. Remember, if anyone else can say it, it is not a good quote.

23. Decide which of the seven news elements fit each of the following stories. Then decide which four you think are the most important and deserve front page coverage. (1) 36 students selected for National Honor Society. Initiation will be next Thursday; (2) Spring break begins in two weeks; (3) New auditorium will be opened after spring break, and the spring play will be presented there April 29-30; (4) Superintendent announces his resignation; (5) Principal announces his resignation; (6) English Department will no longer offer honors classes beginning next fall; (7) Prom has been changed from May 10 to May 17; (8) Teen pregnancy rate at your school is on the rise. Twenty-seven girls have dropped out this semester because of pregnancy; (9) School will begin next year on Aug. 18. This is the first time students have ever attended school before Labor Day; (10) A new housing development in the area will increase enrollment next fall by 200 students. There are already 1,600 students in your school—150 over capacity.

24. Observe everything that takes place during your daily routine at school. Consider at least 10 ideas that could be developed into news stories. Rate each

one of them based on the news elements.

25. Decide which of the 10 ideas you listed in exercise 24 will make the best story. Then compile a list of five people you would interview for more information. Give reasons why you selected those five.

26. Now write a story based on the idea you selected.

27. Invite the drama director or one of the leads of the upcoming school play to class for an interview. Write a story based on that interview.

28. Read the book *The Radical Write* by Bobby Hawthorne, and write a summary of Hawthorne's approach to news writing in high school papers.

29. After reading *The Radical Write*, select a news story which appeared in the last issue of your paper which used a summary lead. Rewrite the lead with a featurized angle. You may have to obtain additional information to get the emotions necessary for a featurized approach.

30. Select a news topic about something that happened within the last month at your school. Write a story with a featurized lead. In some of the exercises above, the directions have said to add facts as necessary. That's because you're writing from a fact sheet that does not include all the necessary facts. Obviously, you would never make up facts for a real story. Do not make up any facts for this story or any other you write where you are doing your own research.

CHAPTER
five

Sports Writing

It's not a chronological world. Sports writers need to remember that. It is rare that sports events occur in order of importance. Yet many high school reporters when writing about a game begin with the first quarter and end with the last quarter regardless of which quarter was the most exciting or which play was the turning point or highlight.

Leads for sports stories must feature the most unusual happening in the game. The writer must always seek what made this game different from all other games he or she has covered. Many high school sports reporters find it easiest to start with the name of the school, but it is never the school that is the most exciting part of a game. It might be a particular offensive play, it might be a strong defense, it might be one player who had an outstanding game, it might be that the weather created sloppy playing conditions, or it might be a key penalty. There are any number of possibilities. Read the following leads and select the one that is weakest.

A. Quarterback Jack Cash and tailback Greg Miles scored 3 touchdowns each as Cash passed for 317 yards and Miles rushed for 187 in Kirkwood's 55-29 romp over Avilla last Saturday.

B. Top-ranked Parkway West relied on the "big play" last Saturday, including touchdown runs of 98 and 95 yards, as it rolled to a 34-7 football win over Parkway North.

C. Jim Jerrell, kicking specialist, booted a 47-yard field goal with :20 left last Saturday to give underdog Blake a 16-14 victory over Red Oak.

D. Workhorse Bill Belew hammered out 182 yards on 44 carries, including touchdown runs of six and four yards as he led Kirkwood to a 20-10 win over Parsons last Saturday.

E. The Kirkwood football Pioneers defeated the Lawnboy Devils 14-10 last Saturday before a small homecoming crowd.

F. Quarterback Ken James, who wasn't supposed to play because of a flu-like illness, ran for two touchdowns and passed for two more as the varsity football team edged Arthur, 28-26, last Saturday at home.

G. Lightly regarded Tawanga struck for three fourth-quarter touchdowns Saturday when Todd Greybull, quarterback, passed for 172 yards to guide the Spartans past DeBois, 21-20.

H. Quarterback Pat Clemons floated a two-point conversion pass through a driving rain to Jamal Abdul, after Kirkwood had recovered a fourth-quarter Kennedy fumble in the end zone for a touchdown Saturday, and the Pioneers turned what would have been a loss into an 8-7 win.

If you selected E as the weakest lead, you are correct. The writer did not zero in on any unusual aspect of the game. Any sports story could begin the way that lead does. Just change the sport, fill in the score, and you have an any-time lead. Obviously, a good sports writer does not want an any-time lead.

A good sports lead includes the highlight or unusual aspect of the game, the two teams involved, the type of sport, the score or outcome, when the game was played, and where it was played. The team involved is particularly important for high school newspapers. The writer must be specific as to whether it's the boys' varsity basketball team, the

Greenwood Invitational
Jan. 29, 2000
Andrews placed first [39 points]

1st Place
- Isai Garcia, 242 lbs. class [1260 lbs.]
- Jay Hughes, super heavyweight [1270 lbs.]
- Aaron Núñez, 114 lbs. class [660 lbs.]

2nd Place
- Adrian Bueno, 114 lbs. class [600 lbs.]
- Chris Núñez, 165 lbs. class [1025 lbs.]
- Travis Horton, 242 lbs. class [1105 lbs.]

3rd Place
- Tyler Ruiz, 220 lbs. class [1000 lbs.]
- Ryan Miller, 275 lbs. class [1065 lbs.]

4th Place
- Tom Garcia, 165 lbs. class [1005 lbs.]
- James Garcia, 198 lbs. class [1000 lbs.]

5th Place
- K.C. White, 181 lbs. class [990 lbs.]

Sandhills Powerlifting
Jan. 15, 2000
Andrews placed second

1st Place
- Aaron Núñez, 114 lbs. class [635 lbs.]

2nd Place
- Saula Arzabala, 132 lbs. class [720 lbs.]
- Ryan Miller, 275 lbs. class [1005 lbs.]

3rd Place
- Adrian Bueno, 114 lbs. class [510 lbs.]
- Daniel Ramos, 123 lbs. class [605 lbs.]
- K.C. White, 181 lbs. class [980 lbs.]

4th Place
- Tom Garcia, 165 lbs. class [1220 lbs.]
- Isai Garcia, 220 lbs. class [975 lbs.]

➢ *Quick Reads*
Quick reads can be effective on sports pages. This quick read from the Round Up, Andrews High School, Andrews, TX, does a good job of presenting a look at all winners in two powerlifting meets.

girls' varsity basketball team, the freshman boys' basketball team, or some other basketball team. It is rare for a school to have only one team for each sport.

From the preceding leads, select the one that includes all the items mentioned as necessary for a sports coverage lead. If you selected F, you are correct. It is the only one that includes where the game was played. Note that both time and place are included, but at the end. It is rare for a sports lead to begin with either time or place. Avoid the following as sports leads:

- The date of the game: *Tomorrow the varsity basketball girls will. . .*
- The name of your school, town, or team: *The Kirkwood junior varsity wrestling team will. . .*
- An obvious fact: *It's time for baseball again, and. . .*
- A statement of opinion: *The freshman swimming team had its best meet. . .*
- Non-newsworthy facts: *The girls' tennis team played in the state meet last week. . .*

Advance stories are probably more important for the high school press than coverage stories, because of the time factor. By the time the paper is printed, the coverage of a past event is usually old news. That does not mean that the school paper should ignore coverage. The paper should especially cover important games such as a state or league championship and games against major rivals. Many schools carry advance-coverage stories. The advance part should lead the story, since it is more likely to contain "new information."

By the time your paper is published, those really interested in a sporting event will likely know the score and other facts about the game. That is why the advance should be emphasized. In the advance story, tell the reader as many facts as you can about the upcoming opponent. What is the opponent's record? Has your school played some of the

> **Deciding What to Cover**
> • Because of the large number of both boys' and girls' sports at most schools, it is usually impossible to give equal coverage to each team.
> • Try to cover every team during a season at least once in detail.
> • Try to cover all teams in each issue in sports briefs.
> • Consider the success of a team when determining coverage.
> • Cover outstanding players in feature stories.
> • Be sure to leave some space for off-campus sports.
> • Be sure your reporting is newsworthy; it should be timely.
> • Why and How are often more important than Who and What.
> • Expect the unexpected!

Keeping Score

U-High score listed first, followed by opponent's score. Varsity games preceed j.v. in parentheses; freshman team scores in brackets. Because of an early printer deadline for this issue to accommodate color photos, some games played last week will be reported next issue.

BOYS' BASKETBALL
Mather Tournament, Nov. 22-Dec. 1: **Fenger,** Nov. 22: 44-61; **Lake View,** Nov. 23: 54-50; **Zion Benton,** Nov. 29: 44-48; **Mather,** Nov. 30: 56-59; **Hirsch,** Dec. 1: 56-47; **Ridgewood Tournament,** *freshman team,* Nov. 22-24: **Ridgewood,** Nov. 22: 21-40; **Timothy Christian,** Nov. 23: 23-42; **Quigley,** Nov. 24: 40-32; **De La Salle,** *freshman team,* Dec. 2, home: 21-38; **St. Gregory,** Dec. 4, home, 67-45 (52-36) [42-20]; **North Shore Country Day School,** Dec. 7, home: 66-49 (38-25).

GIRLS' BASKETBALL
Madonna Tournament, *varsity,* Nov. 17-26: **Immaculate Heart of Mary:** 33-56; **Madonna:** 36-25; **St. Gregory:** 80-32; **Good Counsel:** 50-39; **St. Francis de Sales:** 42-61; **Trinity Tournament,** *j.v.,* Nov. 22-27: **Lane Tech:** 14-51; **Immaculate Conception:** 10-39; **St. Benedict:** 26-17; **Elgin Academy,** Nov. 30, there: 41-34 (23-17); **Holy Trinity,** Dec. 4, home: 63-22 (31-20); **Woodlands,** there: 42-34 (17-29).

It is often difficult to give all sports coverage in each issue of a high school paper since most high schools have ten or more sports teams each season. A good way to give some coverage to each team is to run a scorebox. The one above is from the U-High Midway, University High School, Chicago, IL. Note the paragraph of explanation that precedes the scores.

same teams your opponent has? What were the results of those games? Who are the key players for both sides? Are there any injuries? What are the strengths and weaknesses of both teams? What do the coaches and players have to say about the upcoming game?

Remember that the upcoming game includes two schools. Your story must include information about both schools, not just yours. Call the opposing coach and talk to him.

The lead of an advance story should begin with the importance of the event. Again, look for the unusual. Will the game determine the championship? Is it possible that someone will set a record in the game? Is half the team out because of injuries? Has it been 20 years since your school defeated the opponent? Is your team out for revenge? Does the other team have the leading scorer in the area?

Find the unusual element and also include in the lead the type of sport, the teams involved, and when and where the

Quick reads are evident on the above double truck from the Little Hawk, City High School, Iowa City, IA. Fact boxes on records and favorite and worst practices provide the reader with a quick glance at additional information concerning the track team. This is a good way to feature several participants as well as coaches, and readers are more apt to read all the short stories than they are to read three or four longer stories.

game is to be played. In other words, an advance lead is similar to the coverage lead, but without the score or the outcome of the event.

Reporters need to remember that in both advance and coverage stories two teams are always involved. Make sure the opponent gets fair coverage. It's evidence of poor reporting to say, "An opponent's player stopped Bill Blake at the three-yard line." The opponent's players have names. Use them.

Once the lead is written, develop the story in inverted pyramid order like any other news story. Remember, it's not a chronological world. If the fourth quarter was the most important, give its details before going back and summarizing the other quarters. It is not necessary to give a play-by-play account.

In a combination advance/coverage story, the first few paragraphs should be devoted to the upcoming game or games. Be sure to point out the strengths and weaknesses of both teams. Following that, move into a brief summary of recent games. Put the emphasis on outstanding plays and players. After the wrapup of the most recent game, use a smooth transition into the next most recent game. As the games move further away in time, be increasingly brief. Don't make your story so long that it is intimidating to the reader.

Besides advance/coverage stories, don't forget the full advance story—a summary of the upcoming season. Also, don't forget that a summary of a past season can be interesting reading. A summary story should center on emotions—the frustrations, the excitement, the thrills and chills. Assess the expectations of coach and players and apply them to the high and low points of the season. Why weren't the expectations fulfilled? What made the team exceed expectations? Key plays? Key injuries? Give the players and coaches an opportunity to reflect on the season.

Guidelines for the sports reporter include the following:

    1. Have an understanding of the game. Know the rules and the terminology. Most libraries

> ➤ *Some Sports Story No-Nos*
> • *Avoid using* by the score of. *It's not necessary.*
> • *Avoid using clichés like* under the direction of.
> • *Avoid beginning a story with* when *or* where.
> • *Avoid beginning a story with the type of team.*
> • *Avoid printing a complete roster of all the players.*
> • *Avoid editorializing. Leave the writer's opinion out of the copy unless it is a sports column. Let the facts speak for themselves.*
> • *Avoid beginning with the name of the school.*

➢ Creating
Effective Pages

Effective sports pages should include the following:

• Statistics box for each sport.

• Profiles of key players.

• Columns that focus on the unique and unusual aspects of a team.

• Advance stories focusing on the weaknesses and strengths of each team and comparisons of previous games between the two teams.

• Coverage stories if the contest is of major importance.

• Student and faculty involvement in off-campus sports.

have books on almost any sport. The sports editor should check out one on each sport and make a fact sheet for each reporter similar to the one for soccer on page 115. Reporters should remember, however, that rules for sports are constantly changing. Stay updated.

2. Get to know key people such as the athletic director, the coaches, the team managers, and the players, who can provide you with vital information. It is probably best for the same reporter to cover a sport throughout the season. In that way the key people get to know the reporter and vice versa.

3. Keep records. All high school newspaper rooms should have a list of records for each sport. The reporter should be aware if a record is about to be broken. Sometimes state records are available as well as local ones.

4. Keep game programs on file. They can be helpful in providing information on the opponent for an advance story.

5. Observe, observe, observe. Take notes during and after the game. If possible, visit the locker room and get quotes. Use quotes in both advance and coverage stories, but do not overuse them. In taking notes during the game, devise a system for getting down a brief play-by-play account. That is important, as you never know what may be the highlight of the game. Even the time remaining or who controls most of the jump balls could be crucial factors in the outcome. It is probably wise to have someone spotting for the reporter to be sure that information is accurate. The reporter may check the official scorebook after the game to verify his or her own statistics.

Three sports receive preview treatment in the Epitaph, Cupertino High School, Homestead, CA. The Epitaph staff also tied boys' and girls' basketball together by using a gray screen behind the two stories.

The charts on pp. 117-118 are a way to take notes for football. Similar forms could be developed for any sport. Note that there are separate sheets for offense and defense and that players' numbers are used instead of names, to allow faster writing. The reporter can match the numbers and names later. Use the "Comment" boxes to give the type of play. For example, if number 31 rushed for 21 yards, say how—around right end, through the middle, or on a reverse play. Use a new line for each play, which will give you the game in chronological order.

In the charts illustrated, the reporter could use K for Kirkwood and M for Mehlville to keep the plays of the two teams separate. Note that clock time has been included as a statistic. If a football team should score with just seconds to go or three times in less than five minutes, it could be important in the game.

➤ *Sports Sidebars*

Bio boxes or Dewar's Profiles— short tidbits about a team, a coach, a player, a sport— make interesting quick reads.

Consider various bio boxes when planning sports coverage. For example, perhaps you have a full story on the football team's victory over your rival school, and your quarterback had a fantastic performance. You might run a bio box on the quarterback's statistics. You would probably want to box in this bio box either fully or with rule lines at top and bottom to set it off from the main story. Note how the box contrasts boldface type with normal type.

(Continued)

FOUR WEDNESDAY, OCTOBER 23, 1996   **SPORTS**   THE TOWER

S-t-r-e-t-c-h it out: Proper warm-up, cool down habits prove beneficial to athletes' performance

Matt Barry '98
Sports Staff

Although it may not be one of the most enjoyable parts in preparing for sports, a good warm up and stretch can be one of the most important parts of an athlete's workout.

"Stretching is important mainly to stretch the ligaments, tendons and muscles," said Head Trainer Joe Cimino.

"No pain, no gain" is an old saying, but to minimize the pain of exercise and guard against muscle, tendon and ligament strains and tears, stretching can be a helpful idea, according to Russell Whisler's "Stretching Helps." A warm up and stretch before and after a workout is a great way to stay away from preventable injuries.

"The most important time to stretch is after a workout or match," said Cimino. "Your muscles will benefit more when they are warm. Warm tissue is more flexible and you will get a better stretch when your muscles are warm."

Warm up and cool down programs can take as little as five minutes or as long as 15 to 20 minutes, depending on the type of workout, weather condition, and the type of body the person's has, according to Cimino.

"Athletes who are prone to injury or competing in colder weather should take more time on their stretching," said Cimino. "The amount of time spent on stretching really depends on the person's body."

When practices are held in the early morning when it is still cold and damp out, getting in a good stretch is really important before their workout, according to rowing team member Joe Houser '98.

"In colder weather you need to warm them (your muscles) more so they don't tense up," said Houser. "When your muscles tense up, you can really mess them up."

Stretching programs should start with a short walk or jog to get the blood flowing. "Stretching Helps" reports that warm muscles are more supple and easier to stretch. After the body is warm the athlete should do some light stretching, moving the muscles rhythmically to avoid jarring or bouncing, because this can damage muscle fibers. A stretching motion should use the muscle through its full range of movement, holding each position for at least three seconds.

Cimino said the most important muscles to stretch are the large muscle groups. These muscles include the hamstrings, groins, quadriceps, chest and upper back muscles.

"By stretching the larger muscle groups, you also are able to warm up many of the smaller muscles," said Cimino.

For the rowing team, a stretching period usually lasts 10 minutes. Houser said for the stretches to do any good, each one is held for about 20 seconds.

According to boys cross-country Coach Mike Novak, no longer runs, it is more important for the team to get in a good stretch at the end.

"Before a run, the team usually stretches for five minutes or less, depending on the flexibility of the runner," said Novak. "But if we are going for a longer run in which we start at a slow pace, it is more important to get in a good, long stretch at the end of practice."

Not all teams are into stretching though. According to football Head Coach Mike McLeod, since he has been here the team has not done a lot of stretching. McLeod said that about five years ago he and about 16 teams attended a meeting in which Dr. Robert Teitge, one of the top orthopedic surgeons in the area, spoke about stretching. According to Teitge stretching isn't very helpful because it doesn't help two-thirds of the players, and one-third don't stretch correctly.

"When we came here four years ago, people thought we were weird," said McLeod. "But since we have been here, the number of pulls and strains have gone down."

Instead of stretching, the team tries to do a more active warm-up. According to McLeod the team starts off with a light jog and then builds up with various running drills. The warm-up also includes three minutes of jumping rope.

"Sitting down and stretching doesn't add to the mental state of our players," said McLeod.

Injuries are a part of all sports and exercising. Cimino said a large number of unnecessary injuries can be traced back to lack of stretching or improper stretching.

"I would say with the football team that 40 percent of the injuries since practice started in August have been do to lack of stretching," said Cimino.

Cimino said that if any athlete is unsure of how much they should stretch or types of stretching they should be doing, they should check with him or their coach to make sure they are doing the proper warm up.

Although it is often overlooked, stretching should be a part of every athletes' game. Warm ups and cool downs keep athletes healthy and injury-free.

Photo by Jan-Michael Burre '97
BEFORE PRACTICE, Drew Wrosch and Andy Hill, both '00, demonstrate an upper body stretch done by the freshman football team. Stretching is commonly done before and after practice to prevent injury and pain.

The scene behind the scene provides an interesting topic in the above story on stretching from the Tower, *Grosse Pointe South High School, Grosse Pointe, MI. Most athletes go through stretching exercises, but few school newspapers cover the story as well as the* Tower *has.*

In the charts, KO stands for kickoff and P for punts. Comp. and Incom. stand for complete and incomplete. The reporter could simply use a C or an I to indicate which it was. The reporter might want to make the comments section wider to provide more room.

6. Get close to the action, if possible. It is better to be on the sidelines than in the pressbox.
7. Avoid editorializing. Give credit to the other team, and leave out personal biases. Don't make excuses. The weather is not an excuse for a loss: The other team played in the same conditions.
8. Use statistics. A roundup at the end of a sports story can include statistics, if you don't run a scorebox. For example, a basketball story could include leading scorers, leading

Soccer Fact Sheet

Soccer is a boys' or girls' sport that can be played in any season. Each team of 11 players tries to score by advancing the ball without the use of hands, by kicking or "heading" the ball into the opponent's net. In most states, games may end in ties except in tournament play. Rules provide for overtime periods or a series of shots on goal for tie-breakers.

Positions: Goalie, fullback, links (halfbacks), strikers, and wings (forwards), listed in order from goal to midfield.

Kicks: Penalty kick—a kick when a penalty occurs in the penalty area.

High kick—a player kicks too high (official's judgment call) so that it might be dangerous.

Goal kick—when the ball goes out of bounds at the end line, the defending fullback gets to free-kick the ball toward the opposite end of the field.

Free kick—a kick without interference awarded after the other team has been guilty of a foul or penalty.

Corner kick—when the ball goes out of bounds at the end line of the defensive team, the offense is awarded the ball and a free kick from the corner.

Drop kick—when both teams have fouled, the ball is dropped between two opposing players to be put into play.

Common Penalties: Tripping, touching ball with hands, pushing off, high kicking, Moving past the opposing team's fullbacks before the ball (offside).

Common Terms: Assist—passing the ball to another player, enabling him to score.

Ball—round, two-colored ball (usually black and white or red and blue checked).

Center Line—midfield. Play starts here each quarter or after each score.

Dribbling—moving the ball downfield with short kicks.

Goal posts—holding a net. All points are scored by the ball hitting the net.

Halves—two 30- to 45-minute periods with a 10-minute break.

Hands—hitting or catching the ball with hands or any part of the arms.

Headball or header—hitting the ball with the head (legal shot).

Kickoff—one team (by coin choice) begins the game at the center line.

Penalty Area—area marked in front of goal. When penalty occurs in this area, the fault of the defense, the offense gets a free kick on goal with only the goalie defending.

Penalty kick mark—where the penalty shot on goal is taken.

Soccer shoes—spiked.

Shin guards—pads to protect a player's shins.

Shot on goal—a shot taken by an offensive player on the goal.

Sudden death—after overtime period when neither team has scored, a procedure (such as kicks on goal) is adopted to determine the winner.

Throw-in—when the ball goes out of bounds, the team not at fault is awarded a throw-in. It must be done with both feet on the ground and with both hands coming from over the head.

Quarterback:
C. T. Hall

- **Passes completed:**
27 of 33
- **Total passing yards:** 522
- **Total running yards:** 212
- **Total yardage:** 734
- **Passes for touchdowns:** 4
- **Rushing touchdowns:** 2
- **Total points:** 36
- **Passes completed after four games:** 96 of 112
- **Total passing yardage for season:** 1,477
- **Total rushing yardage for season:** 623
- **Total yardage for season:** 2,100

➢ **Be Prepared**

• *Be familiar with the sport. Know the difference between offense and defense.*

• *Know the sports terminology. Understand what "the top of the key" means in basketball.*

• *Be familiar with the coaches and the coaching staff.*

• *Be familiar with the players. Use a questionnaire to get information on each one, including academic achievements.*

• *Know the rules of the game. Get a rule book.*

• *Be familiar with the opponent. Use the telephone to find out about key players and statistics.*

• *Keep a file on each player for ready reference.*

• *Get a roster of the opposing team so you can use jersey numbers when taking notes. That's faster than writing out complete names.*

rebounders, most assists, and most steals. Again, give the opponents credit. If someone on the opposing team scores 50 points, name him and tell how he did it.

9. Cover more than major sports, and give girls' sports equal coverage with boys'. The sports that draw the most fans may deserve the most coverage, but it's the job of the school press to build up enthusiasm for all sports.

10. Write for the average reader. Not all readers are knowledgeable about the sport. If a rare term is used, explain it briefly.

11. Avoid flowery words, but use figures of speech if they are appropriate.

12. Be prepared to spend a great deal of time covering a sport. You need to ask questions before the game, during the game, and after the game. Know what you are going to ask. Ask why questions as well as fact-related ones. Avoid asking questions that can be answered with "Yes" or "No."

13. Do not let the coach influence you. The coach may love to make excuses for losses and try to avoid reporters. Be tactful in getting your information, but be persistent.

14. Make the reader feel as if he witnessed the event. For readers who were there, help them recall the thrills and disappointments of the event. For those who were not there, help them visualize what happened. Visual description is important.

15. Be accurate. Make sure that the score is correct, names are correct, spelling is correct.

16. Go to practice as often as possible; it will give you a better understanding of the team.

17. Clip articles on opposing teams from your town newspaper. Information therein can be valuable for advance stories.

Game __Kirkwood vs. Mehlville__

Date __October 13__

Quarter __First__

OFFENSE

Rushing			Passing			Kickoff and Punt Returns			Punts and Kickoffs			Interceptions, Fumbles, and Penalties			Clock Time
Jersey No.	+ or -	Comments	No. to No.	Comp. or Incomp.	Comments	KO or P	Jersey No.	Yardage + or -	KO or P	Kicker	Yardage	Jersey No.	+ or -	Comments	

Game __Kirkwood vs. Mehlville__

Date __October 13__

Quarter __First__

DEFENSE

Rushing, yards yielded	Passing, yards yielded	Tackles, clean and alone	Blocked PAT or punt	Fumbles recovered	Interceptions	Penalty by opponents	Clock Time

Catching the Ultimate wave

■ Newly formed league welcomes new members to enjoy their "obsession."

By Andy Moher
Sports Staff

Ultimate Frisbee, one of the fastest growing sports in the nation, has become one of the newest Intramurals sports at OPRF. The league, which will meet on Thursdays, has already attracted over 40 players and six teams.

The idea for the new league was started last year by seniors John Bokum and Dan Moses. A meeting was held September 9 in the fieldhouse to determine the potential of the league. Six captains were named and told to form evenly balanced teams.

"I was very surprised with the turnout that we had," said intramurals director Ricky Baker. " It was the first time that we had given the kids responsibility, and they responded in huge numbers."

"We've been playing Ultimate for almost five years," said Bokum. "This league should increase the following of the game, and help the younger players keep it alive."

Ultimate is played with boundaries on all sides, and two balanced teams. Each player is given ten seconds to find a teammate to throw to if guarded, or turn the frisbee over. The league will consist of two twelve minute halves per game, and will play at Ridgeland Park.

"Ultimate is not just a one-dimensional game, like a lot of people think," said Moses. "It is an extremely active game for versatile athletes, and the games get very competitive."

Ultimate is described as "football with a frisbee," according to senior Steve Schouten. He stated, "Ultimate becomes an obsession once you play it enough. The truly devoted play the game any time, in any conditions." Schouten was backed up during the September 26 sign-up meeting at Ridgeland Park. Despite driving rains and gusty winds, about 25 players showed up to scrimmage. That was not surprising considering a devoted following of about 20 players show up daily and on weekends to play Ultimate at Scoville Park.

"I was very proud to see the great turnout in such inclement weather," said Baker. " It was important that the kids get the league off the ground themselves."

The league, however, is not limited to the

AT SCOVILLE PARK seniors Greg Davies and John Bokum play Ultimate frisbee with junior Colin Stoetzner.

Photo by Louisa Wialwark/Trapeze

Scoville Park crowd. There will be a number of "rookie" players in the new league.

"All of the players in the new league are not real experienced," said senior Zack Priceman. "There are a lot of people who have never or rarely played that just want to be part of the experience."

"Ultimate is a sport that anybody can play," said Schouten. "We started playing at Scoville a few years ago with ten kids, and its grown fast since then. We've had games there with forty or fifty kids. The game is so great because anybody can just show up and play."

The league will begin on Thursday, October 3 from 3:30 to 5:00 at Ridgeland Park.

"We really have a good mix of people in this league," said Baker. "The league has a lot of different social groups, and several girls have signed up to play. It has a lot of people that would not normally get involved in the intramural program."

"This is outstanding that students can find an activity that they can enjoy with a school atmosphere," he added. "We try to create activities that students can enjoy within school walls. Hopefully, this league will spread the knowledge of Ultimate and make it even more popular. We are hoping that this league will grow and become an annual affair."

Sports staffs should look for stories that involve their students in off-campus sports. The above story from the Trapeze, *Oak Park Forest High School, IL, does a good job of explaining Ultimate Frisbee to the reader.*

18. Be aware of crowd reaction; sometimes it can be an angle for your story.

19. Avoid sports jargon, such as *roundballers* for the basketball team or *mermaids* for the girls' swim team.

20. Use action verbs and specific adjectives, but avoid clichés. Use the appropriate verb; there are many better than *beat*. For example, when the margin of victory is close, the

➤ *Top 10*

Sports staff members on newspaper staffs might consider ranking the top 10 teams in their area for various sports. Include in the ranking the number of first place votes each team received. An example follows:

Rank School   (Firsts)
Record   Last ranking

1. Ellis   (2)
15-0   1
2. Beech   (1)
14-0   2
3. Portland   (1)
14-0   3
4. White House   (1)
14-0   4
5. Indian Lake
13-2   6
6. Nannie Berry
12-3   5
7. Knox Doss
10-5   Unranked
8. Brentwood
11-4   7
9. Hawkins
11-4   8
10. Hunter
10-5   9

GIRLS IN FOOTBALL
Two Westside Middle School students tackle opposing teams, along with gender barriers

By Joel Wane

Two middle school girls battled through the pressures of playing a man's sport and are now taking the field.

"Quit playing like a bunch of girls," along with many other exclamatory phrases, may not be appropriate next year when two girls step out onto the football field.

Sarah McManus, a 5-2, 95-pound eighth grader is a deep defensive back for the Middle school. Lindsay Egars, a 5-7 115-pound eighth grader is an offensive tackle and a deep linebacker for the same team. Both of them see a lot of playing time during the games.

"We both have been accepted by our teammates," McManus said. "It doesn't seem like they have any problems with us playing."

Being accepted by the team has been the result of hard work at practice. Teammates see the girls as being two members contributing to the team.

"At the start of the season there were some doubters out there, but they proved those guys wrong,"

said Doug Passmore, a teammate of the two girls. "They are two very good players, who have put a lot of guys on their butts. Putting guys on their butts have made doubters into believers."

Eighth grade coach Jerry Rowslowski was one of those doubters at the beginning of the season. Coming out day after day with intensity has made him a believer.

"I'm very proud of them for coming out for football and sticking it out," Rowslowski said. "We have had a lot of guys quit, but not these girls; they've got a lot of heart. It is the first time in my 36-year career that girls have played for me."

Playing opposing teams has been hard to deal with for the girls.

"It has been very tough because all you really want to do is concentrate on the game, but sometimes you get distracted by another player talking trash," McManus said.

The girls' goal is to play football at Westside next

year. Working hard to achieve this goal is definitely their plan.

"I'm not sure yet if I'm going to play football next year or not, but I would very much like to," Egars said. "It depends on if I feel I gained enough strength over the off-season to compete at the high school level. I think Sarah feels the same way."

Freshman football coach Brett Froendt doesn't find anything wrong with girls playing football.

"I think that it is great that the girls are playing football," Froendt said. "If they want to compete in football, nothing should stop them."

Eighth grade football ended this week. Will it have been their last game? Or could they break the barrier on girls playing football at the high school level? These questions can only be answered over time.

"Playing next year would be a very big step for me, but if I feel that I have gotten that much better over the summer, I might make the next step," McManus said.

The unusual makes for good stories as indicated in the above sports story from the Lance, Westside High School, Omaha, NE. Good quotes carry the story forward.

➤ Points to Ponder

Another sidebar a staff might use on a sports page would be a Points to Ponder brief. For example, you might use the following on a basketball game. Note again the contrast between boldface type and normal type.

Points to Ponder on the Tigers

Phased in: A man-on-man defense for the first time, instead of a zone defense. The new defense led to 15 turnovers by the Statesmen, a team that had been averaging only five turnovers per game. The Tigers had been forcing their opponents to turn the ball over an average of six times a game prior to the win over the Statesmen.

Beating the best: The Statesmen were undefeated coming into the game and had a first place ranking in the area. The Tigers were not in the top 10.

They came from behind: The Tigers

(Continued)

writer might use *edged, squeezed by, nicked,* or *clipped.* When the margin is wide, the writer could use *squashed, annihilated, smashed, clobbered, slaughtered, overpowered, lambasted,* or *trounced.*

21. Read good professional sports writing; it will help you to improve your own writing.

22. Write the story while it is fresh in your mind. If you put your notes aside for a few days, you will forget the details of that thrilling or disappointing play.

Sports briefs are also an important part of any newspaper. It is impossible to give all sports teams a full story in each issue. Therefore, a newspaper staff should consider including a sports briefs column. Each brief may be two to three inches in length and include the team's record, a summary of upcoming events, and a summary of past events.

Even though they are short, briefs are important to the teams involved. Try to cover all teams—freshman, sophomore, and varsity—during a season. Also, be sure to cover both girls' and boys' sports.

In a brief, a reporter must write succinctly. There is no room for unnecessary words. This means that the name of the school or its initials, the year, and the mascot will probably not be included. The reader knows what year it is and what school he attends. Avoid phrases like "by the score of"; simply say, "The girls beat Avilla, 4-3."

If you do not have room for briefs, at least consider scoreboards for some sports. This helps a paper record a history of all games. Keep the scoreboard simple. The second example below is better than the first.

Us	Opponent	Them
29	Mehlville	28
19	House Springs	22

Opponent	Score
Mehlville	29-28
House Springs	19-22

In sports that deal with places rather than scores, a possible structure would be:

Tournament	Results
Parkway Invitational	2nd of 10
Hazelwood Invitational	3rd of 12

The purpose of scoreboards is to provide instant, though incomplete, information. Use them only when you do not have space for briefs or complete stories. Run the scoreboards at the bottom of a page as a single design element. It is permissible to print scoreboards in six-point type; anything smaller would be unreadable for many.

Besides coverage and advance stories, good sports pages also carry features and columns, which are covered in later chapters.

Outstanding sports players provide material for interesting personality features. Personality profiles should be written on players from both on-campus and off-campus sports teams. Perhaps your school has someone training for the Olympics; he or she would make an interesting profile.

trailed by 11 after three quarters, but four straight three-point baskets gave the team a 57-56 lead that it never lost. **They spread the ball around:** *Four Tigers scored in double figures with Watson Malone Dill leading the way with 22 points.*

➢ *Possible Stories*

• *Focus on people involved—team managers, water boys, coaches, players.*

• *Talk about emotions players have before, during, and after the game.*

• *Write about ways coaches have to motivate players.*

• *Look for individual statistics that show positive things about what the players are doing—especially during losing seasons.*

• *Talk to people who make a sporting event happen, including the custodians who line the field.*

• *Write about record-setting statistics that had an impact on the season.*

Sports features can be more than just profiles. Take a look at each sport for possible feature topics. Some ideas are listed below.

➢ *A Fresh Look*
• *Look for a fresh angle to each story.*
• *Be original. Look for a human interest angle.*
• *Emphasize dramatic moments.*
• *Use expressive language.*
• *Help the reader relive the game or the season.*
• *Use action verbs and a lot of visual detail to inform and to entertain.*

Football—How much does it cost each player?
How much does it cost the school?
What are some unusual happenings on the bus?
Have there been any injuries?

Cross-country—How many miles does the average participant run during a season?
How much preparation time is necessary?
What are some of the distractions runners have observed during practice?
What does the coach do while the boys and the girls are running?

Basketball—what happens during timeouts and halftime?
Which fans have never missed a game?
What is an official's life like?
What is it like to be a benchwarmer?

Wrestling—How many spectators really know what is happening on the mat?
How do players condition for the sport?
What must wrestlers endure to stay within the weight limits?

Baseball—What does it take to prepare a field for play?
What effect does a rainout have on a team?
What are the feelings of players when they make errors?

Track—What are the all-time records?
What are unique conditioning methods used by performers?
What is the cost of equipment?

Tennis—How many balls are used during a season?
What types of racquets do players prefer?
What is the key to preparation?

Swimming—How many gallons of water does it take to fill the pool?

How often is the water changed?

What are the thoughts of a lifeguard?

Off-campus sports—Does anyone play racquetball?

Is skiing a popular sport?

Is anyone preparing for the Olympics?

Is there a horse riding champion at school?

Does anyone go inline skating?

Does anyone skateboard?

Does anyone sail?

The list of possible feature ideas is endless. Some schools have written features on players' superstitions, on equality of boys' and girls' sports, on collecting baseball cards, and on ballooning. Whatever the topic, the writer should follow the guidelines for feature writing as given in Chapter 6. The key to good sports features is good interviewing. Use quotes and let the interviewee tell the story. Avoid the weak "Player of the Week" or "Player of the Month." If you want to write a personality profile, choose an athlete who has done something unusual in his/her sport. Find a focus for the profile and concentrate on that focus: Observe the athlete in action. Observe him/her before the game, during the game, after the game. Get to know your subject.

Sports is a world of fierce competition and a world of heroes. The good sports writer captures that world in words. Remember that sports is not a chronological world but a world of unusual, exciting happenings. A good sports writer does more than see a game; she hears it, feels it, and records it, and in so doing she touches the lives of many sports personalities.

EXERCISES

1. Analyze the leads presented earlier in this chapter. List the strengths and weaknesses of each.

> ➢ *Writing the Sports Brief*
>
> • *Create a beat system so each sport is covered in each issue. This means the same reporter will be covering the team all season.*
>
> • *The reporter should meet with the coach weekly to ask for scores and highlights.*
>
> • *Start the brief with the upcoming games and the important facts about them. Then report the most recent scores. List scores with the winning team first.*
>
> • *Include the team's overall record.*
>
> • *Include a brief summary of outstanding players.*
>
> • *Try to cover every sport in every issue, but keep each report brief. That's why they're called sports briefs.*
>
> • *Use a graphic symbol to introduce each brief.*

➢ *Superstitions*
Look for unique angles to your story. This might include superstitions, such as the following:
• *Wearing school colors the day of the game.*
• *Wearing the same pair of socks, the same underwear, the same shoes, etc.*
• *Teammates shaving heads.*
• *Teammates getting tattoos.*
• *Eating the same food the day of each game.*
• *Making the sign of the cross before a play.*
• *Carrying a rabbit's foot or some other type of charm.*

2. Write a lead based on information in the following football scorebox. Add facts as necessary. Scorebox lists points in the order scored.

Kirkwood	21	21	6	7—55
Red Oak	11	6	0	12—29

Red Oak—FG Knisley 32
Kirk—Wylie 85 kickoff return (Carroll kick)
Kirk—Hall 2 run (Carroll kick)
Kirk—Jones 32 run (Carroll kick)
Red Oak—Englert 5 pass from Havern
    (Moyer pass from Havern)
Kirk—Hall 4 run (Carroll kick)
Red Oak—Block 7 pass from Havern (run failed)
Kirk—Wylie 14 run (Carroll kick)
Kirk—Hall 16 run (kick failed)
Kirk—Wylie 16 run (Carroll kick)
Red Oak—Medwick 2 run (pass failed)
Red Oak—Chatman 3 run (pass failed)

The preceding scoreboard can be interpreted in the following way:

The first score was made by Red Oak when Knisley kicked a 32-yard field goal. The second score was made by Kirkwood when Wylie returned a kickoff for 85 yards. Carroll kicked the extra point. Hall scored for Kirkwood on a two-yard run, and Jones scored for Kirkwood on a 32-yard run. Carroll kicked points after each. Red Oak scored on a five-yard pass from Englert to Havern, and Red Oak scored a two-point conversion on a pass from Havern to Moyer. Kirkwood scored on a four-yard run by Hall and a PAT (point after touchdown) by Carroll. Red Oak then scored on a seven-yard pass from Havern to Block. A run for the extra point failed. Kirkwood scored three touchdowns on a 14-yard run by Wylie, a 16-yard run by Hall, and a 16-

Questions to Ask
Players, Coaches or Fans

• What was the most memorable play of the season? Why?

• What challenges did the team face?

• What made the season exciting?

• What was the strength of the team?

• What was the weakness of the team?

• How was team spirit and morale maintained?

• What happened in the locker room at half-time?

• Who were the most challenging opponents?

• Who were the key players for both sides?

• Did injuries affect the team?

• What do you want to see happen next season?

• What was the biggest disappointment of the year?

• How do players feel when they lose or make mistakes?

➢ Fiction Writing
Techniques for
Sports Writers

• *Strong characters.*
• *Good story line.*
• *Conflict.*
• *Climax.*
• *Resolution.*

yard run by Wylie. Carroll missed the middle of the three PAT's. Red Oak scored the last two touchdowns of the game on a two-yard run by Medwick and a three-yard run by Chatman. Pass conversion attempts failed after both.

3.   After you have written the lead for the scoreboard, add additional facts and write the complete story.

4.   Write a complete basketball coverage story based on the following information. Add facts as necessary, but do not change those given.

Your school vs. Ladue.

Game at your school last Tuesday.

Ladue won 54-40 as they sank 20 of 21 free throws.

Your school hit two of 10 free throws.

Marta Jones led your school's scorers with 32 points.

Your school led at half, 21-18.

Ladue led at the end of the third quarter, 32-28.

Your school tied the score at 34-34.

Ladue then hit 12 straight free throws to break open the game, taking a 46-34 lead.

Ladue's last eight points also came on free throws.

Your school committed 12 fouls in the last quarter.

Jones's 32 points gave her a total of 619 for the season, a school record.

Highest previous total was by Shari Joplin— 617 points—set five years ago.

Your school's season record is now 6-2 in conference.

Ladue won the conference with a 7-1 record.

Both teams will meet again next week in the first round of regionals.

Your school defeated Ladue earlier this year, 62-60.

Your school's season record is now 23-2, and Ladue's is 24-1.

Your school's other loss was to Blake, 60-58, in double overtime.

Ladue beat Blake, 72-60.

Ladue's top player, Jackie Jamison, 5'11" center, is averaging 22 points per game.

Ladue will start five seniors. Your school will start three seniors and two juniors.

5. Write a sports story based on the following football facts. Add facts as necessary, but don't change those given.

Your school defeated Bloomingdale in the first round of state playoffs, 21-20.

Game played Nov. 16 at Webster, a neutral site.

The win avenged an earlier defeat that Bloomingdale had handed your school, 14-0.

Bloomingdale is the only team to have defeated your school in the last two years—three times total, including a 13-7 loss in last year's first round of state.

All the scoring occurred in the third quarter.

First half statistics: Your school was held to 10 yards rushing and 0 passing. Bloomingdale had 123 yards rushing and 66 yards passing, but had two passes intercepted, fumbled the ball twice, and lost both fumbles. The second fumble occurred at your one-yard line.

Bloomingdale scored first on a 65-yard pass play but missed the extra point. Bloomingdale tallied again when it recovered a fumble at your 10-yard line. Bloomingdale tried for two points, but failed.

Your school struck quickly on a 95-yard kick-off return.

Bloomingdale fumbled the next kickoff, and your school recovered at Bloomingdale's eight-yard line. Your school scored and the kick was good.

Bloomingdale then put together a 65-yard drive and made a two-point conversion to go ahead 20-14.

Your school scored quickly with a 92-yard kickoff return.

The kick was good.

Bloomingdale made it to your five-yard line with : 30 left, but fumbled, and your school held on for the win.

Bloomingdale had 22 first downs to your 8. Bloomingdale had 227 yards rushing to your 22 and 177 yards passing to your 100.

6. Write an advance story based on the following basketball facts. Add facts as necessary, but do not change those given.

Your school to play Avilla this coming Friday at 8 p.m. in a home game.

You have not beaten Avilla in the last ten years, a string of 20 consecutive   losses.

Your record so far this year is 10-0 and Avilla is 9-1.

Avilla's only loss was to Purdy, 77-75. You defeated Purdy, 78-76.

Avilla is led by Jerry Moss, who is averaging 27 points and seven steals per game. Avilla as a team is averaging 83 points per game while holding its opponents to an average of 54 points per game.

Your school is averaging 75 points per game, with your opponents averaging 62 points per game.

Your leading scorer is Bill Powell, with a 22-point-per-game average. Powell suffered a mild concussion during the last game and may not be at full strength.

> *Records Brief*

A possible fact box to add to any type of sports story would be one about records set during a game or during a year. An example for football follows:

Setting Records

• *Indian Lake's 77 points was the most points the Bears had ever scored in a game, eclipsing the old mark of 62 points in 1962.*

• *The 41 first-half points tied a record. The Bears scored 41 in the first half against Knox Doss in 1998.*

• *Quarterback C.T. Hall's passing yardage of 423 broke quarterback Bobby Martin's record of 420 set in 1977.*

• *The 77 points were the most ever scored against the Lindbergh Flyers.*

The outcome of this game will probably determine the conference champion, as there will only be two games left.

Purdy has lost three games, so if Avilla defeats your school it is likely that the two schools will tie for the conference championship. If both should lose their last two games, Purdy could make it a three-way tie.

7. Write a tennis coverage story based on the following facts. Add facts as necessary, but do not change those given.

Your school defeated Roxana in girls' tennis yesterday, 7-0, by winning all four singles matches and the three doubles matches.

Although the score was 7-0, the coach said it was your school's toughest match this year.

Karen Porter, your number one player, edged her opponent, 7-5, 8-6. Karen was behind in both sets, trailing 1-5 in the first and 2-5 in the second. She tied at 5-5 in both. In the second she fell behind 5-6 before winning 8-6. She won the eighth game on a backhand smash that landed just on the end line.

The other three singles players were also extended before winning. All took three sets, which had never happened before to any of them.

The three doubles matches also took three sets.

"I hope someone eliminates Roxana before we have to meet them in state," said Charlotte Grate, senior and number two singles player.

The victory over Roxana made your school's record 8-0 for the year.

8. Write a football lead based on the following scoreboard information. You may add facts as necessary.

```
Alton        7      3      0      0 —10
Charleston 0      0      7      0 —7
```
A—Steve Howard 99 run (Steve Barl kick)
A—FG Barl 27
C—Tom McIntyre, 5 pass from Charles Smith
(Warren Baker kick)

9. Clip five sports stories from exchange papers and analyze them. Make a list of strengths and weaknesses for each one.

10. Clip five leads from sports stories in a professional paper. Analyze the differences in each. Tell which one you think is most effective and why.

11. Rewrite the sports leads for two stories in the last issue of your school paper. Be prepared to defend the changes.

12. Use the charts suggested in this chapter for taking notes at a football game and cover one of your school's games. Write a story based on your notes, or devise similar charts for another sport and write a story on that sport.

13. Write a sports story based on the following facts. Add facts as necessary to make your story complete, and be selective with those given, but do not change any of them. For example, add quotes, names of players, and statistics, both team and individual.

Girls' varsity basketball game last night.

Your school beat Oakville.

Your school's league record is now 6-1, and Oakville's is 5-2.

The victory clinched a tie for the league crown for your school, since only one league game remains. Your school is now in first place, and Oakville is in second, tied with Radium.

Oakville has now lost 13 straight times to your school over the last five seasons. This string includes 10 regular season games and 3 tournament games.

The first-quarter score was your school 11, Oakville 14.

The officials were Harry Jones and Bob Teuton from Smithville.

Boosters group sold popcorn, candy, and soda at the game and made $57.

Score at half was Oakville 37, your school 25.

Score at end of third quarter was 50-35 in favor of Oakville. Oakville's Vicki Roan hit a three-point shot to end the quarter.

Your school's overall record is now 17-3 and Oakville's is 15-4.

Your school took the lead for the first time at 51-50 with 1:27 left in the game. Your school had scored 16 unanswered points to take the lead. Final score of the game was 57-56 in favor of your school. Your school scored two points on free throws after the final buzzer had sounded.

Three of Oakville's starters fouled out of the game, and two of your school's starters fouled out.

One of your school's cheerleaders, Jessica Dowell, was injured in the second quarter when she was run over along the sidelines by a player from Oakville. She was carried off on a stretcher.

Game was played at home.

14. Look at the sentences below and have a class discussion about which ones contain the writer's opinion. Sports writers have a tendency to editorialize. Let the facts speak for themselves.

    A.   Foul problems caused the boys' varsity basketball team to use a slower tempo in last night's game against Biloxi.

    B.   Several players played an outstanding game.

    C.   The entire team did a fantastic job.

    D.   Rebounding was a key factor in the girls'

➢ *Team Statistics*
Comparing the statistics of the two teams in a sidebar box provides a quick read. There are a lot more statistics than the ones below that you might include for football.

First Downs	Ellis	Knox Doss
Rushing	10	0
Passing	10	6
3rd-Down Efficiency		
	8-16	2-13
4th-Down Efficiency		
	2-3	0-7
Total Net Yards		
	520	131
Total Plays		
	77	34
Average Gain		
	3.6	1.0
Net Yards Rushing		
	257	21

varsity basketball team's 72-71 win over Hampton last night. The girls pulled down 37 rebounds to Hampton's 18.

E. Earlier in the year, Manchester lost to Geyer because of poor officiating.

F. The coach attributed the team's loss to injuries to two key players.

G. Coach Dale McCracken said he thought the boys played their best game of the year.

H. The mighty Pioneers will end their dismal season this Saturday when they play Lafayette.

I. There were many standouts in the game.

J. "There were many standouts in the game," said Coach Dale McCracken.

15. Write a sports story that might appear in your newspaper, using only the facts you think are necessary from those given below. It is permissible to make up additional facts as needed, but do not change those given.

Senior Frankie Lozano won the 124-pound state wrestling championship.

The match was last night in Columbia.

Lozano won the state championship as a freshman in the 95-pound class and as a sophomore in the 118-pound class.

Last year as a junior he lost in the state finals in the 124-pound division to a freshman, Patrick McKartney, from Truman High School.

Last night McKartney lost as a sophomore to Lozano. It was McKartney's first loss in high school wrestling. McKartney was 18-0 as a freshman and is 17-1 after his second-place finish to Lozano.

Lozano's record after four years of varsity wrestling is 77-1. His only loss was to McKartney.

Lozano beat McKartney by a 12-11 decision. McKartney had led during the match for two periods until Lozano scored a reversal with one minute left in the third and final period, which put Lozano ahead 12-11.

With 45 seconds left, Lozano injured his shoulder while riding McKartney. "I had to stay in control of him during those 45 seconds. If he had escaped, the match would have been tied at 12-12, and I don't think my shoulder would have lasted much longer. If he had reversed me, I would have lost 13-12," said Lozano.

Escapes are worth 1 point. Reversals are worth 2 points.

Shortly after the event, a local physician determined that Lozano had dislocated his shoulder.

Mr. Vito Lozano, Frankie's father, moved from the stands to the gym floor, where he yelled out each second for the last 45 seconds. "My son was in control of his opponent with only one good arm after he hurt his shoulder. I wanted him to stay on top and win," said Mr. Lozano.

Most of the 500 fans stood up and joined in the chant led by Mr. Lozano. "I could hear the seconds being yelled out—45! 44! 43!—I guess I just held on and ignored my dislocated shoulder," said the younger Lozano. "Who would have figured I could win the state title with only one good arm?"

16. Based on the following notes that a reporter took at a basketball game, write a sports story. You may add facts as necessary, such as the name of the opposing school and any quotes that might enhance the copy, but do not change any of the facts that are given. You can safely assume that if a team scores three points it was on a three-point shot—not a two-point shot and a free throw. Your team, for example, scored five three-point shots in the first quarter. Be sure to

set the geography of a play by describing the type of play it was, such as a 10-foot jump shot or a tip-in following a rebound. You will need to total points to see who the leading scorer was.

Your school's lineup	Opponent's lineup
Jamal Johnson, center	Rich Strum, guard
Robert Thompson, guard	Demetrias Elston, forward
Alfred Jones, forward	Melvin Irons, guard
Brian Taylor, forward	Tim Seddens, guard
Jason Foster, guard	Tim Stratman, forward
Michael Thompson, guard	Bill Kohm, guard
Darren Baker, forward	Lamar Howard, forward
Andy Stewart, guard	Adam Meinershagen, guard
Scott Stricker, forward	Rich Diffley, center
Tony Gribble, forward	Ronald Loper, guard

FIRST QUARTER

7:05	R. Thompson	3-0
6:43	Rich Diffley	3-2
5:30	Johnson	5-2
4:52	R. Thompson	8-2
3:44	Strum	8-4
3:34	Taylor	10-4
3:21	Elston	10-6
3:06	Foster	13-6
1:50	Strum	13-9
1:14	Foster	16-9
:50	Taylor	18-9
:20	Baker	19-9
:02	Foster	22-9

SECOND QUARTER

7:51	R. Thompson	24-9
7:32	Diffley	24-11
6:47	Diffley	24-12
6:36	Johnson	26-12
6:21	Strum	26-14
6:21	Strum	26-15
6:13	Johnson	28-15
5:56	Johnson	30-15
		(slam)
5:28	R. Thompson	32-15
5:06	Diffley	32-16
5:01	Elston	32-18
4:52	R. Thompson	34-18
4:39	Elston	34-20
4:31	R. Thompson	36-20
4:16	Strum	36-22
3:54	Foster	39-22
3:12	R. Thompson	40-22
3:02	Irons	40-23
2:50	R. Thompson	41-23
	R. Thompson	42-23
2:35	Diffley	42-25
2:18	Strum	42-27
2:00	Diffley	42-29
1:25	Stratman	42-31
:57	R. Thompson	44-31
:27	Irons	44-33
:21	Meinershagen	45-33
	Meinershagen	46-33
:03	Loper	48-33
	(on a steal)	

THIRD QUARTER

7:52	Taylor	49-33
	Taylor	50-33

6:59	R. Thompson	53-33
6:30	Baker	55-33
6:08	R. Thompson	57-33
5:48	Strum	57-36
5:38	Johnson	59-36
	(slam)	
5:19	Diffley	59-39
5:11	Johnson	61-39
	(slam)	
4:46	Baker	62-39
4:26	Johnson	64-39
	(slam)	
4:03	Diffley	64-41
3:34	Strum	64-42
	Strum	64-43
3:16	Johnson	66-43
2:36	Johnson	68-43
1:27	Stratman	68-45
Baker fouled out		
:41	Foster	71-45
:29	Irons	71-46
	Irons	71-47
:18	Taylor	72-47
:01	Irons	72-49

FOURTH QUARTER

7:46	Elston	72-50
	Elston	72-51
7:06	Johnson	74-51
	(slam)	
6:44	Irons	74-52
	Irons	74-53
6:18	Strum	74-55
5:15	R. Thompson	77-55
4:57	Irons	77-56
4:50	R. Thompson	78-56
	R. Thompson	79-56

4:37	Diffley	79-58
4:08	Meinershagen	79-59
	Meinershagen	79-60
3:58	Stricker	80-60
3:45	Howard	80-62
3:34	R. Thompson	82-62
3:24	Meinershagen	82-64
2:45	Strum	82-65
	Strum	82-66
2:34	Johnson	84-66
2:09	R. Thompson	85-66
	R. Thompson	86-66
1:59	Strum	86-67
	Strum	86-68
1:42	Stricker	88-68
1:25	M. Thompson	90-68
1:11	Diffley	90-70
:54	Stratman	90-71
:51	Stricker	91-71
	Stricker	92-71
:25	Gribble	94-71
:16	Strum	94-74
:09	M. Thompson	96-74

Biggest point production for your team since beating the same opponent in 1978. Your team had 13 turnovers and your opponent had 11. Your team was 17 of 23 from the free throw line.

17. Write a sports story based on the following facts:

Your team loses to your opponent 74-72.

Your team was ranked #1 in state and the opponent was #2.

Sellout crowd of 3,600 at opponent's gym.

Telecast on Prime cable TV.

Your school's record slipped to 15-2, the opponent's record became 16-2.

This was the opponent's second win over your team this year. They won the first game, 74-72, also.

Opponent took a 13-point lead with 6:25 left in the second quarter, but with 2:00 left in the second quarter your team tied the opponent 32-32.

Lamont Jackson, center, led your team's comeback with 11 points in the second quarter.

Game was still tied, 38-38, at half.

Scott Highbench, forward, scored 12 points for the opponent in the third quarter, but the rest of his team managed only four points. Dan Jessup, guard, scored 10 points for your team in the third quarter, and your team led 58-54 after three quarters.

Jackson finished with 23 points and 11 rebounds. He opened the fourth quarter with two free throws and a tip-in after a rebound to give your team a 62-54 lead.

Highbench hit a three-pointer at the 3:30 mark to cut the deficit to two points.

Bill Herron, the opponent's center, tied the game on a layup.

Lavon Porter, your guard, scored 15 points in the game—9 of those in the first quarter. A three-pointer by Porter gave your team a 71-68 lead, but Herron connected on a five-foot jumper to make it 71-60.

Guard Sean Black's pass went off Porter's hands and out of bounds—your team's eighth turnover of the game, so your opponent got the ball back.

Highbench drove the baseline with :55 left. He scored to put the opponent on top 72-71. Highbench finished with 31 points, six rebounds, and five assists.

Jackson rebounded a missed three-pointer by Herron, and he was fouled. He missed the free throw. Joe DeLargy, opponent's guard, pulled down the rebound. He was fouled, and he made both free throws to give the opponent a 74-71 lead.

Porter missed a three-point attempt with :08 left. He was fouled with :05 left, and he made the first free throw to make it 74-72. He purposely missed the second free throw and Brent Jones, forward, rebounded for your team. He put up a shot from the low post and the ball rolled around the rim and off as the buzzer sounded to end the game.

18. In some of the above exercises the directions have said "add facts as necessary, but don't change any given." Obviously, if a reporter was covering a sports activity, he cannot add facts, if the facts he adds were not part of the original event. However, when writing from a pre-given fact sheet, it is difficult for the creator to include all facts that might be needed for a complete story. For example, in exercise 2, first names of players were not included in the set of facts. You should have made up first names to make your story complete. You would never make up names of players when covering a live-action sporting event of your choice. Select a school sport and cover the live action. Take notes. Then write a story based on the facts you obtained.

19. In exercise 18, you probably chose a sport you were familiar with. Now, select a sport you are not familiar with and write a coverage or advance story about that sport. Since you are not familiar with the sport, go to the library and check out a book that describes the sport, including typical terminology that will help you describe the action.

20. Take the terms you learned by doing exercise 19 and mount them on poster board and post in the room for other reporters to use when they cover the same sport.

CHAPTER
SIX

Feature Writing

Feature stories give the journalist a chance to be creative, to delve into a topic of interest to the average reader. Feature stories may entertain, but they also inform the reader of an event, a situation, or an aspect of life.

Feature stories are of several types. Each has its own purpose. Professional publications use all types. So should high school publications.

Human Interest Feature. Human interest stories primarily play on the emotions of the readers to make them smile, laugh, frown, or cry. They are customarily based on something unusual and are no more than 300 words in length.

The human interest story usually has an element of suspense and a surprise ending. Many are based on a timely news event. Many are simply anecdotes about an unusual happening. "Look for the unusual" should be four key words in any reporter's vocabulary, but they are especially important for feature writers. Human interest stories may just make the reader say, "Wow." Note the following story written by an Associated Press reporter when Elvis Presley, a rock and roll singer, died.

A disc jockey and three employees of radio station KFAL in Fulton, MO, have this story of their own to tell about Elvis Presley.

It happened to them Tuesday.

Disc jockey Stu Brunner was handed a record by a station employee, along with a request it be played for the woman's sister-in-law. He tried to play one side of the record and the needle just slid across it. He tried to play the opposite side and the needle skipped and the record wouldn't play at all.

The first side he tried to play was Presley's "Bringing It Back." The flip side was "Pieces of My Life."

Brunner apologized on the air for the record skipping.

Five minutes later he and three others at the station received the bulletin that Presley had died in Memphis.

Station personnel said they played the record the next day and it played perfectly.

Embarrassing moments can also make interesting human interest stories. Be careful not to offend if you report these stories, and be sure to verify all information. All human interest stories should include who, what, when, where, and why. Newspaper staffs might consider a human interest column called "Remember When." The following examples appeared in a "Remember When" column in *The Kirkwood Call*, Kirkwood High School, Kirkwood, MO.

Remember when after the opening session of Awareness Week, Jan. 27, in which Rick Nattress, Blues hockey player, spoke, Jason Carrawell, freshman, attempted to get up off the gym floor, but fell back down because someone had tied his shoelaces together. It took him 10 minutes to get all the knots out.

Remember when David Leech, math department head, asked, "Is number 25 done with circumscribed or inscribed rectangles?"

"Circumcised," responded Garret Hoffman, senior, in Leech's fifth hour Calculus class, Feb. 23.

Remember when Bill Jacobs, senior, went to the movies and when he came back from the bathroom, his fly was open. When his friend told him, he

> ➢ *Using Dialogue*
> • *Dialogue aids the writer in developing a personality. In real life you rarely know much about people until you hear them talk. The way they says things, the words they use, the emphasis, the dialect, and the subject define their personalities.*
> • *To write good dialogue, you must know the personality you are writing about inside out.*
> • *You don't need to use he said or she replied on every line. Dialogue can be written without conversational tags. The fact that the individuals speak alternately makes clear who's talking. It also quickens the pace and heightens reality.*

slid up on the edge of his seat and zipped his pants shut. In doing so, he caught the hair of the girl in front of him in his zipper.

Jacobs was unable to unzip the zipper because of the bad lighting, so he and the girl had to negotiate out of the darkened theater and into the lobby in order to free her hair.

Sights and Sounds Feature. These are fun to write and offer a different viewpoint of a school campus or other location. The ingredients of a sights and sounds feature are implicit in the name. Select a classroom or any school location and write down all the sights and sounds occurring during a one-hour period or an entire day; then write a story based on those sights and sounds. Another method is to station all the staff reporters at different sites on campus in the same time period (perhaps for 10 minutes), and have them write down sights and sounds; turn all notes over to one reporter to compile a feature that captures a slice of life at the school. Another idea is to station reporters throughout a stadium and capture 10 minutes of sights and sounds at a football game.

Personality Profile. A personality sketch concerns the life, interests, and accomplishments of a well-known or interesting person. Information for such an article must come from an interview. Be careful not to lose focus. A good personality profile focuses on one aspect of a person's life, not several. Make that person come alive visually. Include physical traits (a long, raw-boned finger, curly hair, bags under the eyes, imbedded wrinkles, fluttery eyebrows) as well as personality traits. What makes the person tick? Why does he do the things he does? If you do a personality profile, be sure you do your homework first. Interview the people involved with the person's life. These secondary sources—parents, friends, teachers, coaches—will provide keys to the individual's personality.

Use the following guidelines when writing a personality profile:

➢ *Using Verbs and Adverbs*

• *Strong verbs and adverbs can improve the effect of one's writing.*

• *Verbs are action words. Don't say* A man walked down the street. *Instead, say* A man swaggered down the street *or* A man stumbled down the street.

142

Sights and Sounds

• Stories that capture the sights and sounds of an event help that event come alive for the reader.

• Sights and sounds stories can be based on almost any event, such as halftime at a football or basketball game, academic classes, or play practice. The following lead for a sights and sounds story is from The Kirkwood Call, *Kirkwood High School, Kirkwood, MO.*

> Dull yellow lights illuminated the stage, March 20, as the shop crew members brought out their tools and started working.
>
> The sound of hammers pounding nails into wood filled the auditorium as the members assembled set pieces.
>
> Dave Oesch and Andy Benedicktus, seniors, and Chris Leech, sophomore, lined the stage-right extension up with its tapemarks.
>
> "Is that center stage?" asked John Dean, crew director, as he supervised them.
>
> "No," replied Leech.
>
> "Well, then get the edge in the center," Dean told him.
>
> They made the adjustment by moving the extension a bit to the right, and then Oesch and Benedicktus hammered more support legs onto it.
>
> Oesch then gently stood on the extension to see if it would hold his weight.
>
> "Does it feel balanced?" asked Benedicktus.
>
> "Not yet," Oesch replied. He then grabbed a three-foot long 1 x 4 and sawed about two inches off one end and hammered it between two legs as a crossbrace.

The story continues with more sights and sounds about the crew creating the set for the fall play.

• *That the average chocolate bar has 8 insect legs in it?*

• *That "stewardesses" is the longest word typed using only the left hand?*

• *That if you keep a goldfish in a dark room, it will eventually turn white?*

• *That the sentence "the quick brown fox jumps over the lazy dog" uses every letter in the English alphabet?*

• *That the names of all the continents end with the same letter that they start with?*

• *That if the population of China walked past you in single file, the line would never end because of the rate of reproduction.*

• *That you share your birthday with at least 9 million other people in the world?*

• *That one square inch of human skin contains 625 sweat glands?*

• *That the "funny bone" is not a bone but a nerve.*

• *That most people blink about 25,000 times a day.*

• *That a human sheds a complete layer of skin every four weeks?*

• *That when you blush, your stomach lining also reddens?*

Trivia provides interesting reading. The above appeared in the Fourth Estate, Laguna Blanca School, Santa Barbara, CA. Use the items presented for story ideas. For example, you could find out when students were born and do a story on the date mentioned most often. You could also do a story on blinking or on blushing. Ideas for feature stories may be found anywhere.

the **Features**

Highland Park Bagpipe October 11, 1996

ARE YOU A COMPULSIVE GAMBLER?

GAMBLING on the rules

◆ *Card sharks study the probablity of drawing a winning hand during open periods*

BY JOHN MABERRY

BREAKING THE RULES Gambling in the Commons has become a diversion for students.

Betting more than greenback$

◆*From drag racing to high stakes gambling, Highland Park students do it all.*

BY JEB ORY

Why do I do it? Speed. I get a rush. I get to be the 'king of the hill' when we win.

-senior Brandon Schmidt

Dividing a feature story into two or more related stories normally improves readership. The above page from the Bagpipe, Highland Park High School, Dallas, TX, also includes a sidebar to help someone determine if he or she is a compulsive gambler.

1. Try to avoid a stereotyped pattern. Don't ask trite questions: "What is your favorite food, color, recording artist, actor, or movie?"

2. Reveal personality through incidents. Permit the reader to see your subject in action. If your profile is on a football player, put him on the field showing what he does best.

3. A personality sketch is more than a description. It permits the person's words and manners to bring her to life.

4. Make your personality seem natural and human.

5. The reason for the sketch should be made clear early in the story. If the sketch is on a prominent student, such as the Student Council president, make that known in the first paragraph.

6. Do not give an encyclopedic listing of your subject's life and accomplishments. Select the facts that individualize the person and suggest what he is like. Your account should permit your readers to know the subject intimately.

7. Reveal character through your subject's speech, action, appearance, and what others say about her.

> Feature Characteristics

- They vary in length from 200 words or less to several thousand.
- They read like non-fiction novels because the characters come alive just as in fiction stories.
- Good features are based on observations.
- They get readers to react and make them feel as if they were part of the event or part of the person's life.
- Quality features make the reader think and care.
- They have strong openings as well as strong conclusions. The ending is often the best remembered part of a feature.
- Most features are people stories. So, the readers should see the people physically and hear them talk.
- Strong interviewing techniques are evident in feature writing.

Historical Feature. Such features center around events such as a national holiday, a school's birthday, or a traditional event. Do not overuse them. Features on Halloween and Valentine's Day appear in school papers across the country, and in some they appear annually. Be fresh with your approach. Find something that concerns your readers. An article tracing the history of integration on your campus, or the history of Homecoming, or of clubs, or of a school tradition would probably be more interesting to the readers than a feature on Thanksgiving or Christmas.

Informative Feature. This type of feature requires a great deal of research, since its purpose is to present specialized knowledge about a particular subject. Topics might include

stress OVERLOAD

by Carly Wray
CONTRIBUTING WRITER

The alarm sounds at 5:30 a.m., only four hours after senior Andrew Buck collapsed on his books in a deep sleep.

With the final performance as the lead in *Blithe Spirit* the night before, he only finished half of the mound of AP homework residing on his desk.

"I heard your senior year is supposed to be a breeze," Buck said. "That hasn't been true for me."

Through a constant influx of homework, meetings and work hours, many students like Buck struggle with too much to do in too little time.

School takes on the role of lead stressor for many students, especially those who join Buck in honors and Advanced Placement (AP) classes. AP classes operate on a college level, producing a heavy work load each night. Many students overload themselves with honors classes, sometimes taking as many as six at the same time.

Enrolling in an AP course not only binds students to hours of assignments but to a certain level of expectation as well. When a student is in advanced classes, both parents and teachers automatically expect high grades and exceptional work. Living up to a preset standard can often prove to be more stressful than the class itself.

After the bell rings at 2:45

p.m., school still provides an ample amount of stress and work through the magical world of extracurricular activities. Meetings, fund raisers, competitions, concerts and games for a vast array of after school groups and teams are always taking place. Not unlike Buck, many students find themselves trying to divide their time and dedication between three or four clubs and organizations. Rushing from one commitment to the next every day can slowly tear at a teenager's patience and ambition. Most students join up due to the fun and interest level involved. The fun, unfortunately, can begin to disappear when it is taken on in too great of proportions.

"I participate in my activities because they are fulfilling and interesting to me," sophomore Clint Davis said. "It does seem sometimes, though, that there are not enough hours in the day."

Beyond the classwork and club gatherings, many students have yet another form of stress during the week. Adolescents between the ages of 15 and 18 are working more and more each year. Some students are responsible for helping put food on the table, while others work to cover personal expenses. The average working week for teens is 15 to 20 hours, usually for no more than minimum wage.

"I work 15 hours a week. I usually don't sleep during the week and try to catch up on the weekends," senior Valerie Nelson said.

This is a popular situation among the population of high schools. Most students claim that they get, if any at all, between three to six hours a night.

Outside of the demands of organizations and other work, stress is a major factor internally for today's teenagers.

"Students generally face more moral dilemmas than adults. It is stressful for a student to deal with conflicts between the way your beliefs work and the demands of your peers," psychologist Dr. Charles Overstreet said. "This kind of dissension leads to the popular adolescent depression and defensiveness." Overstreet works with students, primarily through Tarrant County Junior College.

Still, some students and adults regard teenagers as a stress-free group.

"I personally don't believe that there is very much stress in

high school. There is not that much to worry about," student Chris Lockwood said.

Could it be that adolescents are simply more capable of dealing with a busy schedule?

"Adolescents are very resilient. They are more future oriented. If [students] are in a job that looks like an unchanging entity, they are understanding that it is a temporary situation," Dr. Overstreet said.

For those students who feel like the work load is never going to change, there are a few important things to remember. Psychiatrists say that students need to make sure that they are prioritizing, organizing and trying to relax as much as possible.

"I try not to take life too seriously," sophomore Nick Wilson said. Teenagers need to keep at least a small amount of time open for fun. After all, these are the care free days.

Informative features like the one on stress from the Colt, *Arlington High School, Arlington, TX, are usually well read because they deal with topics that most teenagers can relate to. Note the good quotes used throughout the article, including ones from an expert on the topic.*

phobias, college finances, differences in automobile insurance policies, or alcohol and drug programs.

An informative feature can become an *in-depth article* if the writer interviews as many people as possible on the topic. If a topic has several aspects, it is usually a good idea to divide it into three or four articles to enhance readability. The reader is more likely to read three or four short articles than to spend a greater amount of time on one article.

An informative feature is also sometimes known as an interpretive story. An interpretive story might also be news, but more often than not it falls into the feature category. The interpretive story centers around a problem or issue to which the readers can relate—juvenile delinquency, recycling, drug usage, pressure, depression, dress codes, state education laws, draft laws, college entrance exams, college finances, curricu-

> *Journal Writing*

Keeping a journal is a great way to improve one's writing and a great way to gain ideas for feature stories. All good writers should keep a journal. Consider reading Bob Greene's Be True to Your School.

Greene, a newspaper columnist, kept a journal when he was in high school in 1964. A journalism teacher asked Greene to write something every day, and those daily writings later became a book. Greene went to high school in the 1960s, but many of the trials and tribulations he faced are still being faced by teens today. That's why the book is a great resource for feature ideas.

lum developments. Any problem or issue that confronts the reader is a potential interpretive topic.

The writer must be sure that his or her report is objective. There are always several viewpoints, and the reporter must present them all. The reporter must also provide sufficient background information to give the reader a thorough understanding of the problem. This may require a lot of research before he or she ever starts writing.

Research will include reading newspapers, magazines, and books on the topic and conducting interviews with experts (recognized authorities). The reporter will also interview students and teachers to get their opinions on the issue and to localize the story. The more information the reporter has, the greater the reliability of the content. In reality, the interpretive reporter becomes something of an expert on the topic.

The *Reader's Guide to Periodical Literature* will be a valuable tool for the student who is writing an informative feature. Upon obtaining a list of magazine articles, the reporter must then spend time scanning each article to decide the direction of the piece.

The reporter might use the following questions to evaluate the information he or she has obtained from reading and interviewing:

1. Do I have statistics from scientific surveys?
2. Have I thoroughly documented my information?
3. Do I have all viewpoints represented?
4. Are there gaps in my information? Have I failed to answer any questions?
5. Are some of my interviewees recognized authorities?

A well-written, informative feature will be among the best-read articles in a high school newspaper because it deals with an issue of major concern to the reader and because it provides information that is not readily known. A good informative feature takes time to write; plan it for several issues in the future. Give the reporter time to research thoroughly.

> ➢ *Possible Feature Story Ideas*
> - *Life in the inner city of a large metropolitan area.*
> - *Favorite foods.*
> - *Breakfast habits.*
> - *Life in a wheelchair.*
> - *Life of a deaf person or life of a blind person.*
> - *Serving food in a soup kitchen.*
> - *The effects of MTV.*
> - *Students' attitudes toward learning.*
> - *Barbie dolls.*
> - *Death.*
> - *Divorce.*
> - *Stress.*
> - *Stereotypes.*
> - *Family relationships.*
> - *Teenage mothers/ Teenage fathers.*
> - *Jobs and their effect on student grades.*
> - *Life of a diabetic.*
> - *Cars—favorite type, insurance, getting a driver's license, personalized license plates.*

➢ **Figures of Speech**

• *Simile: Use* like *or as to show comparison.*

• *Metaphor: Uses comparison without the word* like *or as.*

• *Personification: Makes comparisons by giving inanimate objects human characteristics.*

• *Oxymoron: When the adjective contradicts the noun, such as* jumbo shrimp.

• *Synecdoche: Using a part of something to represent the whole, such as* threads *for clothes.*

• *Onomatopoeia: When words suggest their meanings, such as* plop.

• *Alliteration: Repeats the same letter or sound, such as* jauntily joyful.

• *Hyperbole: An exaggeration made on purpose.*

• *Allusion: Referring to someone or something that is well known, such as a well-known phrase.*

News Feature. A timely news happening serves as the basis for a news feature. For example, a fire is a news story. A second story on the aftermath of the fire could capture the human interest angles of the event. This type of feature is also called a *sidebar*—a story that accompanies the main story.

Personal Experience Feature. This type of story is seldom used in school papers. A first-person account should be written only by a person who is well known, or who has been involved in an unusual situation or one that many readers could identify with, such as a suicide attempt or being trapped in an elevator.

Photo Feature. This type of feature usually allots more space to photos than to copy. Photographs are attention grabbers, so use this type of feature when you have outstanding photos that tell the story better than a block of copy would. Be sure to caption the photographs so that readers know exactly what is happening.

How-to Feature. For this feature to be successful, it must have a subject that is timely, interesting, and new. The writer merely explains to the reader the practical steps to follow in order to do or make something.

Consumer Report. This feature is designed to aid the reader in the selection of goods and services in the marketplace by providing pertinent information, such as comparison of prices, quality of products, and quality of services.

Other types of features include adventure, travel, society, humor, and autobiographical.

Regardless of the type of feature, it is necessary for a feature writer to be observant, to react to what she has observed, and to think about what she has observed before she starts to write. Most good feature ideas come through simple observation. Rod Vahl, a former newspaper sponsor at Davenport High School, Davenport, IA, always urged his students to "take a walk" when they could not come up with a feature story idea. He was telling them to "get out of their chair and go out and look for a story."

Good journalists generate story ideas by continually observing their environment. That means the reporter is aware of everything around her. As the reporter takes her walk, she listens to conversations in the hallway. These conversations might lead to stories about what teenagers are concerned with, such as peer rejection. The reporter also notices bulletin boards. She might see a flyer about college scholarships that could lead to a feature on college costs. She sticks her head inside classrooms. She might notice a student building a grandfather clock in shop class, which could lead to a personality profile. She might stop and chat with the principal and find out that the principal is on his way to a meeting to discuss learning styles. This might lead to a feature story on what helps students learn.

The walk should not stop at school. It should continue through the neighborhood. She might notice on her walk that a freshman boy uses a key to unlock his house at 3:30 p.m. This could lead to a story on "latchkey kids"—those kids who have working parents so no one is at home when they arrive from school. She might also notice several teenagers going into a church, which could lead to a feature story on church youth groups and their activities. She might see five classmates working at a fast-food restaurant, which could lead to a feature story on jobs.

When a journalist "takes a walk" she becomes aware of all teenagers and the totality of their lives. There is no reason for a reporter ever to say, "I don't have any story ideas."

When the writer has an idea for a story, the following guidelines should be followed:

> ➢ *Reading and Writing*
>
> *By reading good writing, students can become better writers. A must on everyone's list of good reading is Rick Bragg's* All Over but the Shoutin.' *This book is a collection of his stories that won the Pulitzer Prize for feature writing in 1996. Bragg encourages feature writers to be proud of their work. He says his notebooks are always filled with observations. Observing is the first step in the writing process. Bragg also says he will often go back and interview a person more than once to gather his information.*

1. Research. Research. Research. A writer needs to interview people and read books or articles on the topic.
2. Focus. That means to zero in on one aspect. The writer should always decide the purpose of the article before beginning to write. That purpose should be the focus. For example, dieting is a broad topic; zero in on one aspect such as improper dieting that might lead to anorexia nervosa.

Though, in theory, students under the age of 18 cannot be professionally pierced without parental consent, scores of pierced teenagers clearly disprove this claim. Why is so little being done to stop these

H⚭p Schemes

by Eliza Byington

ALTHOUGH MOST TRENDS ORIGINATE AND BECOME popularized by teenagers, body piercing, one of the latest styles, is restricted to those over the age of 18. Though some places will pierce minors if they can establish parental consent, many parlours will turn away teens even when accompanied by a guardian. However, this restriction does not seem to deter hordes of youth, eager to jump on the band wagon and pierce themselves. For them, piercing has become a means of self expression less permanent than tattoos. In addition, a highly visible tattoo may cause an uproar at school or home, where as a stud in some one's nose or belly button may go unnoticed. With piercing's growth in popularity, teens are finding ways around the age limit. In fact, many places do not strictly enforce this rule, while others ignore it all together.

"If someone wants a piercing bad enough," Christopher Ellerd, manager of Atomic Tattoo said, "they will find a place that does not card. They are common enough."

Just like the age requirement for tattoos, the rule is intended to protect young people. However, because the responsibility falls exclusively on the piercer, a conflict of interest results. There are no legal repercussions for piercing a minor and no authority figure to enforce the rule; piercing has not yet been approved by any state or federal agency and thus receives no government regulation. In short, the people who are paid to pierce are the ones who decide whether or not they will pierce minors. This practice can be dangerous, as many teens may not know the risks involved.

"Any place that pierces minors has no morals," Ellerd said. "The rules are made to protect people from having a bad experience. It actually hurts my business if people have a bad experience with piercing."

But many teens tend to be less careful about who pierces them and more interested in just getting it done. This can be dangerous in terms of whether or not the piercer is certified and uses sterile materials.

"I went to get a nose ring when I was 16," senior Megan Black said. "I just walked in and got it done. I did have to fill out a sheet that asked my age and drivers license number. Of course I had to lie, but that was as far as 'carding' went."

However, if enforced, the age restriction can be useful in preventing conflicts between parents and teens.

"There are a lot of places where there is no way around the rule," senior Dee Dee McCabe said. "When enforced, the rule really does serve a useful purpose."

However, parents who depend on the rule to protect their children may be in for a rude awakening when their son or daughter comes home with a piercing.

"When my mother saw it, she went ape," Megan said. "She took away my car, my stereo and every privilege I ever had. I took it out after about 18 hours because I valued my freedom more than having an extra hole in my head."

670136942895378
Texas State Juvenile Penitentiary

" I did have to fill out a sheet that asked my age and drivers license number. Of course I had to lie, but that was as far as 'carding' went."

Senior Megan Black

Beauty is in the eye of the beholder

Pleasures of Today

• In the Sara tribe of Central Africa women's lips are split and then stretched by saucer shaped plugs. Perforations in the cheeks for the insertion of ornaments are also common.

• Many Hindu women in India stain their teeth bright red to improve their appearance.

• Several East African peoples will constrict their arms or legs with tight bands to cause permanent swelling of the limbs.

• The Padaung women of Burma place a brass neck ring with a length of about 15 inches to elongate their necks.

• Scarification, found primarily in Africa and Australia, is the formation of raised scars in decorative patterns by cutting the skin and rubbing irritants such as dung or dirt into the cuts.

• Among several African peoples, girls are secluded for several months during puberty and artificially fattened with special diets for aesthetic reasons.

Perspectives of the Past

• The ancient Mayans believed that cross eyes were beautiful so they induced this quality by hanging an object between a baby's eyes.

• In 1500 b.c. Egyptian women removed every hair from their heads using special gold tweezers and, with buffing cloths, polished their bare scalps to a shine.

• The ancient Maori tribe of New Zealand tattooed complex spiral designs on their face and buttocks. Fine tattoos were held as a sign of good breeding.

• In the late 1800's it was considered fashionable for English women to wear gold rings through their nipples. Wearing such rings was believed to enhance the size and shape of the breasts.

Fads usually make for interesting stories as in the above example on body piercing from the Featherduster, *Westlake High School, Austin, TX. Note the sidebar on Pleasures of Today and Perspectives of the Past.*

3. Read features in the professional press. Become aware of techniques used by professional writers. Most good writers are avid readers.

4. Describe. Describe. Describe. Good feature writing paints a visual picture for readers. They should feel that they are actually witnessing the scenes that unfold. Vivid detail is essential. Force readers to use all their senses: sight, touch, taste, smell, and sound. The sights and sounds of the event should come alive

through choice of words. The writer must be able to describe the people featured in the piece, especially in personality profiles. Weave the physical description of a person throughout a story; don't lump it into one paragraph. One way to work in physical description is to tie it in with the attribution of a quote or paraphrase: *"You should be dead!" he yelled as he pointed with his long, raw-boned finger.*

5. Use direct quotations. Let the interviewee tell the story. Keep any personal reference out of the copy.

6. Do not editorialize. A writer's opinion belongs in editorials and columns, not features. Opinion in features should occur only in direct quotes. Be sure to balance the quotes if there are two sides to the issue.

7. Use statistics. Statistics can add a dimension to a story. For example, a story on a fire in a Chicago elementary school noted that no lives would have been lost if the fire had struck 1,200 seconds later, because school would have been out for the day. That simple statistic gives readers something extra to think about and further plays on their emotions.

8. Dig deep for facts. Gather more material than you can ever use. Be selective with the facts, but tell the complete story.

9. Use figures of speech. Use simile and metaphor for comparisons. Use hyperbole for exaggerations that readers know are exaggerations. Use personification by giving inanimate objects human characteristics.

10. Prepare yourself for interviews. Make a list of necessary questions. Make an appointment for each interview, and let the interviewee know how long you think it will take. Be on time. Do

➢ *Creating Visuals with Words*

You can make scenes come alive visually if you ask yourself these questions before writing:

• What are the first words that come to mind when you think about the event or topic you're writing about?

• What are the first images that come to mind—the sights, the sounds, the smells?

• Why is this topic important to the reader?

• What was the biggest challenge facing the people involved?

• What surprised you about the outcome?

• What did you find about this event that was different from similar events?

• What revealing quotes were you able to obtain?

• What will be your unusual angle—your focus?

Now take the answers you have to the above questions and turn those answers into a Pulitzer Prize–winning story.

➢ *Conducting the Interview*

• *Identify yourself and your purpose.*

• *Set up a time for the interview.*

• *Try to conduct the interview in person. It's too easy for someone to say "No comment" on the phone and then hang up. It's also impossible to see facial gestures.*

• *Avoid whether or not questions, questions of more than three sentences, questions that begin with an apology, and yes or no questions.*

• *Clarify jargon and spelling.*

• *Concentrate on how and why questions.*

• *Follow-up questions should clarify and expand on the interviewee's comments.*

• *Conclude by asking for permission to recontact in order to verify information and quotes. Be sure to thank the interviewee for his or her time.*

not be concerned about getting all of your advance questions answered. You will probably get a better response if you do not have to refer constantly to your notes. Listen to the respondent's answers. Answers should lead to further questions. Use a tape recorder if the interviewee gives permission. Keep control of the interview. If you cannot use a tape recorder and you see that the interview is going too fast, tell the interviewee that what he has to say is important and you want to get it right. Then ask him to repeat what he just said. Develop your own personal shorthand to speed notetaking. A good system is to drop most vowels. For example: *A gd wy to spll wrds whn tkng nts is to lv out the vwls (A good way to spell words when taking notes is to leave out the vowels).* Thank the interviewee for his time, and leave things open in case you might need more information by asking something like: "May I call you as I write the story, if I find I need more data?"

11. Localize the copy. Be sure that the feature concerns your readers. Use students, faculty members, and parents for information. For example, if you write a feature on abortion, the copy should be more than what readers have already read in the daily paper or a magazine. Add fresh information by interviewing school and district personnel.

12. Play on people's emotions. Make readers shed a tear, or evoke a chuckle from them.

13. For best results, write feature stories in the third person. First person works with personal narratives, but it is not satisfactory for other types. Second person works for direct address leads, but it is a rare writer who can use second person effectively.

'Needling' around with tattoos

She planned for a panther on her back, but after that one, she saw the Chinese symbol for "precious" and decided she wanted it, too. So she put it on her leg.

Tonya Hill, junior, said that is how she ended up getting two tattoos at the same time. Hill said she wanted them because she "thought they would look cute."

Ebony Williams, senior, said she had similar reasons when she had a tattoo, an E, placed on her leg at a friend's house five years ago. Williams said she thought it would look nice and be cool, but after she had it for awhile, she found she did not like it.

"It's ugly," Williams said. "It looks trashy, unattractive and unprofessional."

However, Jade Pounds, junior, said she does not think she will ever regret getting her tattoo -- a rose-surrounded heart with her name -- because she was sure she wanted it before she got it. Pounds said it was her decision, and she said it is important not to get a tattoo because someone else has one. Peer pressure would "take the fun out of it," she said.

Nevertheless, Larry Branam, nurse and director of laser service, said people often "think about today and not about tomorrow" when they get their tattoos.

"Many people don't think through the process," Branam said. "They should think about where they put it, they should think about the design, and they should know it might prevent

them from getting jobs in the future."

Branam said removing a tattoo can be costly, since removing an amateur-made tattoo takes at least two laser treatments and removing professional-made tattoos often requires at least five treatments. Treatments for removal are far more expensive than the tattoo, Branam said.

"Most people who remove their tattoos do it within the first few years," he said. "Sometimes they have one removed because they are allergic to ink, or maybe they have one removed because they regret having obtained one in the first place."

Nicole Chase, senior, said she does not think she will regret the "beautiful and timeless" butterfly tattoo she had placed on her back.

"I was 18 when I got my tattoo, and I felt I had more freedom," Chase said. "The butterfly symbolized that. My parents helped me pay for it as a birthday present."

The price should be unimportant when getting a tattoo, according to Brenda Ansback, owner of the Blue Moon Tattoo studio in Arnold. Ansback said one should be sure to get what one really wants, instead of being "hooked up on the price."

Ansback also said another important thing for anyone who wants a tattoo is to be sure one feels comfortable with the establishment who will do the work.

"It must be clean," Ansback said. "Everything must be individually wrapped and opened in

front of you, and you must feel comfortable with the artist who designs your tattoo."

Christen Cushing, senior, said she has designed five tattoos for friends, and that they sometimes pay her for it. Cushing said they have told her what they want, how big they wanted it and what colors they wanted.

"I don't mind drawing tattoos for others, but I don't plan on getting any for myself," Cushing said. "I'm not into tattoos."

Anna Engestrom

Because their friendship means so much, Erin Canty and Lauren Knight, seniors, had the Chinese symbol for "friendship" tattooed on their hips. (photo by Julie Coppage)

Fads can also be the topic of a feature story. This one in the Kirkwood Call, *Kirkwood High School, Kirkwood, MO, focuses on removing tattoos as well as getting them.*

> *Things to Look for During an Interview*
>
> • *Body language— staring eyes, tapping pencil, hand gestures, hand shakes, chewing gum, shifting positions (shows nervousness).*
>
> • *Interviewee's voice—pitch, volume, speed, inflection (emphasis), articulation, pronunciation (accents), vocabulary, pauses, energy.*

14. Leave no questions unanswered. Don't skirt the hole; fill it. Be sure that all points have been covered. Don't be afraid to ask "Why?"

15. Be positive about what you're writing. Stay away from qualifiers such as *rather* or *slightly*. Make specific, definite statements.

16. Choose a topic that is well known to readers. Be aware that nearly every news event contains several possible features.

17. Have a keen interest in life. To be a successful feature writer, this is a must. Know and understand what makes people react as they do to certain situations.

18. Have a thorough knowledge of the English language. Know how to use words, to turn a phrase that will grip the reader.

19. Avoid repetition in words and in quotes. Don't have four people saying the same thing. Variety

INCREDIBLE BUT TRUE!

4,000 packets of hot sauce!

If Emily Recknor '97, ever has a flat tire, she's in trouble. Rather than the usual jack or spare, the trunk of Recknor's gray Ford Escort contains an estimated 4,000 packets of Taco Bell hot sauce, a collection that has been an ongoing project since the summer of 1995. "I fill up my pockets every time I visit Taco Bell," Recknor said. "My friends give them to me. Last year my family put some in my Christmas stocking."

Though the hot sauce rarely serves any practical purpose, Recknor has found much enjoyment from its presence, an idea spawned by a cousin. Her car is a hatchback, making the collection visible to anyone passing by. "I get a lot of attention from it," Recknor said, "People's reactions can range from utter shock to confusion to dizziness."

Excluding the one packet of ketchup (which has lead to an enjoyable game known as "Find the Ketchup"), the contents of Recknor's trunk are pure Taco Bell. No other restaurants' condiments are present in her car. "Taco John's is my enemy," Recknor said. "I prefer to cross the border."

Recknor has high hopes for the future of her hot sauce packets, including expanding her collection. And she said, "Someday I might turn them all face-up."

by Crissy McMartin

Recknor with her sauce.

photos by Cayenne Stoakes-Hughes

An unusual collection helps the writer from the Little Hawk, *City High School, Iowa City, IA, create an interesting human interest feature. Items found in students' cars might be an idea for an even longer informative feature.*

is important. Use a variety of sentence types. Even sentence fragments can work, if the reader is aware that they are fragments. Fragments can be especially effective when trying to show fast movement of time: *Hurry. Run back. Stop. Too late. She's already dead.*

20. Write an effective lead. There are several ways to begin a feature story:

Descriptive Lead: This is a vivid picture that takes the reader into the story. The reader must be able to see every movement of people you are talking about, including blinking of the eyes. Describe the scenes as they appear; do not make up anything.

Narrative Hook Lead: This is much like the descriptive lead, but it is fictional. It must be fast-moving, and the reader must know it is fiction. You might set it off from the rest of the copy by leaving a space after it or by setting it in boldface or italics. It might be necessary to say something like, "Although the above is fictional, it is indicative of what is happening in today's society, according to...."

Question Lead: Seldom used, because it is difficult to come up with an earth-shaking question, one that the reader really wants to have answered. Avoid question leads that may be answered with *Yes, No,* or *I don't care.*

Quote Leads: Seldom used, because it is difficult to find a quote so exciting that the reader wants to find out more. It is also rare to find a quote that summarizes the content of the feature.

Contrast or Comparison Lead: This type of lead can be most effective when it establishes or suggests relationships that are unusual. It helps to identify something by associating it with the extreme or an opposite. The comparison, however, must be feasible. Even if contrast or comparison is not used in the lead of a feature, it is a good idea to use it throughout the story. It helps the reader identify with the issue.

Suspense Lead: This type of lead usually has an aura of mystery about it. It grabs the reader but leaves him wondering what will happen next.

Striking Statement Lead: Shock is the purpose of this type of lead. The statement should make the reader say "Wow!" or "I didn't know that!"

Summary Lead: Answering who, what, when, where, why, and how can sometimes be an appropriate lead for a feature, but this type of lead tends to be boring. It is best used for news stories.

Direct Address Lead: This type of lead can be effective when the *"you"* addressed can identify with the story. The event must be one that most readers have observed. This lead works best with sights and sounds features. Do not overuse it.

A Few Well-Chosen Words Lead: This type of lead uses sentence fragments on purpose. Be sure the fragments are parallel in construction, and to be effective use at least three. For

➢ *On or Off the Record*
• *On the record:* The reporter can publish everything discussed.
• *Off the record:* The reporter will use information gained only for personal background and perspective and will not publish the information or the source of the information.
• *Not for attribution:* The reporter can use the information without naming the specific person who gave the information.
• *On background:* The reporter can use the information, using a general title as the source (a company spokesperson said).
• *On or off the record comments may be obtained for any type of story. To maintain your credibility, you should honor the interviewee's request.*

example: Dreaded music. Dreaded obstacle. Dreaded movie. In developing the story, the writer would then explain what the dreaded music was, what the dreaded obstacle was, and what the dreaded movie was. The example uses the same adjective in each fragment. That is not necessary. The only requirement is that each sentence fragment be parallel in construction. For example, if a noun in the first sentence fragment is plural, make the noun in each sentence fragment plural.

Satire Lead. This is not an easy lead to write, but it is one that will grab the reader. It takes a special skill to write satire. The writer must stretch the reader's imagination so far that she has no doubt that the lead is not totally true. It might be desirable to set this type of lead in boldface or italic type and leave a line of space between it and the rest of the story. The following satirical lead was used for an article on a school's malfunctioning furnace system. The classrooms were bitterly cold for more than two weeks, and it was impossible for some teachers to move their students elsewhere. After the lead, the writer gave the facts and interviewed students and teachers about the situation.

> Willy Chilly, junior, shivered as he eyed the thermometer during chemistry. Clad in his moon boots, ski pants, scarf, hat, mittens, and down jacket, he reached underneath his desk to turn up his electric blanket.
>
> Discovering that his textbook was frozen shut, Chilly waited in line to thaw it with the bunsen burner. Several of his classmates huddled around the fire that Polly Pyro, senior, built on her desktop, while others drew pictures in the thick frost that covered the walls and chalkboards.
>
> As the bell rang, Chilly unplugged his blanket and skated through the halls to his Algebra II class.

Poetry lead. Do not overuse this type of lead, but it can be effective for some stories. The following lead was for a story on teenage problems.

Speed and pot, alcohol abuse,
Crowbars and paint put to misuse;
Shoplifting, and widespread theft,
Mood-altering drugs, no mind left;
Drunk as a skunk or high as a cloud.
Was there a reason to be so proud?

21. Be careful about granting anonymity when writing sensitive features, or stories of any type for that matter. High school journalists might want to use an anonymous source if the source is providing intimate information about himself or if anonymity allows the source to provide information about someone else. Readers are always skeptical of anonymous sources, however, so it is best to avoid using them at all. If a journalist does grant anonymity, he should do so only if he has his editor's permission, or if refusing to grant it would be a disservice to the news audience. If the information is vital to the story and it cannot be obtained without granting anonymity, then the reporter should do so. The reporter should also make it clear to the source that he might later have to ask to be released from a pledge of confidentiality. If anonymous sources are used in a story, the reporter must also find sources who are willing to go on the record. (This rule does not hold if a story is about the source.) A policy that requires sources to go on the record strengthens the credibility of a publication.

22. Remember that all good features should be emotion-arousing, and the best features are those that cover unique experiences.

23. If possible, link the ending of a feature story to the beginning. Note how the following story

➢ *Use of Adjectives and Adverbs*

• *Avoid using adjectives that are flat and colorless:* He played a great game.

• *Avoid using adjectives that are trite:* The blue ocean.

• *Avoid using redundant adjectives:* He spoke in a muffled whisper.

• *Don't use both a verb and an adverb if just a verb will suffice:* use gripped *rather than* held firmly.

• *Avoid using adjectives that editorialize:* She played a beautiful game.

➢ *Using Quotes*
Quotes should be used when they:
• Express something controversial.
• Express something not likely to be believed by the reader.
• Express the opinion of the interviewee.
• Express something momentous.
• Explain something technical.
• Correct an error.

from *Student Magazine*, Grandview (MO) High School, does that.

"It's no big deal."

She smiles, blinks her long eyelashes, and smooths her red pants against her model-thin legs. First slowly, then with less resistance, she recounts the parts of the accident that nearly paralyzed her. That is, the parts she can remember.

Coming home from a Raytown basketball game on Jan. 28, the car in which Jenny Arbuckle was a passenger ran first off one side of the road, then the other, overturning in a ditch.

"I was just lying there forever, and I was cold. I don't remember any sirens or the ambulance; the next thing I knew I was in the hospital, and I didn't know my boyfriend was sitting right next to me," she said....

..."Really it was the little things that bothered me more than anything. I was afraid I'd have to shave my head, that I would ruin my teeth, and I really cried about track," she said, touching the leg that still has numb patches.

"It's like I said, it's no big deal. I can't wait to get my Mustang, wear my Polos, and sleep on my stomach. I tried that one, it doesn't work," she laughed, probably imagining herself with her face a good six inches above her pillow.

To look at her pretty, unchanged face and watch her eyes shine with enthusiasm when she talks about her car, one would never guess she had come so close to being a different girl for the rest of her life.

But she didn't.

She's still just Jenny, and that is a big deal.

24. Don't ever think there is nothing to write about. If you think you've done every possible

feature story, and you don't want to rehash the same topic over again, it is your job to find a new angle. There is bound to be a fresh angle to the same old story.

25. Consider using polls and surveys to supplement a story. Polls and surveys are discussed in Chapter 8.

26. Be as brief as possible. Just because your story is a feature does not mean you should overwrite. Long stories bore readers.

27. Be clear. When you say something or when you quote someone, be sure you have done it clearly. Leave no guessing to the reader.

28. Tell your story as you might tell it to a friend.

29. Write an effective conclusion. Many high school feature writers think they have to summarize their story. That is not usually necessary, nor is it necessary to congratulate or offer best wishes. Most features conclude naturally; nothing special is needed. When the story has been told, it is time to stop. One effective way of concluding a feature is to link the ending with the beginning. Select some phrase used in the lead and work it into the conclusion. A good, strong quote can also work as a solid conclusion. Regardless of how you end, be sure to leave a lasting thought.

30. Rewrite. Rewrite. Rewrite. Never be satisfied with the first draft. All good writing can only become better through the rewrite process. Good writing is torment. Frustration and a half-full wastebasket will make you a better writer.

EXERCISES

1. Select a person at your school who is well

> *Using Anecdotes*
> • *An anecdote is an incident. It has a point to it. It may be amusing or amazing.*
> • *Reporters should try to obtain them from interviews.*
> • *Anecdotes can make good conclusions for features.*
> • *Anecdotes can be used to illustrate a point.*
> • *Anecdotes can dramatize a significant happening in one's life.*

➤ Getting
Information from
the Web

Feature writers are
turning to the Web
for background infor-
mation on topics.
They need to learn to
evaluate that infor-
mation in order to
know whether it is
factual or not. To do
so, they should ask
themselves the
following questions:

• Is it possible to
tell who authored the
site? Do you know
the person's qualifica-
tions? Is there a way
to contact the person?

• Are biases clearly
stated?

• How recently
has the site been
updated?

• Are sources for
factual information
included so those
accessing can verify
the facts?

• Is the site well
edited? (If the gram-
mar and spelling are
poor, the authors
may also not have
checked their facts.)

known or has done something unusual, and write a personality profile on him or her.

2. Select at least 10 feature stories from your own school's newspaper and exchange papers, and analyze them on their effectiveness. Look back over the guidelines suggested in this chapter, and deter-mine if the stories you chose followed them well. Point out strengths and weaknesses.

3. Make a list of 50 possible feature ideas that your school paper could cover.

4. Write an informative feature based on a topic of your choice. Select a topic such as phobias, runaways, suicide, teenage pregnancy—one that will require some library research to get background information and require you to interview an expert such as a minister, sociologist, psychiatrist, or doctor. Use at least two authoritative interviews, and also include interviews with students and faculty members.

5. Assume that you are writing a personality profile about your journalism teacher. Write a descriptive lead that will capture his/her image and character.

6. Clip 10 feature stories from your daily paper and label each according to type of story and type of lead used.

7. Analyze the front-page news stories of the last three issues of your school paper. Write a news feature based on one of them.

8. Role-play an interview with one of your class-mates. Based on what you find out about the person during the interview, write a personality profile on him/her.

9. Invite the principal to visit your classroom. Have the class interview her for a personality profile. Compare the stories for types of lead used and infor-mation presented.

10. Working with two other students in your class, prepare an in-depth feature on a well-known

topic. Be sure that each student has a different focus for her article. For example, dieting could be divided into three topics: fad diets, junk food, and anorexia nervosa.

11. Use the following facts to write a personality profile. You may add additional facts, but do not change any of the facts given. Be sure to write an effective lead, and try to link the conclusion with the beginning.

Hank Simpson, junior, participated in the International Games for the Disabled in Long Island, NY, last month.

He received a gold medal for equestrian excellence.

Simpson has cerebral palsy, a disability that hampers motor control.

Family members have always encouraged him, he said.

To prepare for international competition, Simpson practiced an average of three times a week last year. Just before participating in the games, he also trained with the rest of the U.S. equestrian contingent.

Because he enjoyed the games, Simpson hopes to become a contender again in four years.

"I made friends from all over the world," he said. "I am now writing to a really neat girl from New Zealand."

"Before the next games, we will compete in Michigan. If I perform well enough to be selected again, I will go on to the games in Australia in four years," he said.

Simpson rides once a week at Three Creeks Farm, where he is a member of Therapeutic Horsemanship, a group that instructs disabled people in riding techniques.

"Three Creeks Farm donates the horses to our organization," said Simpson. "Right now I am

"The most important thing in a story is finding the central idea. It's one thing to be given a topic, but you have to find the idea or the concept within that topic. Once you find that idea or thread, all the other anecdotes, illustrations, and quotes are pearls that hang on this thread. The thread may seem very humble, the pearls very flashy, but it's still the thread that makes the necklace."—Thomas Boswell, Washington Post

training a new horse for Michigan. I have to get him used to my moves and to me as a person."

"When I was born, my legs were wrapped around my neck and my brain cells couldn't get oxygen," said Simpson. "As a result, my physical coordination was affected. My speech and fine motor abilities, including the use of my hands, were impaired."

"When I was young, my family used to work with me on physical therapy five times a day. Now I only have therapy once a week, but my family continues to be supportive. They're wonderful," he said.

Besides a gold medal for equestrian excellence, Simpson also received a silver medal for dressage.

"Dressage is figure skating on a horse," he said.

12. Write a feature story based on the following facts. You may add facts as necessary, but do not change any of those given.

Several organizations at the high school have secret pals. These secret pals exchange gifts on various occasions.

"We have secret pals to promote spirit and unity," said Penelope Smith, Pom Pom sponsor. "We have to get along since we work together, but it's always good for the girls to show their support of each other by exchanging inexpensive gifts."

Pom Pom members exchange gifts twice a month. At the end of the month secret pals identify themselves, and then they select new secret pals.

The newspaper and yearbook staffs also have secret pals.

"I think having secret pals is something both staffs enjoy. It promotes camaraderie," said Bill Stutt, publications sponsor. "However, if someone forgets, it can cause hurt feelings."

➤ *Examples of Descriptive Leads*
• *Rusty wheels squeaked when John Van Matre, junior, pulled in shopping carts at the Warson Woods Schnucks, June 28.*
• *As a loud voice boomed over the intercom, Thomas Eagleton, former U.S. senator, stopped talking in mid-sentence and said, "I've never been this close to God before."*
Lecture Hall A exploded with laughter. Principal Franklin McCallie was the voice on the loudspeaker, introducing Eagleton to the student body.
• *Rumbling noises filled the room as fourth-hour history students in Mike Holley's class moved around E183. Some were in rolling chairs, but others sat in desks spread throughout the room.*

"Having secret pals is a great way for us to become better friends," said Amy Evans, Pom Pom member.

"It is basically just a fun thing we do to get us motivated," said Tim Hall, editor-in-chief of the yearbook. "We usually exchange gifts at main deadlines, holidays, and birthdays."

Carolyn Schramm, yearbook design editor, received a pair of bunny ears last month from her secret pal.

"I almost died when I saw them," said Schramm. "Actually, I've always wanted a pair, and I wore them around for the rest of the day. They're really neat." She also wore them to a dance at the Journalism Education Association's convention in Little Rock, AR, last weekend.

"I got a pair of psychedelic John Lennon-type glasses last week," said Laural MacLaren, Pom Pom member. "They're really cool. Everyone wanted to try them on."

The yearbook has been carrying on the tradition of secret pals for eight years, but the newspaper staff just started this year.

"I thought it would be nice for the newspaper to start secret pals this year," said Lisa Browman, newspaper editor, "since the yearbook staff and Pom Pom have had such great success. The first deadline we exchanged gifts and a couple of guys got dart guns. They got so carried away with them that Mr. Stuff had to confiscate them until the end of the deadline."

Typical gifts are candy bars, comic books, chewing gum, cookies, toys, and helium balloons.

Most students spend an average of $2 for a gift, but some cost as much as $10.

13. In feature writing it is important to capture the sights and sounds of an event. Practice writing

> ➢ *Examples of Suspended Interest Leads*
>
> • *Now you see it. Now you don't. This was the feeling of Kate McClocklin, junior, when two eight-year-old girls stole her wallet, containing about 200 deutsche marks (equal to about $150), during the German American Partnership Program's trip to Salzburg, Germany, June 8-9.*
>
> • *Both saw worlds far from home. Albert Salsich, English teacher, traveled to Greece during the summer, and Amy Fei, German teacher, arrived in the United States to spend one year as an exchange teacher.*
>
> • *It was a family affair. Debra Shrout, English teacher, and Steve Platte, history teacher, taught their own children in their classrooms.*

about sights and sounds by making your own lists of favorite things that impact the senses. For example, one person might include on his list of favorite sounds the following: a crackling fire on a cold winter day; a stadium crowd doing the "wave"; a baby gurgling; a distant police siren. Now make a list of your 10 favorite sounds, your 10 favorite smells, and your 10 favorite sights.

14. Description is important in writing—especially feature writing. Description is the kind of writing that has to do with the way places, people and things present themselves to the senses—the physical appearance of the world. For example, when we write "The banana is yellow," we are referring to the sense of sight. Using a banana as the object, describe it to show the sense of touch, the sense of smell, and the sense of taste. Is there a way to use a banana to describe the sense of sound? Write sentences that use all the senses to describe a car, an elderly man, a small child, a bicycle, and a baseball game.

15. Take the story you wrote for exercise 4 and role play the reader. Pretend you're reading the story for the first time. Did the lead entice you enough to make you want to keep reading? Did you discover the focus of the story quickly? As a reader, do you have any questions that the writer failed to answer? After looking at the story from the reader's viewpoint, rewrite it to make it stronger.

16. Take notes at halftime of some high school sporting event and write a sights and sounds feature, or take notes of a passing period at your school and write a sights and sounds feature. Be sure you include the names of anyone you quote. Do not make up any facts. In some of the above exercises, you were allowed to make up facts because you were writing from a fact sheet. Never make up facts when you're writing your own stories.

CHAPTER
seven

Editorial Writing

It takes only one word to create a furor. For high school newspapers that one word can sometimes create more than furor—it can create anger that could cause a disruption of the educational process. If such anger occurs, it is usually because of some opinion that the paper has voiced on its editorial pages.

The following editorial from *The Kirkwood Call*, Kirkwood High School, Kirkwood, MO, almost did disrupt the educational process. Read the editorial and find the one word that caused the problem.

Black History Segregation
Makes Course Unattractive

One of the results of the civil rights movement of the 1960s has been the encouragement of black studies programs. At Kirkwood its result was the Black History course, which was created in 1969.

It is undeniably true that the history of blacks in America has been for the most part neglected in other history courses. However, though a black history course might seem to provide a remedy for this neglect on the surface, its merit lies mostly in promoting good public relations. In many other ways, a black history course helps nothing whatever.

Presumably, the course was put into the curriculum because black history is sufficiently important to be worthy of study, by all students. In its present form, however, the course is not attractive to white students, as the continually declining involvement in it by whites shows. There is only one white enrolled in the present course.

By making the course a separate elective, the school has insured that no student need take the course, and that many students will not take it.

The very separation of the course from the rest of the social studies department is a two-fold disadvantage. First, it strips the course of much of its educational value. To overemphasize a single aspect of history distorts historical events and their significance. The course has little coherence or relation to other courses.

Also, in teaching black history to predominantly black students, the course may actually promote the racial segregation that it might appear to combat.

If black history is sufficiently important to warrant expanded study, it is important enough to be studied by everyone. A unit (or series of units) on it should be inserted in ordinary American history classes, where it could be integrated with other material. The study of black history could then be made meaningful for whites as well as blacks.

Before the editorial was published, members of the staff discussed possible repercussions. Unanimously they agreed that the editorial would be well received and that it would probably have a positive effect because more white students would be exposed to African American history. That, after all, was the staff's purpose, as it strongly thought that black history should be taught to everyone.

Within minutes after the paper's distribution, the anger became apparent. Some readers (particularly African Americans and the white teacher of the course) objected to the word "If" that begins the last paragraph. The objectors argued that "If" questioned the importance of black history, and that the single word meant *The Call* was attacking black history as a viable subject.

> *Editorial Qualities*
> • *Brevity: Keep them short—about 200-300 words.*
> • *Consequence: Let readers know what the consequences of their actions or lack of actions might be.*
> • *Relevance: Show readers how the issue is relevant to their lives.*
> • *Timeliness: The issue must be pertinent to readers now.*
> • *Forcefulness: The editorial writer must show that the stand he or she has taken is the only one by presenting facts that will convince readers.*

An immediate meeting of the Committee of 12 (composed of six white students and six black students) was called by the principal to help calm the objectors, who were beginning to be disruptive. The editor and adviser of *The Call* attended the meeting. Later that day a faculty meeting was held to discuss the situation, and that night a meeting of concerned parents was held. The series of meetings calmed the situation, allowing the editor and adviser to be convincing as to the editorial's intent. Even so, many of the objectors thought *The Call* should not have run an editorial on the topic at all because it was too sensitive. Several letters to the editor on the subject appeared in the next issue. Even though the editorial created anger, it also did some good. The social studies department met and decided to add a unit on black history to all regular American history courses. Thus, all students would be exposed to some African American history even if they did not take the black history course.

Sensitive issues such as this one should be covered in high school newspapers and yearbooks. Publications do have the right to voice an editorial opinion on anything that is sensitive or controversial. However, editorial writers should choose their words carefully. If the writer of the above editorial had used the word "Since" instead of "If," the uproar probably would not have developed.

It is important for editorial writers to choose words carefully so they do not offend readers unnecessarily. That does not mean that editorials should not offend. When anyone states a critical opinion of someone or something, it is likely to offend. Just be sure that you have researched the editorial so well that the facts support your opinion solidly.

Research is a key factor in editorial writing. Many high school writers simply compose editorials off the top of their head, stating opinions and labeling something good or bad without bothering to get the facts to validate their opinions.

Since most editorials should be based on news stories, the news stories themselves will provide some of the research necessary for the writer. If there is a major weakness in high school editorial pages, it is that few editorials are based on

Editorial

Auditorium needs renovation

Safety hazards and seating problems make the auditorium's long-overdue renovation a priority.

Presently in a woeful state of disrepair, the auditorium curtains and seats have been vandalized, the door to the boys' dressing room is broken and the stage is unstable, making an unsafe environment for performers. This week district workmen were sent to the site to look at the problems, deeming everything but the outdated light system worthy of repairs. The district has allotted a budget for the repairs. This is a promising sign, but the changes need to be made.

The auditorium is the only place on campus where up to one sixth of the student body can gather to watch talented students perform. However, the broken seats reduce its capacity, the poor lighting and vandalized curtains decrease the appeal of the performance and the unstable stage may make it dangerous to perform. These problems do not make it worthwhile for the student body to meet or for clubs to make presentations.

Schurr has previously hosted many important events, such as Jazz at Schurr and various cultural performances. No one will want to perform at Schurr if the auditorium is not cleaned and repaired. Prestigious events deserve an auditorium that is kept in optimal condition. The school cannot expect professional performers to be willing to work in an unsafe environment

Although the district plans to fix many of the problems, the lighting system needs to be replaced as well. Even with a better facility, a poor lighting system will prevent the students from creating truly high quality productions and making important presentations.

It has been hard to maintain a school with so few funds are available. However, the district should follow through on plans to renovate the auditorium so that it can once again showcase the talented students.

The above editorial from the Spartan Scroll, *Schurr High School, Montebello, CA, is based on a front-page news story on the same topic. All papers should try to have at least one editorial in each issue based on a front-page story. This editorial makes its stand in the first paragraph and provides good background to support the stand in the body of the article.*

news stories, and those that are lack proper research. Too many editorials are on such trite topics as the lack of school spirit, the quality of cafeteria food, or the ineffectiveness of the Student Council.

For an editorial page to be vital, it must deal with timely topics, and those timely topics are the news stories that appear in each issue.

Besides use of the news story, research can take other forms, especially if the topic is a national one such as selective service registration or school prayer.

Use the library. *The Reader's Guide,* the *New York Times Index,* and *Research Reports* are three sources for general, and sometimes specific, background information on a subject.

The more you know about the subject, the easier it is to ask intelligent and relevant questions and the easier it is to form an opinion on the subject, including a solution if one is required.

Newspapers are another source of information. They often have news or feature stories that may be relevant to the topic or contain statistics that would help to support a viewpoint.

Although newspapers try to be accurate, because of time pressure they sometimes contain errors, so double-check all facts with another source, if possible.

People are another source. An expert on a subject or some-one involved with a subject is usually glad to talk about it. Learning everything you can about the subject before an inter-view enhances your chances of getting the information you need.

After research is complete, the writer should analyze carefully the information she has gathered. At this point, she may decide not to continue because of her inability to pro-duce a solid stand. A weakness of some editorial writers is that they approach a topic with a preconceived idea of what is right and wrong. Although it is difficult, a good editorial writer does the research and then decides what stand to take.

Following the research, a writer should take time to think about her topic and answer some questions: (1) What can I accomplish with this editorial? (2) Will the topic interest read-ers? (3) If needed, is there a solution? (4) Do I have all the facts? (5) Will publishing this editorial promote the interests of the school (even a negative viewpoint can have a positive effect)? If all those questions can be answered positively, it is time to write the editorial.

An editorial has three main parts. First comes the lead, which is a statement of opinion or the position of the editorial. The first paragraph should immediately give the paper's stand. Editorials should be the opinion of the paper, not of the writer. Some schools have all staff members vote on editorials, with the majority ruling. Others use editorial boards composed of key staff members and sometimes persons off the staff, to decide whether an editorial should be printed. If an individual staff member wants to state an opinion, she should do so in an edi-torial column. Columns are discussed in Chapter 8.

Some editorial writers have difficulty placing the stand of the paper in the lead. Instead they bury it in the conclusion. Analyze the following leads for the stand of each, if one is stated.

➢ *Influencing Readers*
  • Create an open forum.
  • Use non-bylined editorials that are the opinion of the majority of the staff.
  • Use editorials submitted by readers.
  • Use editorials submitted by experts on the issue.
  • Use columns.
  • Use surveys.
  • Use cartoons.
  • Use reviews of books, movies, plays, games, albums, restaurants.
  • Use letters to the editor.

A. Although in many minds August signifies summer, the district and administration made a wise decision in starting school Aug. 31.

B. School organizations that make large mailings can save money by using the district's bulk mailing permit, but apparently several groups are not aware that the permit is available for their use.

C. Scheduling difficulties during registration caused many problems for students, but with the patient help of Assistant Principal Michael Eldridge, the administrator in charge of scheduling, most of the problems disappeared quickly.

D. Lack of organization and poor planning led to the failure of the Girls' Pep Club Big Sister Program.

E. Lack of a definite procedure for electing Student Council representatives caused confusion among the SC officers, club leaders, and teachers. The Council needs to write a set of explicit election guidelines.

It should be apparent that of the five leads only Lead B lacks a specific stand. Lead A's stand is that the administration made a wise decision. Lead C's stand is that the assistant principal helped alleviate problems. Lead D's stand is that Pep Club's program failed because of poor organization and poor planning, and Lead E's stand is that the Council needs a set of written guidelines. Lead B indicates that there is a problem, but it fails to take a stand by expressing a viewpoint about who should inform the organizations of their mailing privileges. A second sentence is necessary, perhaps one like the following:

> The business office should call a meeting of all club presidents, and business personnel should explain mailing privileges.

The second part of an editorial is the body. This is where the writer presents the facts to support the stand.

The conclusion, a summation of the importance of the issue, wraps up the editorial. If it is a critical editorial, it should offer suggestions on how to improve or correct the problem.

Despite popular opinion, the purpose of an editorial is not always to criticize. It can teach, attack, defend, recommend, question, prod, interpret, entertain, advocate, expose, supplement news, increase awareness, explain, argue, commend, commemorate, or praise. The approach, the stand, and the purpose of the editorial determine into which category it falls.

The more common types of editorials found in high school newspapers are the following:

1. **Criticism.** An editorial of criticism must offer a solution. It does no good to criticize if there is no apparent solution. Point out the weaknesses and errors of the situation, and then make suggestions for possible changes.

2. **Praise.** This type of editorial obviously points out the merits of an idea or the superior qualities of a person. Papers should strive for a balance between praise and criticism in editorials. Praise can also include advocating proposals of others or even endorsing someone else's viewpoint.

3. **Moralizing.** Moralizing editorials exhort readers to adopt higher standards of conduct or to develop a better attitude. They often deal with trite topics and do little good because they tend to be preachy.

4. **Interpretation.** The main purpose of an interpretive editorial is to explain why something occurred. It is intended to inform; thus it usually contains less opinion than others.

5. **Entertainment.** Such an editorial is a change of pace. It may take a serious subject and develop it in a lighthearted way in order to avoid

> **Selecting Editorial Topics**
> • Base at least one editorial on a front-page news story.
> • Select topics of interest to teenagers.
> • Localize all topics to show how they affect students.
> • Use local, state, national, and international issues for editorials.

Policy augments stress

Note how the Orange & Black staff at Grand Junction High School, Grand Junction, CO, draws attention to the fact that the above editorial has a news story as its basis.

Divorce not an easy situation

No matter what the circumstances surrounding divorce, all have an effect on children involved.

This effect may be academic, social, financial or emotional, and depends on many variables. It varies upon an individual's personality, family situation and ability to handle stressful situations.

Divorce can affect teenagers' relationships. Teens could become less trusting, defensive, antisocial and withdrawn.

Teenagers whose parents are divorced suffer from up to three times the number of emotional and behavioral problems compared to those live with both biological parents, according to Healthy Kids website.

Both school nurse Kris Purdy and school psychologist Ralph Pajka said talking about feelings a divorce could bring can help. Pajka said nearly half the families in Lakewood have to deal with divorce, and students should not face that alone. However, teens need to remember divorce is not their fault.

It helps to talk about divorce-related feelings, Purdy and Pajka said. While talking about these feelings may presently help teens to deal with the problem, it does not rid them of future problems related to the divorce.

Parents should do their part in helping the transition. They should listen to their child, without placing blame, and make sure the child knows what is happening.

If the parents are having problems dealing with the divorce, the children are likely to as well.

Divorce is never an easy situation, nor is it always a negative one.

Sometimes, divorce can make family relationships stronger because it lessens the tension between family members by separating the conflicting members.

Talking to parents is not the only option. There are youth groups, counselors and religious organizations that may help too.

Divorce is a serious life change and there are ways to get through its effects.

Our viewpoint times editorial

Consumers need to be aware of genetic engineering and its implications

With all the surrounding issues and diverse beliefs about genetically engineered food, it will be a long debate before a resolution is reached.

Some argue corporations promoting genetically engineered foods are sincerely trying to reduce famine and chemical use.

On the other side, some believe these products are being released too quickly into the environment without adequate testing in the pursuit of quick profits. They argue the public is being used a guinea pigs for the testing of these products.

Some are upset that these products are not being held for further testing and say that no production will be held until a health or ecological catastrophe strikes.

These opponents also raise serious question of responsibility for damaged wildlife or health hazards:
• Who is responsible: companies, government regulatory agencies or watchdog groups?
• What if hundreds of thousands of acres of crop land are unusable because an unforeseen toxic cross pollination of or excretion of genetically engineered plants
• What if human health is damaged by these products?

The point is, although most acknowledge you are what you eat, many are hardly aware of the foods we use to build our brains and bodies.

Perhaps the question consumers should consider is should we have to be aware of everything in our food or should those who grow make and sell them be truly responsible for our safety.

The European reaction has been outrage over the idea life itself may be patented and sold. Crops rejected by Europeans are put into American food by companies selling to both because although some American are protesting, the outcry here is not nearly as loud as it is there.

One current idea is to demand labels, so consumers know what they may be eating or what to avoid.

Simply labeling products could cause more confusion because longer and more complex labeling might be more than many people want to take the time to comprehend.

If such generic things like soybeans are genetically engineered, the majority of processed foods you buy will also be. Few know what the effects of processed food are now, and few will take the time to investigate further.

Public awareness is increasing in the United States, but consumers will, in the end, eat what they pay attention to.

Staff editorials do not need bylines, as they should be the opinion of the majority of the staff, not the opinion of one writer. The above editorials are from the Lakewood Times, *Lakewood High School, Lakewood, OH. The newspaper carried in-depth articles on divorce and genetic engineering on other pages in the same issue.*

preachiness. It has a serious point to make, but it does so in a subtle manner.

6. ***Photo editorial.*** One or more self-explanatory pictures might comprise a photo editorial. For example, a picture of a car parked in a no-parking zone, accompanied by a caption, would suffice as a photo editorial. Photo editorials can brighten up an editorial page. Use them selectively, however.

7. **Ten-second editorials.** These may be of any of the above types, but they are designed to be read in about 10 seconds. They have only one brief point to make, and their brevity makes them more readable than longer editorials. Some newspapers have devised descriptive names for their 10-second editorials and grouped them according to praise or criticism. One paper calls them "Pluses and Minuses," another uses "Call Ups and Call Downs."

8. **Sustained editorials.** If a staff feels strongly about an issue, it should not stop at one editorial if nothing happens. For example, if you write an editorial calling for changes to be made in parking regulations, and nothing happens, write the editorial again. Always try to change your approach and come up with additional information. A staff may continue to write editorials on the topic until something is done. This may mean continuing the campaign over more than one year.

9. **Appeal.** This type of editorial appeals to readers for support. It might be support for a tax levy, or a charitable drive, or a particular teacher or learning style. The body of the story would supply facts explaining why readers should give support.

10. **Endorsement.** This type of editorial endorses an idea, a concept, or a person. You might endorse a candidate for office, for example, or a concept such as a seven-hour school day.

11. **Historical perspective.** To put things in historical perspective, the writer must go back in time. He might trace the history of dress codes at school, for example, and then make suggestions concerning the present code.

12. **Prediction.** This is an uncommon type of editorial because it is imprecise. The lead will

> **Other Types of Editorials**
> • Editorial of explanation: Explains what happened, why it happened, and why it is important. It may or may not deal with a controversial issue.
> • Editorial of argumentation: Attempts to persuade readers to adopt a particular viewpoint about an issue, a legislative bill, a tax levy, or a candidate for office. This type of editorial would support or refute a suggestion or an action by a group or an individual. Writers must have solid evidence explaining why their views are valid.
> • Editorial of commemoration: Reminds readers it is time to participate in a celebration of some type, perhaps an anniversary of the school or a specific week, such as National Newspaper Week.

suggest possible consequences if things don't change. The body and conclusion need to offer suggestions for change. For example, the writer might predict that declining enrollment will force the elimination of some classes. A suggestion might be to alternate some courses every other year to preserve them.

A weakness of many editorial staffs is a failure to follow through. If an editorial of criticism offers a solution, but no one takes action to change the situation, the paper should conduct an editorial campaign if it thinks changes are needed for improvement of the school. In other words, the writer should do more research and restate the editorial stand in another issue. Staffs should not drop an issue if they think it is vital. One school carried on an editorial campaign for five years. The staffs over that period of time all thought the school should start a National Honor Society, but the administration failed to take action. Each staff did further research and wrote new editorials. Finally the administration was persuaded.

An editorial is similar to an essay. It has a thesis, facts to back up the thesis, and a conclusion. Keep that in mind when you sit down to write, along with the following guidelines:

1. Make the editorial lively. Spice it up. Find new ways to say things, but don't be flippant or condescending.
2. Be concise, but don't leave out facts. An effective editorial seldom exceeds 300 words in length. Long editorials are not likely to be read in their entirety or at all. Don't be verbose.
3. Write in the third person, except that it is permissible to use the first person *(We)* when referring to the newspaper. Second person *(you)* tends to be preachy, and first person *(I)* means the editorial is the opinion of the writer, not the paper.
4. Cite sources. This gives credibility to the stand.

> ➢ *The "We" Editorial*
> • *Use* we *or* us *when referring to the newspaper staff. Avoid using first person* I, me, *or* our. *Editorials should be the opinion of the majority of the staff—not the opinion of one person.*

However, do not use direct quotes unless the editorial is based on something someone said. The viewpoint should be the paper's, not someone else's.

5. Be objective and fair. Try to see all sides of a situation.

6. Do not write when you are angry. Emotion will cloud your thinking, and it will be harder to present your ideas clearly and logically.

7. Localize national issues. How do issues such as school prayer or minimum wage affect your readers?

8. Criticize policies rather than the person who makes the policies.

9. If you can't make a constructive suggestion, don't criticize.

10. Don't preach. Instead, be persuasive.

11. Offer praise if the situation calls for it.

12. Don't expect miracles. It takes time for action. However, don't back down if you think the issue is important.

13. Keep the writing style simple, but don't write down to your readers.

14. Choose timely topics.

15. Try cartoons to help illustrate a viewpoint. Sometimes a cartoon can stand alone.

16. Make sure the editorial opens with a powerful statement and closes with a general purpose.

17. Don't vacillate. Stick to a single theme to avoid losing the reader.

18. The editorial writer must be *aware, concerned,* and *sensitive.* To be able to come up with a good topic, the editorial writer must be aware of what is happening in the world around her. There is no reason why editorials should be limited to school issues. Any local, state, national, or international issue that pertains to the school's readers is a possible topic. The

➢ *Editorial Checklist*
• *Is the topic interesting to student readers?*
• *Is the stand clear?*
• *Are there facts to support the stand?*
• *Will the headline attract attention?*
• *Is the purpose of the editorial clear?*
• *Does the editorial avoid verbosity?*
• *Is it written in third person?*
• *Is it under 300 words?*

writer must be concerned enough about the issue to be willing to dig out the facts to support an opinion and to be able to present an argument clearly. The writer must also be sensitive to the readers' feelings—why someone might feel strongly about an issue. Always keep the audience in mind.

Editorials are the voice of the newspaper. A paper can freely express its own opinion about any subject it may choose to tackle. Because that opinion reaches a large number of people, the paper can attempt to persuade others to adopt its viewpoint.

With that privilege, however, comes much responsibility: The paper must assure that the argument or opinion is sound, practical, and most important, based on fact. An editorial lacks credibility if it cannot be supported by facts. Do your research and you will have a viable editorial page.

Before writing the editorial, be sure you have planned the topic completely. Use the following form:

Editorial Self-Critique

Editorial Topic _____

Type of Editorial _____

In one sentence, tell what you are trying to say in this editorial. _____

What points will the body of the editorial contain?

1. _____
2. _____
3. _____

How do you plan to conclude this editorial? Will you urge action? If so, what? _____

List written and oral sources below. These are the sources you use to gather facts to support your stand. You should have at least three.

1. _____
2. _____
3. _____

> **Editorial Boards**
> • Consider creating an editorial board to determine editorial content.
> • Editorial boards could be made up of key staff members, the adviser, other teachers, student leaders, administrators, and a few parents. It would probably be best to keep the board under 10 members to enhance communication.
> • Decisions of the editorial board should be binding regarding whether the staff takes a pro or con stance on an issue.
> • The editorial board should determine the newspaper's purpose.
> • The editorial board should set the goals of the publication.
> • The editorial board could decide on editorial campaigns for the publication.

EXERCISES

1. Write leads only, based on the following sets of facts.

A. Administration will change its three lunch shifts to two.

Each lunch shift will be shortened by five minutes, and five minutes will be added to each period of the day.

Present three lunch shifts are 35 minutes each. The new ones will be 30 minutes.

May cause problems for seniors who leave campus for open lunch.

Will give students more academic experiences with longer class periods.

B. Council forms Beautification Committee.

Students on committee plan to hold special days to beautify campus.

Smoking area particularly is a mess.

Some say smoking area will look like a pigpen again days after Council members beautify it.

Council wants students to be proud of their campus.

C. Freshman cheerleaders have to provide own transportation to away games.

B-Team cheerleaders get to ride team bus. Freshman coach won't let freshman cheerleaders ride team bus because he's afraid of discipline problems. Freshman cheerleading sponsor required to attend away games, but she doesn't.

Freshman coach says he might consider letting cheerleaders ride bus if sponsor were along.

Parents object to having to travel up to

Teen curfew: the pros and cons

The Pros

By Andrew Nicolaou
Staff Writer

With the recent approval of the much vaunted curfew by the El Paso City Council, talk about it has flourished as people have tried constantly to decipher what the new law means. Speculation has ranged from possible civil right violations to plans on how to thwart the new ordinance which forbids young people under the age of 16 to be out on the streets after 11p.m. Most discussions have carried with them a negative undertone, but it should be made known that the curfew could very easily bring with it some positive ramifications.

In El Paso, gang violence is becoming a more and more serious problem. The El Paso Police Department has open files on more than 200 gangs with the number steadily increasing and it shows no signs of leveling out or decreasing anytime in the near future. Many Coronadoans are oblivious to this blight on our city, and one wonders if it will take a Jerry Sanchez-like incident among the student body to impress the gravity of the situation upon them. Sanchez, a model Irvin High School student not affiliated with gangs, was killed in a drive-by shooting while leaving a party several weeks ago. Also of importance is the fact that half the crimes committed in El Paso are perpetrated by minors, and most of those crimes occur during the nighttime hours.

With a problem of this magnitude, it is easy to see how El Paso Police and the City Council are desperate for solutions to this dilemma. They may have found something of an answer in the resurrected curfew.

The main complaint many people have about the curfew is that it violates rights that are guaranteed to United States Citizens in the Constitution. However many of the people who are voicing this complaint are unaware of the exemptions, which leave only rape, murder, and theft as unacceptable activities for young people. In reality, anybody under the legal curfew age who is stopped by a policeman and can provide a reasonable explanation as to why they are out past 11p.m. will be given a "Thank you" and sent on their merry way.

Coronado Principal Burl Whatley says that the curfew was "put in place to enforce a parent's responsibility about where their children are, but not by limiting young people's rights as individuals."

Some people may think that this then renders the whole idea impractical. What the curfew does do is allow officers of the law to stop the people under 16 who appear to be doing nothing other than cruising or wandering aimlessly. They can then stop and question those people, something that they previously would not have been able to do unless some minor infraction of the law such as jaywalking or a broken taillight had occurred. From there the police have reasonable cause and can inspect the people in question for drugs, guns, and the other items that so often fall hand in hand with gang membership.

The curfew may not in fact be the best thing that El Paso could do about the gang violence problem, but when looked at in context with bans of athletic headwear and such, it doesn't seem that foolish at all. This new ordinance will not rearrange people's lives; most people will in fact see little or no change in their lives and schedules because of it. Is that really too much to ask for, or do we need another Jerry Sanchez to persuade us?

The Cons

By Liza Torres
Co-Editor In Chief

Although members of the El Paso City Council mean well, the new curfew law just passed does not even begin to address the problem of youth violence in El Paso. The law passed states that anyone under 16 in a public place within city limits after 11 p.m. will be picked up by police and fined $500.

Sounds like a good idea, but this is not the way to go about it. If city council wants to prevent teenagers from committing crimes they need to get tough.

This curfew is a violation of every teenagers rights, rights that as American citizens every person should have. Also, the curfew punishes everyone for the unruly acts of the few. What happened to innocent until proven guilty?

The council should not insist on bringing teens in because it will just make them want to stay out. Besides there are only about 800 police officers for the over 600,000 residents of El Paso. How can they be expected to keep an eye on adult criminals and make sure that all the "little kids" are tucked in at night?

Moreover, the curfew includes several loopholes which teens will surely fall through. One in particular states that the teen on an errand in direct route with written permission from the parent with a brief description of the errand and the teens name will not be fined.

All in all, the curfew does nothing for the police and a lot for teens's sense of humor.

Although it is not always desirable, sometimes presenting a pro and con editorial on the same topic is acceptable. The above editorial columns are from the Explorer, Coronado High School, El Paso, TX. *Since they are bylined, they are the opinions of the writers, not of the staff.*

        30 miles away.

D.   Some teachers not reading daily bulletin. Some students never hear announcements of important activities. Administration not enforcing its rule that teachers read bulletin daily.

Teachers think it wastes too much classtime.

E. Administration sets Wednesday after school, 2:30-3 p.m., as club meeting day. On other days this time is used by teachers to work with students who need extra help or need to make up tests.

Clubs were having a difficult time getting members to attend meetings because they were meeting with teachers. Clubs tried to wait until 3 p.m. to hold meetings, but discovered by that time many members had already left or had to catch the 3:15 p.m. bus.

Therefore, administration compromised and let clubs meet on Wednesdays at 2:30 and asked teachers to have students come in the other four days as needed.

This still poses a problem for students who are members of more than one club.

F. Students lacking in health knowledge.

No class is required, although students do have to take 1 1/2 units of physical education.

School board has suggested that half of the physical education requirement might be a required health course.

2. Clip five editorials from your daily professional newspaper, and clip the news stories on which the editorials are based. The news stories may have appeared in the paper a day or more before the editorial. List the editorial stand and tell why you agree or disagree with it.

3. Clip an editorial from a recent issue of your school paper. Analyze its strengths and weaknesses. Then rewrite it based on new research.

4. Select a news story from the most recent issue of your school paper and write an editorial based on it.

➢ *Making Editorial Decisions*

• *Reach decisions after group discussion.*

• *Have one person write the editorial based on the group's decision.*

• *Read the finished editorial to the entire staff in order to get suggestions for improvement.*

• *Be sure that a majority of the staff approves the editorial's content.*

More sex education needed to protect students' lives

When Magic Johnson announced that he had contracted the AIDS virus, the media eagerly rose to the occasion with a flurry of AIDS facts and statistics.

But once the shock disappears and the hype dies away, students must fall back on the school's minimal sex education offerings to learn about AIDS and other sexually-transmitted diseases.

Currently, the school teaches sex education in Science 1, Biology and Physiology, a system that benefits all students who happen to attend those classes. Students enrolled in other science courses, however, do not have the opportunity to review facts that may mean the difference between life or death.

After all, unlike many other illnesses, once a student contracts the AIDS virus or ignores an STD too long, no doctor can save him.

Students run the risk of joining the estimated 1.5 million Americans who now test HIV-positive. They risk coming down with the painful symptoms of AIDS and devastating their lives prematurely.

To prevent such grief, the school must emphasize sex education in the new science curriculum being developed. More time and effort on the issue of STDs would help students understand the consequences of unsafe sex.

Education about sex must also expand into classes that normally do not teach biology-related topics.

By drilling the same information into students each year, the school can then be sure it has done all it could to prevent the spread of STDs among its teen-agers.

After all, to make education effective, students must also have a future to enjoy what they learned. Knowing what can harm them will help them keep that future.

Class competitions build class spirit, school unity

Now, there's more to lunch than processed cafeteria food.

As the Associated Student Body coordinates class competitions every Friday, students have more to look forward to than choosing what kind of burrito to eat.

Unlike last year, with its skimpy collection of competitions, this year has presented a favorable selection of class activities which offer entertainment and promote student involvement.

With students cheering on their class members, the weekly activities foster class spirit and friendly class rivalry.

But also, by granting students opportunities to interact with one another, the competitions draw classes closer together, building school unity.

Class competitions, which try to create an enjoyable place to eat lunch according to ASB officers, give students incentive to stay on campus, possibly a safer way to spend the lunch period.

In addition to class competitions, ASB has revived music in the quad on Fridays. Although it has failed to be consistent in past years, it further proves that ASB officers have attempted another commendable effort to produce a positive lunchtime environment.

Nevertheless, we find that class competitions and music in the quad remain two of the few aspects of ASB's undertakings worthy of praise.

With those activities established, ASB may be ready to further the campus in other ways. If it uses the same energy required to develop the weekly class competitions, ASB has a good chance at proving successful.

Editorials should be set in the same point size and the same width in each issue of the paper so the reader can quickly identify them. The two above are from the Epitaph, *Cupertino High School, Homestead, CA. Note how the one on top localizes a national story. All stories based on international, national, or state events should be localized.*

5. Take the five editorials you clipped for Exercise 2 and label them according to type. Then find five more editorials from exchange papers and label them.

6. Go through all the issues of your school paper from this year or last year. Count the number of critical editorials and also of praise editorials. Are they about equal in number? If not, think of ways the paper can obtain a better balance.

7. Take one of the following national topics and localize it into an editorial for your school paper: school prayer, reducing minimum wage for teenagers, importance placed on standardized tests, minimum drinking age, higher insurance rates for teenage drivers, registering for selective service, teenage pregnancy, substance abuse programs.

8. Make a list of 10 ideas for editorials for your school newspaper. Do the research needed for two of the ideas, and write the editorials. Read the editorials aloud in class and find out if your classmates agree or disagree with your stand.

9. Write an editorial based on the following news story:

Foreseeing that some would skip classes to get a head start on spring vacation, the administration announced April 5 (one week prior to spring break) that those absent the day before spring break would pay a penalty of no make-up work in classes and an after-school detention for an unexcused absence.

"Since the beginning of the year, I have emphasized to students and parents the importance of being in class the day before break," said Principal Franklin McCallie.

"Students absent before spring break have always been a problem in the district," McCallie continued. "The superintendent asked me to work on this when I came to the district four years ago. We have worked on it, and 186 were absent that

> *Avoid Preachiness*
> • *Instead of telling readers they should do something, write the editorial so readers can form their own opinions about taking action.*
> • *Use specific examples of how people act appropriately rather than telling people they have not acted appropriately.*
> • *Avoid editorials about lack of school spirit, about sportsmanship, about failure to do homework, and about morals. If you write editorials on those topics, you must find a new angle and avoid preachiness.*

day this year, compared to 147 last year."

With consistently high absenteeism the day before break, teachers often cannot conduct regular classes.

McCallie, however, asked teachers to prepare a regular lesson plan and carry through with it.

"I am in the process of having the attendance rule put into the student handbook, with the hope of further improving attendance statistics," McCallie said.

However, many students disagree with McCallie's policy.

"I don't see why they are making this such a big issue," said Mike Burns, senior. "Kids are always being pulled out of classes for trips during the year and that's excused, but they treat this differently."

"The reason I skipped school that day was just to get a head start on my vacation, and to get away from it all," said one senior boy. "They will never stop that."

Your editorial will appear in the newspaper after spring break. An additional fact you have at that time is that only 70 students were absent from school the day before spring break, whereas one year ago 223 were absent. Two days before spring break two years ago, 41 were absent, and two days before spring break this year 38 were absent. Twenty of those absent this year had simply added another day to their spring break; the other 18 were ill. Two years ago, 33 had added another day and eight were ill.

10. Write an editorial either supporting or rejecting the idea of establishing a nationwide exam for high school graduation. You may use the following information from *Time* magazine for your editorial, but you should do some research of your own.

46 million students from kindergarten through high school are subjected to more than

---

> ➢ *Five-Paragraph Essay*
> *Think of your editorial as a five-paragraph essay that you would write in English classes. Five paragraphs is a good length for editorials.*
> • *Put your thesis statement in the lead.*
> • *Use the second, third, and fourth paragraphs for the facts that support your thesis.*
> • *Use the fifth paragraph to restate your thesis in different words.*

150 million standardized tests each year. Only 5% of high school seniors are deemed able to pursue higher mathematical study. The current administration has proposed a national system of exams called the American Achievement Tests. Tests would be taken voluntarily by students across the country in the fourth, eighth, and twelfth grades, yielding uniform yardsticks of performance. The tests would document students' knowledge in math, science, English, history, and geography. White House officials have asked Congress for $12.4 million to start work on developing the exams and the standards that would go with them. Proponents argue that the exams would provide a uniform means for parents to judge a school's performance and compare it with those of other schools in the neighborhood and across the nation. If unhappy with a school, parents could take their child to another. Thus the exams could be used to implement a "school choice" program. They would also be used by college admissions officers and employers. National tests are now being used in Great Britain and Japan. The main argument against the tests is that there is no necessary link between such exercises and better education. Opponents also fear a risk of bias against minority and female students, and they say there is too much testing already and that it would be too expensive.

11. Analyze the following editorial's effectiveness. Does it have a good lead, facts to support the lead, and a good conclusion? What type of editorial is it?

Avilla schools have been receiving rave reviews lately.

But it's going to take money to keep the long-running show a hit.

Nationally, the high school's journalism department has been honored with awards for its newspaper and yearbook.

A comparative guidebook of public schools throughout the country rates Avilla high.

And the majority of local folks—the people who are most important—said in a recent survey that the district is doing an excellent or good job.

District officials are asking for a 38-cent increase to keep doing that job. They've been able to make a 1989 increase last twice as long as projected, but now they're having to borrow from the reserves.

Unlike the federal government, the district can't afford to deficit-spend very long.

The increase requested would allow the district to balance its budget, hire more teachers to handle enrollment growth, start a few new programs, and generally maintain the quality for which the district has been praised.

The price tag requested seems reasonable. Voters need to take this as their cue to vote "yes" on the tax increase.

12. Write an editorial based on the following National Safe-Driving campaign issued by AAA, formerly the American Automobile Association. Do additional research on the topic.

The AAA wants states, parents, and educators to demand more behind-the-wheel training and greater restrictions on licenses for beginners because it claims a teenager is killed every 84 minutes in a traffic accident. It also said 6,300 drivers and passengers ages 15–20 died in traffic crashes last year. In addition it claims that teens count for seven percent of all drivers, but they were involved in 14 percent of the 37,221 fatal crashes two years ago and in 20 percent of the 6.6 million total crashes last year.

The AAA calls its campaign "Licensed to Learn."

➢ *Photo Editorials*

• *Photo editorials should stand alone without the need of a story.*

• *Photo editorials should be self-explanatory, but captions should still be used.*

• *A series of pictures may be used, or just one picture.*

The AAA says that most teen accidents are caused by inexperience, poor driving skills, risk-taking, and poor decision-making. It also says that studies have shown that the risk of having an accident declines sharply after three to four years of experience behind the wheel.

Therefore, AAA is calling for graduated licensing programs in all 50 states. Its three-stage program calls for 16-year-olds to be limited to daytime driving and to require them to take a basic driver education course. A parent or adult over 21 would be required to do some of the training. After six months without an accident or traffic violation, the teen could get an intermediate license after passing a road test. An advanced driver education course would be required, again with some parental participation. A full, unrestricted license could be obtained at age eighteen if the teen had completed at least 12 months on an intermediate license with no accidents or convictions.

Twenty states already have a version of the graduated licensing program. Michigan, for example, requires at least 50 hours of supervised training before a teen can drive alone.

13. Write an editorial supporting or attacking controversial music lyrics. Be sure to do research. Do not write off the top of your head.

14. Write an editorial supporting or opposing the right of a citizen to burn the American flag in protest. Be sure to do research. Do not write off the top of your head.

15. Write a five-paragraph essay on the benefits of block scheduling. You may take the pro side and be in favor of block scheduling, or you may be opposed. Do research. Your first paragraph should state your stand. The next three para-

graphs should include the facts to support your stand, and the fifth paragraph should restate your stand in different words. Writing all your editorials as five-paragraph essays will produce effective editorials, as each requires you to have three facts to support your stand.

16. Write a prediction editorial about how you think the shifts in population might affect your school in the future. Predictions indicate that the current minority races might outnumber caucasians by 2050. Put your editorial in the form of a five-paragraph essay.

17. Write a five-paragraph essay on the benefits of filtering information students may obtain on the Internet. You may take a stand in favor of filtering, or you may take a stand against it. Before writing your paper, do research to find out how other schools and libraries have run into problems or how they have not run into any problems concerning filtering.

18. Now take the five-paragraph essays you have written for 15-17 and expand them to seven-paragraph essays by adding two more facts supporting your viewpoints. Analyze your editorials. Are they better because you added two additional paragraphs? Are they too wordy?

19. Draw three cartoons to illustrate the three editorials you wrote for exercises 16-18.

20. Sidebars or quick reads may also accompany editorials. Based on the research you compiled for the editorials you wrote for 16-18, compile a fact box for each.

21. Now write an editorial on a topic of your choice. Be sure to choose a topic students will be interested in. If you choose a state, national or international issue, be sure to localize it to show how the issue affects your readers.

CHAPTER
eight

Column Writing

To become a successful columnist, one should read the work of successful columnists, including William Safire, Jack Anderson, Nora Ephron, Molly Ivins, Bob Greene, Carl Rowan, Art Buchwald, and Dave Barry. These writers have become so successful that their columns are syndicated in most papers across the United States. At the time of her death, Erma Bombeck had seen many of her popular columns collected and published in book form.

Daily papers also have local columnists who have become favorites among readers in their communities. Column-writing skills are not perfected overnight. Some types of columns, such as humor columns, require certain talents that probably cannot be taught but can be polished through practice. Good columnists at both professional and high school levels are hard to find.

Good column writers must like people. They must be able to see ordinary events with unusual perspectives. They must enjoy doing eventful things. They must be willing to experiment, and they must be curious.

Most columnists write *about* people or write *to* people. A column writer puts forth observations on life, shares emotions, provides an outlet for ideas, and entertains by providing an uplift or evoking a smile or a laugh. He or she sometimes produces tears, also.

Hal Boyle, who for several years was a columnist for the Associated Press, wrote the following about what it is like to write a column:

Columnist: 'Think before you rock 'n roll'

A few days ago I walked into Best Buy to purchase a new compact disc. I wandered around the Jazz section until something I had been looking for caught my eye. I picked it up and, with a little time left on my hands, wandered around the store.

Past the computers, stereos and phones I went, until two large racks in the center of the store obstructed me from going any further. These racks contained what has become one of the most commercially successful items in the history of our country: Grateful Dead Merchandise.

I was disgusted. What was once a band focused entirely on music and an environment conducive to rejecting modern day values has become as commonplace among Americans as the dollar bill. Everywhere I go there are Steal Your Face, (skull with lightning in it), Dancing Bears, and the band's name on cars, backpacks, folders, etc. Sadly, the band made a conscious decision to do this, broadening their spectrum of listeners, thereby creating many problems for themselves.

The last year of the Grateful Dead's touring career came in the summer of 1995. At Deer Creek, a popular concert attraction in Noblesville, Indiana, people with no respect for the community crashed gates, threw themselves around in a drunken stupor and forced the band to cancel the next evening's show. The cause of this "tour from hell" comes from the section of the audience there only because they think

of it as a traveling party.

Because of the tragic ending to one of the greatest bands in history, I have written this column to request something. Another band out there, called Phish, will be at the Omaha Civic Auditorium Nov. 16, and there are a few things that need to be brought to attention. The scene is much like the Grateful Dead in that it is mostly neo-hippies with an urge to follow the band to all its concert locations. Phish also embarks upon extended improvisational "jams" with little framework involved. Although the music is quite different, the similarities in the scene are still there. And this, folks, is why it scares me.

Phish has attained enormous success from bootleg tape trading, word of mouth and touring. They produced four albums without ever having a radio single or a video on MTV. When they finally agreed to produce their own video, the band hated it and vowed never to do it again. So, naturally it angers me when I see people with no respect for the music or the band attending their shows.

This summer I attended two Phish shows at the Red Rocks Amphitheater in Morrison, Co. A favorite place for Phish to play, the band agreed to do something about the increasing problem of ticketless fans. With all the measures they took, a clash still occurred between fans and the police because some idiot, who obviously thought a Phish show was just another party, threw a bottle at a police officer. This

Chris Nilsson

The Village Idiot

sparked what the newspapers were calling a riot and precluded Phish from ever playing at Red Rocks again.

I offer some advice to all Westside students who are considering attending the show. The people who follow Phish need tickets. I don't condone the lifestyle of traveling from city to city and never having a job, but to continue the touring life of my favorite musical group, ticketless fans pose a problem. If those who truly care about the music have their spaces bought by locals who couldn't care anything about the band, the likelihood of conflict escalates.

The reason Red Rocks was such a mess was because the people who drove 2,000 miles to see the band had their tickets bought by careless drunks who didn't care about the music and who just go for the prospect of free-flowing controlled substances. Those without tickets have nothing to do but hang out in the parking lots which provokes overcrowding and clashes with authorities. Therefore, I ask one thing of the people at this school. If you think on Nov. 16 you are going to see Phish to hear the two popular songs you know, get really drunk or stoned, and talk about it later in your Jeep, don't go. Secondly, the band doesn't deserve to be sold out. They have done almost everything to avoid become a sensational rock band. Don't aid in making them so.

The reasons to see the band are simple. It is the greatest live performance ever, it is a non-threatening environment, and nothing else is like it. So, before you think about getting a ticket to see the show, evaluate the reasons for going. Perhaps you can wait and see the Dave Mathews Band instead.

Unorthodox Halloween rituals examined

I would first like to say that my little trilogy of articles will be ended in the next issue, and not in this one due to a lack of space. If I'm going to thoroughly write about the ills of Westside, I need more space than 100 lines.

Halloween is my favorite time of year. I enjoy every aspect of the season, and I usually can't stop reading Stephen King novels in the weeks before the big night. My mind centers on it, thinks about it, and researches it. For some odd reason, I take the season absolutely seriously and I am fascinated by it. I know that a lot of you, with full reason, go out, and have a good time which is exactly what I plan to do myself. However, there is one thing that concerns me about this date, and this is my odd and neurotic fascination with the season, that some people for (and apologize for the terminology) s — s and giggles tend to do really odd and stupid things.

You know that it is that stupid superstition of full moons, and Pagan holidays that seem to get people going. It is my observation that people do one of three things: go out to haunted houses/movies/concerts, party and get drunk, and do odd little festivals and rituals in honor of pagan beliefs, usually as a big joke.

No you know I have nothing against films. I know that many of you know that too well, and as for concerts, haunted houses and getting drunk, well

Brian Grummert

Kafka-esque

knock yourself out. It's the little rituals that bother me, though.

Do not get my religous beliefs mixed up in this. I am Catholic, the only religion that still performs the exorcism behind everyone's back. If you want a realistic view, read the *Exorcist* or *Dark Debts* which were both heavily researched on the exorcism. Note that I said read the Exorcism, because while the movie is interesting, it's not as accurate — most exorcisms take at least three days.

With that view I am going to throw two theories on you as to what will happen if you are doing a little ritual to worship Satan, if you think that's cute. I'll give you a classsical representation and a psychological theory based on what will happen to you through ritual. I'm not saying that I believe in both or either, but I think you should know (possibly) what you are getting into.

I've known people our age who've dealt with "black magic," and the only thing that I've noticed is that a lot of people do not like talking about it when they are done, and wish that they had never started. I do not know if these people were just bluntly insane or if something really happened, but I will reveal a theory presented in *Dark Debts*, which was based on an actual exorcist case. Through the usage of a Ouigi board or basic ritual, people have conjured something up they didn't want to and a serious of posses-

sion takes place. It first takes over the body, the mind, the will, and then the soul. By the time the "demon" takes over the person's body, there isn't much to the person, and the "demon" can have control leading to chaotic behavior and murder.

That is one view point on it, but even the Catholic Church rarely performs exorcisms now because of mental illness and mind tricks. Some people will convince themselves that they are possessed and will act accordingly. These people will do evil acts because, through ritual, they have slowly convinced themselves that they are possessed, and will do their little deeds.

I don't know what to make of all of this. The psychological theory is more credible and there have been documented cases with Dungeons & Dragons. Whatever causes it, just be careful, or just go to a darn haunted house.

Letters to the Editor:

Dear Brian Grummert,
I am writing to you regarding your Sept. 6 column "Neuroticism haunts hall of school." I would like to give my perspective on it, seeing as how you seemed to unknowingly describe my life in your column.

I am a freshman at Colorado College in Colorado Springs, having graduated from Westside last May. I was an Opinion editor of the *Lance*, which is why I received the paper here at my school.

This summer, someone I love was killed, in a car accident ironically enough. You wrote in your column about how something like this is liable to cause stress and how people shouldn't worry about the little things that go wrong every day.

I couldn't agree with you more. It took the loss of a loved one to show me this, and I commend you for having figured that out already. But I do disagree on a point you made earlier in the article. You said you have friends in college who have more work to do than high school students, but they are less stressed

because hey have life all figured out already.
To this I politely say "Ha!"

What I mean is, how old someone is or what institution of learning they attend has nothing to do with the way they assess and handle the stressful situations in life. I know plenty of students at my school who do the same. What matters is how we see ourselves as individuals, existing in a world that isn't really all that fair and nice. I've learned that petty things don't matter, unfortunately I learned the hard way. It's not college that gives us insight and ability to handle difficult situations, it's our own inner strength that we sometimes don't even known we have until we are forced to tap it.

Brian, you made a good point and I think you're on the right track. I just wanted to let you know how I see it, speaking from firsthand experience.

Sincerely,
Sara Kugler

Sara:
I do appreciate your letter, but you should know that when I said that I had friends who were currently in college that had a lower stress level than some of the students here at Westside, I didn't mean that they didn't have more work to do. My point was that stress over little things is common, but even more common at this school for some reason in particular. I think it has to do with ideas based on environment — that people in a certain area tend to have a slightly different trait than those around them, and I think with the idea of stress, it also stands to be true.

Thank you, however, for reacting to my article — I didn't get very much feedback here which means that either no one read it, (the more likely idea) or that people did not understand it which seems to be a common problem with my writing.

Have fun at college though, and don't let the little things in life get to you. — Brian Grummert

Personal columns liven up the editorial pages. The above columns are from the Lance, *Westside High School, Omaha, NE. Note the standardized treatment of the columnists' photos and names. Standing heads are a good way to present a paper's personality. Letters to the editor also offer variety to an editorial page's content.*

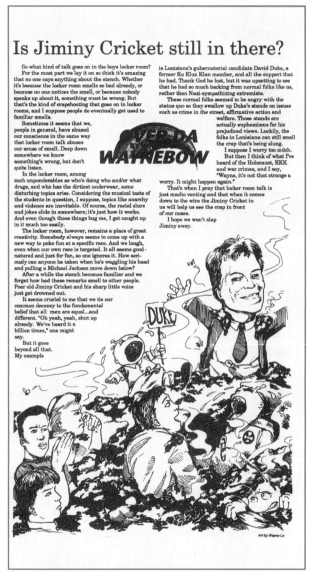

Is Jiminy Cricket still in there?

So what kind of talk goes on in the boys locker room?

For the most part we lay it on so thick it's amazing that no one says anything about the stench. Whether it's because the locker room smells so bad already, or because no one notices the smell, or because nobody speaks up about it, something must be wrong. But that's the kind of crapshooting that goes on in locker rooms, and I suppose people do eventually get used to familiar smells.

Sometimes it seems that we, people in general, have abused our conscience in the same way that locker room talk abuses our sense of smell. Deep down somewhere we know something's wrong, but don't quite listen.

In the locker room, among such unponderables as who's doing who and/or what drugs, and who has the dirtiest underwear, some disturbing topics arise. Considering the musical taste of the students in question, I suppose, topics like anarchy and violence are inevitable. Of course, the racial slurs and jokes slide in somewhere; it's just how it works. And even though these things bug me, I get caught up in it much too easily.

The locker room, however, remains a place of great creativity. Somebody always seems to come up with a new way to poke fun at a specific race. And we laugh, even when our own race is targeted. It all seems good-natured and just for fun, so one ignores it. How seriously can anyone be taken when he's waggling his head and pulling a Michael Jackson move down below?

After a while the stench becomes familiar and we forget how bad these remarks smell to other people. Poor old Jiminy Cricket and his sharp little voice just get drowned out.

It seems crucial to me that we tie our common decency to the fundamental belief that all men are equal...and different. "Oh yeah, yeah, shut up already. We've heard it a billion times," one might say.

But it goes beyond all that. My example

is Louisiana's gubernatorial candidate David Duke, a former Ku Klux Klan member, and all the support that he had. Thank God he lost, but it was upsetting to see that he had so much backing from normal folks like us, rather than Nazi-sympathizing extremists.

These normal folks seemed to be angry with the status quo so they swallow up Duke's stands on issues such as crime in the street, affirmative action and welfare. Those stands are actually euphemisms for his prejudiced views. Luckily, the folks in Louisiana can still smell the crap that's being slung.

I suppose I worry too much.

But then I think of what I've heard of the Holocaust, KKK and war crimes, and I say, "Wayne, it's not that strange a worry. It might happen again."

That's when I pray that locker room talk is just macho venting and that when it comes down to the wire the Jiminy Cricket in us will help us see the crap in front of our noses.

I hope we won't slap Jiminy away.

Art by Wayne Lo

Clever titles add to a column's appeal, Wayne Lo chose "Over Da Waynebow" for his column in the Epitaph, Cupertino High School, Cupertino, CA.

It enlarges the soul, but wrinkles the brain.

There are those who believe that writing a column is an easy racket, but Don Marquis said it best long ago when he described this peculiar form of industry as "digging a grave."

> ➤ *Tips on Writing Reviews*

• *Use first person I in a limited way. It is always best to keep the writer out of the article as much as possible.*

• *Byline the article. The byline should make it unnecessary to use first person I.*

• *Avoid quoting others—other reviewers or other readers. The review should be your reaction—not someone else's.*

• *Make the reader want to see the movie, read the book, view the concert, hear the album, or visit the restaurant—or evoke the opposite feelings. State your viewpoints about what you are reviewing in such a clear way that the reader will know what you're thinking.*

It takes no unusual equipment to become a columnist. But you do need an insatiable curiosity about life, a pair of ears bent from listening to others.

The question a columnist is asked most often is, "Where do you get your ideas?" The answer to this is you don't "get" ideas. You beg, borrow or steal them—or excavate them out of a numb skull with the cold chisel of necessity.

> ➢ *Editorial*
> *Column Content*
> • *Varies from issue to issue.*
> • *May cover the news behind the news.*
> • *May deal with unusual events.*
> • *May interpret the news.*
> • *May include the human side of the news.*
> • *May praise or may be critical.*
> • *Must be based on solid research and good interviewing.*

Ideas for columns are everywhere. Erma Bombeck said that many of hers came from her readers. News, sports, and feature stories should spur ideas for columns.

For a column to be successful, it should appear regularly, have approximately the same position each time, and have the same typographic style. This element of consistency helps the reader identify with the column. Give the column a standing head, but allow space for a second deck head that will change each time to describe the column's content. All columns should carry a byline.

Depending on type, a column may appear on the editorial page, the feature page, or the sports page. Since most columns contain the writer's opinion, they may supplement the editorials on the editorial page.

High school papers should consider, at a minimum, running an editorial column, a review column, a humor column, and a sports column in nearly every issue. An opportunity to write columns may create in some writers the desire to make a career as a columnist.

EDITORIAL COLUMNS

An editorial column differs little from a regular editorial except that, since it is one person's opinion, it is permissible (but not necessary) to use first person "I."

Editorial columns are usually but not always written by the editor of the paper. Topics may center around school life or community, state, and national events as they apply to the students. All copy should be localized, and timeliness is important.

Like editorials, editorial columns should be kept short to enhance readability, and they should have an introduction, a body, and a conclusion.

REVIEW COLUMNS

Reviews should be used in all student newspapers because (1) they can promote an interest in art, and (2) they can help the reader develop discriminating taste.

The general qualifications of a good reviewer are:
1. Honesty
2. Integrity
3. Openmindedness. The reviewer must approach each work of art with a willingness to be convinced that it is well done.
4. Humility
5. Charity. The reviewer must realize that criticism need not be destructive.
6. Background, experience, and maturity. These, for a student journalist, are usually unfound qualities. However, if a student really has the desire to be a good reviewer, he or she can gain them through hard work. For example, a good movie or music reviewer will read widely in the field and maintain a file of information for reference when making comparisons and contrasts. Review columns are of several types.

Book reviews seldom appear in high school papers, but they should. Papers should consider reviewing library books; most librarians will provide copies of newly acquired books. School papers may also review newly published books, but that can be costly if someone has to purchase the books. Select publications for review books that the average teenager is apt to read. A book reviewer should be a good reader as well as a good writer. An avid reader should be able to differentiate between literature and trash.

➢ *Roads to Success*

Jim Bishop, former American journalist, said there were three secrets to becoming a good columnist:

- *Begin with a true incident.*
- *Fill in the missing pieces.*
- *Add a punch line.*

Bishop gave this advice in the book Read All About It, *which Jim Trelease edited. The book is a must-read for all would-be columnists. Bishop was noted for his taglines (the ending punch). They are memorable.*

Columnist explores sincerity, personal optimism

I'm starting to doubt the sincerity of a lot of people lately, including myself. I just think everyone is depressing or phony. It is weird.

I read this book, "The Catcher In The Rye", by J.D. Salinger, and I was, I don't know, inspired and disturbed by how honest the book was.

It shows people being fake, but they don't even see how awful they are acting.

After I read the book, I kept analyzing people and their behavior. It is strange. A few days later I watched the "Charlie Brown Christmas Special" on television.

It is the same one that is on every year, where Charlie Brown directs the Christmas Pageant and everyone hates the tree he picks out.

As I watched it, I remembered myself watching it as a little kid. It freaked me out. As a little kid I always thought that Charlie Brown was stupid.

I liked the other characters, like Pep-

permint Patti, and basically everyone else on the show, with the exception of Linus and Pigpen.

Now I realize how brilliant Charlie Brown really is. I never understood it before. I just never paid enough attention I guess. He sees things the way I think people should see things.

I think it's sad, that as a child I never put it together that the show was named after Charlie Brown for a reason.

He makes the most sense of all the other characters on the show.

He questions people, and he notices some of society's pathetically obvious flaws that most people choose not to think about.

It is like, my older sister once wrote, "Who cares about poverty when there is poetry in the air? The leg-less war veteran can stand ringing his bell outside of the coffee shop all day long. They'll choose their iced cappuccinos over him every time."

She's right you know. But thinking this way scares a lot of people.

Well, it scares me at least, not too much, but a little. I have been called a pessimist more times than I can count in the last couple of months, and it just kills me.

I honestly always thought I was an optimist; I still think I am. I think I'm just realistic about things.

When I am happy about something, people wonder what I have to smile

about, but when I'm grouchy, people think I'm a pessimist. There is no happy-medium. I can't ever just be content; people don't understand the concept. It just wouldn't be enough for them.

Now lets get back to Charlie Brown. No one was ever happy to see him, because he was their idea of a pessimist.

If you take a closer look, Charlie Brown just had a big heart. He didn't choose the smallest tree because he wanted it to ruin the pageant; he picked it so he could save it and give it a better life.

It may be a small thing to care about. I mean these are fiction, the book and the cartoon. It is all made up, but it is based on reality. Don't just read this book or watch the cartoon, take a look around, think about it, absorb it, and apply it.

It could make the world a better place, even if you are the only one who notices.

I DON'T WANT TO HEAR A LOT OF WHINING SO I'LL SHUT UP

By Emily Troutner

Column topics can reflect on past experiences as this one in the Blazer, *Fairbury Jr.-Sr. High School, Fairbury, NE, does. The writer reflects on how she used to think about Charlie Brown and how her perception of the cartoon character later changes.*

The book reviewer should avoid clichés *(This is a truly interesting and enjoyable book)* or opinion without a basis *(This book is one of the most meaningful of our times)*. The reviewer should always seek an original point of view.

Book reviews should be concerned with the significance of the work. How does the book compare with similar ones on the same subject or with others by the same author? All good reviews contain comparison and contrast when possible. Give only a brief summary of a novel or book. Deal less with content than with telling the reader how the novel or book deals with human lives and values. Are characters real and convincing? Is the craftsmanship good? From what point of view does the author tell the story?

Wrap up a book review by giving the number of pages and the publisher's name.

Film reviews often appear in high school papers. Because papers are not published daily, a lack of timeliness sometimes hampers the film reviewer at the high school level. Select a film that has just opened in town in the hope that it will still be showing when the paper comes out. If possible, view a film before it is available to the public. Some movie chains make advanced viewing possible, especially in metropolitan areas.

Like book reviews, film reviews should deal as little as possible with the plot, and they should never divulge a surprise ending or plot twist.

Film reviews should also compare and contrast. Compare the actors' roles with previous roles, compare the director's work with previous films he or she has directed, compare the plot with other movies with similar plots.

The review should assess the story itself. Is it a good story? Is the dialogue fresh, convincing, real? Is the film an adaptation of a novel or play? If so, make comparisons. If original, what type is it: action adventure, comedy, drama? Discuss the camera work, the acting, the sets, the overall production. Sometimes the costuming or the scenery makes the film worth seeing even though the acting and directing lack strength. Other times the costumes and setting make the production laughable.

At the end of the review include the film's rating: G, PG, PG-13, R, NC-17, or X. Since high school readers may not legally view X-rated films, it is probably not a good idea to review them in high school papers. Use discretion when reviewing NC-17s as well, since many of your readers are not legally old enough to see them either. If your school is in a large metropolitan area, let the reader know where the film is playing. Use the following guidelines when writing a movie review:

1. Give just enough of the plot to arouse interest and to provide proof for your opinion of the movie.
2. Note which human emotions the movie appeals to.
3. Was the movie made for a specific purpose? Does it relate to the group it was intended for?
4. Is the movie well cast?
5. Is the dialogue realistic? Is it too simplistic?
6. What is the quality of the cinematography and sound? Does the movie use any interesting special effects? Is it excessively violent?

7. Is the plot interesting? Believable? Is the ending satisfactory (do not reveal it)?

Play reviews are difficult to write at the high school level because of the timeliness factor. If there is a professional play in town, chances are that it will be around for only a week or two. By the time the paper comes out, it will no longer be showing. Like all types of reviews, the main reason for writing a play review is to advise readers either to see it or skip it.

School plays may be reviewed, but the timeliness problem is even more difficult. Most school plays are performed for only two or three nights. Some school papers review a rehearsal of a school play. If that is done, it must be made clear to the reader that it is a rehearsal being reviewed. It is a rare play that really "comes together" before opening night. Reviewers of high school plays must also keep in mind that the performers are amateurs and should be treated as such. Be kind, but be honest in evaluation.

Because of the timeliness factor, most play reviews appear in high school papers after the last performance. In such cases, the review should make readers sorry they missed it or glad they did not waste their money. The same is true for *concert* reviews. Most concerts are one- or two-night stands, so it is usually impossible for a reviewer to urge attendance based on his opinion of the concert. It is possible, however, to remind the readers of the strengths and weaknesses of past concerts by this performer. On rare occasions, the reviewer may be able to catch the concert in another town before it comes to his hometown. Again, comparison and contrast are important in concert and play reviews.

Restaurant reviews offer the writer more opportunities because restaurants are not likely to close before the paper appears. Comparison and contrast are also important in restaurant reviews. If the review is about a new Chinese restaurant, compare it to other Chinese restaurants in town. It is usually best to write on new restaurants, before many readers have visited them. A review will either encourage or discourage such a visit.

Comparing several restaurants in one review is effective in this example from the Chronicle, Harvard-Westlake School, North Hollywood, CA. The use of rating stars is a quick way to convey the writer's thinking.

Restaurant reviews should include prices of main menu items. List enough to give the reader an idea of the types of food served and a range of prices. Some papers run a photocopy of the menu with the review.

Be sure to discuss atmosphere and service. Sometimes a good atmosphere and outstanding service are reason enough to eat at a restaurant even if the food is only average. On the other hand, if food is outstanding but service is poor, it can be a detracting factor.

The conclusion of a restaurant review should provide the address, hours of operation, and whether reservations are necessary. Be sure to visit the establishment more than once. It is unfair to try its menu and service only once. It is also a good idea to take someone with you. That way, you can sample menu items other than the one you order. You might also consider doing a consumer report on similar types of restaurants. For example, visit four fast-food restaurants and compare the sizes (number of fries or weight) and prices of their small french fries.

Reviews of compact discs or cassettes should also be part of school papers, as should reviews of digital video discs. Some writers still refer to these as album reviews—dating back to the day when performers recorded their work on 33 1/3 rpm albums or 78 rpm albums. Reviews of musical recordings tend to be overused in high school papers. Papers should strive to achieve balance in types of reviews.

Cassette or compact disc reviews should compare and contrast similar music by the same recording artist or group. Be sure to discuss instrumentals as well as vocals. Select two or three songs and give more details about them. If one of the songs has also been released as a single, that should be pointed out.

It is permissible to use some of the lyrics; however, do not reproduce a song word for word, which could be a violation of copyright law. Reproducing part (not a substantial part) of a copyrighted work is permissible if it is for nonprofit educational purposes and if it does not affect the sales of the work.

Material that cannot be copyrighted includes phrases, slogans, and titles. Even exact reproduction of an advertising slogan such as M & M's "It Melts in Your Mouth, Not in Your Hand" would not normally constitute copyright infringement. But be aware that such slogans could be trademark-protected. Nike did copyright "Just Do It." Corporate logos can be copyright-protected or trademark-protected. You can't use a Coca-Cola can, for example, or any reasonable facsimile of the can, without permission. Materials remain under copyright for 50 years beyond the death of an author or creator.

At the end of the review, it is a good idea to include the name of the recording company and the price of the cassette versus the price of the compact disc.

Use the following guidelines when writing a cassette or compact disc review:

1. Do the lyrics convey a message?
2. Has this message been used by the group or artist before?
3. Does the vocalist's voice convey genuine emotion? Are backup singers supportive?
4. Is the style imitative or revolutionary? Describe

the style: rock, classical, country, rap, etc.

5. Is the instrumentation well done? What instrument is dominant? Are there any special effects?
6. Is there an interesting story behind the lyrics, the artist, the songs?
7. How does the recording compare with other works by the same artist or group and with works by other artists or groups?
8. What have other critics said about the recording?

Television reviews, like film reviews, should be based on current shows. The best times to write TV reviews are in September or October when new programming is debuting or later when a show has been dropped and replaced. It is best to review a series rather than a one-time performance. Another good time to review shows is when the networks test out mid-season replacement shows.

Besides comedies and dramas, it is also possible to review TV news programs. Review the news coverage of all major networks, for example, comparing and contrasting how each reports the news generally or covers a particular story.

Regardless of the type of review, start your article with a statement of opinion, and then back up that opinion with examples. If you are attending a live presentation, do not overreact to the audience's impression. Rely on your own judgment.

HUMOR COLUMNS

Humor columns are popular in high school papers if they are well written. Too many school papers lack humor. If you have someone who can write satire, use it.

Humor columns can be devoted to both wit and humor. Wit shows the resemblance between two things, is concisely stated, and appeals to the intellect. Humor, on the other hand, shows contrast, is stated in detail, and appeals to the emotions. Humor is more popular than wit with most students. A good column contains only original humor, is mostly about

> ➢ *Satire*
> • *Publishing satire and humor sometimes prompts threats of lawsuits by individuals who find themselves the subject of ridicule.*
> • *Humor and satire are protected from libel suits as long as readers understand the material is not to be taken seriously.*
> • *If a reporter means for something to be a joke, be sure the readers recognize it as a joke.*
> • *Label a humor column clearly, and if it is a parody, tell the reader that it is a parody and is not to be taken seriously.*
> • *Any time you are not reporting factual information, let the reader know what you are doing.*

school life, and avoids trivial items.

Variety is important in humor columns, and it can be achieved in many ways.

A pun, which is a play on words that are spelled the same way or have the same sound but different meanings, is an example of wit that amuses some readers.

Humorous verse is effective. It can be a sonnet, ballad, or any form of poetry. Original verse is desirable, but sometimes a paraphrase of familiar verses can be entertaining.

The school anecdote may also be used. An anecdote is a brief account of an amusing incident.

Parody, in which the language and style of a well-known author are imitated to produce a humorous effect, is usually well accepted in school newspapers.

The use of caricature and burlesque are other ways of achieving variety in a humor column. Caricature exaggerates the features of a person, place, or thing; burlesque imitates something serious in a lighthearted way or vice versa.

People like to laugh. High school papers should give readers a taste of humor along with the serious. That can be done without resorting to gossip columns and the April Fool type of humor.

Instead, run a regular humor column and deal with topics that relate to teenagers. Humor column ideas include:

1. Getting up in the morning to get ready for school.
2. Messy bedrooms.
3. Milestones in a teenager's life.
4. Senioritis.
5. Song titles.
6. Shopping.
7. It never seems to fail. . ..
8. Problems with contact lenses or glasses.
9. Dating.
10. Driver's education.
11. Junk food.
12. Boredom in the classroom.

➢ **The Sports Column**

• *Avoid writing about non-school topics unless a majority of readers would be interested in that topic. Readers can learn about professional teams in the professional press.*

• *Write about ways to develop an athlete, differences between boys' and girls' sports, about the outcome of a particular game, about prospects of various teams, about how a team prepares for a game, about selection of referees and umpires, about how the athletic director creates the sports schedule, about alumni who are playing college or pro sports, about the role of the trainers, about records, about the thrilling plays and the chilling plays.*

Any subject that interests teens is a potential humor column. Read good humor columnists for ideas. Erma Bombeck, for example, often wrote on topics that teenagers could relate to, such as brother-sister affection, leftovers, doing the dishes, carpooling, and staying in fashion.

Select a topic, stretch the imagination a little, turn the sublime into the ridiculous, and you have a humor column. Be careful not to offend when you stretch the imagination. The purpose of humor columns is to entertain, but not at the expense of someone else.

SPORTS COLUMNS

Sports columns are much like editorial columns, but they are usually written by the sports editor and comment on sports events and personalities. It is acceptable to use first person in sports columns, but most sports columnists still use third person for effect.

Sports columns usually deal with serious topics, but sometimes they report human-interest sidelights about amusing incidents that happen in the locker room.

Possible topics for sports columns might be a coach's or a player's comments about the game, predictions of the outcome of future games, or an analysis of the financing of sports events. Sports columns may criticize or praise, depending on the circumstances; they may deal with intramural sports as well as interscholastic sports. Physical education may also be discussed in sports columns. For example, one Missouri school spoke out against differences in grading boys and girls in physical education. The column called for equality in grading, and it obtained action when the administration changed its grading policy.

If the column deals with predictions on the outcome of games, it requires some research. Don't predict that your team will win if its record is 0-10 and the opponent's is 10-0 unless you have some sound reasons for predicting an upset.

LETTERS TO THE EDITOR

Give the readers a chance to present their viewpoints by

> ➣ *Sports Column Content*
> • *May profile key players.*
> • *May discuss rules of a sport.*
> • *May discuss the school mascot.*
> • *May talk about the referees and the umpires.*
> • *May talk about game rules.*
> • *May include traditions.*
> • *May discuss superstitions and good luck charms.*

➤ **Advice Columns**

Advice columns seldom appear in high school papers because most students have little experience to offer sound advice. Even Ann Landers, whose real name was Esther Lederer, relied heavily on experts before answering many letters.

Lederer died June 22, 2003. She wrote her column for 47 years. It appeared in over 1,200 papers worldwide with an estimated readership of 90 million daily.

CROSS Fire

Is capital punishment unacceptable?

Jennifer Eaglet
Viewpoints Editor

How easy it is to drown our sorrows in a sea of pity for a convicted murderer sentenced to die. We spend our empathy on the men and women who steal lives; how about a tear or two for the victims who hadn't a say in the matter?

Whether or not the death penalty is a deterrent to would-be murders is not a sufficient argument against capital punishment for the fact that justice must be served takes a higher priority.

Capital punishment is not enforced as a scare tactic for someone contemplating a homicide but rather as a way to insure that the murderer is given what is due him or her.

Is it morally decent to allow a man or woman guilty of murder to go without his or her due punishment in order that we may spare

a dollar of tax money? Surely their victims wouldn't think so.

The tired old eighth amendment argument as a basis for opposing capital punishment grows weaker with each heated debate. Protection against cruel and unusual punishment is the right of each American citizen as the Constitution states. Murder victims have these rights abstracted in the blink of an eye, devoid of any say in the matter.

An almost anti-logic seems to have rooted itself within the hollows of many American heads, preaching that we should abstain from afflicting such excruciating pain on the murderer. Was it not his or her choice to steal the life of another? The moment that one commits a murder he or she has voluntarily drained themself of protection against the same form of torture.

Joel Thompson
Reporter

Next Monday when you are sitting in the middle of your B block class and the bright shining voice of Amanda Jensen comes over the intercom to lead us in the Pledge of Allegiance, take a second and think about what you are saluting. Is it the land of the free and the home of the brave as we have all been taught? Yes, certainly it is, but it is much more than that. It is a country that kills people.

Last month the State of Oregon executed Douglas Wright. This was done to act as a deterrent to others. He earned this punishment because of the murders of three homeless men. He promised them jobs, drove them out to the Wasco County desert, and shot them each in the head. These attacks were completely unprovoked. They were the work of a very sick man. Just before the execution

was carried out, Douglas Wright confessed to molesting and killing a young boy over a decade ago. He told of how he just drove down the street and decided to act as the executioner of this innocent child simply because he was alone. Do you honestly think that the death penalty works as a deterrent to people like this? Sadly, no. The people who are candidates for the death penalty are far too sick to be deterred by it. Some of them, like Wesley Allen Dodd just a few years ago, actually request it. They thrive on it.

In this country the death penalty is carried out almost solely on people convicted of murder. We kill these people to keep others from killing. It is one thing for a sick, lonely person to carry out such a savage act, but it horrifies me that the greatest country in the world can do the same.

Pro and con columns are an excellent way to present two points of view. Pro and con articles should be written as columns—not editorials. If the staff does not want to take a stand, then let two writers present their opposing viewpoints in pro and con columns as in the above from the Scroll, Gladstone High School, Gladstone, OR.

running a letters to the editor column. A newspaper that is doing a good job will elicit letters from its readers. Be sure that the content of letters is accurate; readers often write in a moment of anger and do not bother to check the facts. It is not necessary to print all letters received, and it is unwise to run letters that are incorrect. Point out errors to the writer, and if he or she agrees, make the corrections and run the letter. This is possible at the high school level, since circulation is small and it is fairly easy to reach the writer. A professional paper probably would discard the letter rather than taking time to contact the writer. Editors should require letters to be signed, but can withhold the name if requested. Without a name, the editor cannot contact the writer for confirmation.

Every issue of your paper should print the paper's policy

concerning letters with the masthead. A suggested maximum length is 300 words, but good letters might be a little longer.

EXCHANGE COLUMNS

Few high school papers run exchange columns today, but they can provide interesting reading. Check through your exchange papers for unusual things that are occurring at other schools.

Research for an exchange column might support a column in which the writer suggests that innovations tried in other schools be considered at your school.

ALUMNI COLUMNS

Although alumni columns do not usually appear in every issue of a school paper, such columns are a good way to promote news of graduates. Items should deal with well-known graduates or with recent graduates—people present students remember.

POLLS OR SURVEYS

Survey stories are used as standing columns in some school newspapers. Surveys or polls may accompany news, sports, features, or editorials.

One type of survey story is the inquiring reporter story that simply asks a question. This type of story asks only a few people for their opinions, and pictures accompany the responses. The inquiring reporter story can be an interesting feature, but it certainly cannot be considered representative of the student population.

A good survey must be designed scientifically to assure accuracy. The only way to achieve absolute accuracy is to poll the entire population. That would be time-consuming even with computers to do the tabulation. Experts in polling techniques have concluded that it is possible to get a 95-percent confidence level by polling a relatively small number of people. How much is enough?

➢ *Exchange Column Content*
  • *May include comparison of similar events or policies.*
  • *May encourage cooperation between schools.*
  • *May be entertaining.*
  • *May be used to show what is happening at other schools.*
  • *May include information from other school newspapers or from professional papers.*

Population size	Sample size
Infinity	384
500,000	384
100,000	383
50,000	381
10,000	370
5,000	357
3,000	341
2,000	322
1,000	278
Under 1,000	Poll everyone

In other words, if your school has a population of 2,000 students, you could poll 322 of them and achieve a 95 percent confidence rate that the results of your survey are accurate.

A survey can be accurate, however, only if the respondents are selected scientifically and if it is systematic. What makes a survey systematic? There are three essentials: (1) the population to be surveyed must be defined clearly in advance; (2) every member of the population must have a known probability of being included in the sample; and (3) every member of the sample must be asked the same questions and have his or her answers recorded in the same manner.

To assure that every member of a given population has a probability of being included in the survey, the persons selected must be chosen randomly. One way to do that is to put all the names in a box and shake it. Then if you want 322 names, draw them out. Each time a name is drawn, however, it must be placed back in the box; otherwise each person does not have the same chance of being selected. For example, if there are 2,000 names in the box and one name is drawn, that person has 1 in 2,000 chance of being selected. If that person's name is not put back in the box, the next person selected has 1 in 1,999 chance of being selected and so on, until the 322nd person would only have 1 in 1,679 chance of being selected.

Another system is to use a list of random numbers that can be found in a book. Start with a particular number and the book will indicate which numbers should go next in random order.

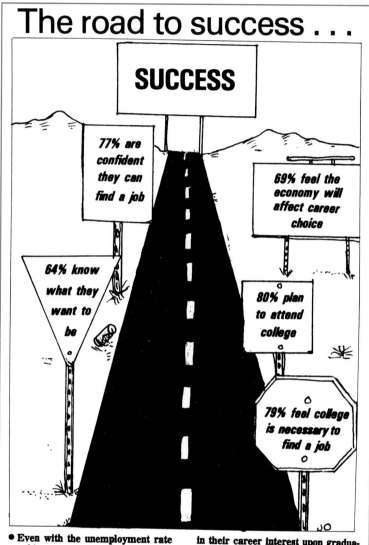

The road to success . . .

SUCCESS

77% are confident they can find a job

69% feel the economy will affect career choice

64% know what they want to be

80% plan to attend college

79% feel college is necessary to find a job

● Even with the unemployment rate reaching over 10% for the first time since the depression, a recent survey conducted by Oracle Design Editor Robin Morse found that students are optimistic about their futures.

The poll, distributed randomly to 10% of the student body last month, sought to determine students' views about their college and career plans.

Over three-fourths of the students are confident that they can find a job in their career interest upon graduation from high school or college.

This optimism, however, is tempered by the feeling of the majority of the students that the economy and the state of the future job market must affect their career choices and that a college degree will be necessary to realize their plans for a "well-paying" job. In fact, 65% feel that a graduate degree will also be a necessary step on the road to success.

By use of artwork, the results of a survey are presented effectively in a story from the Oracle, *West Springfield High School, Springfield, VA.*

Tips for Creating an Infographic

- *Keep it appealing.*
- *Keep it simple.*
- *Keep it accurate.*
- *Dress it up. Don't use simple bar graphs. If you are doing a graphic on smoking, use cigarettes for the bars.*
- *Label it clearly.*
- *Box it in with hairlines, 1/2-point lines or 1-point lines. Wider than that will make the line unappealing.*
- *Keep type and elements one pica away from the lines.*
- *Make it readable. Use sans serif type in 8 to 9 point.*
- *Use headlines.*
- *Don't decorate. Design.*
- *Horizontal and vertical shapes work best.*
- *Research your information.*
- *Plan your infographic to stand alone.*
- *Relate the infographic to your readers' lives.*
- *Approach the infographic like a story—have a beginning, middle, and end.*
- *Gather information from more than one source, if possible.*
- *Use active-voice verbs.*

This would require you to assign a number to each student in your school, if the student body is a population to be surveyed.

Another, but less reliable, way is to select every tenth name or every fifth name in your student directory.

Obviously, all of those ways are time-consuming, but they do assure greater accuracy than simply taking the survey to certain classes and asking individuals to respond. If you select enough respondents, you will gain a general idea of the thinking of the student body, but you need to be careful that the classes used are representative. Do not select all senior classes, for example, as seniors may have different opinions than freshmen. Select your respondents carefully.

Be sure to phrase your questions carefully. Closed-end (multiple-choice) questions are usually the best, because all respondents have the same choices. It is wise, however, to make the final choice "Other" so that the respondent has a chance to give an answer not included in the survey. For example, if you want to find out what musical group is the favorite of students, you might list five that you think are among the top, but make your sixth choice "Other" so that the respondent can name another group if necessary. It is best to put "Be specific" after "Other," so that you will get definite answers. Closed-end surveys are easiest to tabulate, especially when a computer is used for tabulation.

Open-ended question surveys can be valuable, however, if you want complete opinions from the respondents. An open-ended survey requires the respondents to fill in the blanks. For example, you might want to know if students think the minimum wage for teenagers should be increased, or how many students can name the two senators from their state? Open-ended questions do not bias the respondents toward one of the answers you have given them.

Be careful with the phrasing of open-ended questions. Don't combine two issues in one question. For example, don't ask, "Did you choose to go to the Prom because you had the money or because you heard the band was great?"

Phrase questions in terms of "behavioral indicators," rather than looking for subjective expressions of feelings. For example,

> **Using a Table as an Infographic**
> • A table is usually half text and half chart with side-by-side comparisons.
> • Comparisons may run vertically or horizontally.
> • Screen every other line to help guide the reader.
> • Run headings horizontally across the top of the table.
> • Keep any explanation of the table brief.
> • Align any numbers flush left.
> • Design it to stand alone or to run as a sidebar to accompany a story.

ask, "If you could vote today, would you vote to retain the President in office?" instead of "Do you like the President?"

Avoid questions that are biased or loaded. Balance the choices available to the respondent. For example, avoid a question like the following, which is biased:

> School is:
> ——great because of the excellent faculty
> ——great because of the excellent principal
> ——great because students are constantly learning
> Some respondents probably have negative attitudes toward their school.

Some other guidelines follow:

1. Keep your words simple enough for less educated respondents.
2. Keep sentences short and simple.
3. Eliminate stereotyping.
4. When using checklists or multiple-choice responses, keep them short.
5. Eliminate ambiguous words such as *rarely* and *frequently.*
6. Request personal and identifying data about the respondent at the end of the questionnaire. Such data are important if you want a stratified sampling that will indicate boys' opinions as compared to girls' or those of freshmen as compared to seniors. Personal data include age, grade level, and gender for high school surveys. Professional surveys often include educational level of respondents, income level, and geographical location.
7. Be sure each class in the school is represented in your survey unless you want only the opinions of one class.
8. Both genders must be represented (unless you

➢ *The Line Chart*

• *A line chart measures changing quantities over time.*

• *A scale runs vertically along one edge measuring amounts, and another scale runs horizontally along the bottom measuring time. These two scales may be reversed.*

• *Use a background grid to track numbers.*

• *Usually works best with only one statistic.*

attend an all-girl or all-boy school, or unless the question clearly relates to just one sex).

9. Faculty should also be represented in the survey, unless you're just after teenage viewpoints.

10. Be sure all minorities are represented. If 25% of your school is African American, then 25% of your survey respondents should be black.

11. All students and faculty must have an equal opportunity to be represented in the sample.

Statistics gained from conducting surveys are being used in infographics in today's yearbooks and newspapers. An infographic serves as a sidebar (a story with additional information about the topic) to the main story. Information graphics can be used for any topic from the serious to the trivial. *USA Today* uses information graphics on the first page of each of its sections. The following questions were in one issue of *USA Today*.

What percentage of North America is wilderness? Has declaring bankruptcy become more acceptable to Americans? In which year did professional baseball produce the most 20-game winners? What is the average price paid for a video cassette recorder? Which group of people is best at keeping secrets? How much money do Americans spend on prescription glasses? In which month do most no-hitters by professional pitchers occur? How much money does the average credit union member have in savings?

The answers to the preceding questions may not be vital information for the American consumer, but they do add to the average person's knowledge of trivia. School newspaper and yearbook staffs should look at professional publications for information graphic ideas. Most surveys done at a national level can be localized and comparisons made with a survey done at the school level.

Information graphics combine artwork with statistics or

other data. An information graphic must be well done in all aspects.

George Rorick, director of the Knight-Ridder Graphics Network in Washington, DC, says that six essentials are necessary for a good information graphic:

1. Headline—an easy-to-read label.
2. Body—date, perhaps a drawing or cutaway of a map. The body transforms verbal information into visuals.
3. Credit—all information graphics should have a credit line.
4. Explainer—a short sentence or paragraph explaining what the graphic is about and perhaps why the information is important to the reader.
5. Source—a line that identifies the origin of the information, the population polled. In many instances *USA Today* uses information gathered by another polling agency. When it does, the paper always credits the source. High school publications usually conduct their own polls. Their source of information is the student population they poll. The publication should tell how many people were polled.
6. Time—although time is not part of the actual information graphic, Rorick stresses that a good graphic takes time—time to gather the information and time to create.

In *USA Today's* information graphic that answered the question, "Which group of people is best at keeping secrets?" the *headline* was "Who can keep a secret?" The *body* of the graphic had drawings of four types of people with a fifth person whispering a secret to them. The paper gave Aaron Hightower *credit* for creating the graphic. The *explainer* said, "Percentage of those polled who think these professionals are best at keeping personal information confidential:

> *Developing a Style*
> • *Read good columnists, like Dave Barry. Note his style, use of diction, structure, and mechanics.*
> • *Note the difference between voice and style. Voice is the tone of your writing. Tone can be different from column to column and can range from angry to sentimental. Style is the diction, the structure, and the mechanics of your writing. It includes word choice, sentence construction, and rhythm.*
> • *Capture the detail of what it is you are writing about.*
> • *Write in words that the reader will understand. For the most part, use words you would use in conversation.*
> • *Use strong verbs that will add description.*

bankers, 36%; lawyers, 64%; doctors, 66%; and clergy, 74%. The *source* of the information was The Roper Organization.

Few high school publications include all the essentials in their information graphics. That does not mean they do not succeed as graphics. Often the aesthetics of the graphic make it appealing to the reader. However, the person who creates the graphic needs to be sure readers have all questions answered. For example, the *USA Today* graphic on keeping secrets leaves out one important element—how many people were surveyed. Therefore, the percentages lose validity. How many is 36%? Is it 36% of 100 or 36% of 500?

The Roper Organization undoubtedly conducted its survey scientifically, but few high school publications take the time to conduct their surveys in such a manner. They should.

As already mentioned, a high school publication might consider doing a local survey and comparing it to a national survey. For example, a few years ago, *World Almanac* surveyed 5,000 high school students to find out the name of the person they most admired. The students's top 10 were: Tom Cruise, Bill Cosby, Michael Jordan, Eddie Murphy, Kirk Cameron, Bruce Willis, Michael J. Fox, "my mother," Mel Gibson, and Arnold Schwarzenegger. It would be interesting to see whom students at your high school might select in comparison to the above list.

Regardless of the type of question asked, information graphics will fail if the creator tries to jam too much into too small a space or fails to provide enough information.

Creators of graphics are providing a service to the reader. They need to be sure in providing that service that they have answered any question the reader might raise. If they have not, the graphic will fail.

With today's desktop publishing capabilities, it is fairly easy for a newspaper or yearbook to create an information graphic. Many software programs are available. Cricket Graph enables the artist to create a bar or pie graph quickly. PageMaker, Cricket Draw, Aldus Freehand, and Adobe Illustrator are among software programs that make it easier to create visuals.

If the creators include Rorick's six essential ingredients of an information graphic, they should succeed. The reader will then probably look at the graphic as a provider of necessary information rather than just a provider of trivia.

PERSONAL COLUMNS

Any reporter who has had an unusual or interesting experience might turn that experience into a personal column. A personal column differs from a personal experience feature because it appears regularly under a person's byline. A column can also contain opinion, whereas a personal experience feature should stick to the facts. The following article by Nora Ephron, a professional columnist, is an example of a personal column. In a way, she is also making an editorial comment about teaching.

The best teacher I ever had was named Charles Simms, and he taught journalism at Beverly Hills High School in 1956 and 1957. He was young, cute in an owlish way—crew cut, glasses, etc.—and was a gymnast in the 1956 Olympics. He was also the first person any of us knew who had stereo earphones, and he taught us all to play mah-jongg.

The first day of journalism class, Mr. Simms did what just about every journalism teacher does in the beginning—he began to teach us how to write a lead. The way this is normally done is that the teacher dictates a set of facts and the class attempts to write the first paragraph of a news story about them. Who, what, where, when, how, and why. So he read us a set of facts. It went something like this: "Kenneth L. Peters, principal of Beverly Hills High School, announced today that the faculty of the high school will travel to Sacramento on Thursday for a colloquium on new teaching methods. Speaking there will be anthropologist Margaret Mead, educator Robert Maynard Hutchins, and several others."

We all began typing, and after a few minutes we turned in our leads. All of them said approxi-

➢ *The Personal Reflection Column*

• *May be humorous or sentimental.*

• *May use satire to stretch the imagination.*

• *May use anecdotes (humorous or serious) to expand on. Get people to tell their stories.*

• *May use fictional dialogue to develop the article.*

• *May use puns or plays on words to enhance the writing.*

• *May be written in the narrative form.*

• *Must appeal to the readers' emotions, regardless of the type of emotion.*

• *Should make people think: make them talk about your column.*

mately what Mr. Simms had dictated, but in the opposite order ("Margaret Mead and Robert Maynard Hutchins will address the faculty," etc.). Mr. Simms riffled through what we had turned in, smiled, looked up and said: "The lead to the story is, "There will be no school Thursday."

It was an electrifying moment. So that's it, I realized. It's about the point. The classic newspaper lead of who-what-when-where-how-and-why is utterly meaningless if you haven't figured out what the significance of the facts is. What is the point? What does it mean? He planted those questions in my head. And for the year he taught me journalism, every day was like the first; every assignment, every story, every set of facts he provided us had a point buried in it somewhere if you looked hard enough.

He turned the class into a gorgeous intellectual game, and he gave me an enthusiasm for the profession that I have never lost. Also, of course, he taught me something that works just as well in life as it does in journalism.

After teaching at Beverly Hills High School for two years, Charles Simms quit and opened a chain of record stores in Los Angeles. I hope he's a millionaire.

➢ Column Weaknesses
 • Lack of research.
 • Exaggeration of the issue.
 • Omission of facts.
 • Too preachy.
 • Use of personal attacks.
 • Overplaying the issue.
 • Using a superior tone.

EXERCISES

1. Select one of the topics for humor columns suggested in this chapter and write a humor column. Use satire. Stretch the imagination, but be kind.

2. From exchange papers, select one column and be prepared to criticize it in class. Point out its strengths and weaknesses.

3. Choose a current movie that you have seen and write a review of it.

Harassment labeled as male abuse of power

Sexual harassment is not about sex. In fact, it has little to do with sex. Sexual harassment is about power- who has power and how it is exercised in this society. Harassment of women by men is a way in which men abuse this power.

In the United States today, men hold power. Sexual harassment of women persists because in the majority of social, political, work and school situations men dominate women. They hold the highest paying jobs, control the national and international political arena and outnumber full professors at universities three to one.

In the National Association of Independent Schools (of which Harvard-Westlake is a member), less than five percent of the school heads are women. In a world where men dominate, men abuse their power through sexual harassment, and women tolerate the abuse.

They ignore the snide remarks, look straight ahead while construction workers cat call from the other side of the street and if they know the boss or fellow worker, they often pretend it didn't happen.

Women are not the only less powerful group in our culture. Teenagers and university students have little authentic power. Gays, handicapped people, low income families and all racial minorities are groups of people who have experienced the results of being powerless–namely discrimination, exclusion and harassment.

Harassment exists in the society and probably in lesser degree, in our school community. The broadest definition of sexual harassment might include the following behaviors: whistling at girls, cat calling, driving by and screaming, yelling at a group of girls, "mooning" girls, flirting or coming on to girls in an aggressive way.

To some teenagers (male *and* female) this behavior is seen simply as friendly, goofy or flirtatious. Other teens might be more offended. The point is that as people become more aware of these issues, standards change. Increasingly, men and women are realizing that behavior which in the past we labeled

A faculty perspective

Balance of power
by Leni Wildflower

"annoying," (whistles or cat calls) may in fact be a subtle form of sexual harassment.

Whether or not you decide to call any of the above behaviors "sexual harassment," consider the following: If women did any of these actions, would men be offended or feel intimidated? Not likely. These behaviors offend, insult or harass precisely because women are less powerful (sexual objects or victims) and men hold the power.

How do we solve this problem? Talk to each other! Women practice being more patient when talking to guys. Try to get in their heads and use examples and situations which they can understand and identify with. Guys resist getting defensive too quickly. Don't instantly label women "libbers" or "feminists" when they object to some behavior or attitude. We have existing programs on campus where the issue of sexual harassment, among other topics, can be discussed: Peer Counseling, Women's Studies and Upper School Human Development.

National issues serve as good topics for editorial columns, as illustrated in the Chronicle, *Harvard-Westlake School, North Hollywood, CA.*

4. Choose a book from the school library and write a review of it. Try to select a new addition to the library.

5. Read the following review and point out its strengths and weaknesses.

When visiting a music store, today's CD buyer confronts thousands of wide-ranging choices. Genres such as rock, rap and dance music all are experiencing a great deal of popularity on radio and Music Television (MTV). The convenient random play feature on a CD player selected the following tracks from recent releases as a cross-section of the current music scene.

"Understanding" by Candlebox, from the album "Lucy." Following the no-standard formula of repeatedly going from soft to loud, this song blends in with much of today's current music trends and style. "Understanding" does not seem to go anywhere until Kevin Martin, vocalist, belts a powerful yell and Peter Klett, guitarist, rips some lead licks, although he does not play an extended solo. Overall, this song represents Candlebox's music better than previous radio hits, like "Far Behind," because it shows its edgier side.

"Nimble" by Fig Dish, from the album "That's What Love Songs Often Do." This quartet from Chicago has produced an excellent power-pop album. The track follows the soft-to-loud format and comes out sounding like a lighter, more poppy Nirvana song. The cheery, almost bouncy, music off-sets vocalist Blake Smith's pained insistence of his correctness.

"Some Might Say" by Oasis, from the album "(What's the Story) Morning Glory." At first listen, it sounds like Oasis wrote the song in the '60s rather than the '90s. The song proves entertaining but not deep as lyrics like, "The sink is full of fishes/She's got dirty dishes on the brain," make hardly any sense. However, the chorus hooks the listener in and does not let go, even hours after the song ends.

"It Might As Well Be You" by Del Amitri, from the album "Twisted." The first thing this band should learn is lines like "I'm looking for something and anything will do/So hey babe it might as well be you" are not lines of great love songs. This cheesy pop song sounds like the melody of a church choir tune, though no choir would accept these poor singers.

"Strawberry" by Everclear, from the album "Sparkle and Fade." From the beginning, it sounds as if the band is going to crank up the volume at any time. Instead, Art Alexakis, guitarist, simply plays with great energy, implying he will break out and rock soon. By not doing so, Everclear sets itself apart from current bands but can also leave the listener a little disappointed.

"Purpose" by 311, from the album "311." Two musical styles, reggae and rock, mix effortlessly in

➢ *Reviewing School Productions*

• *Keep in mind that you are analyzing the performances of amateurs—not professionals.*

• *Make clear your reasons for liking or disliking something.*

• *Don't be afraid to criticize, but give praise where it is warranted.*

• *Be sure to comment on the set design, the lighting, and the costumes.*

• *Include the audience's reaction to the performance. Reaction to the action is important in writing any review.*

• *Compare and contrast to previous productions that were similar in nature.*

this slow-paced number. The band is better at playing rock but also quite adept during the reggae section. The two blend so smoothly that when the first reggae section ends, the listener hardly notices the slip into the loud, fuzzy guitar.

"Typical Situation" by The Dave Matthews Band, from the album "Under the Table and Dreaming." This ridiculously boring song drones on for nearly six minutes. Matthews sounds like he is wearing clothespins on his nose and operating heavy machinery at the same time and repeats the same verses over and over. Half of the song seems positive with lines like, "Everybody's happy," and the other half negative. "We can't do a thing about it," leaves the listener a bit confused (if he or she is still awake).

6. Construct a closed-end survey (multiple-choice responses) on one of the following topics:

A. Favorite recording groups.
B. Favorite movie theaters.
C. Favorite TV programs.
D. Favorite films of the year.
E. Favorite movie stars.
F. Favorite radio stations.

7. Do an open-end survey on the curriculum offerings at your school. Find out which courses are the favorites among students and why, and which are the least favored and why.

8. Find an information graphic in *USA Today* or another professional publication that you think would interest students at your school. Conduct your own survey to find out if your school's students agree with the national survey. Then create an information graphic (combining art with the statistics) that will visually tell the information.

CHAPTER
nine

Headline Writing

Officer shoots
man with knife

The above headline, which appeared in a metropolitan newspaper a few years ago, is indicative of the problem with many headlines: They are ambiguous and don't really say what the writer meant. The story actually dealt with the fact that a knife-wielding man was shot in the leg by a police officer as the man fled from the area.

Sometimes headlines are ambiguous because of their sentence structure, as evidenced in the following example:

Fleeing Car Crashes onto Sofa
After TV Watcher Leaves at Ad

The story dealt with a driver who lost control of his car, crashed into a house, and hit a sofa. The occupant of the house had just left the sofa during a commercial.

To be successful, a headline must relate to the story, lead the reader into the story, fit the allotted space, and be grammatically correct. In addition, if it is a yearbook headline, it must fit the specific year.

Most yearbooks are currently using feature (magazine) headlines rather than sentence (newspaper) headlines, and many newspapers are using feature headlines for feature stories. Feature headlines are usually three words or more in length but do not have a subject or a verb. They often use a play on words, taking a well-known phrase and making it fit the story. For example, *Time* magazine used "A Contempt of Court" as a headline to describe a tennis player's actions during a game. Below are some examples of good feature headlines used in yearbooks:

Goodbye Boss—on a principal who was retiring.

A game that wasn't cryable—on the worst football defeat in the history of the school.

Something to Shout About—on winning a basketball tournament.

Short Changed—on how much money it takes to be a senior.

Dollars for Scholars—on scholarships.

Cafeteria Blues—on not being able to have open lunch.

Politics on parade—on a parade that featured political candidates.

Sneak Preview—on seniors visiting college campuses.

Follow the leaders—on class officers.

All temperature cheers—on cheerleaders who brave all kinds of weather.

She lets her fingers do the walking—on a pianist.

Not for kids only—on children's theater.

We've Got Spirit? Maybe We Do—on student apathy.

A serious kind of horsin' around—on student who trained horses.

Down in the volley—on a losing volleyball team.

A weighty dilemma—on weightlifting.

The fourth time was a charm—on winning the fourth game of the season, after losing the first three.

Artwork can be integral to a headline's design. The Orange & Black, *Grand Junction High School, Grand Junction, CO, uses various shaped cigarette butts for its main headline. A secondary sentence headline explains the feature head.*

A really lovely type of compliment—on a choral group surprising its teacher by singing her a special song.

Those empty stands—on cheerleaders' problems with the lack of fans.

An episode with a cop—on stopping students at 3:30 a.m.

Feature headlines generally create greater interest than do sentence headlines, but sometimes it may be necessary to use a sentence headline as well to help explain the feature. For example, the last two headlines were accompanied by sentence headlines. "Those empty stands" was followed by "Cheerleaders have little support from students," and "An episode with a cop" went on, "Curious officer stops Quill & Scroll members."

Note that in feature headlines the words *a, an,* and *the* are acceptable. Unless part of a title, they are not acceptable in sentence (newspaper) headlines. Most papers use sentence headlines for news, sports, editorials, and some features.

Some rules for writing sentence headlines follow:

1. Just as with feature heads, strive to make each one an attention grabber.
2. Make sure each head fills the space allotted (normally no more than two counts or two picas under the maximum).
3. Avoid repetition of words or phrases within a head or from spread to spread or story to story. For instance, do not use the word *senior* on each senior portrait page headline of the yearbook, and avoid using the word *team* for each sports story in the newspaper.
4. Use single rather than double quotation marks.
5. Use a comma to replace the word *and*.
6. Do not use *a, an*, or *the*, except in titles.
7. Separate related thoughts with a semicolon.

➢ *Possible Fonts*
- *For body type, consider Goudy, Berkeley, or New Century Schoolbook. If you want a sans serif look, consider Helvetica, Franklin, Univers, or Poppl-Laudatio.*
- *For accent type and a grunge look, consider Crackhouse or Wooly Bully.*
- *For caption copy, consider Goudy, Palatino, Caslon, or Times.*
- *For display type, consider Brush Script, Cloister, or Boulevard.*

Try to place the semicolon at the end of the first line of a two-line head, and avoid using it in a one-line head.

Principal makes presentation; discusses attendance policy

Note that in the preceding headline the subject is the same in both lines, so it is not necessary to repeat it. If the second line has a different subject, then it must be used in that line.

8. Do not editorialize, unless the headline is for an editorial or opinion column. Opinion should be obvious in an editorial headline.

9. Every headline should contain a subject and a verb; however, avoid beginning a headline with a verb.

10. Avoid using forms of the verb *to be*, such as *is, are, was,* and *were*. However, it is acceptable to use *to be* for the future tense. Try to be consistent in style when using future tense: Use either *to be* or *will be* for all stories.

11. Use only well-known abbreviations. In most schools, SC is a well-known abbreviation for Student Council. YMCA and YWCA are other common abbreviations. Do not use periods in abbreviations.

12. Do not begin a headline with an arabic numeral.

13. Use the future tense for future stories and the present tense for both past and present stories.

14. Keep related words on the same line (prepositions with their objects, adjectives with their nouns, verbs with their objects, parts of names, abbreviations, and hyphenated words).

15. Avoid clichés—words or expressions that appear so frequently in headlines that they become monotonous or weak in meaning.

16. Use information from the lead for your headline, except for feature stories. Feature headlines may come from any part of the story.
17. Use full names of persons, unless the person is well known.
18. Use strong verbs to show action.
19. Use the active voice, not the passive.

Avoid use of label headlines—headlines of a few words that do little more than identify a page or a story. For example, *Varsity Basketball* as a headline for a yearbook spread on the team is boring. It does not fit the specific year, and it certainly lacks excitement. Be creative, but make sure the headline fits the story.

Most high school yearbooks and newspapers use the flush left style of headline. Flush left means that each line of the headline is set even with the left-hand margin.

Other headline styles include the following:

Hanging Indention. This type of headline should have at least three lines. The first completely fills the column, and succeeding lines are indented one more em. An em is a type measure that is the width of the letter *m* in the size and style of type being used.

Cross-line. A single line of type filling the column or space allotted to it.

Inverted Pyramid. This type of headline should have three or more lines of type. The first line fills the entire column, and the succeeding lines decrease by the same number of units on each side and are centered.

Drop-line. This type of headline has two or more lines, with each succeeding line indented on the left by one em.

Centered Headline. As the name indicates, this type of headline is centered above the column. It need not completely fill the space but is rarely more than two counts under the maximum.

Following are examples of the types of headlines mentioned here.

➢ *Using the Dominant Photo for a Picture Story Headline*

• *The dominant photo can direct the reader to the story's content.*

• *The dominant photo should be a top-quality print with lots of emotion or action.*

• *After looking at the photo, decide what verb best describes the action.*

• *Determine who is in the photo.*

• *Now list adjectives and adverbs that would describe the noun and the verb.*

• *Now write the headline for the story using some of the words in your list.*

➤ **Woven Words**

Another style of headline is one where the words appear to be woven together. In this style, ascenders from the bottom line overlap descenders from the top line. To make each line stand out more, it is wise to contrast each one in shades of color. Designers can create this headline style by using negative leading (setting the leading at a smaller number than the point size) or by setting one line of the head as a separate piece of copy and then moving it manually onto the other line of the headline.

It All Adds UP

EVERY MINUTE COUNTS

New twists to the rules and regulations force students to prepare for any

QUICK CHANGE

POINT IN THE RIGHT DIRECTION

CREDIT

"I try to start my homework right when I get home and I do as much as I can. I try to find time at school to finish whatever I didn't finish the night before."
Dan Watanapongse, junior

PARTIAL CREDIT

"I usually spend an hour at night on my homework and hurry to finish the rest in the morning and during classes and lectures."
Barry Smith, freshman

NO CREDIT

"The only time management that I worry about is ignoring the time so that I can manage to make school go by faster." Janet Oi, senior

At first glance, little had changed. The same classes and for the most part, the same people occupied the same space. But little by little, the changes listed in the latest edition of the handbook came into sight.

The North Office tackled handling attendance in addition to its infamous disciplinary responsibilities. "My first reaction is that they caught me parking in the teacher's lot," Amy Sobolewski, junior, said.

To curb the ditching problem, the School Board decided to deduct three percent from a student's grade for ditching. "I'm really worried about my grades so the three percent rule really discourages me from ditching," Mike Rawlings, sophomore, said.

The tardy policy loosened to allow for stalled engines, broken alarm clocks or just running late. Instead of usual three tardies, hurried teens received an extra tardy for first hour only. "I felt that it was unnecessary. Bosses don't give extentions to people who come in late in the morning any more than they do for those who come in late from lunch," Mrs. Mary Yorke, English teacher, said.

As the seven minutes between classes seemed to grow shorter, students clamored for new lockers and the administration complied, moving the teens as many as seven lockers. "The administration should have either kept us at our same lockers or moved us to the larger lockers seniors had in previous years. Moving us down one or two spaces was just an inconvenience," Jamie Gardner, senior, said.

Student negligence forced the cafeteria to replace the metal "silver"ware with plastic counterparts, despite a "Save the Silver" crusade led by Mrs. Mary Yorke's English Literature Class. "We were really sick and tired of using Ken and Barbie stuff. We go the regular silverware but then people started throwing it away so we got the other stuff back," Becky Boilek, senior, said.

Students also faced the consequences of breaking rules. "Going out to lunch is worth two detentions because you get better food. You'd have to get busted at least three or four times before getting caught would even cross your mind," Matt Mertz, sophomore, said.

GIVE A HOOT, DON'T POLLUTE
Tossing his fork into the pan, Nick Schneider, junior contributes to the school's new recycling program. The effort to keep the "silver" war instead of plastic utensils failed due to a lack of students' participation.

FOR OFFICIAL USE ONLY
Checking over attendance records with Mr. Jack King, dean of students, Julie Zimmerman, junior, learns to check a student's class schedule.

Read-in heads are good ways to catch the reader's attention. Note how the first three lines lead into the main line of the head in the Paragon, *Munster High School, Munster, IN. Note the effective use of typography throughout the page.*

Ed Goodman Inspires
Varied Imaginations   **FLUSH LEFT**

Teachers Need
  Bigger Increase   **HANGING INDENTION**
    In Wage Package

Wage increase breeds discontent	CROSS-LINE
Strokers to host state champion in home battle	DROP-LINE
Two Spanish classes to host festivals for community	INVERTED PYRAMID
Two win awards	CENTERED HEADLINE

A yearbook or newspaper should use only one of the above types of heads on a page or spread. Yearbooks should not mix the types within a section. It is important to remain consistent.

Writing a headline that is an attention-grabber and that fits in the allotted space is difficult. Headlines must be long enough to fill the space but never go beyond that space. Each style and size of headline has a prescribed number of units. A headline that contains too few units will not fill the space, and one that has too many units cannot be used at all. As a general rule, each line of a headline should come within two counts or two picas of the maximum or fill the space entirely. If it is a two-line headline, the second line should be at least as long as the first.

A secondary headline under the main headline is called a deck. Each succeeding deck is in a smaller type size. Some stories in large newspapers are long enough to require two or three decks. School papers seldom use more than one deck because of the small size of the publication. However, both yearbooks and newspapers are using more than one deck as staffs learn how to use typography effectively to enhance design. Refer to Chapters 11 and 12 on newspaper and yearbook design for more information on typography. A one-deck headline means that each line in that deck is of the same size

➢ *Getting the Right Type*
  • *Type should set the mood.*
  • *Type should convey a tone.*
  • *Type should bring personality to a publication.*
  • *Use a maximum of three to four typefaces throughout the publication. Vary the use of these styles (roman, bold, italic) to create a more distinctive design look.*
  • *Choose one typeface for all body copy, one typeface for all headlines, one typeface for subheads, and one typeface for all captions.*
  • *Yearbooks will normally be consistent with type usage within a section of the book. Newspapers are normally consistent throughout the publication but may change headline fonts to fit the mood of a story.*

and typeface. However, a deck may be more than one line in length. For example:

> Pioneers down Lancers, 3-0,
> in muddy, defensive battle
> before standing-room crowd
>
> ## Win clinches district berth

The first three lines are one deck, and the fourth line is a second deck.

One eye-catching device that is used for variety is the kicker, sometimes called a tagline. A kicker precedes the main headline. It is always short, and the type may be underlined for emphasis. Some publications use an ellipsis after the kicker. Often witty or humorous, the kicker is used to draw attention to the main headline.

A kicker is half the size of the main headline. A point is a vertical measurement for the height of type; there are 72 points in an inch. A 72-point headline would be a one-inch headline. However, most points are not true to size, because printers allow for leading between lines of type. If a main headline were 36-point type, the kicker would be 18-point. Kickers are normally used only with one-line heads; the main line is indented two ems, with the kicker flush left. Following is an example of a kicker with a mainline.

Cold weather hits ...

Temperature drops below freezing

The kicker above is in 12-point type, and the main headline is in 24-point type. The main headline above should have been one line—not two.

Hammer heads are also used, especially in yearbooks. A

> Type-Casting
• Clean-cut types: Traditional serif or sans serif fonts like Palatino, Times, Helvetica, Avant Garde.
• Artistic types: Sculpted, etched, sketched types that look like they sound—Tekton
• Curvy types: A handwritten look like Brush Script, Freestyle Script, Boulevard.
• Multi-cultural types: Contrasted by diversity of letter strokes: Hallmarke Light, **Bold or Black.**
• Shy Types: Italicized traditional serif or sans serif type like Helvetica Regular
• Physical types: Varied letter width of traditional serif or sans serif type: Helvetica Narrow, Hallmarke Condensed Black, Hallmarke Condensed Bold.
• Chaotic types: Unique alignment and inconsistent letter strokes: Mistral, Reporter No. 2.

Contrasting gray with black creates an interesting headline effect in the Kirkwood Call, Kirkwood High School, Kirkwood, MO.

hammer head is the opposite of a kicker: It is a main headline that precedes a smaller headline. If the hammer head is 48-point, the smaller headline following will be 24-point. Normally the hammer head completely fills the space, and the smaller head is centered under it. The following is an example of a hammer head:

Drowning in 'Purple Rain'
Storm delays Prince's concert at Arena

The main line of the preceding hammer head is in 24-point. The sentence head below it is in 12-point type. Note that single quote marks are used around the song title 'Purple Rain.' Always use single quote marks in headlines.

Subheads may be used to break up long stories. As a general rule, any story of seven paragraphs or more could use subheads. Subheads, which relate to the material in the following paragraph, are used every two to three paragraphs.

Type Definitions

• *Old English or Text: Since it is ornate, it is usually hard to read. Do not use text type in all caps; it is probably not a good choice for anything besides announcements.*

• *Old Style Roman: These fonts have serifs (hooks or feet on ends of letters). There is minimal difference between the thick and thin parts of each letter, which helps the reader skim across the tops of letters quickly. It is considered the most readable type and is often used for body copy and captions.*

• *Modern Roman: These fonts also have serifs but there is a lot of difference between the thin and thick parts of the letters. As such, it is not as readable as Old Style Roman, so it works best for headlines.*

• *Square Serif or Slab Serif. This type looks as if it has little blocks for serifs. It works well for logos and display heads.*

• *Sans Serif: These fonts have no serifs. In French, sans means "without." These fonts work well in headlines, but are usually more difficult to read in body copy.*

• *Scripts/Cursives: These fonts resemble handwriting. Do not use in all caps, but they work well in heads.*

Never use only one subhead. Most subheads are crosslines (one line) in the same size or slightly larger type than the body copy and set in boldface for contrast.

Yet another type of headline is the wicket, two or more lines of secondary headline above one primary headline. The primary is usually a feature, and the secondary is usually a sentence. However, the four lines together can create a complete sentence as in the following example:

Five inches of rain

creates muddy field

as Chiefs, Bears go

Slip, Sliding Away

Note that the primary headline is twice the size of the secondary head. It is not necessary for the two decks to form a sentence. The three top lines can stand alone as a sentence head, with the bottom line standing alone as a feature head.

Another type of headline is the slammer. A slammer is a two-part head that uses a boldface phrase to lead into the main headline, which is not bold. Both parts of the head are the same size. The following example is in 24-point type.

Turkey Day: Pioneers regain Bell

Sidesaddle heads are also used by a lot of papers. This style places the head to the left of the story, rather than above. It works best with a boxed horizontal story. Each line can be flush left, flush right, or centered.

Another type of head is the raw wrap or dutch wrap. The head is placed above the first column of a story, and the remaining columns of text wrap up to the right of the headline. This can be risky in the middle of a page. If one is used, it needs to be separated from the story above it with a cutoff rule (discussed in Chapter 11).

Other ways of obtaining contrast in type styles are to use roman (straight vertical lettering) or italic (slanted lettering). Generally it is not acceptable to get contrast by mixing serif (letters with hooks) and sans serif (letters without hooks). However, if used consistently, this mixture can be effective.

In fact, as long as one is consistent in usage throughout a section of a yearbook, it is possible to mix cursive fonts with roman fonts. Be creative, but don't overdo. Always be sure that

➢ *Faces, Fonts and Families*
  • *A typeface is a single style variation in a type family, such as light, bold, or condensed.*
  • *Most experts define font as all the upper and lower case letters of the alphabet. It includes all the numbers and basic symbols in one point size of type. By that definition, one font would be 10-point Bookman type. However, when desktop publishing began, a font became a type family in any point size and family variation. Bookman then became a font—not a family as in the former definition.*
  • *A family then is all fonts with the same name. A type family is a progression of design widths, with corresponding italics, condensed, expanded, and ornamental styles.*

Problems involving trash, smoking, lines, theft prompt administration to ask SC for help with

ISSUES

Soda sold for more than 50 cents a can in January.

Principal Franklin McCallie closed the soda and candy machines the first two weeks of January, so Steve Thomas, junior, brought sodas for himself and his friends. However, people who did not know Thomas paid him $1-$2 for one.

"I started bringing sodas to school basically from the first day the machines were closed," said Thomas. "My friends and I drank them during lunch or after school, but people I didn't even know offered to buy a can. I ended up making a profit out of it."

McCallie closed the machines after going to Student Council (SC) and asking for help on how to deal with the trash problem. He also wanted SC to think of solutions for three other major ISSUES--long lunch lines, theft, and smoking--which were affecting the student body.

Coming up with solutions for the four ISSUES proved to be difficult, according to Jennifer Steinman, president.

"It was hard to find solutions," said Steinman, "because we knew McCallie would never accept some of our ideas."

One proposal SC presented that McCallie did accept was closing the soda and candy machines.

"We made announcements every day threatening to close the machines if the trash problem didn't get any better, but apparently it didn't work," said Eric O'Neill, sophomore, "so McCallie closed everything down."

Another ISSUE that caused controversy was smoking.

Cars pass by as Sara Roock and Jane Roettger, juniors, try to flag down customers for the wreath sale, Dec. 1. The Beautification Committee IS-SUED 297 wreaths.

SC proposed that the first time an administrator caught a student smoking he should receive five IVC'S. For each additional time, the administration added another day to the suspension.

"I don't think our proposal was harsh enough," said Mary Duncan, senior. "I think we ignored the fact that not only are minors smoking illegally on public property, but they're also violating a school policy."

Stealing was the final ISSUE SC dealt with.

"There wasn't much we could do about it except make announcements," said Chris Hahs, secretary. "What was Student Council going to do? Call in the Equalizer to check out every theft?"

Photographs can enhance headlines, as illustrated in the Pioneer, *Kirkwood High School, Kirkwood, MO. By dropping out the background around the photograph, the yearbook staff was able to use it effectively with the headline.*

any mixture of fonts complement each other.

Fitting headlines to fill a space has become easier with the use of computers. Students can go to the computer and keep playing around until a headline fits. Be careful, however, not to make headlines too large or too small just to fit a space. As a guideline, don't vary the size by more than one point up or down. If a headline is to be 36 point in size, don't make it any less than 35 or more than 37. Also, don't overuse tightening or loosening of letters and words. It is easy to close up or open up space between letters and words on computers. However, this can cause a noticeable variance in spacing from story to story or from spread to spread.

It is also wise to write headlines before sitting down at a computer to fit them to a space. The process is speedier if the writer has an idea in mind first. Also, if you create your own counting guide for the font you use for most headlines, you can get close to an exact fit before ever going to the computer. For example, if you know that in 24-point Garamond you get an average of 5 characters per inch, it would be simple to write a headline with approximately 20 characters for a four-inch space.

In case you are not using a computer, you can use a headline schedule your printer gives you to count headlines.

Every publication has its own headline schedule. Generally, however, printers use the following counting guide:

> Lowercase *m* and *w*—1½
> Lowercase *f,l,i,r,t,*—½
> All other lowercase letters—1
> Uppercase *I*—1
> Uppercase *M* and *W*—2
> All other uppercase—1½
> Numerals—1
> Spaces between words—1
> $ and &—1½
> ? and %—1
> Single quote marks, commas, periods, semi-colons, colons, apostrophes, and parentheses —½

The printer's typestyle book will show how many counts

> ➤ *Tracking and Kerning*
> • *Tracking means closing up the space between all letters and words.*
> • *Kerning is closing up the space between individual letters and individual words.*
> • *Most software programs have a default in tracking that is normal. However, tight tracking can sometimes look better than normal, especially in headlines.*
> • *Normal: I love journalism.*
> • *Tight: I love journalism.*
> • *Very tight: I love journalism.*
> • *To kern between letters in PageMaker, hold down the Command key and use the left arrow to close up space and the right arrow to open up space.*

Tips for Using Type

- *Experiment. Print out a variety of fonts in various sizes and combinations to compare readability.*
- *Create a font notebook so designers can readily see what a font looks like.*
- *If you don't have a font notebook, use key caps to find out what various fonts look like.*
- *Avoid anything below 10 point for body copy and 8 point for captions in yearbooks, and avoid anything below 9 point for body copy for newspapers.*
- *Contrast is important. If you use a serif typeface for the main headline, then consider a sans serif for the subhead.*
- *Black, white, and gray are available colors. Try screening type to achieve a different look.*
- *Avoid setting headlines, subheads, and body copy in all capital letters, as they are difficult to read.*
- *Avoid setting body copy and captions on black or colored backgrounds, as they are difficult to read.*

are available per column width of type. For example, if a 36-point headline has a 12-count per column, the writer would double that count for two columns. Usually, one count is added for the vertical space between columns in headlines of 36-point or smaller. Remember that headlines are counted line by line. In the preceding example, a two-line, 36-point headline, two columns wide, would count 25 per line.

There is no one way to count a headline. Some people simply write down the headline and count it letter for letter. For example, *Video Games Under Fire* counts 22½.

Note that each word of the headline in the preceding example is capitalized; such a headline is called an upstyle head. Few publications today use upstyle heads. The more usual style is downstyle, which capitalizes only the first word of the headline and proper nouns. In other words, it is written just as you would write a sentence:

Video games under fire

Note that periods are not used at the end of headlines.

Some writers prefer to count headlines by pairing the fractions as they count. For example: in *Video games under fire*:

Vi	2 (paired; 1½ + ½ =2)
d, e, o	3, 4, 5
space	6
g, a	7, 8
m	9 and 10 (the writer glanced ahead and paired the *m* with the *r* in under)
e, s	11, 12
space	13
u,n,d,e	14, 15, 16, 17
space	18
f, i	19
r	19 1/2
e	20 1/2

Another method used to count headlines is to mark the full units above the line and the half units below the line, as follows:

```
 I   2 3 4 5    6 789 10   II 12 13 14 15  16        17
/  / / / /     / / / / /  /  / / / / /            /
V i d e o    g a m e s    u n d e r   f i r e
/             /               /     / / \
17½           18½             19   19½ 20 20½
```

It is more important to be accurate than fast, but deadlines make speed important also.

➤ *Ascenders and Descenders*

• *Ascending characters are b, d, f, h, k. l, and t. They rise above the x-height of a letter (the height of the letter x) and may not always align at the top.*

• *Descending characters are g, j, p, q, and y. They descend below the x-height and baseline and usually align at the bottom.*

• *Leading (space) between lines must be sufficient to allow for the ascenders and descenders. Ascenders should not touch the line above and descenders should not touch the line below, unless you're doing a woven words headline.*

Fitting a headline can be faster if the headline writer develops a good vocabulary, so that she can immediately replace a short verb with a longer one if necessary, or vice versa. For example, synonyms for *find* would include: *determine, encounter, discover, uncover, declare, decide*. A good idea is to have a counted list of commonly used verbs so that a headline writer can check immediately whether a certain word will fit.

Do not violate the rules of good usage just to make a headline fit. Avoid libelous statements, poor grammar, misspelling, and sensationalism.

"Will Dad Kill Us?" is an example of a headline that could be considered sensational. The story dealt with the supposed fear that children in a town felt after one father had killed his children. The story did not indicate how many children were living in fear. The headline seems to distort the importance of murderous dads to the story.

Don't try to be humorous in headlines. Some staffs think it is clever to use alliteration, but it usually backfires. For example:

Bountiful busy bicyclists bustle briskly by

Joggers jaunt for joyance

Frisbee frolicking finds fans

All three are mouthfuls, and few readers would be amused by them. The goal is to attract attention to the story without going overboard. Good headlines take time to write, but speed comes with practice. Remember, the key to a good headline is that it fits the story and at the same time attracts attention. You might use *antithesis* to show the opposite. For example, one yearbook used "Gentle Jocks" on a story about girl athletes. You might also use *allusion* to refer to a well-known expression or person. One yearbook used "It rained on our parade" for a story about a storm during a parade. Don't forget that using a play on words is one of the most effective ways to write a feature headline. For example, one newspaper used "Caught standing in the reign" for the

> **Keeping Count**
> Counting headlines has become part of journalism's historic past as schools and printers around the country are mostly using computers today to set type. Nevertheless, students should have a knowledge of the way things used to be, when it was more difficult to write headlines that fit the allotted space. Students should practice writing headlines using the counting methods discussed on pages 227-229 in order to get a feel for the methods that were still being used near the end of the 20th century.

Teachers react to announcements of honorary awards

They said he was the best.

H.L. Hall, journalism teacher, became highly suspicious when Mrs. Barbara Zelle, registrar, telephoned him, seventh hour, Dec. 6, to tell him Principal Franklin McCallie wanted him at the office to pick up a fax immediately.

"I couldn't think of any fax which would be that important," Hall said.

Upon entering the office, Hall received a balloon bouquet and a decorated cookie which read "Best in Nation."

Earlier that day Hall had received a letter from the Journalism Education Association (JEA), naming him as the first "Yearbook Adviser of the Year."

"A yearbook adviser in Michigan (Gloria Olman) nominated me for the award," Hall said. "She gathered several letters of support, and I also solicited letters. All the letters were really special, and they will be keepsakes for me."

Hall left the evening he received the news from JEA to speak in Boston, and when he arrived home, Dec. 10, another surprise awaited him.

"The Pioneer staff left a congratulatory sign in my yard," Hall said. "The ground was frozen, so it kept falling over. My wife ended up tying it to a tree, so I would see it when I got home."

Besides Hall's award which included a $1,000 scholarship for one of his students, Bob Becker, science teacher, also received recognition when Synaps, a CD-ROM company, asked him to put together a program for chemistry teachers and professors. Becker completed the project, earning $1,000 for the Science Department.

Becker also received the regional American Chemical Society (ACS) award at a convention in Joplin.

"The award was a surprise," he said. "I hadn't planned on going to Joplin as I was already speaking in Oklahoma City at the time, but the ACS insisted I come. I found out later why. I was honored, but it was a weird situation."

Using contrasting fonts, and using a feature head and a secondary sentence head help explain this copy about several teachers who received awards in the Pioneer, *Kirkwood High School, Kirkwood, MO.*

➢ Try Tucking

Tucking words inside other words or tucking words inside letters, such as the letter o is also an effective headline design. It is visually attractive to the reader, and it provides a way to visually link information.

crowning of the Homecoming queen. Following are other examples of headlines that use plays on words.

Hair today, gone tomorrow—for a story on hairstyles.

Clip off the old block—for a story about a touchdown that was called back because of an illegal block.

When soap gets in their eyes—for a story on soap operas.

Too many tows to count—for a story on illegally parked cars.

A melon folly day—for a story on a watermelon bust.

The cruising is over—for a story on Tom Cruise's marriage.

Chairman of the boards—for a story on skateboarding.

To get ideas for headlines, you might look closely at the photo that goes with the story, especially the dominant

Type Legibility

• Large amounts of body type should be broken up to avoid grayness. The use of subheads, initial letters, and pulled quotes can often be effective.

• Line width should range from no less than one lower case alphabet (26 letters) to no more than two lower case alphabets (52 letters). Another formula is to double the point size in picas as an optimum line width. Thus, a maximum line width for 10-point type would be 20 picas, plus or minus four picas. The range then would be 16-24 picas.

• Do not mix too many families in selecting body and headline type.

• One to two points of leading is best for most body type. One point is most common for roman typefaces while most sans serif faces, because of their vertical stress, require two points of leading.

• Avoid italic type, reverse type, and bold type for large amounts of body type.

• Use sans serif type on backgrounds. Filling patterns as dots may make roman type appear fuzzy.

• Type margins can be arranged or justified, ragged right, ragged left, centered, and symmetrical. Body type should be justified or ragged right.

photo if you're working on a yearbook spread or a photo story for the newspaper. Often the dominant photo shows part of the information presented in the copy. Look at the photo, and write down key words that come to mind. If the dominant photo is of a hurler throwing the discus, and his feat is mentioned in the copy, the headline could be "A Mighty Throw." Of course, you wouldn't use that if it wasn't "a mighty throw."

Use of rule lines, screens, initial letters, and a variety of type sizes can add graphic appeal to a head. Even grunge fonts have become popular for special circumstances. The different look of grunge fonts helps to create appeal. Literally thousands of grunge fonts have cropped up, and many magazines are using them for headlines and advertisements. Grunge fonts are also appearing on greeting cards, CD covers, and television commercials. Designers refer to these fonts as grunge because they usually have a distressed look about them. They also tend to have unusual names. Wooly Bully would be one type of grunge font and Where's Marty would be another. Display type faces add personality and impact to a newspaper or yearbook page. They might be acceptable for headlines, but they are not acceptable for body type. Designers also need to keep in mind that just because a particular font is fun today, it may not be appropriate for years, and yearbooks will be around for years. Nevertheless, a yearbook does portray one particular year, so using fun fonts to tell the story of that year is satisfactory. Type must be readable, but it can also be entertaining. The real secret of writing good headlines is choosing the right font to convey a feeling and then having the ability to juggle words and to think of synonyms. A headline writer should have a *Roget's Thesaurus* at hand.

EXERCISES

1. Count the following headlines (count each line separately) and point out any rules that have been violated:

A. Representatives
   well received by Parkway's student body
B. Faculty topples students by
   overwhelming margin
C. False Fire Alarm Witnessed
   by North's Skaters
D. PIONEERS OUTSCORED BY
   WEST LADUE MUSTANGS
E. New Year and Resolutions
   Keep 16 Students Active

> Type Definitions
> • Backslant: Type slanted to the left.
> • Body type: Type below 14 points in size.
> • Display type: Type 14 points or larger.
> • Em: Square of space. The size of the square depends upon the size of type. An em space is often used for paragraph indents.
> • Italic: Type slanted to the right.
> • Justified: Type that is even on the left and right margins as opposed to unjustified type such as ragged right or left.
> • Posture: The angle of type, such as backslant, roman, and italic.
> • Swashed: Ornate extended serifs available on some type families.
> • Typography: The use and arrangement of type.

➢ Ragged Right
Vs. Justified

• "One of the things that bugs me now is the huge amount of type set ragged right. That's an irritation to the eye. When we have to do a job over and over again, the only way we can do it is rhythmically. Justified type makes that process easier. The eye does not have to adjust to a different sweep on each line."—Edmund C. Arnold, author

• "Ragged-right reads better. In setting justified copy, the type-setter (whether a person or a programmed machine) often has to spread out the space between words to make the lines come out the right length. The resulting uneven spacing affects the visual rhythm of each line and disturbs reading. It makes the eye stumble, as it tries to compensate for these imbalances. That is tiring work. ."—Jan V. White, author

F.   Statistics Prove Kids Are Worse Today

G.   Promoters of Tacky Day
     Refused a Fair Hearing

H.   Social Studies Classes to
     Offer Several Mini Courses

I.   Future of Boys' Pep Club
     Discussed by Faculty

J.   Newspaper Sales Lagging
     According to Martino

K.   *Gone with the Wind* to be
     Shown to history classes

L.   Fair Sponsored by
     German and French classes

M.   Ancient history classes
     visit prehistoric pit

N.   Kirkwood R-7 to Implement
     Reorganization next year

O.   Educationally disadvantaged students
     find new hope at alternative school

P.   OFFICERS PRICE, RICE GIVE
     LEGAL COUNSELING

Q.   KHS Students Tutoring
     During Independent Hour

R.   MEDITATORS SHATTER MYTHS

S.   Quiz will reveal philosophic powers

T.   *Popeye, Our Gang, Blondie*
     Topic for Nostalgia Freaks

U.   Name change to 'Nicks'
     possibly just for kicks

V.   LEARNING RESOURCE CENTER
     INTEGRAL PART OF PROGRAM

W.   Hall's Stick Pounds
     Eardrums into Submission

X.   Halloween Witches On
     Tap for Halloween Dance

Y.   auditions precede play; cast,
     crew join newest production

Z.   Gets seminary post

2. Go through a file of last year's newspapers and make a list of verbs used most often. Then compile a list of synonyms for those verbs. Count each one and post the list in the classroom for all headline writers to use. Do a similar exercise for the last issue of the yearbook.

3. Write a feature headline, 21 count in length, for the following story. Then write a 40-count sentence headline. If you are using a computer, make your feature headline 36 points in size and 45 picas wide, and make your sentence headline 18 points in size and 40-45 picas wide.

"We tried as hard as we could, but the other team pulled us across the line," said Sandy Berg.

Kirkwood's Distributive Education Club of America (DECA) members competed with particpants from 11 other districts in a mock Olympics, including a tug-of-war, at Greensfelder Park, Oct. 9, and took first place, as they won two out of three tugs. Berg was referring to the second of three tugs, which they lost.

"The Olympics helped us get to know DECA members from other schools," said Jim Graves, sponsor.

4. Write a feature headline, 18-count in length, for the following story. Then write a 38-count sentence headline. If you are using a computer, make your feature headline 30 points in size and 30 picas wide and your sentence headline 15 points in size and 25-30 picas wide.

"We can bounce our signals off the moon," said Chris Winslow, junior.

Winslow was one of the 12 Radio Club members who met to use radios.

"We really worked to increase our range and our ease of operating," said David Mote, president.

Factors to Consider When Choosing Justified or Ragged Right Type

• *Readability: One study found that ragged right type is easier to read for most people, but other studies found little difference in the readability.*

• *Suitability: Which style creates the most suitable image for your publication. Justified type creates a quiet, traditional, formal look, and ragged right creates a more active, more contemporary, more informal look.*

• *Producibility: All word processing programs and page layout programs allow for either ragged right or justified. You should avoid using justified type without automatic hyphenation.*

• *Line width: If the line width is short, ragged right usually works best. When type is justified in a short line, gaping holes often appear between words.*

• *Space: On the average, justified copy usually fills about 3% less space than the same copy set ragged right.*

"We had good range, especially with our new 2000-watt radio," said Winslow. "It operated through the antenna on top of North building. We talked to people all over."

"I talked to people from all over the world, like Mexico and Brazil," said Lisa Liss, senior. "It's hard to believe that little box can transmit your voice so far. The club made me more aware of the world."

5. Write a two-line sentence head, 24-count in length, for the following story. Remember that the

second line should be as long as or longer than the top line. Do not go over the maximum, and make the minimum no more than two under the maximum. If you are using a computer, make your headline 24 points in size and 24 picas wide.

Placing video game machines in quick shops, grocery stores, and game rooms has prompted increased concern about the hazardous effects on local businesses.

These establishments provide a center for entertainment and amusement, but they also encounter the frustrating problem of theft, disruption and disturbances as a result of such games.

These stores often place two or three video machines in their establishments to attract students and children in hopes that more business and profit will result. Some businesses have introduced special bonuses to attract players.

"The Wonder Corporation has established a policy where for every 'A' on a report card a student receives a free token," said a Wonder Corporation worker. "We hope that it will bring more business into the arcade and Sears store."

Although business has increased, the machines have created various problems.

"Overcrowding, theft, and distractions are all problems caused by the two machines in the store," said Mike Walt, salesperson at Magic Market on Geyer Road. "We constantly have problems with kids stealing from the store before and after using the machines," Walt said. "We also have a major problem with loitering."

6.   Study all the headlines in the last issue of your school paper. Point out the weaknesses and strengths of each. Rewrite those that are weak, using the original count.

7.   Count all the headlines in the last issue of

➤ *Feature Head Ideas*

More Than Passing Fancy—for a story on note passing.

One Life to Loaf—for a story on procrastination.

Waking Up Is Hard To Do—for a story on getting ready for school.

Return to Sender—for a story on teachers who graduated from the same high school.

Flu or False—for a story on excuses for being absent.

your school paper, using the headline count in this chapter or the one used by your publication.

8. Study all of the headlines in the last edition of your school yearbook. Point out the weaknesses and strengths of each one. Rewrite five of those that are weak.

9. Count the headlines in the last edition of your school yearbook, using the headline count in this chapter or the one used by your yearbook.

10. Select a newspaper or a yearbook from your exchange file and be prepared in class to discuss types of headlines used and the good and bad features of each headline.

11. Count all headlines on the front page of your daily newspaper for one week, using your headline count. Bring your counts to class and compare them with those of your classmates.

12. Go back to exercises 3 to 5 and write a wicket headline for each. If you are not using a computer, make each of the 3 lines of the secondary headline 16 counts, and make the primary line 32 counts. If you are using a computer, set your first three lines in 16-point type, 18 picas wide, and make your primary headline 32-point type, 30 picas wide.

13. Write a hammer head for the following. Your teacher can give you the maximum counts, the pica widths, and the point size for each deck.

A picnic in the park. A deceiving balloon. A sinking boat.

All of these events were part of the itineraries of students Prom night, May 18.

The evening started early for three couples who went on a picnic and limousine ride.

"We went to get Chinese food after the limo picked us up, and then we ate it at Laumeier Park," said Chad Garrison, senior. "On the way there, when we stopped at stop signs, we rolled down the windows halfway and acted like we were movie stars."

"We had a fun time, but Alison (Moskoff, junior) got bit on the head by a bug, and she was upset about it," said Garrison.

Other prom-goers experienced confusion at the Prom.

"When I was eating dinner I felt something under the table, and when I pulled it out it was a silver balloon. I noticed a blue circle on the bottom, and I thought maybe the people at the table with the balloon under it would win a prize. I was concerned that other people would take it and I wouldn't get my prize," said Laura Hook, senior.

"Later I heard it was just part of the decorations, and it was supposed to be floating around the room."

The problems continued after Prom for some students. Twenty-eight people went to Mike Swoboda's cabin at Innsbrook Estates.

"Around nine in the morning everyone was getting a little restless because our horseback riding plans got canceled, so we decided to liven things up and go for a boat ride," said LeeAnn Hurley, junior. "The johnboat was only supposed to hold two people, but we were able to pack in six.

"The boat held all our weight, but once we started moving, the boat gradually sank lower and water began to trickle over the sides. It took us 15 minutes to paddle the boat 10 feet back to the dock."

14. Write a kicker and a one-line primary head for the following story. Your teacher will give you the point size, count, and width.

For the first time they were recognized as an official team.

The school district made boys' volleyball an official varsity school-sponsored sport. This was the first such team in the state.

"The sport itself hasn't changed, but since the

team is school-sponsored the public is more aware of the sport, and we get more publicity," said Cory Miller, outside hitter.

Brian Clawson, middle hitter, did not think the status had changed.

"Only our school recognized the sport, so nothing changed with the other schools," said Clawson. "We just didn't have to pay for any of the equipment this year as we have in the past."

15. Write headlines for the stories (5 to 8 and 10) at the end of Chapter 10. Your teacher will give you types and sizes.

CHAPTER
ten

Writing Yearbook Copy

Yearbooks are history books. That simple fact means that if yearbooks are to present a complete history of the year, copy must appear on each two-page spread. Make a commitment to include each student in copy at least once. When students know they are in the book, they are more apt to want to buy a copy. If you can't get each student in copy, try for a candid photo. Students deserve more coverage in a book than just a portrait picture. The goal of the yearbook staff should be thorough coverage. Give newsworthy events top priority. It is impossible to tell the history of the year with just photographs. The average photograph is probably shot at about 1/250 of a second. That means if a yearbook contains 500 candid photos (action shots only), it will have captured exactly two seconds of time. There is no way the history of a school year can be told in two seconds even if a picture is worth a thousand words. A wide variety of copy styles should be used to avoid monotony. Each staff member should strive to use a different format for presenting copy in each section of the book.

Many staffs have trouble coming up with enough ideas that are different from the copy of the previous year. It helps to have several "thinking" sessions during the early planning stages to determine what is new or different about the year in question.

These new or different things should help the staff select a theme that fits the year. A theme may be a logo or a phrase of two to six words; it is used to give the book continuity. The theme is usually used on the cover, on the end sheets, in the opening section, on the divider pages, and in the closing section. Copy in those areas develops the theme.

A theme should fit a particular school for a specific year. Do not select a theme that will fit any school year, unless you have a unique way to develop it.

The yearbook staff at Van Buren High School, Van Buren, AR, selected "There's One in Every Crowd" for its theme one year. Although it could have fit almost any school anywhere, the staff developed it so well that it worked, even though it could have been used any year.

The book's cover featured five questions in a multiple-choice list from which the reader could select his or her type of person in the crowd. This was continued on the end sheets and in the table of contents. In each section of the book the staff provided choices for the reader to make as to what type of person he or she was in the crowd. Under Student Life, for example, choices included Summer Bum, Hopeful, Queen, Escort, Preppy, Cruiser, Brown Bagger, and Snoozer. The concept of "There's One in Every Crowd" was continued in the index, where labels for people were used to separate letters of the alphabet. For example, the word for *U* was *unemployed*, and the word for *W* was *worriers*.

The general theme worked well for Van Buren's staff, but most schools select themes based on the specific year. The *Pioneer* at Kirkwood High School, Kirkwood, MO, selected the theme "A Common Ground" to mark the dedication of a new outside area at school, The Commons. For the first time all math teachers were located in one building, and all science teachers in one building; thus, both faculties had a common ground. The school closed its last portable building used for classrooms; all classrooms were housed in permanent buildings, creating another common ground. The school also voluntarily integrated with St. Louis city schools, thus creating a common ground for students from both districts. All of these events made "A Common Ground" a natural choice for the *Pioneer's* theme.

The staff found ways to use the word *common* in many sections of the book. It did a special section on "A Common Day in the Life of ...." The section covered more than 20 faculty members and students and showed how each one commonly spent a day. One of the portrait sections dealt with common

➢ *Considerations for Selecting a Theme*

• *All staff members should participate. A yearbook does not belong to the editor or the adviser.*

• *Look through magazines to collect words or phrases.*

• *Analyze your student body and your school. What makes the students tick? What new is happening at your school?*

• *Avoid clichés and overused concepts.*

• *As you narrow the possibilities, think about how a particular idea could be presented graphically and how it could be photographed.*

• *Envision how the theme idea might be carried throughout the book.*

• *Does the idea relate to this year at this school?*

• *How will you present the theme graphically?*

sayings, another featured common facts, and the index covered common names. These mini-themes throughout the book helped the staff further develop its overall theme. Mini-themes are often spin-offs of the book's overall theme. They tie a section together the way a main theme unifies the book. It is not necessary to have a phrase as a theme, but it does help a staff unify the book's contents. A graphic device or logo can also help unify a book. A staff might be wise to use a logo if nothing new is happening and no phrase fits the specific year. Don't contrive a phrase just to have a theme.

Be creative with the theme copy. Keep it short, but keep it lively. It is possible to use a parody (a takeoff on a well-known song, poem, or piece of literature). One school did a takeoff on *Catcher in the Rye* by J.D. Salinger for its theme "Well, It's About Time."

Poetry is another way to present theme copy. One school used poetry to present its theme, "It's not as easy as 1,2,3." Following is the opening theme copy:

> Beneath the surface one could see
> It wasn't as easy as 1,2,3.
> Dr. Rich Ehlers left behind
> His assistant principalship when he resigned.
> 45 candidates applied for the position,
> and 6 of those faced an inquisition.
> Terry Proffitt won the race,
> Filling Ehlers' empty space.
> 25 North Central Committees shifted into gear
> For an evaluation which occurred every 7th year.
> Faculty, parents, and students played their parts,
> Examining the school and filling out charts.
> There were 5 officers for grades 11 and 10,
> And 6 full hours for the Writing Center's den.
> As one could see, making things new
> Wasn't as easy as 1 and 2.

Another good presentation of theme copy is a conversational approach, as in the following example from Bay Village High School, Bay Village, OH, to present its theme, "What's the Catch?"

➢ *Finding a Theme*

• It is better to have no theme than to have a contrived one. If there is no main story of the year, develop a logo or concept that can be carried throughout the book.

• Even if there is a specific theme, you still need a visual unifier—a logo, a graphic, a color.

• Stretch your mind. Try to come up with a unique theme. Avoid ones used by other schools. If you do use a theme phrase that another school has used, be sure to be creative about how you present it. Don't copy what another school has already done.

• If possible, tie the theme in to all sections of the book, but don't overdo it.

• Short, catchy phrases of no more than three or four words usually make the best themes.

Oh no will you look at it now. They've got a blue fish on the cover of the yearbook! What does a fish have to do with Bay High?

Please be reasonable. At least they have some blue and white this time around.

Yeah, I guess. But who wants an ugly fish on their yearbook?

What's the deal here?

What's the catch?

Huh? What catch?

Avoid opinion in theme copy. Too many staffs expound on what a wonderful school they have. That may be true, but let the facts speak for themselves.

If you can't come up with a specific theme for the year, consider using a concept instead. Some books have been successful with a concept. In doing so, they have also broken away from the traditional sections—Student Life, Academics, Sports, Organizations and Portraits.

For example, the *Paragon* at Munster High School in Munster, IN, used three sections for one of its books. The sections were Wants, Options, and Needs. The staff included Academics and People in the Needs section, Student Life in the Wants section, and Sports and Clubs in the Options section. The *Pioneer* staff at Kirkwood High School used Inside, Outside, and Coming Together. In the Inside section they included everything that took place indoors. In the Outside section they included everything that took place outdoors, and the traditional People section was in the Coming Together part. This meant they mixed sports, academics, organizations, and student life in the other two sections. The Outside section was grouped around spin-offs, including Out to Learn, Out for Football, and Out to Serve. There were also spin-offs in the Inside section, including In the Money, In the Spotlight, In the Know, and In Competition.

Another book that used the three-section approach was the *American* from Independence High School in San Jose, CA. The *American* staff divided its book into School Life, After School, and People. The School Life section covered the seven

➢ *Conceptual Themes*

If nothing new is happening at your school, and it is impossible to select a theme phrase that fits the school year, consider a conceptual theme. There are still steps a staff must consider.

• Coverage, instead of a theme phrase, will determine the book's organization.

• Select a single word or a collection of related words, along with page design, color, and graphics, that will create a unifying effect.

• Consider reorganizing the book into nontraditional sections.

• Name these nontraditional sections with the related words you have selected.

• For example, the Deka staff at Huntington North High School in Indiana one year divided its book into six sections. They labeled the sections as Fundamentals, Camaraderie, Commitment, Applause, Leadership, and Community. The staff unified the book

(Continued)

academic periods. It also included clubs and school support groups. The After School section covered events that occurred after the school day, including sports.

The *Mascot* staff at Mexico High School in Mexico, MO, also used three sections: Opening, Life Journal, and Reference. There was no theme statement on the cover. Instead the staff used two graphic elements—a blue spiral and a black rectangle to begin the theme development. The Opening section included Red Letter Days, and the Life Journal section covered the year's events in chronological order. The staff covered each week on its own spread. The Reference section included sports, people, group photos, and an index. The book concluded with more Red Letter Days from the second half of the school year.

There is not a limitation regarding the number of sections a staff may use in a concept book. The *Pioneer* used four sections one year in developing a magazine concept. They were Entertainment, Expressions, Events, and Sports. The Entertainment section included Student Life and Fine Arts, the Expressions section included clubs and portraits, the Events section included everyday events, current events, and special events. The book included special features in each section.

Selection of theme or concept can help a staff get started on finding subjects to write about for the year. Certain topics such as sports, clubs, and academics are covered annually, but the staff should look for different ways to present them. For example, rather than covering one club in a spread, a staff could do its club coverage by topics such as fundraisers, banquets, and initiations. A similar plan could be used for academics. Instead of one spread to each department, coverage might be by field trips, projects, laboratories, skits, and music. This type of coverage might require continued copy blocks. For example, adequate coverage of projects would probably take more than one spread.

Staffs should seek as many different ways as possible to present copy. Surveys, questions and answers, quotations, lists, infographics (discussed in Chapter 8) and the traditional summary article are ways to consider. Even a sights and sounds feature (discussed in Chapter 6) can work well. It is probably

through consistent design and type.

• Several schools have used a calendar concept to present its coverage. A school in Missouri, for example, used a monthly concept, and a school in Iowa used a day-by-day approach.

• Another possible concept would be to present the book like a magazine and have sections for sports, entertainment, personalities, and news.

• Another possible concept would be to have only one section. The Wings yearbook staff at Arrowhead Christian Academy in Redlands, CA, used that approach in its 2002 edition.

• Proofreaders need a dictionary, a thesaurus, and a good grammar book for reference.

• Proofreading means reading the copy at least twice and marking the errors.

• Proofreading means more than just correcting spelling and grammar. It also means looking for inaccuracies in fact, looking for illogical order, looking for balanced coverage, and looking for any missing information necessary to reader understanding.

• Always check numbers, dates, titles, and quote attributions. Be sure percentages add up to 100.

Know kidding

Moments too embarrassing to believe

"During gym, Sarah Nichols got this bright idea that she was going to jump over the net if someone would hold it down, so I volunteered. Well I "accidentally" let go to see Sarah fall in front of the whole class. I don't think she'll do that again"
HEATHER *Davis*

"One day at football practice someone threw the ball at me. It hit my finger and bounced off my foot and almost landed in the practice field rather than the playing field. I ended up getting laughed at and my finger getting jammed."
MATT *Davis*

"In our Horticulture class, some of us volunteered to water the plants. This woman came around the corner while we we watering them and said, 'Girls, that one you are watering is artificial.'"
LATOSHA *Jennings*

Embarrassing moments make interesting quick reads. The ones above are from the Mascot, Mexico High School, Mexico, MO. Note the use of contrasting shades of type and the use of italic type with roman. Also, note the woven words in the headline with negative leading between "Know" and "kidding." The Mascot's theme was Everybody Knows..., and that is the reason for the word "Know" in the headline instead of "No."

best to be consistent within a section—i.e., do all sports copy the same way—but change presentation from section to section to add variety and increase readability.

The quick read story is one way to gain readability. Surveys show that 51% of all copy four paragraphs or less will be read. Longer copy has less readability. When determining the content of a spread, break that content down into various types of quick reads that might be used as sidebars. This would include factoids, maps, bio boxes, and timelines.

Following are some rules for writing yearbook copy:

1. Write in the past tense. Since a yearbook is a history book, it is logical that the story be told as if it has already happened. That is sometimes difficult to remember when a book is delivered in the spring before the end of school. Most spring-delivery books have a final publication

deadline of late February or early March. Nevertheless, writers must refer to events scheduled for April and May in the past tense. This is sometimes a gamble, as some planned events may never materialize. To be safe, a staff should consider doing a spring supplement to cover activities after the deadline for the main book. The whole problem of timing has led several schools to adopt late-summer or early-fall publication, which enables a staff to cover the full year without a supplement.

2. Normally write in the third person. The first person *I* is too personal. The history of one year should be about all people, not just the writer's personal involvement. However, if a staff decides to use first person, it should byline the copy so the reader knows who *I* is. Sometimes *I* can refer to the student body as a whole, but it takes a skilled writer to make it work. The same is true for first person *We*. Also avoid first person *our* and *us*. Second person *You* should also be avoided—it is rare that all students can identify with every activity. Using *he, she,* and *it* is much more specific.

3. Be specific. Avoid generalities. Don't say that four students were National Merit Finalists without naming them. Don't name them without saying why you are naming them.

4. Do not editorialize. Keep the writer's opinion out of the copy. Let the facts speak for themselves. The reader can make up her own mind if something was good or bad.

5. Use quotes. This is the way to get opinion into the book, but it is the reader's opinion, not the writer's. If you are dealing with a controversial issue, be sure that the quotes are balanced. Present both sides. By using quotes, the writer lets the reader tell part of the story, and read-

➢ *Characteristics of Concept Books*
   • *Books have fewer sections.*
   • *Chronological development is more common.*
   • *Generally the book is structured around a general concept word or words.*
   • *Typography helps to develop the concept.*
   • *Packaging is used to group stories.*
   • *Some subjects cover more than one spread.*
   • *A wider variety of methods is used to tell the story.*
   • *Concept books usually take more planning and more creativity.*

➢ *Graphically Speaking*
   • *Select an appropriate typeface to present the theme or concept.*
   • *Color, lines, foil, typeface, and texture are all elements the yearbook staff needs to consider in order to be sure the theme has the appropriate tone.*
   • *Present the graphic devices on the cover and repeat them on theme-related pages (title page, opening, dividers, closing).*

er involvement often sells books. There are other ways to include the reader in copy. One book used letters to the editor, which gave the readers a chance to state their viewpoints about issues that arose during the year. Be sure that all opinion is attributed: The reader has the right to know who said what.

6. Follow style rules. Be sure that grammar and spelling are correct.

7. Write in the active voice, not passive. Active voice was discussed in Chapter 3; review the comments made there.

8. Avoid the phrase *this year*, unless it is needed for comparison. Most books have the year on the cover; therefore, it is not necessary to use the year with a date. You need not say *Oct. 12, 1990* if the book covers the 1990-91 school year; simply say *Oct. 12*.

9. Avoid beginning copy with *a, an*, and *the*. Use impact words; make the reader take notice.

10. Keep paragraphs to 40 words or less to enhance readability. Short paragraphs look less formidable to the reader.

11. Write leads that make the scene, event, or person come alive. Feature the most important thing in the lead. (See discussion of leads later in this chapter.)

12. Avoid using the name of the school in copy. It should be used only if needed for comparison.

13. Consider four or more briefs to fill a copy area rather than one long story. Briefs are read. Long copy looks boring.

14. The words *team, chorus, band,* and *choir* are singular and take the singular pronoun *its*.

15. Do not use the phrase *due to* for *because of. Due* is an adjective, not a compound preposition.

16. Do not use *stated* loosely for *said. Stated* should be used only if someone is making an

Conducting the Interview

- *Plan questions that will produce interesting, unusual answers.*
- *Find out as much about the interviewee as possible before conducting the interview.*
- *Plan questions that will elicit personal responses. Be sure the quotes you obtain are not ones that just anyone could say.*
- *Set the interview at a time when neither you nor the interviewee will be rushed.*
- *Listen carefully to all responses, as the answers may provide you with additional questions and may even take you in a different direction.*
- *Be sure to ask for the correct spelling of all names and titles.*
- *Check the quotes for accuracy and context.*
- *Get a phone number to contact for additional information.*
- *If your story is about an issue and not about one person, be sure to balance your sources. If the issue is one that is pertinent to the entire student body, then be sure your sources are 25% freshmen, 25% sophomores, 25% juniors, and 25% seniors. Also be sure to balance between male and female and between ethnicities.*

official statement. Actually, there is no better word for *said* than *said*, unless another word—like *yelled*—describes the way a person said something.

17. Avoid using the verb *feels* when you mean *thinks* or *believes*. People tell you their thoughts, not their feelings.

18. Bury attributions for best effect. Place the speaker in the middle or at the end of the quote.

➤ *Writing Leads*
• *Avoid beginning with dates.*

• *Avoid using the same style throughout the book. Change from section to section.*

• *Avoid wordiness. Keep leads short.*

• *Avoid beginning with* The purpose of ... , Under the direction of ..., *and the name of a club or sports team, such as* The Latin Club ... *or* The varsity basketball team ....

• *Avoid beginning with a direct quote, unless it is an astonishing statement.*

• *Avoid beginning with a question, unless the reader would be dying to know the answer to the question or unless the answer is astonishing.*

19. Vary word usage within a sentence and within a paragraph. Use synonyms where appropriate.

20. Use statistics appropriately. They add to the history of a year. Do, however, avoid long lists of statistics.

21. Use a variety of copy presentations. Some forms and styles to consider: question and answer; survey results and statistical analysis; dialogue and dramatization; lists; first-person accounts; remember whens (anecdotes); journal reports; and interpretive analysis. If a survey is used, it could be presented as an information graphic.

22. Use sidebars (short stories related to the main story). For example, a copy block on an organization might zero in on one major event the group participated in during the year. A sidebar, perhaps entitled "Facts on File," could briefly explain other activities. Sidebars must expand coverage. They should not feature someone who has been featured elsewhere in the book. They should feature the unique, the unusual, the unexpected. You need a tight focus in the sidebar. Quote boxes can serve as sidebars. A student portrait might be included with the quote. Quote boxes must ask questions that are somehow related to the topic of the spread. It might even be necessary to write an introduction to the question so the reader understands how the question ties in with the rest of the spread.

23. Use transitions well, so the reader is carried from one thought to the next.

24. Use descriptive words to make copy come alive.

25. Learn to interview well. Dig deep for meaningful, unusual quotes.

26. Consider using a mini-magazine to develop one aspect of the year more fully. A mini-magazine can be used in any section of the book.

It usually has more copy than photo space.

27. Be sensitive to your subjects' feelings. Paint your subjects in as positive a light as possible.

28. Never stop listening. That is how you get outstanding quotes.

29. Write, rewrite, and rewrite! Rewriting is the secret to good writing. Read the story aloud to yourself so you can hear grammatical mistakes and awkward phrasing. It might also be a good idea to have a friend read your copy to see if he has any questions.

30. Maintain good copy flow. The following basic structure will help: Lead, Transition, Quote, Fact, Transition, Quote, Fact.

31. Avoid clichés. Some common offenders are "tried and true," "short but sweet," "fast and furious," "A good time was had by all," "It's lonely at the top," "Grin and bear it," "Go ahead … make my day," "This was a rebuilding year," "Their dedication paid off," "out of the blue," "icing on the cake," and "for all the marbles."

The preceding rules are general ones for regular yearbook copy. There are, however, specific rules for specific types of copy.

SPORTS COPY

1. Be sure that the copy does not merely rehash the scoreboard. It is not necessary to have a paragraph on each game of the year and to repeat the score. Each sport should have a scoreboard in the yearbook for individual game results.

2. Sports copy should capture the highlights of the important games. Space does not allow for complete coverage of every game. Help the reader recall the thrills and disappointments of the year. A yearbook sports writer should attend every game of the season and take notes. Then he can select which games to use

➢ *Creating Sidebars*

• *If the sidebar is a quote box, use quotes that are not part of the main story in order to present additional information to the reader.*

• *Sidebars do not have to go on the side of a page to be considered a sidebar. They may also go along the bottom of the page or at other appropriate places.*

• *Use them to entertain when possible. Humor should be part of any good book. However, don't use humor to embarrass someone needlessly.*

• *Choose a variety of quick read formats to present the additional information.*

Personality profiles work well in yearbooks in almost any section. When doing a profile, write a complete story on a person, but then consider doing a bio box for other pertinent information. The types of questions a reporter might ask the interviewee are endless, as are the number of questions. An example follows. Please note how the question is in boldface and the response is in normal type. Consider some form of type contrast when doing bio boxes.

Favorite book: The Shining by Stephen King.

Least favorite moment: When I ripped a seam in my jeans at an indoor movie one night, and I had to go around with a hole in the seat of my pants the rest of the evening. I tried to keep it covered, but it was rather obvious.

Favorite moment: Being crowned Homecoming Queen last October. I couldn't believe I was following in my mother's and my sister's footsteps.

Dreams for the future: To become president of the United States. I want to undo all the wrongs previous politicians have created.

Combining the scoreboard with the copy was a unique treatment in the *Pioneer*, Kirkwood High School, Kirkwood, MO. A brief paragraph giving a highlight of each game, or in this case each meet, gave the reader a quick glimpse at the sport.

in his copy.

3. Include statistics, both team and individual. Who was the leading scorer? Who made the most tackles? Who made the most saves? Were any records broken? Statistics add to the history of the year; they should be part of each sports copy block.

4. Avoid talking about the future. Coaches love to ignore a losing season and predict how much better the team should be the next year. As a history book, however, a yearbook should deal with one year only, unless a comparison with another year is needed.

5. Do not make excuses for losing teams. Coaches like to blame the weather or key injuries. Sometimes an injury can be devastating, but it is doubtful that the weather contributed to a poor season, since the opponents had to play under the same conditions.

6. Make the scenes come alive visually. Let the reader see that wild run for the winning

touchdown, let them see that twisting, turning basketball player go in for the winning layup, let them see the fans going wild in the stands.

ACADEMIC COPY

1. Be sure that the copy covers accomplishments for the year rather than merely listing goals of a department. The reader can determine the goals by seeing the accomplishments.

2. Copy should emphasize student involvement. Tell what the students did rather than what the teachers did. A separate section of the book should cover the faculty and such matters as faculty honors, moonlighting, sponsorships, and coaches. The academic section should tell what the students did in the classroom: projects completed, speakers heard, and experiments conducted. This section could also include field trips, academic contests, and personal achievements.

3. Avoid listing courses offered; this is "any year" type of information. Copy should deal with the specific year. If a new course was offered, however, student reaction to that course would be appropriate.

4. Be sure to cover all of the academic programs. That includes coverage of math classes, for instance, even though nothing new may have occurred in those classrooms. Coverage could be on how students prepare for a math examination, or on the sights and sounds of a classroom on a given day. Students spent at least six hours a day in classrooms, so coverage of the academic side of school is important for a complete picture of the school year.

5. Make classroom scenes come alive visually. Help the reader see the cake falling in the home economics lab, the student grimace as a frog is dissected, the frustration of a physical educa-

> **Sports Feature**

"A couple of wrong turns, and Ginny Broffitt, senior, Jenny Pringle, junior, Allison Page, freshman, and Melissa McGivern, junior, were lost.

'We found ourselves running around a bunch of dead guys," Broffitt said. The four cross-country runners got lost trying to find their way into Hickory Hill Park while coming back from the annual cross-country Bait Shop run. Out of the 85 people who participated on the August 29 run, only these four managed to get lost.

'The best part was when the little girl and her mom had a water stop for us on the way back. We were dumb and ran right by the original one,' Pringle said.

The run this year took on extra meaning when coaches Steve Sherwood and Jayme Skay brought up the idea of collecting pledges to raise money for a team tent.

'It was very

(Continued)

tion student when he misses the bull's-eye in archery for the seventh consecutive day, etc.

CLUBS/ORGANIZATIONS

1. Avoid discussing the goals and purposes of the group. The reader can grasp the purpose by reading about the accomplishments.
2. Focus on one or two main activities of the group. Do not try to cover all activities in detail. It is better to make one or two activities come alive visually than to attempt to give a paragraph to each activity.
3. Avoid listing names of officers. Those should be included in the caption for the group picture. If there is no group picture, quote officers in the copy and identify each in the attribution.
4. Avoid stating the sponsor's name in the copy, unless quoted. If a group picture is available, include the sponsor with the rest of the group and identify him/her in the caption.
5. Try to feature a unique angle. If an organization does the same thing year after year, it is the writer's job to find something new about that traditional event. Don't be content with repeating last year's copy.

In all types of copy the writer's primary purpose is to make the scene come alive visually. This needs to begin in the opening paragraph and continue throughout the copy. The writer must construct a lead that will grab the reader and carry him into the rest of the copy. Several leads work well for yearbook copy. Many of them were discussed in Chapter 6 on feature writing. Two other leads the writer might consider are the astonisher lead and the allusion lead.

An *astonisher lead* is used to emphasize something extremely important or startling:

> It was a secret. No one knew it was to be done.—*Pioneer*, Kirkwood High School, Kirkwood, MO.

impressive,' Skay said. 'We have great traditions of cross-country at City. We had great parental support, and very few walked.'

Enough money was raised to purchase the tent, which costs $1,500. The tent will have City's name on it, and will be used for shade, as well as for the runners to put their stuff under.

'The pledges motivated more people to run,' Broffitt said. 'While we were on the way out (to the Bait Shop) we passed a bunch of cows, and on the way back we got them to moo at us. It was the highlight of the run, seeing which one of us could moo the best.'"—Red & Black, *City High School, Iowa City, IA*

Inflation has taken a bite into everything, including love.—*Small Change*, Bay High School, Bay Village, OH.

An *allusion lead* is used to refer to something or someone well known. It may be the name of a person, a familiar line from a book or song, or the name of a movie or book:

It was raining, it was pouring. But no one in the Civic Center Coliseum was snoring.—*Colonel*, William Fleming High School, Roanoke, VA.

They're heeeeere!!
And not only are they here, they're everywhere!! Every day, college-bound seniors receive hundreds of phone calls and mail from colleges and universities— *Mascot*, Mexico High School, Mexico, MO.

A staff should try for a variety of leads to avoid monotony. Once a lead is written, the writer's job becomes easier. Remember that the key is to zero in on one aspect of the year for each sport, each club, each organization, each academic department, each student life activity. Don't get too broad, or the writing will lose focus. Create that single effect. Then create motion and sensory perceptions to make the copy come alive. Report the information accurately, and you will have copy that will be read.

One of the best ways to present copy is by capturing the sights and sounds of an event. This type of copy does not require interviewing. It may require asking someone his or her name, but the key is for the writer to take down everything she sees and hears at an event, which will supply all the quotes she needs. Writing sights-and-sounds copy requires keen observation and strong listening skills. It can be used anywhere in the book. The following was written for the academics section. Notice the use of *A Few Well-Chosen Words* as a lead. The writer used *(Un)* in parentheses to show comparison and contrast, since some students loved what was happening and others did not.

> ➢ *Coverage Ideas*
> • *Look through magazines for ideas. For example,* Entertainment Weekly *has a column entitled "What People Were Talking About This Week." That would make a great story idea for any yearbook. It could be changed to "What Students Were Talking About This Month."*
> • *Look for special anniversaries—1996 was the 100th anniversary of the car. A spread on students and their cars would be good any year, but more so on an anniversary year.*
> • *Do a survey to find out student interests. Base some spreads around those interests.*
> • *Look for national surveys of teenage interest. Survey your students on the same topic and make comparisons between the national survey and your survey.*

➤ *Timelines*

Another type of quick read is to provide the reader with a timeline. This copy from the Pioneer, *Kirkwood High School, Kirkwood, MO, was from a day in July. The* Pioneer *used the date for the headline.*

Mind
Live and learn through trial and error

Gods and goddesses beheaded mere mortals while Samantha Orme-Rogers, sophomore, sang "Twinkle, Twinkle Little Star" in Mrs. Linda Ford's English 10 class, Sept. 13. The class acted out the "God Court" in which the gods of ancient mythology put mortals on trial for various crimes and determined their punishments if found guilty. Students stretched their MINDs by learning about various gods' personalities before acting out their characteristics during the trials. Although she pleaded innocent, the class charged Orme-Rogers with writing bad poetry and not being able to sing, and one of her punishments was to sing in front of the class.

> "The class charged me guilty and made me sing in front of them. It was really embarrassing."
> --Samantha Orme-Rogers

Minutes before the start of the Youth In Government picnic, Sept. 9, Mike McDonald, sergeant-at-arms, and Steve Williamson, political whip, rushed through the aisles of Shop 'N Save when they realized they had not bought any soda for the picnic. McDonald and Williamson used their MINDs in order to bargain-shop, and they returned to the picnic with four cases of soda and time to spare.

Kissing strangers and eating endless amounts of french fries were both part of senior Sarah Paulsen's one-month stay in Madrid during the summer, June 24-July 24. Paulsen expanded her MIND by learning about different aspects of Spanish culture during her stay. Although she became used to the custom of greeting by kissing on the cheek, she never grew accustomed to the food, so her host mother usually made her french fries.

Counterweight fly systems, access to the Internet and computerized theater lights were just a few of the additions to the school as a result of renovations to the library, the Keating Center and the old auditorium. According to Mrs. Marge Nardie, librarian, the new facilities helped students broaden their MINDs.

Mind/Divider

This divider spread from the Pioneer, *Kirkwood High School, Kirkwood, MO, helps carry forth the concept of Mind, Body, and Soul. The staff divided the book into those three parts. It included student life, clubs, and academics in the Mind section, student life, clubs, and sports in the Body section, and student life, clubs, and portraits in the Soul section.*

(Un)Dreaded music. (Un)Dreaded obstacle. (Un)Dreaded movie.

Country hit tunes sounded throughout East 183 during third hour, April 27, as Teddy Garret,

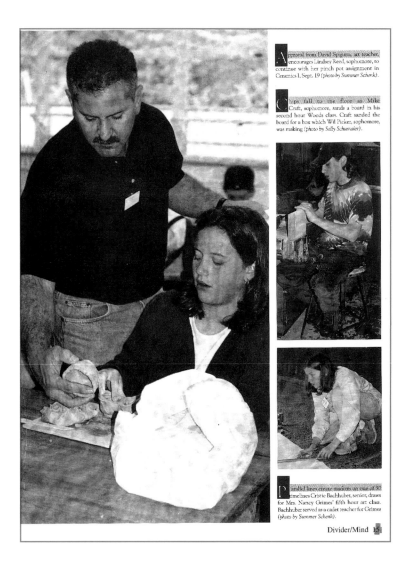

Quote boxes provide a good way to include a lot of readers' comments in copy. The above is from the Trail, *Fairbury Jr.-Sr. High School, Fairbury, NE.*

Initial letters and the use of gray help draw the readers' attention to the captions on this page from the Pioneer, *Kirkwood High School, Kirkwood, MO.*

sophomore, covered his ears and made a sour face to show his disgust with the music.

"Turn off the tape!" screamed Garrett.

Laughing at Garrett's expression and comment, Mike Holley, world history teacher, turned

➢ **Academics**

Finding unique ways to cover academics is a challenge for most yearbook staffs. The Heritage staff at Horizon High School in Scottsdale, AZ, added a sidebar entitled "Great Expectations" to broaden its academic coverage.

Double Vision

◆ Seen It...

Sumo Wrestler. Jaime Escalante. Greg Drummond.

All of these came together when the Girls' Pep Club (GPC) and Boys' Pep Club (BPC) performed a skit at both the afternoon and evening pep tallies, Nov. 22.

The skit was a "Family Feud" set up with Kirkwood characters competing against Webster characters. Erica Purcell, vice-president, played Tim Souhrada, football co-captain.

"I tried to walk like him," Purcell said. "I used little details to dress like him, such as a brown curly wig, black pants and a red shirt under my jersey. People knew he often wore black pants."

According to Purcell, students also knew other inside jokes.

"The first part of the skit was funnier than the second half," she said, "because the students watching it understood the things we were playing off of, like stuff (Principal Franklin) McCallie says, and why Jaime Escalante was in the skit. Parents at the second half didn't understand as much."

Adam Wilson, spirit man, and Erica Purcell, vice-president, vote, Sept. 13 (photo by Carey Zeigler).

◆ Heard It...

Screams erupted from the bleachers as Kara Sheban, treasurer, held a whipped-cream pie threateningly close to social studies teacher John Merrit's face.

Meritt competed against Cassie O'Brian, walking counselor, in the cheering contest at the afternoon pep assembly, Nov. 22.

Both faculty members stood on ladders and, judged by the volume of the side of the gym they represented, moved up one or two rungs.

GPC members smashed a pie in the face of the one who climbed to the top first. Pies flew in the faces of both contestants when McCallie called a tie between the two halves.

"I knew I was going to get hit by a pie when Jim Velten (athletic director) took my tie," Meritt said. "I didn't think, though, that I should have been hit. My half of the gym was clearly the loudest."

◆ Lived It...

Neon. Plaid. Argyle.

In order to make meetings more interesting, GPC members decided to give each meeting a theme. Members dressed up and participated in contests for Disco, Tacky Day and Halloween.

"We were looking for something fun to do at meetings that would make them more appealing and attract more people," Laura Bross, co-president, said. "We had a disco contest where people could stand up and dance for a prize. People were wearing everything from bell-bottoms to a checkered dress. The prizes were candy, and we even gave away the disco mix used for the contest. At other meetings, we had contests for the best Halloween costume and for the person dressed the tackiest."

Beats of the "Kirkwood Honk" sound from the Frisco Bell, Nov. 23, as Laura Bross, co-president, rings it (photo by Carey Zeigler).

◆ Learned It...

Bulldozers blocked their path.

Construction stopped GPC members attempting to deliver a football door sign to senior Nick Berry's house, Nov. 22. They ended up learning a new route to his house.

"First we got lost," Bross said. "All the streets looked the same, and when we finally turned down the right street, it was blocked off by bulldozers because of construction. We went up to some guys getting into their car and asked them. It was kind of scary because it was late at night."

Girls' Pep Club/Clubs 183

Clubs copy in the Pioneer, Kirkwood High School, Kirkwood, MO, looks like a series of briefs under the headlines "Seen It ...", "Heard It ...", "Lived It ...", "Learned It ..." The staff wrote each copy block in this section in this style rather than writing one long copy block.

---

the volume of the ghettoblaster up.

In response, Garrett slumped his shoulders, shook his head, and slouched over.

However, the music did not seem to bother Sarah Hook, sophomore, as she showed off her *Roger Rabbit* dance steps to the class.

Holley also joined in the dancing.

As Maureen Houston, sophomore, tried to maneuver around Holley to get to the trash can,

Holley took hold of her hands and swung her around the room. Houston escaped from the captivity.

Hook, however, folded her hands and pleaded with Holley to dance with her.

"And get Hook germs?" joked Holley.

The two stopped dancing and Holley brought in a television and VCR so he could show a documentary. He fast-forwarded the tape until he found a specific part.

Oohs and ahhs sounded throughout the room as students watched the deaths of numerous people on the guillotine. Blood dripped from the sharp blade as bodies became headless and heads became bodiless.

Jennifer Saltger, sophomore, shuddered at what she saw. Salter turned her head away from the TV and squeezed her eyes shut.

"That is the most revolting thing I have ever seen!" exclaimed Salter.

Thriving on the class's response, Holley played the scene again.

Salter became even more upset, placed her hands on her stomach, leaned over, and acted as if she were going to be sick.

Again Holley rewound the movie.

Involved and intrigued, Dave Statzel, sophomore, switched desks for a better view.

"This is awesome," Statzel said, "I'm watching an R-rated movie in history class."

> Mexico finished with 11 shots, only 3 fewer than the NCMC rival Pirates in one game. | Lights were added to the soccer field at the beginning of this season. | Rock Bridge's coach and Mexico's coach Goodman went to college together. | There were two exchange students on the team.

➤ *Little Known Facts*
Small trivia tidbits about the soccer team ads to the coverage in the Mascot, *Mexico High School, Mexico, MO.*

One of the difficult aspects of writing for a yearbook is that the copy must fit an allotted space. That may mean that you have a lot of editing to do. Sometimes the design artist can eliminate some photographs or other elements of a design in order to give the copywriter more space, but more often than not, a long copy block will have to be chopped. That is why all writing must be tight and concise. Use as few words as possible. Be sparing with adjectives and adverbs, but do not eliminate them entirely, since they are necessary for visual

2-our goes down under

History students take a trip to see a side of school few ever see--in the old steam heat tunnels underneath MHS

Happy to give a tour, Mr. Charles Lind, athletic director, walks a group through the newly completed complex.

Most days, students take textbooks, notebooks, and pens to class. On Oct. 24, A.P. American History students took hard hats, flashlights, and shovels. During second hour that day, Mrs. Ginny Raney's class took a field trip to see a side of the school few see—the underneath side.

Raney's class was discussing historical preservation of buildings and how people at MHS are preserving the school's history. The tour of the original building, built in 1927, began with the school memorabilia case, then went to the original front entrance, and Emmons Hall. The final stop was at the trap door leading to the tunnels.

"During our tour of the building, Mr. Charles Lind invited us to tour the tunnels," Raney said. "If he had not mentioned it, we would not have gone through them."

The class entered the tunnels through Lind's office, and came out in the weight room. "We got lost," Rob Lee, junior, said, "but it was too hard to turn around so we just kept going."

The tour was not mandatory, but all the students were eager to do something that has been done by only a few.

"It was really neat," Lynn Houf, junior and only female to complete the tunnel tour, said, "because nobody else got to do it and not many people know about the tunnels."

The tour also gave students a chance to look for the statue of Minerva. Minerva moved from the old McMillan High School to MHS when it opened, was once placed in the front hall. When the school was being renovated the white, plaster statue disappeared. Some people believe that the statue was put in a sealed storage room but nobody has been able to locate the statue.

"There were a couple of places where we could go two ways," Houf said. "I would do it again to be able to go the ways we didn't go."

Using a comparison and contrast lead, the writer for the Bulldog, Mexico *High School, Mexico, MO, grabs the reader quickly in the above copy. The fact that the writer is dealing with an unusual topic also makes the article interesting.*

➤ *Organization Copy*

Instead of placing all the quotes in one long copy block, the Red & White *staff at City High School, Iowa City, IA, highlighted five students in a sidebar quote box.*

description.

Be sure that you understand how to fit copy to a specific space. If you use a computer, you don't have to spend as much time fitting copy. With a computer, all you have to do is set your column widths and decide on your pica length. Then you just type copy to fit the predetermined space. At one time, however, yearbook staffs had to fit copy by using a yearbook-company guide.

Yearbook companies used to provide yearbook staffs a copy-fitting guide for each size and style of type. The guide showed how many characters and how many lines will fit in a set space. For example, the Korinna type chart below shows that in 8-point type you get an average of 3.6 characters per pica and eight lines of type in six picas. Each type style differs in characters per pica and lines per pica.

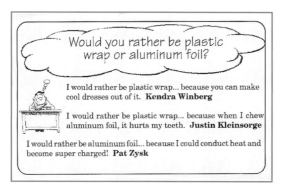

Would you rather be plastic wrap or aluminum foil?

I would rather be plastic wrap... because you can make cool dresses out of it. **Kendra Winberg**

I would rather be plastic wrap... because when I chew aluminum foil, it hurts my teeth. **Justin Kleinsorge**

I would rather be aluminum foil... because I could conduct heat and become super charged! **Pat Zysk**

Quick reads appeal to the readers as the above trivia question in the Bulldog, Mexico High School, Mexico, MO. Questions like the above are also a good way to add humor to the book. This sidebar appeared in the portrait section.

KORINNA TYPE-FITTING GUIDE—WIDTH
Average characters per inch/pica

Lowercase	6-pt.	7-pt.	8-pt.	9-pt.	10-pt.	11-pt.	12-pt.	14-pt.	18-pt.
per inch	29	24	21	19	17	15	14	12	9.5
per pica	4.8	4.1	3.6	3.2	2.9	2.6	2.4	2.0	1.6

KORINNA TYPE-FITTING GUIDE—DEPTH
Average lines per pica*

Picas	4	6	8	10	12	14	16	18	20	22	24	26	28	30
6 pt.	6	10	13	17	20	24	27	30	34	37	41	44	48	51
7 pt.	6	9	11	14	17	20	23	26	29	31	34	37	40	43
8 pt.	5	8	10	13	16	18	21	24	27	29	32	34	37	40
9 pt.	4	7	9	11	13	16	18	20	22	24	27	29	31	33
10 pt.	4	6	8	10	13	15	17	19	21	24	26	28	30	32
11 pt.	4	5	7	9	11	13	15	16	18	20	22	24	25	27
12 pt.	3	5	7	9	11	12	14	16	18	20	22	24	25	27

*Lines per pica based on the point size of type. In a copy block 14 picas in depth, for example, you can fit 24 lines of 6-point type.

EXERCISES

1. From your own or another school's yearbook, select one block of student life copy, one of sports copy, one of academic copy, and one of clubs/organizations copy.

Analyze each for effectiveness. Make a list of weaknesses and strengths of each copy block. Be prepared to discuss in class.

2. Since schools are using computers today,

Defining the era

coping- a round metal pole horizontally attached to the top of a halfpipe or ramp

air- when the entire board is over the coping

deck- wooden part of the board

griptape- a rough paper much like sandpaper that sticks to the deck of the board

halfpipe- a half cylindrical skating surface made of plywood with outside supports

kickflip- board spins around once. To complete a kickflip, kick left foot out so board flips once under your body

nose- front part of the board

tail- back part of the board

ollie- usually the first trick learned, the ollie forms the basis for all other tricks. To finish an ollie, kick down on the tail of the board with right foot and drag left foot up so the left foot ends on the nose of the board

trucks- two metal bars that attach the wheels to the deck

➢ *Glossary of Terms*

Sports pages are a good place to include a glossary of terms as a sidebar. The above sidebar on skateboarding terms is from the Paragon, *Munster High School, Munster, IN.*

students don't need to use the old copy-fitting guides which yearbook companies provide. Nevertheless, counting copy in such a manner is a piece of history that should not be forgotten. Therefore, using the type-fitting guide in this chapter, determine the character width and the lines in depth for each of the following in four type sizes: 6-point, 8-point, 10-point, 12-point. Round all answers up.

  A.   12 picas wide and 14 picas deep.
  B.   14 picas wide and 12 picas deep.
  C.   15 picas wide and 6 picas deep.
  D.   18 picas wide and 21 picas deep.
  E.   21 picas wide and 18 picas deep.

3.   Based on the rules for writing yearbook copy, state what is wrong with each of the following sentences or paragraphs:

  A.   Anne Crawford was crowned homecoming queen.
  B.   Medieval humor was displayed in the play "Grammer Gurton's Needle."
  C.   Awards were earned and presented to students in many different fields and areas.
  D.   Our own prom took place on Friday, April 29, at 8:00 p.m. and extended until 6:00 a.m. with afterglow.
  E.   Out of school is where most students would like to be, at one time or another. Even though only one third or less of the day is spent in school, time seems to drag on, especially when the weather is favorable. So when we become free of scholastic burdens, how do we spend the remainder of the day? There are a number of socially acceptable ways. There are also other activities that can't be expanded on for fear our adviser would have to search the job market and employment pages. In light of this

Types of Quick Reads

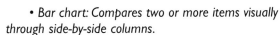

• **Bar chart:** Compares two or more items visually through side-by-side columns.

• **Bio box** (also known as Dewar's Profile): Brief profiles of people or organizations in the news. This is usually written in list form and itemized by key characteristics.

• **Checklist:** A list of guidelines or questions that itemizes key points.

• **Diagram:** A drawing that shows how something works.

• **Fact box:** Short bits of information that give readers a quick look at the 5 W's behind a story.

• **Fever or line chart:** Measures change over time by plotting points on a graph.

• **Glossary:** A list of specialized words and definitions that helps readers understand a topic better.

• **Map:** A visual way to present geographical information.

• **Opinion poll:** A sampling of opinion gathered scientifically.

• **Pie chart:** Compares parts that make up a whole, usually in percentages.

• **Quote collection:** A series of quotes related to the main topic.

• **Quiz:** A list of questions with answers.

• **Ratings:** A list of items that lets critics make predictions or evaluations.

• **Step-by-step guide:** A graphic that breaks down a process one step at a time.

• **Timeline:** a chronology of events highlighting key moments in the history of a person, place, or issue.

fact, things such as work, hobbies, and just playing out life must suffice. Work could be the most important element away from school. It teaches us that everyone has his or her own place in society, how to get along with others, and diligence, which are ways of raising status for the future.

F.   The senior class was an active and involved class.

G.   Money raising was the most important activity for the junior class.

H.   Placing first at regionals enabled us to go to sectionals. We placed seventh at sectionals as a team, and Jerry Jones came in seventh all around.

I.   Attitude, along with cooperation, made our sophomore team a successful group.

J.   A strong staff in the science department came up with excellent advanced science programs in Biology, Ecology, Chemistry, and Physics.

K.   The strength in the English department was having many qualified teachers and in teaching proper usage of verbs, adverbs, nouns, adjectives, and pronouns.

L.   New policies made for a very busy year. We had a new attendance policy and dress code installed, and parental permission slips for English films were instituted for PG ratings. Students' attendance at such films was optional if they or their parents had objections to the subject matter. The principals were also busy scheduling, advising, disciplining, and attending school events.

M.   The yearbook staff worked hard to recap the year's events.

PLaNtin' trEeS
cHeESe
**Key clubbers raise money
to help prevent teen suicides,
while LEAF beautifies school,
international club tries food**

"Hey don't shovel dirt on me!" Anne Genthe, co-vice-president, yelled to Adam Spies, president.

Members of Leading Environmental Awareness into the Future participated in Beautification Day, Sept. 19, by planting trees and picking up trash.

Genthe and Suzanne Zitzmann, junior, planted a tree while Spies helped a group of Student Council members pick up trash lying around campus.

"So would anyone like flaming cheese?" Albert Salsich, International Club sponsor, asked members of the International Club while eating dinner with them at Cafe Olympia, Feb. 12.

"Oh gross! That's disgusting!" Terence Whitaker, junior, yelled as he spit out a mouthful of the cheese.

After the group figured out the bill and bought some Greek candy, they piled into Salsich's van to travel back home.

"Buy valentines for only $2!" Katie Fernandez, secretary, yelled to shoppers at West County Mall, Feb. 14.

Members of Key Club sold valentines for Kids Under Twenty-One, an organization which raised money to help prevent teen suicide.

Shoppers bought the valentines to put on a tree located in the mall. Some wrote messages to someone they knew that died from suicide, others bought them to simply support the organization.

➢ *Club Briefs*

Sometimes space problems require staffs to cover more than one organization on a spread. One brief on each group guarantees equal coverage. The above copy is from the Pioneer, *Kirkwood High School, Kirkwood, MO. Notice the typography treatment in the headline. The original headline was much larger with the secondary headline being two lines rather than four.*

N. The purpose of Bible Club was to attempt to maximize Christian fellowship among students.

O. Completing a 5-2-1 season, the frosh-soph football team had a successful year. The season featured victories over Reeds, Mound Springs, Smithtown, and Lincoln by scores of 10-7, 13-7, 20-3, and 10-9, respectively.

P. Next year looks bright for the Junior Varsity Team if the upcoming sophomores can stay healthy during the season. There should be a big bunch of freshmen to look forward to next year also.

Q. Cheerleading takes a lot of practice, determination, and continuing interest. In these ways cheering is like participating in a sport, but there is no way to measure success. Cheering is hard work, but it is fun and gives us a genuine feeling of accomplishment.

R. Physics isn't what you'd expect it to be. I remember at the beginning of the year, when we were studying the concepts of motion, we talked a lot about free fall. I really enjoyed Physics, because I was able to learn aspects of the subject by experiencing the real happenings. It was really fun and a lot easier with a good and willing teacher behind you.

4. Write a copy block describing a scene that contains a great deal of movement. Increase the effect of motion by careful choice of words. Following are suggestions of scenes you might describe:

A. a school hallway between classes

B. the parking lot at lunch hour or at the end of school

C. an auto race

What would you do . . . if you could add one store to Munster

"We need a store for tests and term papers. If you needed a paper, they'd have one completed. For test answers, you'd tell them what teacher you have and they'd hand you answers."
Ralph Topete, senior

"I'd open a surf shop and sell beach stuff. I'd name it 'IWannaSurf.' We need a surf shop for those who attempt surfing on Lake Michigan or for vacations."
Beth Sliwa, junior

"I'd open up a coffee shop. I'd call it 'House of Coffee.' My waiters would serve coffee in G-strings and do stripteases."
Meredith Nelson, sophomore

"A music store. I'd sell rap, no country, no disco, no techno, and punk because I respect people who listen to punk. I'd name it 'The Music Store.' "
Jimmy Howard, freshman

➢ *Community Highlights*
Advertising pages are a great place to include coverage about the community. The Paragon staff at Munster High School, Munster, IN, chose a question approach. This question tells the reader what types of stores are not part of the Munster community.

District 5-4A

Triple Jump
■ 4th, Shelia Medina, 33'6½"
Shot Put
■ 2nd, Jessica Sisk, 34'1"
■ 3rd, Angela Kennedy, 32'9"
100-meter hurdles
■ 1st, Jessie Mathews, 15.56
High Jump
■ 3rd, Jessie Mathews, 4'10"
300-meter hurdles
■ 3rd, Liz Kessler, 50.38
1600-meter relay
■ 3rd, Jessie Mathews, Jalyn Mathews, Jessica Perser and Ashlei Lashbrook, 4:22

➤ *Stats Box*
Instead of including statistics in the main copy block, the Mustang *staff from Andrews High School, Andrews, TX, chose to run a separate stats box on its girls' track spread. Statistics are part of the history of the year and should be part of sports coverage.*

D.	the school band at halftime during a football game

E.	the Pom Pom squad at halftime of a basketball game

F.	a basketball player driving for the hoop

G.	kites flying on the March wind

H.	a swimmer trying to win a race

I.	two dancers at a school dance

Write the copy to fit in 10-point type, 21 picas wide and 24 picas long.

5.	Write a copy block based on the following facts. Your teacher will give you point size, character width, and depth. Add information as necessary but do not change given facts.

Bad ice storm hit town New Year's Eve.

Many homes were without power. Some didn't have power restored until Jan. 5.

"This is one of the worst ice storms in history for this area, with more than 100,000 residences in the dark," said Dave Murray, television meteorologist. "We can compare this storm to the one in 1972, although that one was probably more severe."

Ice froze on power lines, and transformers exploded throughout the town.

Matt Meyer, senior, felt his family was "pretty lucky to have power, because I slept under an electric blanket."

Some were able to watch the Bowl games on television, since they never lost power.

"Our lights flickered, but they never went out," said Whitney Hermann, sophomore.

Ice freezing on tree limbs caused many limbs to fall.

"At 3:30 p.m. New Year's Eve, our neighbor's tree, with a three-and-a-half-foot base, fell into our driveway," said Dave Roach, senior. "It took the lines right off the house. The city came and removed it around midnight."

"Our whole family sat in front of the fire and popped corn and heated coffee over the flames," said Beth Dionne, senior. Her family was one of the unlucky ones without power.

"My parents had some people over," said Steve Hunsicker, senior. "The power went off before the guests arrived, and came on right when they were leaving," he chuckled.

For Mr. John Tomasovic, father of Sue Tomasovic, senior, the loss of electricity almost ruined his business as a florist. "The heaters in our greenhouse are electric," said Sue. "We had to convert to gasoline heaters." According to Sue, her family stayed up New Year's Eve pouring the gasoline. "We used 105 gallons—enough to get to Florida and back twice," she said.

Sue Keil, junior, and her family experienced 84 hours without electricity. "We got so cold and bitter that we checked into a hotel," she said. "We were going to send the bill to the electric company," she joked. "While we were at home, we'd walk into rooms and automatically turn on the light switch," Sue said. "It just goes to show how much we take for granted."

6. Write a copy block based on the following facts. Add information as necessary but do not change the given facts. Your teacher will give you the point size, character width, and depth.

Girls' cross-country team finished season by placing second in state.

State meet was held in Hough Park at state capital, Nov. 18.

Girls lost by one point to Lindberg, 83-84.

Chris Ridenour, sophomore, took first place, setting a state record of 15:29.

He was dropping them like bad habits. Andrew Murray, guard, seemed to have the magic touch against Lindbergh as he sank four three-pointers, leading the Pioneers to a 65-37 victory. Murray led the team with 12 points. The victory improved the team's record to 9-3 overall and 1-0 in the Suburban West. The team's 65 points were spread out among 10 players, with eight scoring five or more.

➤ *Sports Stats*
Statistics on one game can also be run as a sidebar. The Pioneer staff at Kirkwood High School, Kirkwood, MO, focused on one conference game to indicate that the top scorer was only one of 10 players to connect in the game.

Head for Surveys

movies that made you

cry
1. Titanic (19)
2. Armageddon (18)
3. Stepmom (11)
4. Patch Adams (10)
5. What Dreams May Come (7)

scream
1. Halloween H2O (26)
2. Urban Legends (23)
3. I Still Know What You Did Last Summer (9)
4. Scream 2 (13)
5. 8mm (2)

laugh
1. There's Something About Mary (57)
2. Waterboy (25)
3. Rush Hour (11)
4. Office Space (8)
5. Half Baked (6)

gasp
1. 8mm (10)
2. Halloween H2O (5)
3. Urban Legends (5)
4. There's Something About Mary (4)
5. Titanic (3)

197 seniors surveyed

➢ *Surveys*

Conducting surveys is a good way to find out what the student body is thinking on various topics. Note that the Paragon staff, Munster High School, Munster, IN, indicated the total number of students surveyed and then showed a specific number for each response. It would also be a good idea to show a percentage after each number so the reader does not have to figure out the percentages on his or her own.

She finished eight seconds and 70 yards ahead of second-place finisher Esther Corrigan of Rosary.

Ridenour also finished first among 118 girls at the AAU Nationals, Nov. 24, in Raleigh, N.C.

This was the first girls' cross-country team ever at your school.

They never finished lower than fourth in any meet and captured first in your own neighborhood's dual and first in the Suburban North Invitational.

Susan Jones finished second behind Ridenour in all but two meets. She placed third at district and fifteenth at state.

The other five girls on the squad were Betsy Doerr, freshman; Joan Parks, senior; Kathleen Boyd, sophomore; Barbara Peterson, senior; and Jane Cravens, sophomore.

With only one senior on the squad, the team has a bright future.

"I ran about two hours per day during the cross-country season," said Ridenour, "so it was really a great feeling to be first in state."

"At first I was stunned," said Peterson. "I couldn't believe we had gotten so close and not made it. We were all crying—not only because we hadn't gotten first, but because we had gotten second!"

The girls gave the coach a lot of credit.

"Coach Bill Pullen made me serious about running," said Doerr. "He gave us hard workouts, but they really helped me improve."

"Although I always came in behind Chris," said Jones, "it didn't keep me from trying my hardest."

"I worked for my coach, my team, and myself," said Cravens. "Competition was great, but I ran for the enjoyment of it, too. There is no freer feeling in the world than running!"

The team finished second at the Northwest Invitational, the Hazelwood Invitational, the

Suburban West Conference, District, and State. They were third at the Ladue Invitational and fourth at the Webster Invitational.

7. Write a copy block based on the following information. Add facts as necessary, but do not change the given facts. Your teacher will give you point size, character width, and depth.

Birthday celebrations—many different ways to celebrate.

It was a surprise party for Debbie McGhee, junior. She had been baby-sitting one Friday night and came home at 11 p.m. to a completely dark house. When she opened the front door, blinding lights and party horns shocked her as a houseful of friends shouted "Surprise! Happy birthday, Debbie." They had all pitched in to buy her a stereo.

Tina McGhee, sophomore, received presents from two guys. "I received a necklace and a heart-shaped cake from one of my boyfriends. My other boyfriend beat that by buying me two huge stuffed elephants. He also gave me 16 red roses and flew me to Kansas City to eat at the Golden Ox!"

Othelia Larsen, senior, received a balloon bouquet from her parents during sixth-hour class, plus a cake from the bakery to share with her classmates.

One senior boy decided to show off his birthday suit as he streaked through the school, March 7. Administrators chased him but could not catch him. Friends who knew the boy said he was just celebrating his birthday.

Tom Boss, senior, brought sparkling grape juice in a bucket of ice and placed it in an unused locker. Then during his independent hour, he celebrated with Jake Hall, senior. It was Tom's birthday. A teacher saw them and reported the incident to the administration, who questioned both boys about possession of alcohol on campus.

RUNNING FOR CANCER
Community joins together for Relay for Life run-a-thon

FIRST PERSON

As I walked into the University of Iowa Recreation Building, with an arm full of bagels and fellow teammate Alison Page '02, my eyes darted around trying to find my team. With a spot all picked out, Hillary Mills '00, was standing on top of the bleachers putting up signs and streamers so everyone knew that the City High Girls cross-country team would be there running for the day.

Mills had put together a team of girl's cross-country runners to raise money and spend a Sunday running for the Relay for Life. I had never been part of this awesome event and was excited to volunteer my time. With our team raising just over our goal of $1000 we had already put in a great effort to help find a cure for cancer. Now a twelve-hour day of running was to be put in. We split the day into half an hour increments with someone from our team always on the track. A half an hour of running by yourself in a circle can sometimes be a boring thing so Mills and I spiced it up with a few "WOOOOOOOOHOOOOOOO's" that echoed through the building.

The enthusiasm my teammates and I shared was absolutely amazing. Everyone was so excited to be there and everyone around us seemed to be glad we were there. We were running for a cure. A cure for cancer, to help save the lives of those we love. To be part of such a wonderful day was an awesome experience that no one can take away. My heart has now changed, and life has become so much more precious.
Kaye Sparks

➢ *First-Person Copy*

Sometimes it is best to have a student who participated in the event to write the copy rather than have someone on the yearbook staff write it. The Red & White staff at City High School in Iowa City, IA, had a participant write about experiences in a run-a-thon.

September was the month with the most student birthdays—177. When school started, September 5, the youngest student in school was 14-year-old Stacie Rockewell. She celebrated her fifteenth birthday January 6.

8. Write a copy block based on the following information. Add facts as necessary but do not change the given facts. Your teacher will give you the point size, character width, and depth.

Homecoming football game—your school vs. opponent (make up name).

Your school loses 48-0, the worst defeat in the 63 years the rival game has been played.

8,000 fans in attendance for the kickoff. The opponents kick to your school.

On the kickoff, Leon Jones, sophomore tailback, catches the ball at the eight-yard line and returns it to his own 30. On the first play from scrimmage, Jones gains 12 yards. Three more running plays, however, gain only six yards, and your team punts. The opponents take over on their eight. In 15 plays the opponents go 92 yards, with Joel Hall, running back, scoring from the three. This was the first of seven touchdowns by the opponent.

Your school was the underdog in the game, although Jones was the conference's leading rusher, with 720 yards in 42 carries going into the game, and you had the leading pass receiver (Alvin Hawkins) in the conference, with 23 prior to game time.

Several major colleges have shown an interest in recruiting both Jones and Hawkins.

The opponent entered the game with an 8-0-1 record, and your team was 2-6. The opponent ranked second in the conference in offense.

➤ Theme Copy

"Everybody knows *the names of faces of starters and stars.*

Nobody knows *the importance of learning fundamentals and waiting in the wings.*

Everybody knows *whipped cream will disguise students at the Food Fight.*

Nobody knows *what to expect from a dancing turkey or carrot-eating contest.*

Everybody knows *to show up for the traditional events.*

Nobody knows *the headache of bringing back the bonfire.*

At MHS unity forms from traditions Everybody knows, *possibility comes from new ideas* Nobody knows, *and individuality develops through what made us say* Who Knows."—*Copy from the* Mascot, *Mexico High School, Mexico, MO, for the theme* Everybody Knows....

The staff divided the book into three sections—Everybody Knows, Nobody Knows and Who Knows. In

(Continued)

Traditionally, the underdog has won this game.

Your team came close to scoring only once. It trailed 14-0 at halftime, but moved to the opponent's 29-yard line in the third quarter before Jones fumbled. The opponent then drove 71 yards for its third touchdown.

"It wasn't even cryable," said Karen Burno, senior.

9. Have every student in your class go to different places on campus and take notes of everything seen and heard for a five-minute period. Make copies of each one's notes, and have each write sights-and-sounds copy capturing five minutes of time at your school. Students should go to a variety of places—classrooms, the main office, bathrooms, hallways, etc. All should take notes for the same five-minute period such as 1:45-1:50 p.m. Be sure each person gets the name and identification of anyone quoted. Students should be told the pica length and width and point size of the copy so that they write to fit a space.

10. Write copy based on the following facts. You may add facts as necessary, but do not change any facts given. Your teacher will give you the length, width, and point size of your copy.

Student jobs. Carie Roock, sophomore, worked at Six Flags in the Calico Kitchen from May until mid-November. "I worked there because it was fun and it gave me something to do over the summer," Roock said. "I also made a lot of good friends." "It was really embarrassing once," Roock said, "when I was carrying a box of chicken to be separated. When I walked out of the freezer, I slipped on a piece of chicken and went flying under a table."

Sara Crutcher, junior, worked at the Sock Market in the Galleria. "On my second day of work I was the only employee there," Crutcher said. "It turned out someone wanted to pay by credit card, and I had no

the Everybody Knows section, it included student life, clubs, sports, and portraits. In the Nobody Knows section it included academics and junior varsity sports, and in Who Knows, it included advertising and the index.

➢ *Divider Copy*

"Familiar faces fill the classrooms and streets, faithful fans follow the sports teams, and secrets are few and far between. Welcome to Mexico, where cars you pass on the streets are those of your neighbors, first-grade teachers, or coaches. Where the checker at the grocery store will likely know your name, and the graduation fireworks light up most parts of town. Welcome to a place where adversities and advantages come from what everybody knows.— Copy from the Mascot, Mexico High School, Mexico, MO, for the theme Everybody Knows...

271

idea what to do. I didn't like being left alone."

Mike Hall, senior, worked 65 hours a week at the Happy Times Swim Camp and at Country Surf Swimming Pool during the summer. He taught kids how to swim at Happy Times. "I liked Happy Times because it was rewarding. I saw kids come in with no ability, and at the end of the session they could swim," Hall said. At Country Surf, Hall worked with Art Stout, math teacher. Stout was the pool manager. "One day it was about 110 degrees, and all the lifeguards were beat, so Mr. Stout gave us a break and got up on the lifeguard stand. I thought it was funny to see such a high-ranking teacher on the stand," said Hall.

Nick Vespa, junior, worked at Johnny Mac's Sporting Goods store during the summer and the school year. "It was hard because I had to remember these little details, and one detail could throw everything off. I could end up sending Red Bud jerseys to Parkmoor and they would not be pleased," he said, "but I was working with people and that's what I like to do."

Chris Claywell, junior, worked at Modern Auto Parts where his mother was co-owner. "It was a junkyard, basically," said Claywell. "Everyone else was out of high school, and I had to do the jobs no one else wanted. My mom had me go through the car junkyard and pick up all the nuts and bolts off the ground."

11. The topic for your spread is stress. Write the story, and then write three quick reads that could be used as sidebars with the main copy.

12. The topic for your spread is boredom. Write the story, and then write three quick reads that could be used as sidebars with the main copy.

13. Select a student on which to write a personality profile. Be sure to select someone well-known

---

go figure

Aside from those engrossed in a world full of Hollywood fads and neverending rages, students stayed true to individual styles and interests.

1: aspired to acquire an all-body tattoo
2: loyally watched the television show "Dragonball 7"
3: turned up the volume to the sounds of Garth Brooks, their favorite music artist
4: held true to their nationality, hoping to tattoo the Serbian coat of arms somewhere upon their body
20: raced to their favorite store Target time and time again for everyday wants and needs
68: glued themselves to their television sets every Wednesday night for the newest episode of "Beverly Hills 90210"

Source: 340 students surveyed

➢ *Facts and Figures*

Numbers often tell a large part of the story of a year. The above copy from the Paragon, Munster High School, Munster, IN adds an interesting note to the year's history.

or someone who has done something unusual. Then do a bio box as a sidebar to accompany the main story.

14. Write a short paper explaining whether or not the following lead and conclusion to a story which appeared in *U.S. Today* is effective. The story was about how parents dealt with raising their son, a son who had been normal until he was four years old and contracted viral encephalitis. In a matter of days, he was blind and unable to walk, sit up, or take food or fluids by mouth. The story appeared in *U.S. Today* five years later.

Lead— She remembers the last time her son Patrick spoke.

Conclusion— "Tomorrow is not guaranteed for any of us."–a quote by the mother

15. Clip 10 leads and 10 conclusions from 10 articles in any magazines and discuss whether or not you think they are effective.

16. Now find 10 leads and 10 conclusions in your own yearbook or in exchange yearbooks and discuss their effectiveness.

17. For exercises 5-8 in above, create an appropriate sidebar—a quick read like a Fact Box or a Quote Box—to accompany your story. Be creative.

18. To help students realize the importance of description, have each student choose an object in the room and write a description. Read aloud and have other students guess the object. You can do the same thing by having each student choose another student in the room to describe. Then read the descriptions aloud to see if the other students can guess which student was described.

19. Ask students to develop a possible list of coverage ideas. Give the students a series of prompts, such as the following:

- I am most afraid of...
- I am happy when...
- The greatest asset I would like most people to have would be...

➢ *Top 10 Lists*

Listing the top 10 responses to questionnaires is a good way to add some humor to a publication. The one below is from the Heritage at Horizon High School, Scottsdale, AZ. Note how the staff used parallel construction by starting each number with an ing word.

Top 10 Strangest Sophomore Behaviors

10. Eating fries with chocolate ice cream.

9. Dressing up disco style.

8. Collecting hippos.

7. Wearing Mickey Mouse ears to school.

6. Eating pretzels with sour cream.

5. Going to bed early to get up early to study.

4. Walking through the rain to get hair curly.

3. Drooling while sleeping.

2. Throwing freshmen in the trash.

1. Walking imaginary dogs to school.

(answers taken from 200 responses to a December survey)

➢ *In-Depth*
Quotes

"Every Thursday, I had a voice lesson at my teacher's house. Ever since sixth grade, I've taken lessons from the same woman, Nancy St. James. Every week we did silly exercises and scales and then we worked on classical pieces. I worked on Italian, English and French songs and arias. In November, I was preparing for college auditions so we focused on particular songs for the schools. My teacher and I were good friends, and I loved going to my lesson each week."—Jane Ellis, senior

Too many quotes in yearbooks are shallow and often include information that anyone at any school could say. This quote from the Pioneer, Kirkwood High School, Kirkwood, MO, provides meaningful information.

• If I could have one wish, I...
• Sometimes my friends...
• I am sad when...
• My earliest childhood memory is...
• I laugh when...
• I felt I had to lie when...
• One specific thing I would like to remember about today would be...
• One specific thing I would like to forget about today would be...

20. Make a list of someone's personality traits by describing the contents of their backback, or the contents of their purse, or the contents of their car, or the contents of their locker. Use these personality traits in writing a complete story on the person. Do not make up any facts. In some of the exercises above, you were allowed to make up facts because you were writing from a fact sheet that contained incomplete information. However, when you write stories based on your own research, you should never make up facts.

CHAPTER
eleven

Newspaper Design

Computers have changed the way staffs design newspapers, but the basic rules remain. Content still dictates design. Content (copy, headlines, photographs, and illustrations) is more important than design. The content of a story should not suffer just to make a page more attractive; however, if a story is not packaged attractively, the reader may never look at it.

Any design artist should keep in mind four main goals: (1) to display news according to its importance; (2) to give the page an orderly, attractive appearance; (3) to guide the reader through the page; and (4) to give the newspaper a personality.

Although all four goals are important, the last is especially so. It would be terribly boring if every school newspaper in the United States looked exactly the same. It would also be monotonous if a paper remained static in design from year to year. Newspaper staffs change personnel annually, so the paper should go through a redesign each year.

Papers can gain personality in several ways. Type style used for the nameplate and page headings can help. Use of standing headings for columns can establish personality, as can repeated use of the same size tool lines for standing stories such as news briefs. Methods of bylining stories and size and width of type can also be part of a personality.

A page can be designed in different ways. The key is to be consistent. Modular design became popular in the early 1980s for both professional and school papers. In modular design every element on the page is rectangular in shape.

Pictures and the headlines and stories they accompany may be considered as one element.

The following are suggested layout rules for modular design. They may be varied to fit individual needs. The key again is to be consistent.

➢ **Creating Teams**
• Page design requires staff members to work in teams, as no one person can do it all.
• Teams could consist of a photo editor, a photographer, a designer, a writer, and a copyeditor.
• Team members should work together to decide how best to present a topic—what information to present and how to present it.
• Analyze all the options from quote boxes to factoids to bio boxes.

1. Graphics are secondary to content. Content should determine graphics, and never be sacrificed for graphics.
2. Use uppercase heads rarely. Downstyle—capitalizing first word and proper nouns—works best.
3. Use large photos, or at least vary photo size.
4. Crop photos tightly, usually within one pica of the center of interest. Learn to use a scaleograph or a proportion wheel to enlarge or reduce photographs to fit the space. Your printing company can provide you with these devices.
5. Use both horizontal and vertical rectangles; the best design moves both horizontally and vertically.
6. Two important words are *space* and *distance*. Horizontals should be used for stories seven inches or longer. Shorter ones may go vertical.
7. Consider using an "On the Inside" box on the cover.
8. Contrast is important—in width of tool lines, in heaviness of type, and so on. Contrast head shades—nameplate—one word can be black, another gray. In doing so, it becomes unnecessary to space between words. Other types of contrast would be to use outline lettering with solid lettering, and gray lines to contrast with black ones.
9. Consider using initial letters to begin stories, headlines, and captions. Do not overuse.
10. Use some open boxes rather than enclosing a story on all four sides. Put tool lines on the

Newsmagazines, including the Arlingtonian, Upper Arlington High School, Upper Arlington, OH, often use artwork on the cover to illustrate the main story of the issue.

top and bottom, for example, or break out of the box with a photo, an illustration, or a headline.

11. Consider using gray screens behind stories. A 20% gray is generally heavy enough.

12. There must be a center of visual interest

> **Online Publications**

In 2000, some schools, including Hanover Central in Indiana had dropped their print publications and started a Web-based publication. Hanover Central called its new Web paper the CyberCat, a spinoff of the print newspaper, the Cat's Eye. Print design rules don't always apply to Web pages. The HTML language used to create a Web page doesn't adapt easily to the "drag and drop" approach of desktop publishing. It is easy to spend a lot of time designing eye-catching graphics, but you need to remember content is still of utmost importance. You don't need to invest in a digital camera to get good pictures, but a digital camera stream-lines the process of getting good pictures online. Mastering any software take time, but one can begin with a basic Web page authoring program, a scanner, and image editing software, such as Adobe Photoshop or PhotoDeluxe.

➢ Advantages of
Web Publications

Advantages of an
online publication
over a print publica-
tion include:

• Staffs may post
daily information and
announcement
updates that are not
newsworthy in a bi-
weekly or monthly
print publication.
Staffs can also post
hard news quickly. If
a fire occurs, that
story can be online
the same day.

• Costs are usually
less to create an
online publication
than to do a printed
version, especially if
the school district
provides the host
computer for the
Web site.

• Because Web
papers are inexpen-
sive, staffs can easier
incorporate spot
color, color photos,
animation, even video
and audio clips, as
well as links to related
topics and interactive
feedback forms.

• Story length is
not as important as
there is literally no
space restriction. It is
also easier to display
photos larger, but
certain limitations
may exist based on

(Continued)

Well-planned white space enhances this design in the HiLite, Carmel High
School, Carmel, IN. The contrasting shades of type in the headline as well
as the contrasting sizes of type also make this design strong. A large dominant photograph and a pulled quote help draw the reader to the page.

(CVI) on each page, where the reader's eyes
go first. A CVI is usually achieved by having a
dominant element (ordinarily a photo) that
is at least twice the size of anything else on
the page. This is particularly important when
designing a double truck (facing pages).

278

MAKING THE

grade

1 SUPERIOR

2 VERY GOOD

3 GOOD

4 ACCEPTABLE

5 FAIR

6 PASSING

7 FAILING

Teachers and students differ on 'Honor' Roll

By Jodi Blazek

Honor roll, according to some students really isn't much of an honor anymore. In the last 15 years the percentage of juniors and seniors on the honor roll has practically doubled. In 1967, 18 percent of the senior class and 15.5 percent of the junior class were on the honor roll, compared to now, in 1982, 34 percent of all seniors and 31 percent of all juniors are on the honor roll, vice-principal in charge of student services, Don Darnell said.

According to Darnell, there are a number of factors contributing to this. One is the pressure from the student's parents. Harold Baker, math teacher, said, "The parents encourage the kids to do well, but in some cases it's the students who put presure on themselves, thinking their parents will get mad if they don't get good grades."

"My parents don't make a real big deal about my being on the honor roll—it would be a bigger deal if I weren't," though," junior Dirck Fuller said.

Another factor contributing to the high percentage of students on the honor roll, Darnell said, is the lowering of academic standards. This means that the demands from a teacher could be less strict. "Teachers in the past taught classes in a higher concentrated way. Today we have a better teaching method, the students know exactly what they are being tested on," Darnell said.

Also, "the goals and objectives differ. The teachers are getting along better with students," Darnell said. Now, basic classes are being taught nationwide so that every student is learning the same things which make putting together an ACT a lot easier, he added.

What does being on the honor roll actually mean to some students?

"I feel like I have really accomplished something that is hard to achieve," senior, Doug Kline said.

Stuart Scott, junior, said, "it's going to help you in applying for colleges and scholarships."

"Basically, it's too easy to get on," Fuller said. "It doesn't mean much when you are just one of 30 percent of your entire class that made honor roll."

"There are the people who take really easy classes and get on honor roll and then people who take hard classes like pre-cal afd composition, they deserve something better," Watmore said. "The people who take the easy classes just aren't going to be prepared," she added.

"Unless you want to be a vegetable all your life, you should take hard classes," Kline said. "You have to be prepared for life in general."

"Most anybody can get on honor roll taking easy classes, but it's really something when you can take hard classes and make honor roll. You have to take hard classes for a challenge," Scott said.

Honor roll should have to be an honor, Fuller said. "You should have to work for it."

Baker feels that people need to think of what they can learn because there are too many grade conscious people.

English teacher Melissa Beall said, "People are in for a rude awakening in college if they don't take classes now to prepare them for later. Doing things to prepare you for the rest of your life—that's what education is all about."

Judy Bogle, math teacher, said, "You should take classes beneficial to your future. Hard classes for some might not be hard for others."

Pass/fail grade options are a cop-out to saving a good grade point average, some have said.

"It's okay for some kids that really need it, but some do it to screw off," Watmore said. "If I took it I wouldn't be trying as hard with a pass/fail; I wouldn't be learning as much."

"It's good for students who are worried about their grades," Fuller said. "Also, it's good for someone who wants to take a class that they are interested in and not necessarily good at. It can be over used, though."

Beall said. "Pass/fail is good for someone who wants to learn a lot but doesn't have the time to devote to the class, especially classes like Debate, that take a lot of out-of-school time. It could be good to take off some pressure."

> "It's the personal satisfaction that you get, being on honor roll is just a reward for achieving good grades." — Stuart Scott

Baker said he agrees with "the philosophy that lets students take a course without fear of lowering their grade point average if they're taking the class for a learning experience. Maybe there shouldn't be an option with required courses."

All together with the disadvantages and advantages to honor roll, Darnell feels that honor roll really is an honor. The only way it wouldn't be is if it was an unusual school where 50-75 percent of the students were on it—then it wouldn't be much of an honor, he said.

"People on honor roll are usually trying hard anyway." Beall said.

Lincoln Northeast has 20.4 percent of the total school population on honor roll. Lincoln High has 21 percent of the senior class and 23 percent of the junior class on honor roll. Lincoln East has a sweeping 44 percent of the seniors and 43 percent of juniors on honor roll.

Citywide requirements for honor roll are 20 hours of one's and/or two's and no failing grades. In 1967 and 1968 however, Southeast's requirements were 20 hours of one's and/or two's and no grades falling below a four. Kline and Watmore find that honor roll is a big confidence booster.

Taking the opposite view, Scott and Fuller bring out points on why honor roll isn't an "honor" anymore.

Agreeing that taking hard classes gives you much more future preparation, Watmore and Kline said that to be an honor, honor roll must take into consideration the more difficult classes over the easier classes.

Wrapping copy around a quote and use of effective typography to the left of the copy distinguish this design from the Clarion, Lincoln Southeast High School, Lincoln, NE.

13. Consider combining two photos, for example, a silhouette above a rectangle.

14. Distance between elements should be 1 pica—between head and copy, photo and copy, or photo and caption.

15. Consider positioning copy in a U-shape or an L-shape around a picture. You can also U-shape a story around a related story or around artwork, or U-shape artwork or a photograph around copy.

16. Try to avoid a vertical drop of more than six inches before going to the second column of a story, or you might lose your reader.

17. Consider using a dutch wrap, in which the head goes across only the first column of copy and type runs alongside it in the second column. This works best for two-column sto-

memory constraints.

• *Parents, alumni and other community members are more likely to see the Web paper because of its easy access.*

• *Stories on the Web are easily archived and remain available online long after most papers are tossed out.*

• *Hard copies may be printed, if desired.*

• *Corrections can be posted quickly and stories can be updated as needed. Editors can even update from their homes if they have remote access to the school's server.*

• *A resource links page facilitates Web surfing for academic and social topics.*

• *Web page authoring programs make it relatively easy to create pages without having to learn HTML.*

• *A good digital camera will cut photography expenses. Using a digital camera streamlines the process of getting images online. It usually takes less time to prepare an image from a digital camera than one that has been scanned.*

➢ *Increasing*
Visual Activity

• *Think packaging.
Don't think page
design.*

• *Think TV. Use a
remote control to
take readers through
the pages. Readers
use a remote control
to scan TV channels.
Publications need to
be designed the
same way—a way to
get the readers to
stop at each chan-
nel—on each page.*

• *Increase points of
entry to help reader
get into the story. The
three main magnets
(points of entry) are
the photos, captions,
and headlines.*

• *Eighty percent of
all readers enter a
page through a photo.*

• *Captions are the
most read copy on a
page. That's why
National Geographic
has an entire staff
writing captions.
Perhaps yearbook
staffs should also
have a caption staff.*

ries and at the top of the page. In the middle of a page, a tool line will be needed to separate the story above a dutch wrap. A three-line head works best with the dutch wrap.

18. Consider blending photos and art.

19. Block ads across the bottom of a page horizontally or up the side of a page vertically. The largest ads should be placed at the bottom of the page, with smaller ads on top.

20. Consider using a tripod head. This three-part headline has one line to the left that is twice the size of two more lines to the right and is usually separated by a colon. For example, if you had a 48-point head on the left, you would have two lines of 24-point on the right. See Chapter 9 for an example.

21. Flush left heads work best.

22. When using two photos with a story, it is best to use one vertical and one horizontal.

23. It is permissible to continue stories from one page to another, but try to continue all stories to the same page.

24. Consider using some ragged-right copy to contrast with flush right.

25. Consider using some interline spacing—two points between paragraphs, for example.

26. Keep nameplate in the top four inches of the page.

27. Vary column width, but don't go too wide. The ideal width is 13 to 16 picas; try to avoid going wider than 24 picas, and type narrower than 8 picas will create problems with too many hyphenated words. In some cases, a one-syllable word is all that will fit on a narrow line, and the computer may space between letters so it will fill the line. That is why you should not have narrow lines. Inconsistent letter-spaced words are ugly.

A strong infographic enhances this feature page in the Kirkwood Call, Kirkwood High School, Kirkwood, MO. The staff has used the page to package stories about flying, including an opinion column by a writer who was close to the girls whose parents died in the crash.

➤ Disadvantages of Internet Publications

• Not everyone wants to sit at a computer to "read the paper." Therefore staffs must provide content and interaction that's not possible in a print version to give the readers a real reason to visit the site.

• Good technical support is not always easy to find. Staffs need to get their school's technology technician and coordinator on board with their efforts.

• There will be some down time when servers crash.

• Some Web page authoring programs do not help staffs manage the site. Consider using programs like Adobe Go Live!, Adobe PageMill, or Claris HomePage.

• Web pages display differently from computer to computer. The most obvious variables include the browser used for viewing, the screen size and the viewable window size. Staffs will have no control over which of these their readers may use. It is best to create pages so readers can easily view them on a 640x480 pixel screen, which can easily be viewed on 12"–15" monitors. Staffs also need to be aware that PC and Macintosh computers tend to display the screens differently.

• Designers tend to want to create eye-popping graphics for their Web pages. There's nothing wrong with that as long as they realize how much time it takes and as long as content doesn't suffer as a result.

➢ **Creating a Package Step-by-Step**

• *Have page editors brainstorm to develop a story idea.*

• *Once the idea has been selected (death, for example), decide on what the main story will focus. Assume the focus will be on suicide.*

• *The team (writer(s), photographer, designer, and page editor) working on the page decide which sidebar options they will use with the main story. The page editor makes assignments.*

• *Page editor follows up with each team member about angles being pursued.*

• *Designer creates page on computer. Team members decide on photo sizes, write captions, and write headlines.*

28. Design logo to be common with all standing stories (columns). Create visual continuity by using the same typeface on nameplate and masthead.

29. Emphasize the date of the paper in the nameplate more than volume and issue number.

30. A single photo on a page should be above the fold.

31. The average story on a page should not exceed 12 inches in length. If you use longer ones, be sure to break up the gray with initial letters, pulled quotes, artwork, photographs, boldface type, or some graphic device that will make the article more appealing.

32. Avoid use of italic heads and kickers.

33. Two inches of type is the minimum for one column. If a story runs more than one column, be sure that each column contains at least two inches of type. In other words, if you run a story in three columns and L-shape it around a photograph in the second and third columns, be sure that there is at least two inches of copy in both the second and third columns.

34. Never bump heads at top of the page. It is best not to bump heads anywhere. Heads help break up a gray page. When they are placed side by side, large areas of unbroken gray usually result.

35. Consider achieving contrast by using serif type for standing column heads and sans serif for other heads, or vice versa. However, do not mix serif and sans serif for nonstanding heads.

36. On double trucks, put the CVI near the middle.

37. Keep body copy off the gutter of a double truck. Run pictures, artwork, and headlines across the gutter.

38. Avoid boxing stories next to ads, especially if

Inside boxes on the front page of the Buzz, *Bonneville High School, Idaho Falls, ID, lure the reader to stories on the inside pages. Note how the staff also uses bullets beside its secondary heads.*

story and ad both have photos.

39. Try to experiment once you have mastered the basics.

40. Consider using photographs where you have dropped out the background. These are called COBs (cutout background). Partial COBs are

➤ *Survey Results*

The following statistics and statements are from studies that the Poynter Institute conducted.

• *Ninety percent of readers enter pages through large photos, artwork, or headlines.*

• *Surveys show headlines are more apt to be read if a photo is nearby.*

• *Photographs and information graphics markedly increase text comprehension and story interest.*

• *Readers see 80% of the artwork and 75% of the photographs in a paper.*

• *Readers see 56% of the headlines, but they are aware of only 25% of the text, and they read just a portion of that.*

• *Only about 13% of the articles in a paper are read in-depth—that is, at least half is read.*

• *Text is the last thing people see in a paper.*

• *Most papers jump stories from one page to the next, but research shows readers are lost at the jump.*

➤ *Creating a*
Design Handbook
  • *Consider every*
design element (the
nameplate, the body
text, the standing
heads, the display
fonts).
  • *Decide on the*
architecture of each
page (grids, headlines,
briefs, ads, rules, and
boxes).
  • *Decide on all*
secondary elements
(liftout quotes, logos,
bylines, jump lines,
cutlines, credit lines).
  • *Include ideas*
gained from profes-
sional publications—
ideas that you might
use for special stories.

also effective. A partial COB might cut out the background around a person's head, for example, but leave the rest of the background.

41. Remember that form follows function.
42. Provide contrast by using different weights and sizes of types.
43. Every page should have a photo, artwork, or a graphic element.
44. Run pictures at the top of a page to help prevent tombstoning or bumping heads.
45. Remember that simpler is better. Don't overdesign.
46. Give your paper its own personality. Elements that create personality are: nameplate, menus (on-the-inside boxes), logos, standing heads, boxes, bylines, folios, masthead, typography, column width, lines, shadings, justified vs. ragged-right type, color.
47. Remember the four major principles of good makeup—harmony, proportion, balance, and fitness. Harmony means selecting type and border in a way that promotes unity, neatness, and orderliness. Limit head fonts to one type—two at the most. Be sure all typefaces complement each other. Proportion means a pleasing arrangement of all elements on a page. The size of the page should dictate the size of type used. Balance means the arrangement of heads, stories, illustrations, and boxes in such a way that each item seems to have a proper place. Fitness means that the paper's design fits the image of the school. If the student body is conservative, a more conservative design is indicated. If the student body is liberal, then a more modern, upbeat design would be best. Again, form follows function. Determine the function of your paper, and you will be able to determine

design.

48. Be daring. Try new ideas. Don't just copy from other sources. A new idea may not work, but you will never know if you don't try. Set as a goal each year to do something different from what you did the previous year.

Another design style is the more traditional method called brace or focus makeup. This style may be used when one story is more important than any other. The most important story is placed in the upper right corner of the page. Heads are arranged diagonally from lower left to upper right. Two-column heads and photographs scattered throughout the page can help offset the weight of the major story in the upper right.

Elements in a brace design do not have to be rectangular, although some may be. Rules for the traditional design are the following:

1. Do not run a story out from under its head.
2. Do not put a picture between a headline and its story. Arrange the elements in order of photograph, headline, story, or headline, story, photograph.
3. Don't let the last line of a paragraph begin a new column, especially if it does not go at least two thirds of the way across the column. Such a line is called a widow; it often leaves unattractive white space at the top of a column.
4. Keep the nameplate in the upper third of the page.
5. Keep stronger heads at the top of the page. In other words, graduate heads downward with the large point size at the top of the page and the smaller sizes at the bottom. It is possible, however, to have all heads on a page the same size if all stories are of equal importance.
6. Do not tombstone heads (using the same size

➤ **Possible Formats**
• *Tabloid: This page size (11 x 17) is one-half that of the broadsheet. This size page allows the staff to vary column widths on the page, which helps add more visual variety.*

• *Magapaper: The front page of this paper is 8 1/2 x 11 in size, but when it opens up to the inside pages, it becomes tabloid in size. The front page size allows the staff to create a paper with a magazine look.*

• *News magazine: The size of this paper is usually 8 1/2 x 11 or 9 x 12, and it tends to look more like a magazine throughout.*

• *Other sizes are also used, including a 10 x 14, the size of Parade magazine, which appears in several Sunday newspapers.*

• *Broadsheet: The size of most daily newspapers. This size has become more popular in the school settings in recent years. This is a full-size newspaper measuring roughly 14 x 23 inches.*

A successful example of making the design fit the story is this layout from the Echoes, *Abraham Lincoln High School, Council Bluffs, IA.*

and style of head side by side).

7. Avoid placing heads next to each other, even if they are of different sizes and styles. Headlines are used to break up gray areas, and placing them next to each other does not accomplish that.

8. Ads should be pyramided at bottom of page, with the largest ad in the lower right corner and smaller ads to the left and on top. It is possible, however, to do a two-page ad spread in a well shape, with the largest ads in

the lower left corner on the left page and in the lower right corner on the right page.

9. Scatter pictures throughout the page. Pictures have greater impact than anything else; by scattering them, you can guide the reader more effectively.

10. Make pictures large enough that faces can be seen. Generally, try to make a face at least the size of a dime, or better yet, a thumb.

11. Be sure that pictures fill column space.

12. Be sure that headlines fit the allotted space.

13. Use subheads or boldfacing to break up long stories.

14. Caption all photos.

15. Don't mix type families on a page.

16. Avoid vertical type.

All the rules for the modular layout also pertain to traditional style except for No. 1. In modular layout it is permissible to place a headline to the left of copy, or to place it in the middle of the column or columns of a story that goes across more than one column.

Regardless of the design style used, a paper should strive to be distinctive. Dare to be different. Sometimes experiments fail, but it is only through experimentation that a new look becomes possible. Be sure to make each page different. For example, set editorials in larger type to make them distinctive. Also, be consistent from issue to issue in placement and type size of editorials so that the reader can recognize them easily.

Editorial pages sometimes lack pizzazz. Try to think of ways to make them livelier. Research shows that editorial pages have low readership. That may be because the page design never changes. Be sure to place the masthead at the bottom of the page. Place the editorials at the top. Cartoons will usually be read, so scatter them throughout the page. Use larger body type for editorials. If you use 9 point for other stories, use 10 or 11 point for editorials. Use wider

> *Terminology*
> • *Doglegs:
> L-shaped columns of
> text wrapped around
> another element, such
> as a photograph.*
> • *Double truck:
> Two facing pages on
> the same sheet of
> paper treated as one
> unit.*
> • *Drop shadow: A
> thin shadow effect
> added to characters
> in a headline.*
> • *Dutch wrap or
> raw wrap: Text that
> extends into a column alongside its
> headline, normally to
> the right of the head.*
> • *Ear: Text or a
> graphic element on
> either side of a newspaper's flag.*
> • *Flag or nameplate: The name of a
> newspaper on page
> one.*
> • *Graf: Slang for
> paragraph.*
> • *Hairline: The
> thinnest rule line.*
> • *Halftone: A photograph that has
> been converted into a
> pattern of tiny dots.
> This means photos
> can be reproduced in
> shades of gray.*
> • *Hanging Indent:
> Type set with the first
> line flush left and all
> other lines in that
> paragraph indented.*

One trend in front-page design today is to make the main story a feature, rather than hard news. Readership surveys generally show readers prefer features over untimely news stories. The above front page from the HiLite, Carmel High School, Carmel, IN, begins its feature story on smoking on page 1 and then continues it on page 6. Most readers would probably not jump to page 5 for a news story, but they would make the jump for this interesting feature.

Three smokers share feelings

TOBACCO RULES EVOLVE OVER YEARS

Smokers now pay the price

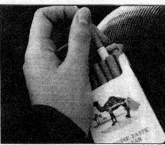

Abell

A smoker handles one of the many packs of cigarettes used each day by students meeting after school. One cigarette soon will be lighted.

Sarah Ford Photo

> "My dad gets so drunk he's like, 'Here have a beer.'"
> "NATASHA"

> "I know all the effects. I really only think about (what cigarettes will do to me) when my mom gets on me. Then, I usually just wish she'd leave me the – alone. I know it's bad for me, but I don't care."
> "NATASHA"

> "Hey, I make good grades. I only had two F's."
> "CARL"

CONTINUES FROM THE FRONT PAGE

in school.

"Do you know what happens when you can't smoke for a while?" Carl asks while he takes another satisfying taste of his Camel Light. He says that without a cigarette, he's not the same. He becomes edgy, and his temper suddenly gets a very short fuse.

Natasha has experienced the same feeling when she can't get her hands on tobacco. "You wanna bite people's heads off and start fighting. People bother you when you don't have a cigarette."

All three admit to being addicted. Carl has been hooked for at least two years. Amy and Natasha aren't sure when that point came for them. None of them really think much about what smoking will do to them in the future. "I know all the effects. I really only think about (what cigarettes will do to me) when my mom gets on me. Then, I usually just wish she'd leave me – alone," Natasha said. "I know it's bad for me, but I don't care."

Carl offers some advice to Natasha. "If you smoke weed, then you won't get any cancer. But I don't smoke weed."

Natasha laughs at this and reputes him. "Listen to the way he talks. He's definitely a pothead."

Slowly, the discussion goes back to what keeps the three smoking. Natasha says that her life is saturated by cigarettes, and their constant presence keeps her going. "If you see someone smoking a cigarette, you just want to light one up."

Amy offers a bit of her experiences. "You feel sick if you don't smoke." Natasha's face lights up as as she agrees. "Yeah, you start hacking — up, like tar."

Carl has been sitting quietly this whole time since the topic of stopping smoking came up. He looks into nowhere as if deep in thought and then speaks. He says he really needs tobacco, and he's felt the need physically many times. As an example, he talks about what happened to him the day before. "Yesterday, me and my brother was — tearing up the whole house 'cause we couldn't find a cigarette."

Politics

Government doesn't really play too big of a role in their lives, but they do have their opinions. "— President (stinks)," Carl says. "He's an —."

Amy says the President isn't the only aspect of politics that stinks. "The government's —. It's —. That's not what life's about. It ain't about that. Nobody — has control over anything. We're all going to die."

None of them seems to believe the government can do much to help them in their future, and Natasha is the only one who thinks she'll vote when she becomes old enough.

Grades

One subject that does affect their future is their grades. Carl becomes defensive immediately when asked about his. "Hey, I make good grades. I only had two F's," he says half-jokingly.

Natasha teases him, "Those aren't good grades."

While grades are somewhat important to them, they don't hold much respect for teachers. They can all name off teachers they hate. "The — teachers don't even notice (pot use in school), and if they do, it's way too late," Natasha says to explain what she defines as the stupidity of teachers. She alleges she has been in various areas of the school and smelled pot with teachers nearby, and they have done nothing. She continues off the subject about her own marijuana use. "I used to smoke bud all the time until I got on probation. Then, I quit. I'm feelin' pretty good about it, too."

Amy gives a laugh. "I didn't. I'm on probation, and I smoked weed all weekend."

Carl says he thinks drugs are prominent in many students' lives. "Lots of people come to school trippin' (on hallucinogens) or high. It's true." The two girls tell him to shut up as if this information were a secret that must be withheld. Soon, though, all three are comfortable talking about it.

"I never got high in school," Natasha says. "I always got high right after, though. You know, to relieve the stress of the day, just get really stoned 'til you can't move. When I started coming down (from the high), I'd just go to sleep."

Lost cigarette

At this point, Natasha realizes her cigarette is missing. She looks around, and then looks down at Amy's hand. "Did you take my cigarette?" she demands.

Amy can't help but give a playful smile and place her hand out of Natasha's reach.

"What the —? Give me my — cigarette! Give it to me!" Natasha demands once again. She jumps up, and they fight over the lit cigarette.

Carl ignores all of this. He says, "You know, the reason that a lot of people smoke is that they're bored most of the time."

Eventually, the stolen cigarette ordeal is ended, and the three are asked whether smoking has anything to do with rebelling against authority.

"— no!" Carl says vehemently.

"Maybe unconsciously," Amy says. Natasha agrees with her.

With the subject back on smoking, Natasha tells a story. She goes into details about a choir concert she was performing at where she and a couple friends walked out. They just stood outside and smoked during the concert. "We like left and had a cigarette right on the trail."

Amy says her family first got her started smoking cigarettes. "My dad's been smoking cigarettes around me my whole life. I tried my first cigarette in kindergarten."

Not to be outdone, Carl says, "I drank beer in kindergarten. My dad used to give me a beer."

Parents playing a role in their children's substance abuse seems to be uniform between the three. Natasha says her dad has given her alcohol. "My dad gets so drunk he's like, 'Here, have a beer.'"

Their future

They have all used more than pot before. None of them think any of this drug use will really hurt their future as adults. "Going to work. Coming home to feed the kids. —!" Amy says.

Everyone laughs at this comment, including Amy. "My kids aren't goin' to school. My kids are gonna be —," Amy says.

Seriousness comes back, and Amy says she'll probably be an artist 10 years from now when she has kids. "Or a stripper," she adds.

When Carl is asked what he wants to do, it takes a little time to ponder the question. "I've thought about bein' a special effects designer."

Natasha says she wants to be a music teacher. "I want to be like Mr. (Michael) Pote. Mr. Pote is really cool. He's the music theory teacher."

At this, Carl decides it's time to leave. They get up and strap their bags on their shoulders. With a wave of their hands, the three walk off into the slowly darkening sky. Stripper, special effects designer and music teacher, side by side.

STUDENTS WHO use tobacco may face even more risk with the recently proposed changes in tobacco policy.

At the Sept. 30 school board meeting, the school board discussed the possibility of a change to send students with tobacco problems to a court appearance where they could be ticketed and fined for their offense.

According to Administrative Assistant Mr. John Abell, the proposal continues a trend of getting tougher on tobacco in this school and in the state. "There was a time when the law did not directly concern itself with age (regarding tobacco)," Abell said.

The law up to 1988 was vague and consisted mainly of an approach of not allowing the sale of tobacco to those under 18, as stated in *Indiana Code*. It did not clearly define in writing whether students could use or possess tobacco.

However, in 1988 Indiana adopted a new tobacco policy that stated no one under 18 could purchase or accept tobacco under any circumstances for personal use. This clarification of rules prompted the school to make a change in school policy and ban any tobacco use or possession.

The current school rules consist of a smoking clinic after the first tobacco offense, a five-day out-of-school suspension after the second offense and a semester expulsion for any offense after that. *By Wayne Hsiung*

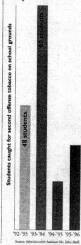

Students caught for second offense tobacco on school grounds

'92-'93 '93-'94 '94-'95 '95-'96

Source: Administrative Assistant Mr. John Abell

column widths for editorials, but remember not to set them wider than 24 picas. Use ragged right for columns. Try to use photographs on the page—perhaps a photo of a musical group for a music review, or promotional pictures to go with a movie review. Information graphics can make an editorial page more attractive. Boston boxes—sentences that summarize the editorial—can also enliven a page. Other features of editorial pages are the masthead (staff box and abbreviated editorial policy), editorial columns, and letters to the editor.

Maintain harmony on a page by limiting varieties of typefaces—preferably use just one—and by selecting tool lines that complement the headlines in style. Create balance by carefully arranging the heads, stories, illustrations, and ads on a page. Establish personality by being consistent with nameplate, page headings, and standing columns, and achieve proportion by arranging elements on a page in relation to all other elements. Keep in mind that proportion can be obtained both vertically and horizontally.

Use of graphics can help create good proportion. In today's newspapers, graphics are very much "in." Use of tool lines, shadow boxes, quote boxes, initial letters, full cutout photographs, infographics, bullets, and partial cutouts give pages a special dimension that helps set them apart from the ordinary. Master the basics. Then experiment. Eye-appealing designs can get a story read. Don't be afraid to be creative, but don't let content suffer just to add that extra creative touch.

It is best to keep design simple. When using tool lines, keep them to hairline, 1 point, or 2 point. If you use anything larger than that, consider screening them to a percentage of gray. Larger lines in 100% black will look overpowering. If you can afford color, try tool lines in a spot color. Lines are the designer's best tools to show relationships—to create packages of elements. Lines make it easy to tie headline, copy, artwork, and photographs together as one. Lines can also help break up extremely gray areas. Let the size and content of the story determine the thickness of the line to be used. Remember, not every story or page needs to have lines. It is possible to overuse lines. Don't overuse any one graphic device.

Color plays a prominent role in design today. Everything points to the use of more color, but use it judiciously.

Bullets are especially effective with captions. Any geometric shape (triangles, squares, circles, parallelograms) will work. They can also be effective to break up long stories, and they work well with headlines.

Some designers refer to bullets as gimcracks, or splashy showy objects of little value or use. In design, however, they can be used to break up long, gray areas. Besides bullets, checkmarks or stars may also be used to call attention to major points in articles or to highlight items in a list. For example: Contemporary newspapers use:

- Color
- Briefs
- Graphic devices
- Modular layout

Some newspapers use gimcracks as a signal to readers that they have reached the end of the article. A series of three or four stars is sometimes used to separate short articles.

Be careful when using full or partial cutout photographs. To begin with, it is not easy to find a picture where the background can be dropped out. If you do find a picture, be careful in cutting out around the center of interest. Use a sharp blade and a steady hand.

Patterns and screens can enhance a design, but be careful that patterns are not too busy, and be sure they fit the story. Remember, content should dictate design. Patterns and screens tell the reader that this story is important; is it more important than other stories on the page? Also, be careful when using tool lines. Thick, heavy tool lines attract attention. Is it the tool lines you want the reader to see first?

Infographics can also enhance a design. If a survey is part

➤ *Use of Art*
• *Fills: Fill patterns of 10-30% can be used behind type. Normally 10% works better to be sure the type is readable. Fills of 40–100% require reversed type.*
• *Infographics: Using pie charts, bar charts, fever graphs, and other types of infographics can add to a page's appeal.*
• *Boxes: Four-sided boxes can add impact, but so can boxes that have no side lines— just top and bottom. Also, consider breaking elements out of their boxes to avoid boxing in the element totally.*
• *Reverses: Use reverse type sparingly, but it can work well for headlines.*
• *Line art: Hand-drawn artwork can be effective if the art is well done. It is preferable not to use clip art, as the work should be student-produced.*

➤ **Terminology**

• *Porkchop: A half column mug shot.*

• *Refer: A line or paragraph referring to a related story somewhere else in the paper.*

• *Register: Aligning different color plates or overlays so they're positioned perfectly when they print.*

• *RGB: An acronym for red, green, blue.*

• *Rule: A printing term for a straight line.*

• *Runaround: Text that wraps around another element, like a photo.*

• *Screen: A pattern of tiny dots used to create halftones.*

• *Sidesaddle head: A headline placed to the left of a story.*

• *Skyboxes or skylines: Teasers that run above the nameplate on page one. They are called skyboxes if they're boxed or skylines if they are just a line of type.*

• *Table: A type of sidebar that stacks words or numbers in rows for comparative purposes.*

• *TIFF: Tagged image file format—a computer format for saving scanned images.*

• *Widow or orphan: A short word or phrase that makes up the last line of text in a paragraph and that begins a new column of text.*

of your story, present the results as an infographic. Combining art with type can be eye-catching.

Effective use of white space can add to design, providing visual relief for the reader. Extra leading between lines is one way to use white space. It is also permissible to use white space in corners—especially in corners of photo stories. White space can also be used effectively around headlines. For example, you might run a headline across four columns, but run the story across only three and one-half columns, the other half column being left empty. This is referred to as a drop column. It is obviously white space left on purpose. Using kickers and wickets for headline styles is another effective way to work in white space. Do not trap large amounts of white space between photos or between headlines and copy.

Typography

Typography is also important in creating a pleasing design. An understanding of type sizes and faces is a necessity.

The selection of a typeface for body copy is important, since body type is the major element in a newspaper. Body type is used for all articles, cutlines, and bylines. The typeface chosen must be readable. All printing companies have a limited number of typefaces. Therefore, if a staff uses a commercial printer it must choose among those available. The accompanying illustration shows the way a printer might list the typefaces carried.

TEXT TYPES

The following type faces are available for body or text type:

This is 8 Palatino.

This is 8 Palatino bold.

This is 8 Palatino italic.

This is 9 Palatino.

This is 9 Palatino bold.

Former Blood member expresses regrets

Kim Miller

> I only had one brother, and he didn't live with me, so I really didn't have anyone to associate with. When I joined the bloods, I had something to belong to.

> We started selling drugs (including cocaine, crack, and marijuana), carrying guns, and we really got into it with our rival gang, the Crips.

> My mother was looking forward to me graduating. I felt that I let her and my whole family down, and I did. I decided then to get out of the gang.

> Getting involved in a gang is not worth it. Eventually, there are only two places gang members can go--the jail or the grave.

In 1990, Jack Smith (not his real name) was a 17-year-old senior at KHS. He attended classes and fully intended to graduate with his class in the spring. Unfortunately, his extracurricular activities included being a member of the Bloods. He sold drugs, carried a gun, and stood solidly by his "brothers." This allegiance led to a fight with a rival Crip member and ended with a 90-day suspension from school. With this suspension, Smith lost all hopes of graduating.

Though Smith never lost his dream of graduating with his class, he hopes that his story of involvement with gangs will make students think twice before joining one.

Smith's cousin, a Blood from L.A., first introduced him to gangs when he was a freshman in 1988.

"When I was a freshman, my cousin talked to me and my friends about being part of a gang. He told us how much money we would make and how exciting the violence would be," said Smith. "At the time, it [being in a gang] was something new. Being young and immature, we didn't see what was wrong with [gangs], so we went along with it."

From mid 1988 to the end of 1989, gang membership declined in St. Louis, according to Smith.

"It was really just me and my friends in the beginning, and we didn't do anything because there weren't any Crips to get into it with," he said.

As the activity and popularity of gangs increased by the end of 1989, so did Smith's involvement with the Bloods. He attributes this to his growing need to fit in somewhere.

"My grades had dropped, and I was ineligible to play football. My friends in school who were keeping me away from gangs were eligible and playing football. I wasn't able to hang with them, so I stayed with guys from the gang," Smith said. "I only had one brother, and he didn't live with me, so I really didn't have anyone to associate with. When I joined the Bloods, I had something to belong to."

The time Smith got involved with the Bloods also marked the period of tremendous growth among gangs. With an explosive number of gang members in St. Louis, the group's activities changed dramatically.

"We started selling drugs (including cocaine, crack, and marijuana), carrying guns, and we were really into it with our rival gang, the Crips," he said. "I got more involved with the gang and its activities after my cousin was arrested. I was looked upon as a leader because of the association with my cousin."

Besides having the feeling that gang members looked up to him, Smith listed three other benefits of being in the group.

"Money, protection, and friendship, were provided by the gang," said Smith, "but the downside was trying to keep my involvement a secret from family.

"I tried to keep it [involvement in gangs] away from home as much as possible. After being in the Bloods for a year, my mother noticed that I was wearing a lot of red. Each time she asked me if I was in a gang, I just lied to her and told her I wasn't," Smith said. "I think I did a good job, since my mother didn't find out until I started getting in trouble at school."

Rivalry between the Bloods and the Crips caused Smith's troubles in school.

"I got kicked out because I fought with Bob Johnson (not his real name) of the Crips," said Smith. "I tried keeping my involvement with gangs away from school as much as possible, but [Johnson] kept pushing it. Me and my friends would walk down the halls, and [Johnson] and his friends would bump into us or say something to us. Out in Meacham Park, our gangs fought a lot. This was just the principle of the gangs, that Bloods and Crips hated each other."

It was Smith's fight with Johnson which resulted in a 90-day suspension from school. This absence caused Smith to fall three credits short of graduation requirements.

"My mother was looking forward to me graduating," Smith said. "I felt that I let her and my whole family down, and I did. I decided then to get out of the gang."

Smith's decision became definite after an incident between the two gangs. The summer after Smith's suspension, a fellow Bloods gang member murdered Johnson in Meacham Park.

"[Johnson] is dead now. He lost his life over a color. It wasn't worth it," said Smith.

To become totally independent from his gang, Smith could not return to KHS.

"I knew that if I came back to KHS I would be in the same boat again, because my friends would still be there," he said.

Smith moved, and now works to complete three credits and earn his high school diploma.

Smith said he is grateful to be out of gangs today.

"Getting involved in a gang is not worth it," said Smith. "Eventually, there are only two places gang members can go—the jail or the grave. I'm glad I got out before I went to either one."

Pulled quotes are an effective way to add appeal to design. The Kirkwood Call, *Kirkwood High School, Kirkwood, MO, has used quotes to create a sidebar effect with a layered look.*

This is 9 Palatino italic.

This is 10 Optima.

This is 10 I Optima Oblique.

This is 10 B Optima Bold.

This is 10 BI Optima Bold Oblique

This is 8 Century Old Style.

This is 8 Century Old Style Bold.

This is 8 Century Old Style italic.

This is 9 Century Old Style.

➤ *Scanning Images*

• *Avoid large file sizes. To ensure files remain small, crop scanned images to the size it will appear on the page.*

• *Use the correct resolution. The proper resolution for scanned images is 225 PPI at the final size. Too low a resolution will result in a pixelated image.*

• *Pictures that look like they are what you want on the screen may print too dark. If the picture looks a little light on the screen, it is probably right for printing.*

• *Be wary of digital cameras. They are more useful for small images because they usually result in low resolution. Enlarging digital images may cause pixelated photos.*

• *In PhotoShop, use the "dust and scratches" filter along with the lasso tool to remove each flaw individually. Use the "unsharp mask" filter to sharpen the entire image.*

• *Remember when you save a*

(Continued)

293

This is 9 Century Old Style bold.
This is 9 Century Old Style italic.

Note that the typefaces in the chart allow a staff to choose either lightface, italic, or boldface type. Staffs should select a typeface that allows for this contrast, which makes it possible to highlight words or phrases within copy.

Body type is usually 8-point or 9-point. Smaller type is difficult to read. If a staff selects 8-point, it might consider using 9-point or even 10-point for editorials to distinguish them from news copy.

The trend is toward even larger type, especially for opening paragraphs. You might consider beginning a story with 12-point type, and then reverting to 10.5- or 11-point type. Large type gives a paper a clean appearance. More color and larger photographs also attract the reader. However, if page sizes get smaller in the future, photos will also get smaller.

Spacing between lines (leading) also may make copy more readable. As a general guideline, use 1-point or 2-point for leading.

Another possibility is to set copy ragged right (unjustified). This technique should be used sparingly, to highlight a special story, or perhaps a standing column. An example follows:

There is a new war waging. It is not violent, it is not hostile or threatening, but it is competitive in the highest sense. Another battle takes place every time someone turns on a television, opens a magazine, or wheels a shopping cart down the aisle of a grocery store. The new war is not between countries or people, but between the fiercely competitive soft drink industries.

After selection of a body type, the staff needs to choose headline typefaces that are complementary. Be sure to base selection of a typeface on content and on a pleasing

---

photo as a JPEG that they lose quality as they are saved and reopened, so try to save them only once.

• Adjust the brightness and contrast by using the "curves" control in PhotoShop. Using the "brightness" and "contrast" controls reduces the quality of the scan. The "brightness" and "contrast" controls work better with line art.

> *Coding Headlines on Designs*

To tell someone the type of headline to write for a story, use the following coding formula that will indicate (1) the column width, (2) the point size, and (3) the number of lines. For example, a 4-36-2 would be a four-column head, 36-point in size, two lines in length. Designers could mark their page designs accordingly, so anyone on staff could then write the head. The designer should also indicate the font to be used.

conjunction with the rest of the paper.

Typefaces are either serif (with letters having hooks or strokes that project from the main stem) or sans serif (without serifs). They are also either roman (with straight letters and usually with serifs) or italic (with slanting letters).

Type families are available in several sizes. As a general rule, the largest headline on a page should be at least 36-point in size; however, with typography playing such an important role in modern design, the largest head on a page may be much larger.

Illustrated here is Helvetica type, in both roman and italic, from 14-point to 60-point.

➢ *Designing Headlines*
  • *Heads one column wide probably need to be 3–4 lines in depth.*
  • *Heads two columns wide should be two to three lines in depth.*
  • *Heads three columns wide should be one to two lines in depth.*
  • *Heads more than three columns wide should probably be one line in depth.*

14pt. ABCD abcdefghijklmnopqrstuvwxyz

18pt. ABCD abcdefghijklmnopqrs

24pt. ABCD abcdefghijkl

30pt. ABCD abcdefghi

36pt. ABCD abcde

42pt. ABCD abcd

48pt. ABCD abc

60pt. ABC abc

14pt. *ABCD abcdefghijklmnopqrstuvwxyz*

18pt. *ABCD abcdefghijklmnopqrs*

24pt. *ABCD abcdefghijkl*

30pt. *ABCD abcdefghi*

36pt. *ABCD abcde*

42pt. *ABCD abcd*

48pt. *ABCD ab*

60pt. *ABC ab*

As you can see, Helvetica is a sans serif font. Serif fonts probably work best for body type, and either serif or sans serif can be effective for headlines. The lines below are all Garamond, a serif font.

ABCD abcd—Garamond Light
ABCD abcd—Garamond Italic
ABCD abcd—Garamond Bold
ABCD abcd—Garamond Bold Italic

Most type today is set by computer. Two machines—the video display terminal (VDT) and the optical character reader (OCR)—have made this possible.

The VDT keyboard resembles that of a typewriter. As the reporter types a story, it appears on a display screen in front of her, and she can make corrections, deletions, and insertions immediately. Such a process makes copyediting

➤ Creating a Mood

• Readers should get a "feel" for the type of publication you are trying to produce.

• To create a feeling of power, you could use bold sans serif typefaces for headlines. You could also use large photos and large artwork with heavy lines. Body type should be sans serif, and headlines should be large.

• To create a feeling of dignity, you could use roman typefaces. You should also allow for more white space, and photos will be somewhat smaller and loosely cropped. Head sizes should be no larger than 36-point.

• To create a design that depicts action, use a mixture of typefaces. Also use a lot of color, and crop photos tightly.

• Novelty typefaces can also create a specific mood.

fast. When the reporter is finished with the story, she activates a printer that prints the story rapidly. When the printed copy has been edited, the phototypesetter can be programmed to reprint it in a specified typeface, type size, and pica width. The story is then run through a waxer so that it can be trimmed and pasted up in its assigned space on the layout. When the page has been completely pasted up, the sheet is photographed. A printing plate is then prepared from the photographic negative.

The OCR method is similar. The reporter types the story and edits it on the same machine; then he feeds it into the OCR. As the OCR reads the copy, a phototypesetter prints it out in a predetermined type size, typeface, and pica width. The pasteup procedure is the same as with the VDT.

Most schools today use Macintosh or IBM computers for all their typesetting. It is easy to use programs like PageMaker, Quark Express, and Ready, Set, Go for headlines, captions, and body copy. A large variety of fonts and sizes are available. It is also easy to add graphics to the fonts by using various software programs, including Aldus Freehand and Adobe Illustrator.

Page Design

Before going to the computer to draw a page layout, a staff should still create a dummy (rough draft) by hand. It will be easier to complete a design on the computer if a rough sketch has been made first. If you don't use a computer, a dummy is essential. Use the layout sheets that your printer uses, and key all items carefully so that anyone looking at the dummy would know immediately what to do. Use X's to indicate headlines, horizontal lines to indicate width of copy, and rectangular shapes to indicate photos. The photo boxes may be marked with an X or blacked in. Include all special instructions. If you plan to use tool lines around an element, indicate where the line is to go and its size. If you plan to use a quote box with copy, indicate it by beginning and ending the quote box with quotation marks.

Some staffs paste up their pages themselves and can use

> ➤ *Designing Cutlines*
> • *Be sure cutlines look different from the body text.*
> • *Generally place a caption below the photo, but regardless of placement be sure it is next to the photo it is describing.*
> • *It is possible for two or more photos to share a common cutline. Just be sure you make it clear to the reader which part of the caption goes with which photo.*

the dummy as a guideline for placement of elements. Doing their own pasteups gives them experience in shortening lengthy copy, leading short copy to fill space, and cropping photographs to fit spaces.

Staffs quickly learn the value of writing copy to fit. It saves everyone working with a page design a lot of time if the original copy is close to the right length. Of course, with a computer, it is easy to get the copy to fit eventually, but if you know you can get 400 words in a 10-inch space, why not write 400 words to begin with? If the reporter writes 800 words, the editor will have to do a lot of cutting. That takes time. It is not easy to pad or cut copy and still maintain transitions and follow rules of style.

To understand design fully, it is necessary to understand terminology. Learn the terms and definitions that follow.

Nameplate—also called a *flag*. It is usually found at the top of page one and contains name of paper, issue number, volume number, and name and address of the school.

Folio—identifying line on each page. It may be at the top or bottom, but most papers place it at the top. It specifies the contents of the page (news, features, sports, opinions, entertainment, etc.) plus the page number, the date of the issue, and the name of the publication. It is normally separated from the rest of the paper by a 1- or 2-point rule.

Standing headline—used to identify content (usually columns) that appears in every issue of the paper. It often contains the name of the column and the name and/or photo of the writer.

Banner headline—a head that goes across the entire page. It is usually used for the main story on the page.

Primary/secondary headlines—used to combine a large line of type with a smaller line or lines of type.

Teasers—also known as *menus*. These are used on the front page to promote stories on the inside. They are sometimes called *refers*, but they really are different: Refers advise, but teasers advertise. Refers guide the reader to stories inside the paper. Teasers, through an attention-getting head, try to attract the reader to another page. Most supermarket tabloids are covered with teasers. Most dignified

---

➢ *The Dominant Photo*

• *Normally you want one photo substantially larger than any other on a page. Two photos of the same size on a page compete for the reader's attention.*

• *Photos of the same size block a sense of movement on the page.*

• *Photos, like mugs or sequential action ones, might work best as the same size.*

• *Make the dominant photo the one that has the strongest content, the one that goes with the most important story.*

• *On a photo spread, the dominant photo should be the one that shows the greatest emotion, the most dramatic moment, the greatest facial expressions, with the highest image quality.*

SAY what?

"I think anyone who comes to watch a game here is going to be very impressed with the building."
◆ADAM DEADMARSH

The Orange & Black staff at Grand Junction High School, Grand Junction, CO, used contrast to effectively box in pulled quotes that it placed in the middle of the story. Note how "SAY" is in all capital letters, but "what" is not. Also notice how the headline is reversed out of a black box and the quote itself is centered and set on a gray background.

GULP

Public speaking frightens teens

NIKKI MUSELES

John's heart begins racing as he stumbles to the front of the classroom. He starts to tremble, clears his throat and begins, "Uh, my report . . . um . . . is on uh . . um . . ."

Situations similar to this are quite common in Churchill classrooms, according to many Churchill teachers They find that many of their students have a fear of speaking in front of a large group. English teacher Judy Webster explains, "I can always tell when someone is really nervous, because they talk too fast—they just run away with it- and they have trouble getting their breath." Webster continues, "A common manifestation of nervousness is to have difficulties swallowing and breathing."

This weakness places students at a disadvantage, according to a recent article in *Working Mother*. The article, entitled "Speech! Speech!" states, "To get ahead in today's world, developing some degree of competence in public speaking is vital."

The article admits, however, "It ain't easy" for someone to accustom himself to speaking before a large group. Therefore, the author, Barbara Kaye Greenleaf, suggests certain hints to aid the inexperienced speaker, For example, Greenleaf emphasizes that "There is no substitute for practice when it comes to public speaking." She explains that "the only way to totally overcome nervousness is by frequently speaking in front of large groups."

In addition, it is very important for the speaker to be prepared. Webster explains, "Students who aren't prepared are the most nervous. That's why I always suggest that they prepare notecards and outlines. That firm structure should definitely help them to calm down."

Senior Jaime Kotchek agrees with Webster. "I don't usually get too nervous," he explains, "except when I'm not ready. Then, I really get worried."

The article suggests easing nerves through another method of preparation—reading the presentation into a tape recorder and then playing it back. This will help the speaker to learn his lines, as well as allow him to hear it himself and possibly find ways to improve the speech.

For the person who is just too frightened to attempt public speaking, the article suggests taking a public speaking course. Churchill offers such a course, taught by Eileen Freiman. Freiman remarks, "The benefit of a speech class is that an individual has many experiences giving a variety of different speeches throughout the year. The bottom line is," she continues, "that it gives a person confidence, so that later in life, when one is called upon to speak before a group, one is mentally prepared."

Graphic by Shau-Fai Tse

Art can have as great an impact as a good photograph when it is as well done as the drawing in the Churchill Observer, *Winston Churchill High School, Potomac, MD.*

Effective packaging is evident in the above design from the Orange &
Black, *Grand Junction High School, Grand Junction, CO. The articles tie in a
local angle with national stories. In addition, the paper conducted a survey
to discover the types of businesses where the high school's students worked.*

newspapers use a more refined approach.

Wraparound—text wrapping around another element,
such as a photo or a liftout quote. Some papers call it a
runaround. If it snakes around a cutout photograph or a non-
rectangular piece of art, it is called a *skew.* Be sure a wraparound does not disturb the flow of text: If you stop the
reader, the text is not wrapping around the other element.

Byline—the writer's name. Some papers also include staff
position of the writer.

Initial cap—a large capital letter set into the opening of
various paragraphs throughout a story; also called *drop cap*
or *dingbat.*

Reverse head—a white headline set on a dark background.

Deck—a section of a headline using a different size of
type. For example, it may be a smaller headline below a main
headline. The main headline would be one deck, and the

An effective headline treatment plus the cutout photograph add to the appeal of the "Singled Out" column from the Campus, Huntington North High School, Huntington, IN.

➤ Design Checklist
- Is the design easy for the reader to follow?
- Are all stories designed in rectangular shapes?
- Have butted headlines been avoided?
- Do photos and artwork face toward the stories they accompany?
- Would boxing a story or setting it on a color screen help separate it from another story or help add emphasis?
- Are headlines designed to attract attention?
- Do fonts complement each other?
- Is there a dominant element?

smaller headline would be another deck.

Cutline—also called *caption*. It provides information about a photo or piece of artwork. A cutline should touch the photo it describes. When cutlines run beside photos, be sure they are at least 6 picas wide. When they run below the picture, which is typical placement, be sure they square off even on both sides of the photo. Cutlines wider than 30 picas should be divided into two legs if they're more than 1 line deep.

➤ Developing
Continuity
• The nameplate
should set the tone
for the rest of your
paper. Select a font
that establishes your
personality.
• Use the font you
select in your name-
plate, in your folios
and in your standing
heads. Also, repeat
any graphic device
used in the name-
plate in your folios.
• Be consistent
with font and place-
ment of all bylines.
• Be consistent
with font and lead-ins
for all captions.
• Be consistent
with font and design
for all liftout quotes.

Jump line—tells the reader what page the story is continued on.

Liftout quote—also *pullout quote, popout quote, quote box,*
or *breakout*. This is a quote pulled from the story and given
graphic emphasis.

Gutter—the white space running vertically between
pages of a two-page spread.

Bastard measure—columns of type set in a different
width than the standard width.

Cutoff rule—any line used to separate elements on a page.

Sidebar—a story or other element such as an infographic that accompanies the main story.

Photo credit—line giving the photographer's name, usually placed at the end of a cutline.

Jump head—head used on a story continued from one
page to another. If you jump a story to another page, be sure
to jump at least six inches to make it worth the reader's
time. Be sure to have at least four inches of the story on a
page before you jump it.

Double truck—two facing pages printed across the gutter. Try to keep ads off a double truck. Normally all elements
on a double truck are related. There may be three or more
stories on one similar topic—depression, for example.
Infographics and pictures would deal with the same topic.

Subhead—boldface line or lines of type used in the middle of a story to break up gray areas.

Sig—a special label set into stories giving typographic
emphasis to an article; also called *bug* or *logo*.

Elements—there are five basic elements on a page: headlines (the oversized type that labels each story); text (the
story itself); photos (pictures that accompany stories); cutlines (type that accompanies photographs); and artwork.

Leading—the vertical space between lines.

Boldface—darker type than the rest of a story. It is used
to highlight words or phrases within text. It should be used
sparingly.

Italics—slanted letters used for editor's notes and titles.
Italics are also used within stories to emphasize words; use

Double trucks often are hard to design, especially when there is a lack of photos to go with the stories. the Kirkwood Call, Kirkwood High School, Kirkwood, MO, used a survey as its center of visual interest to add appeal to this design.

➢ *Photo Design Guidelines*

• Be sure quality is good—no out-of-focus, dark, or light images.

• Border all photos so the white in the background does not bleed into the white of the page.

• Be sure each photo has a strong center of interest. Avoid large crowd shots where everyone is doing the same thing.

• Crop each photo closely—normally within two to three picas of the center of interest.

• Get in close to the center of interest.

• Remember the rule of thirds. Do not put the center of interest in the middle of the photo.

• Avoid posed photos. Capture the action as it happens.

• Caption every photo.

• Be sure faces are large enough to be seen. Try to make them as large as a dime, if possible.

In Brief

▲ Long plays help freshmen ramble over House Springs

Freshman Football (3-1)

UPCOMING EVENTS: Lindbergh (2-2) will be the team's next challenge at 4 p.m., Oct. 25, in an away game. Results from yesterday's game against Parkway Central (5-0) were not available at press time.

HIGHLIGHTS: Long plays accounted for all five touchdowns in the Pioneers' 38-0 win over House Springs, Oct. 10.

Marcus Wilkerson, running back, scored two touchdowns on 50 and 25 yard runs, respectively. Elmer Telfair, running back, also scored on a 50-yard run in the fourth quarter.

The Pioneers started their scoring in the first quarter following a fumble recovery on the Lions' 40. A 37-yard pass from Mike Ehnes, halfback, to Kevin Ragland, tailback, set up a three-yard touchdown run by Kent Layman, running back.

Sean Macon, quarterback, connected on a 40-yard pass to Steve McMiller, wide receiver, for the Pioneers' fifth touchdown.

Adam Harbaugh, kicker, was successful on three of the two-point conversions, and Ehnes made the other one.

▲ Girls end season with loss to Parkway West in districts

Varsity Softball (5-12)

UPCOMING EVENTS: Season over

HIGHLIGHTS: Even though Parkway West shut out the Pioneers, 5-0, in district action, Oct. 8, they scored a shutout of their own in first-round action when they downed Nerinx, 10-0, Oct. 7. Christy Green, pitcher, only allowed two hits—one in the third inning and one in the fourth. Green, along with Laurie Hecker, centerfielder, served as captains of the squad.

Gray screens and bullets add to the design of the news briefs and the sports briefs in the Kirkwood Call, *Kirkwood High School, Kirkwood, MO.*

sparingly, as large blocks of italics are hard to read.

Agate—a sans serif typeface 5 to 7 points in size. Agate may be used for sports statistics and classified ads.

Legs—a leg is one column of a story. It has two legs if it is set in two columns, and three legs if it is set in three

Our viewpoint
the last word

Kick Butts Day, Smoke-Free Class of 2000, Great American Smoke Out, Kick Butts...

Anti-smoking campaigns should be realistic

Teenagers are often thought of as being too impressionable, too easily swayed and easily taken in by peer pressure.

Anti-Smoking Campaigns everywhere blame peer pressure as a major reason teens smoke. These campaigns offer inventive ways to fight it off.

Yet peer pressure is exactly the tactic used to get students to sign up to be tobacco-free for life in first grade.

Who wouldn't sign up? Supporters of the program gave out shoelaces and bookmarks, and it wasn't as if all your friends weren't doing it.

It is understood Smoke Free Class of 2000 was only intended to help students stay smoke-free, not bind them to a contract for life. Ruth Newlin, who worked with SFC2000, admits this.

It should definitely not be assumed this pledge would physically restrain anyone from not smoking. There is probably not one smoker in the graduating class of 2000 who feels tremendous, if any, guilt when he or she lights up.

Anti-Smoking campaigns targeted toward youth should be commended since they all try to help children stay away from a dangerous substance. Studies show, and America in general accepts, that smoking is harmful to one's health.

Anti-smoking campaigns targeted for the general public are a completely different story.

If campaigns really want children to be tobacco-free, they first need to realize the day will come when it is someone's choice to smoke or not. That no matter how well proponents believe their effectiveness is, someone will still smoke, and they'll have that right until drastic law changes occur.

Students really will listen to honest, well put-together campaigns offering devastating statistics of what smoking can do to the lungs; ones showing real people whose lives have been ravaged by those devastating statistics.

Those campaigns are the type that work.

TV ads that show smoking as the ultimate in cool will not be effective. If children and teens really think kids who smoke are cool, and this is the target audience of the campaigns, children and teens will not trust TV's version of cool to that of real life's.

Smoking campaigns are helpful to some, but if they changed their strategies, they could reach a lot more.

Timesphoto
illustration by Matt
Leifer and Bridget
Rubenking.

➤ **Adding Visuals**

• *Visuals are vital elements in story telling.*

• *Visual decisions are as important as the choice of words, the style of writing, the proper grammar, and the perfect edit.*

• *Color can help create a mood, and it can create movement.*

• *Photos and artwork are the main entry points on a page.*

• *Photos and graphics must communicate clearly. The photos need to tell part of the story—its drama, its importance.*

• *Headlines should support the photos.*

Photo illustrations can add effectiveness to a design. The Lakewood Times *staff at Lakewood High School, Lakewood, OH, used an illustration to highlight its story on anti-smoking.*

columns. Avoid legs longer than 10 inches and shorter than 1 inch. The best lengths are 2 to 6 inches. Avoid wide legs. Thirteen to 16 picas works best, but never go narrower than 8 picas or wider than 24 picas.

Dominant—with two photographs on a page, one should be dominant; that is, at least twice the size of the other. Vary photo sizes on a page, even if you are doing a photo story.

Cut—photograph. Be sure photos face the story they accompany. One large photo is usually better than two small

➤ *Cropping*
Photos

• *Eliminate all unnecessary parts.*

• *Do not amputate body parts. Runners, for example, need feet.*

• *If you cannot leave in the entire body, crop at the waist for best results.*

• *Loose crops can work if the designer is trying to capture a specific mood.*

• *Make the central image as powerful as possible.*

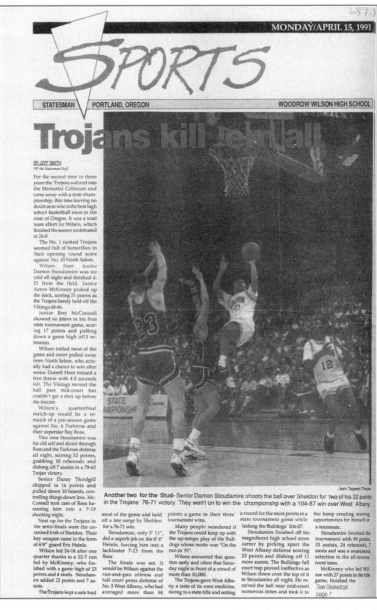

An L-shape design, a large dominant photograph, and overprinting the head on the photograph add to the design in the above page from the Statesman, Woodrow Wilson High School, Portland, OR.

photos because large photos are easier to view.

Halftone—printing process that changes a photograph into a pattern of dots. Halftone dots are created by reshooting the original photo through a halftone screen. Halftone

BEAR THE FACTS

Alief Hastings High School · September 27, 1991 · Issue 1, Volume 17 · Alief, TX 77411

Hitting Close to Home
Recent city-wide crime wave affects Alief area homeowners, students

▽ VERONICA BANNISTER
Entertainment Editor

With drug sales, burglaries, rapes, shootings, and various other crimes being committed all over Houston, some of it has hit home in Alief, especially where juveniles are concerned.

Malicious mischief, window shoot-outs, shoplifting, shootings, and burglaries have increased in Alief. In the Alief police area (known as district 19), which extends west of the Beltway, south of Alief Clodine, and north of the Southwest freeway, an average of 150-175 burglaries, between 35-40 robberies, and 50-60 vehicle break-ins occur each month.

According to local police, the number of burglaries in the neighborhoods around the high schools increases during the off-campus senior lunch periods. Alief police officers have arrested several AISD high school students coming in from lunch after robbing an area home. According to Lt. Jean Watt of the West Side Command Station, the relatively small number of students committing the burglaries is large enough to be of concern to the police.

"If senior off-campus lunches were stopped, most of the high school burglaries during that period would cease," Watt said.

During the day the police officers at the Command Station deal with such juvenile offenses as truency, shoplifting, and car theft. The night crew deals with drunken teenagers, violence, and almost any other crime conceivable.

Teenage crime in Alief decreased over the summer, while the amount of gang violence increased.

"It's not one group having problems with another," Sgt. James Woodruff of the Command Station said. "It's the gangs themselves that are the problem."

Alief area police and high school administrators are working together to help minimize crime around the schools. Early last year police and the schools had a gang awareness meeting to inform the community about the growing problem. Most crimes committed at school are handled by school security. If the crime deals with a gun, stealing, or a fight (depending on the injuries and the reason), Alief security officers take the student(s) to the Command Station.

The police are trying to stop problems by also policing neighborhoods. They want to get the community involved by encouraging people to inform the police of local crime.

One possible solution to the rising crime rate is a teen curfew law (see related story on page 3). This law would require teenagers 17 and under to be off the streets by midnight. Both Watt and Woodruff think that the midnight curfew would be a good idea. "The curfew would help, but it would punish the good kids while inhibiting the worst kids," Woodruff said.

Concerned parents in Alief have given their children a few pointers on being safe while out on the town (see related story on page 5). Many parents agree that teenagers should always go out in groups and not alone because there's safety in numbers. "I want my daughter to know some self defense," Parent Karen North said. "She also has a whistle that she can blow if she's in trouble."

With an increase in juvenile crime, juvenile institutions are becoming overcrowded. According to the *Houston Post*, the number of juveniles in Harris County committed to the Texas Youth Commission (TYC) and the Texas Juvenile Authority has doubled in six years, from 343 in 1986 to 623 so far this year. The *Post* also reported that the rate of violent crimes committed by juveniles in Houston has risen from 11 percent in 1988 to 14 percent in 1990.

TYC facilities lack sufficient funding, which leads the TYC to reduce the stay of many offenders in the facilities. Stays have been reduced from nine months to six months, while some multiple felony offenders are being released after only two or three months.

"All juvenile offenders should be forced to continue schooling," Watt said. "If they don't pass, their parole is revoked and they stay in jail."

Sixteen-year-old Tony Gilbreath, who ran away from a correctional facility, is one example of how serious this problem is. Before being caught, he murdered a 54 year-old man, raped and kidnapped the man's wife, and stole the man's truck. Gilbreath was tried as an adult, and is now serving two life sentences but could be eligible for parole in 15 years.

The *Post* reported that staff members of TYC facilities have been attacked by juvenile offenders, who constantly fight among themselves.

The TYC has requested a $91 million budget for 1992. Their budget currently stands at $69 million.

> ▽ If senior off-campus lunches were stopped, most of the high school burglaries during that period would cease.
> — *Lt. Jean Watt,*
> *West Side Command Station* ▮▮

> ▽ It's not one group having problems with another. It's the gangs themselves that are the problem.
> — *Sgt. James Woodruff,*
> *West Side Command Station* ▮▮

Text wrapped around artwork and pulled quotes create a pleasing design on the front page of the Bear Facts, *Alief Hastings High School, Alief, TX.*

screens are necessary to create gray tones when photos are printed on newspaper presses. Most newspapers use screens with 85 lines to the inch.

Line shot—type of photograph printed without the halftone process. You would use this only if you did not want gray tones. In a line shot all dark tones turn black, and light tones turn white, creating a high-contrast image. This type of photo is best reserved for feature stories.

Flopping—printing a photo backward as a mirror image of itself. Do not do it because it distorts the truth. Anything in a flopped photo turns out backward: If a person parts his hair on the left side, it will be parted on the right side in a flopped photo.

Logo—a word or graphic that is customized in a graphic way. A logo may be type alone, or you may add rules, photos, or other artistic devices.

Standing heads—used for columns. They appear in every issue of the paper in which the column appears.

Widow—line of type at the top of a leg that does not fill at least two thirds of the width of the column.

Rules—also called *lines*. Rules are measured in points. It is best to limit the sizes used to one or two. Rules are most commonly used with bylines and logos. They are also used to box stories, to add dimension to charts, to border photos, and to separate stories and other elements from each other.

Once you understand all the rules of design and the terminology, you should decide how you are going to package the product to make it appealing to the reader.

If your main story on your sports page is on Ultimate Frisbee, you need to think of various ways to cover the sport to make it more appealing to the reader. One long story on Ultimate Frisbee would lose reader appeal. However, dividing the page into several alternative copy sources would aid the reader. For example, you might include a fact box that describes the game to the reader who is not aware of how it is played. You might also include another sidebar on the terminology of the sport. Check the sidebars in this chapter for types of sidebars you might use. You might also have a map of the playing area. You might also include a quote box from players about their reaction to the game. Of course, pictures of actual games would also enhance the coverage.

Pictures have greatest impact on the readers—they want the visual. Various types of quick read visuals have been discussed earlier in this book. Quick reads aid the designer in creating a more visual effect as they help to break up long, gray pieces of copy.

➢ *Using the Centerfold*

• *The centerfold, also known as the double truck, consists of the facing pages in the middle of the paper.*

• *Type can be run across the gutter on the double truck. Therefore, the two pages can be designed as one unit.*

• *Since you can design the two pages as one unit, these pages are often used to develop an in-depth feature topic or an in-depth sports topic. There is space available for several articles and several photos.*

• *Be sure you have a center of visual interest somewhere near the center of the spread.*

• *The double truck could also be used for a photo story.*

• *Be sure to carry the reader both horizontally and vertically with the package on the double truck.*

Using a grid design (narrow columns) is a great way to create a package. In fact, a lot of schools are using grids to design all their pages, as grids tend to give a school greater flexibility and also allow for creative uses of white space.

Create a grid layout sheet by deciding how many vertical columns you want on each page. The number you choose should be based on the size of your paper. For most tabloid papers, an odd number like 7 or 9 usually works best. You can also add horizontal grid lines at equal intervals, like every two inches. Then try to start and stop each element (story, sidebar, photo) at a vertical grid and a horizontal grid.

When you are creating a grid, you should also think about how many packages you want on your page. As already indicated, it is possible to have only one package on a page, but realistically schools don't usually have enough space to have only one package on each page.

To make the grid concept and the packaging concept work, it would be best for you to create a design manual for each student on staff. That way each student would know exactly what the design concept was for every section of the paper.

EXERCISES

1. Study several exchange papers. Select design techniques that they use and discuss why they are or are not effective. List any layout rules that they fail to follow.

2. Study the daily newspaper in your area. Select design techniques that it uses and discuss why these techniques are or are not effective. List any design rules that it fails to follow.

3. Redesign your school newspaper from page one to the back page. Create a new nameplate and

> **Positioning the Elements**

• The lead story on a page should appear somewhere in the upper one-third of the page.

• Create a visual balance for the page by placing photos both above and below the fold.

• Guide your reader through the page by using various transitional devices to grab the reader's attention.

• Position photos so the people in the picture are facing onto the page or toward the story rather than off the page or away from the story.

• Place headlines above stories or to the left of stories for best results. If headline is placed elsewhere, you must use a graphic device, such as a drop cap, to get the reader back to the lead of the story.

• Do not separate the headline and the lead of the story with a photo or artwork.

➢ Sidebars and
Infographics
• Quote collections: Important comments on a topic by readers.
• Bar chart: A way to compare two or more items side by side.
• Pie chart: A way to compare several parts of a whole. Keep to eight slices or less.
• Line or fever chart: A way to show changing quantities over time.
• List: Can be a top 10 list or any number of various components.
• Bio box: Brief profiles of people, places, and things.
• Polls: Surveys that sample public opinion on various topics.
• Timeline: A chronological listing of the order of events.
• Table: Arrangement of data into side-by-side rows for comparative purposes.

(Continued)

create continuity throughout with some standing logo or type style. Using your paper's layout sheets, make a pasted-up dummy of your version. Use pictures and copy from magazines and other papers to create the new look.

4. Find 10 examples of graphic elements discussed in this chapter. Clip them and paste them in a notebook. Label each one and write a sentence or two discussing the effectiveness of each graphic.

5. Design a news page for your paper using some of the following elements. It is not necessary to use all of them. Remember that part of page design is placing the most important stories at the top and the least important ones at the bottom. Always place the most important story first.

List of Stories: 1) Science students test balloon designs; 2) News brief column called Bottom Lines (3 stories); 3) National Honor Society adopts needy family; 4) Students to vote on adopting an honor code; 5) School board votes that boys may not run for Homecoming Queen; 6) School board votes to extend the length of the school day next year by 40 minutes.

List of Pictures: 1) Picture of balloon designs by science students; 2) Picture of National Honor Society members packing food items for needy family; 3) Picture of Student Council officers speaking at the school board meeting protesting the lengthened school year.

As part of your design, create a graphic (perhaps a bullet) as a lead-in for captions, and create a byline design for each story. Make bylines consistent. Also create a folio (page content, name of paper, and date) for the top or bottom of the page.

Remember that your design should carry the reader from top to bottom and from left to right. Be sure to vary column widths. If you are using a mini tabloid paper (8½ x 11 or 9½ x 12 in size), use 2 to 4 columns on your paper. If you are using a tabloid size (about 11½ x 17), use between 3 and 6 columns. If you are using a broadsheet (about 14½ x 24 in size), use 4 to 8 columns. No column should be wider than 24 picas or narrower than 8 picas.

6. Select one sport at your school and design a page based on that sport. Create a grid pattern of 7 vertical columns. Decide on types of sidebars you would use with the main story. If you have a computer, create the design on the computer after you have hand-drawn an original one. Think about how you're going to package together all the related items about the sport you choose.

7. Select a feature topic such as depression or stress and create a packaged design for one page. Decide how many vertical columns you want, but make the number between 7 and 11 based on the size of your paper. Brainstorm for alternative copy approaches to the main story. Draw your design by hand, but if you have a computer, use it for the final design.

• *Step-by-step guide: Showing the reader how to understand a process of some type in a step-by-step order.*

• *Question and answer: A way to get answers to hypothetical questions.*

• *Glossary of terms: A list of defined words.*

• *Quiz: A way to test reader's knowledge of a topic.*

• *Checklist: A way to itemize key points in an article.*

• *Diagram: A drawing to show how something works.*

• *Map: A way to present geographical information.*

➢ *Knowing Technology*

"In a world of technology, the learners inherit the earth. The learned are prepared for a world that no longer exists."—Eric Hoffer, philosopher

twelve

Yearbook Design

It's appealing! It's interesting! It's new! It attracts the eye to every element on the page! It's well rounded! It's exciting!

It would be fantastic if all yearbook readers could pick up the annual and make those comments about the design of each spread. Good design can create excitement.

In trying to cover every event of the year, yearbook staffs may write tremendously appealing copy and take exciting pictures, but they must also package the copy and photographs in an interesting way to attract the reader. The key to design is using the space available in an effective way.

Layout and design are terms that are used interchangeably by most yearbook staffs, but they are not the same. Layout refers to the arrangement of elements (headlines, copy, captions, artwork, photographs, and white space) on a page. Design is the planning that goes into the placement of each element to determine its effect on the overall appearance of the page. Design requires a knowledge of the computer, of photography, of typography, and of printing. A designer applies creative touches to a layout.

A design must be attractive, but it must do more than merely please the eye. It must tell a story with the help of its four basic elements: pictures, copy, artwork, and white space. Copy includes body text, captions, and headlines. Artwork includes drawings, tool lines (gray, black, white, or any spot color), and other graphic elements such as spot color, partial cutouts, or shadow boxes. Graphics are discussed later in the chapter.

Several design styles are used in yearbooks, but there are certain rules to be followed with any style:

1. Design facing pages as one unit. That means that all pages in the book are designed as part of two-page spreads except for the first and last pages.
2. Achieve balance. Balance may be either formal or informal. In formal balance, facing pages are mirror images of each other. In informal balance, the designer maintains a balanced ink distribution with a variety of sizes and shapes so that one page does not mirror the other. Informal balance is generally more appealing because it does not become monotonous.
3. Maintain dominance. Dominance is best obtained through correct use of photographs. If possible, make one photograph on a spread at least 2 1/2 times the size of any other photograph. Place that dominant photograph near the middle of the two-page spread. That will draw the reader's eyes to the center and from there to the other elements. Dominance may also be obtained by severely cropping a picture (eliminating all unnecessary portions), by using a special effect (a photographic distortion such as a fish-eye 360° lens), by using a second color on a photograph (duotone), or by using a full-color (four-color) photograph on a spread with black-and-white photographs. Regardless of other methods used, however, dominance should usually be obtained by size; sheer size is appealing. The dominant photo is usually the center of visual interest (CVI). The CVI can be anywhere on the spread, but it usually works best near the center. A dramatic dominant photo with a strong CVI would be one with strong action and strong facial expressions. The subject and the action in the photo should direct the reader's eye to the center of the spread rather

➤ *Layout Vs. Design*

  • *Layout is a general term used when referring to the arrangement of photographs, headlines, copy, captions, and white space on a spread.*

  • *Design is the act of determining the effect of an element's placement on a spread. Design adds those creative touches to a spread to give it reader appeal. Design is a process, not a product.*

➤ *Adding Variety*

• *Although there needs to be some consistency in design within the same section of a book, no two spreads should look exactly the same.*

• *Vary copy length and copy placement from spread to spread.*

• *Vary number of photos and size of photos from spread to spread.*

• *Flopping layouts from spread to spread does not add a lot of variety.*

• *Tweak the type to add variety. Take a font and change its weight, its size, and its placement.*

The Decamhian, Del Campo High School, Fair Oaks, CA, used its front end sheets for the table of contents. The staff used spinoffs from its theme for its division titles, but it still told its readers the contents of each division. Note the absence of a "Table of Contents" heading. It is not necessary.

than off the page. Consider placing copy next to the CVI, which helps guide the reader to the copy.

4. Repeat the dominant shape. If the dominant is vertical, have at least one more vertical picture on the spread.

5. Contradict the dominant shape. If the dominant is vertical, have at least one horizontal or one square on a page.

6. Use only rectangular photographs, unless circu-

lar or other odd-shaped photographs are used for a specific purpose such as conveying a theme. Cookie-cutter shapes should be avoided, because unity becomes difficult to maintain.

7. Make all people in pictures on the sides of pages (external elements) face in toward the gutter of the book. People looking off the page impel the reader to move to the next page. People facing inward create a natural eye flow from one element to the next.

8. Link the facing pages by using a consistent internal margin at the gutter or by bleeding a picture across the gutter from one page to the other. Linkage may also be obtained by continuing a copy block from one page to the other or by running a headline from one page to another. Be careful when running either copy or a headline across the gutter that letters are not trapped in the gutter. At the same time, do not create extra wide margins to avoid trapping the letters in the gutter.

9. Obtain unity on each spread by using a specific design style. Obtain unity within a section of the book by using the same design concept throughout. Obtain unity on portrait pages by paneling the portraits in a block so that a series of pictures appears as one element.

10. Maintain consistent internal margins between all elements. If one pica is adopted as the internal margin between photographs, that same one-pica margin should be used between captions and photographs, copy and headlines, copy and photographs, copy and captions, and artwork and copy. One pica is probably the easiest internal margin to work with; however, it can be more or less. If you use more than a two-pica margin, you may waste valuable space. Some

➤ *Creating Linkage*

• *Create a horizontal eyeline across the two pages somewhere other than the middle. A dominant photograph might stop the eyeline.*

• *Bleed photos across the gutter to link the two pages.*

• *Repeat graphic elements from page to page to link the two pages of a spread.*

Use of a sidebar to accompany the main story and headlines for the captions enhance the above design from the Highlander, Highland Park High School, Dallas, TX.

yearbook printers use 1/8-inch squares on their layout sheets, and an 1/8-inch internal margin works well in that instance. Even the gutter margin should be consistent with other internal margins. If you use one pica as your internal margin, you will probably need to leave two picas at the gutter, as some of the space at the gutter will be lost in the binding. Once you have mastered consistent internal margins, start experimenting. It is possible to have more than 1 pica between elements. Planned white space can be appealing. Books today are experimenting with drop columns, dropping only one element into a column and leaving the rest of the column empty. This means the internal margin will be wider between some elements, but it is also obvious that the white space was left on purpose.

11. Keep external margins consistent. Most printers mark external margins on their layout sheets, but it is not necessary to follow those. You may set your own external margins, but they should seldom exceed one inch on the sides, top, or bottom. To establish the external margins, one element on each side, top, and bottom must stop at the margin you set. All other elements must either stop there, bleed all the way to the edge of the page, or stop at least 6 picas in from the margin you set. The 6-pica rule is necessary to avoid a ragged look.

12. Be aware of eyeline across the spread. If a caption in the upper left corner of a spread stops 6 picas inside the external margin, it is best to stop the caption—or whatever element is used in the upper right corner of the spread—6 picas in also.

13. Avoid ragged internal margins. If elements do not align top and bottom, try to offset them

> *A Step-by-Step Approach to Creating a Spread*

• *Determine the number of grids or columns you will use.*

• *Set the external margins top and bottom. The side external margins will be set by your grid width and the number of grids used.*

• *Place your dominant photo near the middle.*

• *Add the rest of the photos. Be sure at least one contradicts the dominant shape and at least one repeats the dominant shape. Vary size and shape of all photos.*

• *Establish an eyeline across the spread to achieve linkage.*

• *Add the captions. Make them consistent in width. Avoid trapping captions between photos.*

• *Add the body copy and the headline.*

• *Add any sidebars.*

• *Place the folios.*

Twenty-five photographs appear on this two-page spread in the Heritage, Horizon High School, Scottsdale, AZ. The six clustered photographs that go with the headline "The More the Merrier" become the dominant element on the spread. Longer captions for some of the photos serve as the copy on the spread.

Effective use of white space (the rail to the left of the copy block) is evident on this spread in the Paragon, Munster High School, Munster, IN. The staff has also used woven words in the headline and has used contrasting type with shades of gray. Note the contrast in the caption headlines as well.

The *Pioneer, Kirkwood High School, Kirkwood, MO,* continued its theme continuity in the index by running a bio box on selected seniors' "final days." The *Pioneer* used a monthly calendar for its concept, so the index was part of the month of May. Index pages should include photos and copy to make them more appealing to the reader.

by a minimum of 6 picas. That will avoid a ragged look and provide better eye movement throughout the spread.

14. Control white space. Copy and white space work best to the outside of a spread. White

space in each corner of the spread helps the layout breathe. If white space appears on the inside, it may appear to be trapped, but some designers claim there is no such thing as trapped white space if it is planned white space. That is the key to design. Be sure the white space doesn't just happen. Make it planned. Unplanned white space on the inside makes a spread appear unplanned and sloppy. It is possible to place copy to the inside, but don't trap it between heavier elements (pictures), and be careful with the gutter margins. White space can be attractive, depending on how the designer uses it. White space in corners helps balance the spread. If you leave white space in the lower right corner, try to leave some in the upper left corner for better balance. You do not have to leave the same amount in both corners, however. Do not fill the entire spread. Leave some white space in the corners. White space in the margins can serve as a framing device, and white space above a headline can call attention to the typography.

15. Count heads precisely. Headlines that are too short often violate internal margins, whereas headlines that run too long often violate external margins.

16. Place headlines so that they lead the reader into the copy. The best placement is either above or to the left of copy. Headlines serve as a drawing force and should perform their function—to get the reader to read the copy.

17. Do not overuse special effects. Using a screen over a poor picture will make it worse. Use screens for a purpose. Avoid duotones (second color) on photos. Pink, red, green, blue, or yellow people do not look natural.

➤ *Single-Page Designs*

• *Although traditionally yearbooks are designed in double-page spreads (except for the first and last pages), single-page designs can work.*

• *Small books with limited space might want to consider single-page designs.*

• *Book staffs that want more thorough coverage might also consider single-page spreads.*

• *Single-page designs are created just like double-page ones, but there will be no bleeding of pictures across the gutter.*

• *Organization coverage might be designed as single pages, with each organization receiving one page. There will also be a primary copy block on each page.*

• *More photos (usually three to five) will likely be used in a single-page design.*

➢ *Graphics to Avoid*

• *Ghosted photographs: If the photo is of excellent quality, its quality should shine through. Ghosting it ruins its quality. Type placed on a ghosted photograph is hard to read.*

• *Body type or caption type in color: Colored type is harder to read.*

• *Hand lettering: This type of letter usually looks childish and does not work in professionally designed publications.*

• *Polarized or solarized pictures: These photos have a dull or gray look that lessens the impact of the photographs.*

• *Thick rule lines: Lines thicker than 2 or 3 point usually detract the reader's attention from the rest of the spread.*

• *Patterned background screens: Type overprinted on such screens is hard to read.*

18. Keep copy and caption widths consistent within a section of the book. Generally, copy should not be set wider than 18 to 24 picas; a wider measure looks boring. In isolated instances caption widths may be different on a spread. For example, if you run a picture with copy, the caption width will be the same as the copy, but other caption widths on the same spread might be different.

19. Do not number or letter photos and captions. That makes the reader work to match them. Place the captions by their photographs rather than lumping them together. Captions work best in clusters of two placed in the corners of the two-page spread.

20. Generally avoid using more than seven photographs per spread. This is not a hard-and-fast rule, but if you use no more than seven it is easier to place captions next to photographs, and it avoids having a crowded-looking spread. It is possible to place more than seven pictures on a page, but when you do, you will probably have to make your dominant smaller. There's nothing wrong with that as long as you still maintain some consistency with your design. Some schools are placing 10-15 photos on a spread. This may mean they will have to cluster captions together and number photos and captions. This is not considered to be reader-friendly. You can probably use more than seven photographs and still keep the captions next to the individual photographs through careful planning.

21. If you bleed a photograph across the gutter, do not catch a person's face or any other center of interest in the gutter.

22. Crop pictures tightly. Generally, crop within two picas of the center of interest; however,

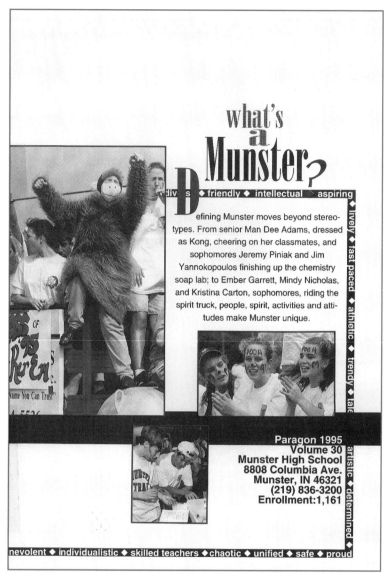

➢ *Caption Treatment*

Yearbook staffs should create an entry point for captions. The Pioneer *staff, Kirkwood High School, Kirkwood, MO, used a headline to grab the reader's attention, and it set the caption on a gray background to match the gray background it used behind the headline on the page. Note the contrasting type sizes in the headline and the use of reverse print.*

"What's a Munster?" was an obvious theme for the Paragon *staff at Munster High School, Munster, IN. Note the strong photographs on the title page and the excellent design of pages 2-3 and 4-5 to carry out the theme. Strong use of white space, including extra leading between lines of type, makes these theme pages come alive.*

extra space is sometimes needed around the center of interest. For example, if a cross-country runner is struggling to get up a hill, leave some space in front of the runner to let the reader see how difficult the hill is.

➢ *Maintaining Consistency*

- *Keep the number of columns or grids per spread the same within a section.*
- *Keep copy starters (such as an initial letter) the same within a section.*
- *Keep caption starters (such as boldfacing and putting in small caps the first three words) the same within a section.*
- *Keep fonts consistent within a section, but adapt it to add some variety. Changing the set width, changing the tracking, or using bold, italics, or small caps can make the same font look different.*
- *Keep caption widths the same.*
- *Keep copy width the same.*

reality check

66

People from Munster get a bad rap. Not everyone is snobby and superficial. I'm from Munster, and I'm not stuck up . . . am I?

**Tim Paliga
junior**

Danny Branch

Jaime Dausch
Jason Winterfeldt

Allowing the truth to appear, Jaime Dausch and Jason Winterfeldt, juniors, share secrets and Ulrich Weber, senior, edits his composition. While displaying Munster's athletic side, Scott Zimmerman, junior, plows through a group of players and Danny Branch, senior, shows a silly side while dancing with a boa. Reality came alive when students got involved in activities such as athletics and clubs, or just acted goofy with friends and classmates to let Munster's true side shine.

ted ◆ fast paced ◆ athletic ◆

2
Opening

23. Use at least 10-point type for body copy and 8-point type for caption copy. For opening, closing, and dividing copy, 12- or 14-point type is preferable.

24. Select photographs that have strong centers of interest. Avoid crowd shots that do not have one or two people doing something different from the rest of the group. It is best to tell the photographers to get in close. Zero in on one to four people for best results.

shredded

As students react to outlandish lies created about Munster, they strive to tear apart false accusations

Look, you might think you know exactly what makes this school tick. Well, maybe you should think again, because when people say the school consisted of arrogant, isolated, proper, wealthy, critical and haughty students, the truth needs to expose itself. So get ready, here it comes.

◆ While leading spirit training sessions, Mr. Steve Cronk, new assistant principal, along with cheerleaders, poms and some faculty, proved it was never to late to learn new tricks. At first, everyone thought that the whole idea would fail tremendously, but shocked students loved it.

◆ Dissolving a self-centered reputation, 49 Advisories adopted 57 Salvation Army Angels during the holiday season. With an average five presents per child, three cars, packed from floor to ceiling with the packages, delivered the gifts to ensure needy Calumet Region children a happy holiday.

Ulrich Weber
Scott Zimmerman

Striving to stay focused, Amy Herron, junior, photographs the Homecoming pep rally festivities amid hundreds of pieces of distracting confetti. Digging for the truth, students moved beyond Munster myths through jobs, homework, friends and sports.

what's a Munster?

◆ intellectual ◆ fashionable ◆ skilled teachers ◆ aspiring ◆ resourceful

3 | Opening

➢ *Avoiding Redundancy*

• *Create several templates for each section.*

• *Be sure each template has changed some aspect of the design, such as moving the copy from the top right to the lower left.*

• *Change the size and shapes of photos. Use a horizontal dominant on one and a vertical dominant on another.*

• *Change the number of lines in the secondary headline.*

25. Be sure the title page (page 1) design includes space for the name of the school, the name of the book, the address (city, state, zip code), the year, and the volume number. The title page information might also include enrollment figures and telephone number.

26. Choose headline types carefully and be sure they fit the overall design concept. Headlines should be large enough to attract attention; 24-point is the usual minimum.

➢ *Rule Lines*

Varying the thicknesses of the rule lines makes for an attractive design in the Paragon, *Munster High School, Munster, IN. The yearbook staff chose not to box in the sidebar totally, which gives it breathing room.*

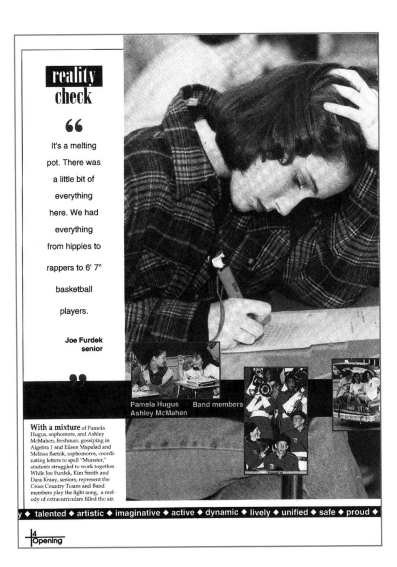

27. Do not bleed pictures together in the gutter.
28. Use graphics only if they serve a purpose. The graphics discussed in Chapter 10 may also be used in yearbooks and magazines.
29. Keep the budget in mind when designing pages. Remember that most yearbooks are printed in 16-page signatures. If you plan to use color in the book, it is cheaper to use color in one signature than to spread it throughout the

More than an upper-middle class suburban school, diversity flourished with students ranging from Greek to German and preppy to alternative. With the additions of Japanese and ceramics classes, students could express their individuality through an expanded curriculum.

> **Background Patterns**
>
> The background pattern for this quote in the Trail, *Fairbury High School, Fairbury, NE,* draws attention to the copy. Sometimes background patterns can be too busy, so select them carefully.

book. It is cheaper still to use color on only one side (a flat) of a signature, since the book is printed in flats. A flat is every other spread in a signature. For example, pages 1, 4-5, 8-9, 12-13, and 16 make up one flat and pages 2-3, 6-7, 10-11, and 14-15 make up the other flat.

30. Be consistent. Create a design concept for the book and follow it for each spread. A different look for each spread will be obtained because

➤ *Tips for Type*
• Artistic types can create a mood for a spread, but avoid too much artiness in design.

• Avoid using city fonts (Geneva, Monaco, etc.). They are generally bitmap fonts and often do not print cleanly.

• Use leading for effect. Extra space between lines of type can add pleasing white space to a design.

• Avoid using too many typefaces. Generally three to four per section is sufficient. Some staffs use three or four per book.

copy will not always be in the same place, the dominant size will be different, and the number of photos used will vary.

31. Select typefaces carefully. Suggestions concerning typefaces are made in Chapter 11.

32. Become familiar with the layout sheet the yearbook company provides your school. These sheets come in three sizes—7 3/4" x 10 1/2", 8 1/2" x 11", and 9" x 12". The sheet is divided into small squares (picas). Remember, there are 6 picas to an inch. Picas can be divided into points. There are 12 points to a pica. Type and rule lines are usually measured in points. Also, notice that the layout sheet is for two pages. Therefore, you should always design two pages (a spread) at the same time. The only pages designed as single units are the first and last pages of a book. The area down the center of the spread is a gutter. This is where the printer binds the book. If you extend (bleed) a picture across the gutter from one page to another, be careful not to catch a person's face on the gutter. This is not apt to happen on a natural spread—the middle two pages of a 16-page signature—because natural spreads are not cut apart in the binding process. Do not cross the gutter with any typographic element. If you do, you may lose letters, and it is difficult to align the type on both sides of the gutter. The thick 1-pica (12-point) line around the edge of a layout sheet is the bleed line (outside edge) and the trim line (inside edge). If you bleed a picture to the edge of the page, bleed it to the outside of that line, but remember that the trim line for all pages is the inside of that line.

33. Master the basics, and then experiment. It is possible to violate any of the above rules and

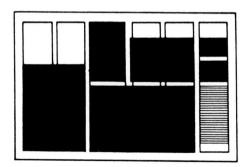

COLUMNAR/GRID

still have an excellent design. For example, it is possible to place copy and captions inside through careful planning. It is also possible to use white space attractively on the inside through careful planning. Rules are guidelines. You can disregard some of the guidelines and still create pages that will attract readers. The decisions for design are yours. Just avoid a cluttered or a disjointed look.

The preceding rules pertain regardless of the layout style used. Many types of layout are possible. Most books use a variation of a particular style throughout the book, but it is possible to use different styles from section to section. Just be sure that all styles complement one another.

Columnar design. This is probably the design used by most books today. Begin a columnar design (if you are working with an even number of columns) by establishing a starting line 1 pica out on both sides of the gutter. Then measure the distance from that line to the side external margin you have established. Determine the number of columns you want on the page. Let's say that the total distance you measured was 47 picas and you want to establish three columns on each page. Since you must leave a one-pica margin between columns, you must subtract two from the 47 to get the number of working picas. Divide the 45 by number of columns (3) to get the pica width of each column; in this case, 15. If the working pica width does not divide evenly, the leftover has to

➢ *Cutout Backgrounds*
Dropping the background out from around a photo creates a special effect. Instead of dropping out the entire background, a partial cutout can also work. For example, in the photo above, the staff might have just dropped out the background around the girl's head.

329

The Layout Sheet

• *Layout sheets come in three sizes—7¾ x 10 ½, 8½ x 11, and 9 x 12.*

• *Layout sheets are divided into small grids called picas. There are six picas to one inch.*

• *Picas can be divided into smaller units called points. There are 72 points to an inch, or 12 points to one pica.*

• *Layout sheets are two pages wide.*

• *The center area of a layout sheet is called the gutter—the space between the two pages.*

• *Books are usually printed in signatures (16 pages). The middle two pages of a signature (pages 8-9, 24-25, 40-41, 56-57, 72-73, 88-89, 104-105, etc.) are called natural spreads. Photographs can be bled across the gutter on these spreads without a break in the printing. Type should never be bled across the gutter, as letters would get lost in the binding process.*

• *Layout sheets indicate suggested external margins. For the most part, those should be followed. Elements closer than three picas to the edge of a page may be trimmed in the printing process.*

• *Photos may bleed beyond the external margin to the edge of the page.*

be added to the external margin. If you are working with an odd number of columns, figure out the total picas needed and start measuring from the outside rather than at the gutter. You normally need to make the column that runs across the gutter wider than the other columns to compensate for space lost in binding.

Columns need not be the same width. It is possible to have two columns the same width and a third column a different width; that is called a two-plus columnar design. It is also possible to work with four or five columns per page, but columns narrower than 9 picas are difficult to set and to read. Columnar design has many variations. It is possible to design column widths over a two-page spread, thus creating a seven- or eight-column design.

Once you have established column widths, all elements start and stop at a column. Of course, elements may be wider than one column, but everything is measured in columns. For example, the dominant picture can be as wide as four columns, and the smallest picture only one column wide. Be consistent throughout a section about column width. If you use a six-columnar design on one spread in the sports section, you should use six-column on all spreads unless you have a special section (perhaps a minimagazine) within sports. The minimag could have a different design. You might also run special features (off-campus sports, for example) scattered throughout the sports section. If you have four special-feature spreads, those four pages could have a different design than the rest of the sports section. Be consistent with the design on those four spreads, however.

Don't forget the possibility of using a drop column as a plus column. A drop column that has only one or two elements dropped into it can add some pleasing white space to a design. A drop column may be left completely empty, but a headline or small photo in the column helps to define it and bridge the space between the other elements on the spread.

In creating a columnar design (or any type of design, for that matter), design the spread from the center out, and be sure that all elements start and stop at a column. The following guidelines could be used for determining column widths based on the size of the book you are creating. When you are working with even columns, always leave two picas blank at the gutter (one on each side).

For a 9" x 12" book, use the following:
- 4 columns (24-pica columns). Remember that body type should never be wider than 24 picas; 20 picas is preferable.

> ➢ *Guidelines on Bleeds*
> - *Bleed toward the center of the spread to eliminate balance problems.*
> - *Avoid bleeding more than one photo to a single side (top, bottom, left, right).*
> - *If you bleed a photo to the left, consider also bleeding one to the right for better balance.*
> - *Avoid bleeding to the corners.*

➢ *Layout Symbols*

• The layout symbol for a photo is a box with an X drawn through it. A bled photograph must extend through the trimline on the edge of the page.

• Artwork is shown on the layout sheet as a box without an X.

• Show type on a layout with brackets. A top bracket shows where copy begins and a bottom one shows where copy ends. Brackets for headlines can be placed to the left and right showing where the head begins on the left and ends on the right.

• 5 columns per spread (19-pica columns with a 20-pica gutter column).
• 6 columns per spread (15-pica columns).
• 7 columns per spread (13-pica columns with 14 for the gutter column).
• 8 columns per spread (11-pica columns).
• 9 columns per spread (10-pica columns with a 12-pica gutter column).
• 10 columns per spread (9-pica columns).
• 11 columns per spread (8-pica columns).
• 4 regular columns and one plus column per spread (22 picas for the regular columns and 9 for the plus column).
• 5 regular columns and one plus column per spread (18 picas for the regular columns and 6 picas for the plus column).
• 6 regular columns and one plus column (12 picas for the regular columns and 23 picas for the plus column).
• 7 regular columns and one plus column (10 picas for the regular columns and 4 for the plus column).
• 4 regular columns with two plus columns (18 picas for the regular columns and 10 picas for the two plus columns).
• 6 regular columns with two plus columns (12 picas for the regular columns and 8 picas for the two plus columns).
• 5 regular columns with two plus columns (11 picas for the regular columns and 20 picas for the plus columns).
• 7 regular columns with two plus columns (9 picas for the regular columns and 15 for the two plus columns).

For an 8½" x 11" book, use the following:
• 4 columns per spread (23-pica columns).
• 5 columns per spread (18-pica columns).

- 6 columns per spread (15-pica columns).
- 7 columns per spread (12-pica columns).
- 8 columns per spread (11-pica columns).
- 9 columns per spread (9-pica columns with 12 at the gutter).
- 10 columns per spread (8-pica columns).
- 4 regular columns per spread and one plus column (20 picas per column for the regular columns and 12 picas for the plus column).
- 5 regular columns per spread and one plus column (16 picas per column for the regular columns and 11 picas for the plus column).
- 6 regular columns per spread and one plus column (11 picas per column for the regular columns and 24 picas for the plus columns).
- 7 regular columns per spread and one plus column (9 picas per column for the regular columns and 26 pica for the plus column).
- 4 regular columns per spread and two plus columns (17 picas per column for the regular columns and 11 for the two plus columns).
- 6 regular columns per spread and two plus columns (12 picas per column for the regular columns and 8 picas per column for the two plus columns).
- 5 regular columns per spread and two plus columns (10 picas per column for the regular columns and 20 picas per column for the two plus columns).
- 7 regular columns per spread and two plus columns (8 picas per column for the regular columns and 16 picas per column for the two plus columns).

For a 7¾" x 10½" book, use the following:
- 4 columns per spread (20-pica columns).
- 5 columns per spread (16-pica columns).
- 6 columns per spread (13-pica columns).

➤ *Comparison and Contrast*

Contrasting boldface with normal type and contrasting gray with black creates an attractive appearance in this quick read in the Mascot, Mexico High School, Mexico, MO. The gray background also adds to the design.

24 Grids

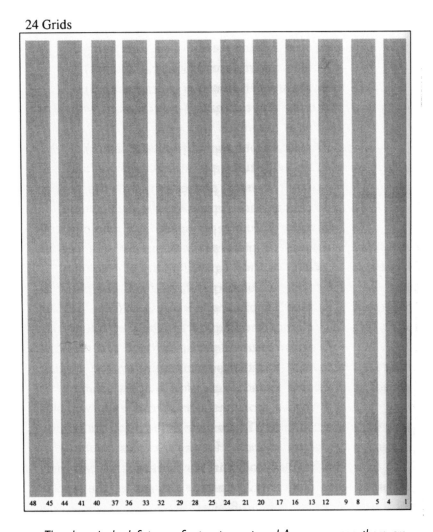

E ven though he found him-self both frustrated and stressed out, David Dunn waited until the last minute to get his schoolwork finished. Despite how important his studies were, he had so many other things to do, and it wasn't always easy to prioritize.

➤ **Initial Letters**

Using large letters, sometimes called dingbats, to begin copy or captions helps attract the reader. The Mustang *staff at Andrews High School in Andrews, TX, used the same font it used for its main headline on the spread.*

The above is the left page of a two-page spread. As you can see, there are 12 grids on the page. If you combine the two pages, you would have 24 grids. Each grid is 3 picas wide. There is 1 pica between each grid, and there would be 2 picas between the grids at the gutter. The first grid starts at pica number 1, and the 12th grid ends at pica 48. In creating a design, it is permissible to start and stop at any grid. However, it is still best to be consistent with caption widths. The key is to be consistent within a section. If you made the caption for the dominant picture a different width than other captions, that would be satisfactory as long as you did that on each spread within a section of the book.

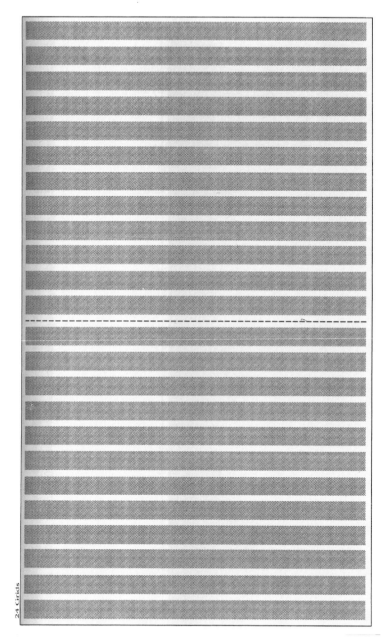

24 Grids

Each page of the two-page spread above has 12 grids. The dotted line in the center is the middle (gutter) of the two pages. The number of grids you want on a spread is up to you, but it is not advisable to go narrower than 2 to 3 picas. It is difficult to write copy that narrow. Therefore, most copy and caption blocks should probably be at least two grids wide in the above 24-grid design.

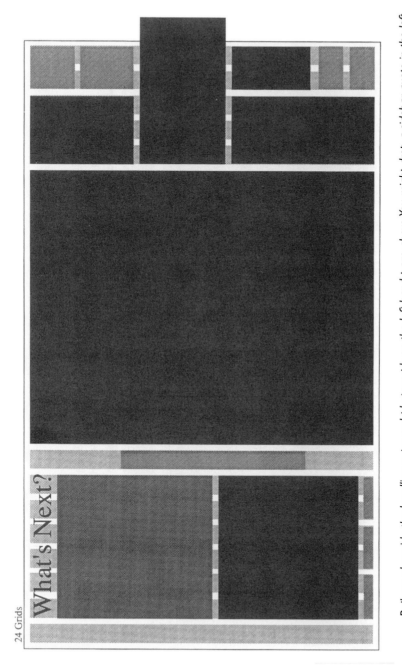

24 Grids

What's Next?

Rails go alongside the headline, copy, and photograph on the left-hand page above. You might drop a sidebar quote in the left rail. Rails 3 picas wide, however, are pretty narrow for any large type. A caption for the dominant photo has been dropped into the right rail. All other captions are two grids wide. The caption below the photo on the left-hand page has been divided into three blocks—each block goes across two grids. It would be possible to treat that caption differently than the rest and have it run across all six grids. You might want to use all six grids if the caption was for a group photo, for example. The picture on the far right bleeds off the page. Bleeding to the edge of the page is permissible in grid design.

- 7 columns per spread (11-pica columns with 12 at the gutter).
- 8 columns per spread (10-pica columns).
- 4 regular columns per spread and one plus column (8 picas per column for the regular columns and 12 picas for the plus column).
- 5 regular columns per spread and one plus column (15 picas per column for the regular columns and 8 picas for the plus column).
- 6 regular columns per spread and one plus column (10 picas per column for the regular columns and 22 picas for the plus column).
- 4 regular columns per spread and two plus columns (15 picas per column for the regular columns and 10 picas per column for the two plus columns).
- 6 regular columns per spread and two plus columns (11 picas per column for the regular columns and 8 picas per column for the two plus columns).
- 5 regular columns per spread and two plus columns (9 picas per column for the regular columns and 18 picas per column for the two plus columns).

Change column structure from section to section in a book to add variety to design. Also, if you use a drop column or a plus column, float that column to different areas of a spread. It does not have to stay in the same place all the time. Don't allow any two sections to resemble each other. It is also possible to mix column widths on a spread. You might use four columns of one width on the left page, for example, and three of a different width on the right.

Freestyle design is also popular. With this design, a standard width is established for captions and copy, but the photos are placed without regard to column guides. Some books use freestyle design in the opening and closing sections of the book.

Graduated License passed in Indiana requiring adults over 21 to be in the car the first 60 days after teens receive their licenses.

➢ *Index Design*
Besides using an initial letter, the Paragon staff at Munster High School, Munster, IN, also used planned white space underneath the "G" to make the statement stand out. The staff used a statement that began with the letter that started the next section of the index.

Some Design Terminology

• *Bullets: Dots, circles, triangles, and other dingbats used to break up paragraphs, to begin captions, and to highlight items in fact boxes.*

• *Duotones: Using a spot color on a black-and-white photograph. These are usually not acceptable because people don't look good with a color over their faces.*

• *Kerning: Adjustment of space between letters.*

• *Planned white space: Used for isolation. Using grids as a design allows a mini-column for planned white space. Used to set apart a copy block, a dominant photo, a group shot, or a sidebar of any kind.*

• *Process color combinations: Achieved by screening percentages of the four process colors (cyan, magenta, yellow, black).*

• *Rails: These are the width of a single grid and are rails of white space.*

• *Sausage columns: Wide columns of text with dingbats used instead of paragraph indentations. Type is normally 12 point or larger.*

Even though columns are easy to work with, some schools today have found that using grids allows them to have more variety in design. The premise, however, is the same as columnar design. Grids are really columns, but they are much narrower than the normal column—perhaps only 3 or 4 picas wide. Be sure to leave 1 pica between grids just as you leave 1 pica between columns. Grids may run both vertically and horizontally. Staffs using computers may create grids by establishing a series of guidelines on the spread to show where

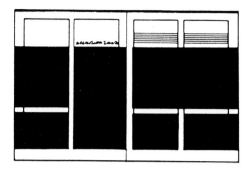

MODULAR

SWISSAIR SUFFERS

On Sept. 2 SwissAir Flight 111 from New York to Geneva crash landed in the water near Halifax, Nova Scotia. All of the passengers and crew, totaling 229 people, were killed in the crash.

Just 11 minutes before Flight 111 went down flight attendants were serving dinner and pilots still believed that they would be able to land the plane safely. Based on data recovered from the plane's black box, investigators have discovered that the real emergency was detected when the cockpit began to fill with smoke. The black box data recorder then picked up problems with the flight control computer and other navigational systems. Within 30 seconds of that, copilot Stefan Loew reported that he had lost all his main instruments.

Jeff Saunders

> ➤ *Reverse Type*

Setting white type on a black or dark gray background can work as long as the type is large enough to be readable. This quick read in the Red & White, City High School, Iowa City, IA, *could also have been reversed out of a dark color background. Be careful about reversing type on a yellow background, which usually makes the type difficult to read.*

each grid starts and stops. Grids can be effectively set up using software programs like PageMaker.

It is possible to create as many as 15 grids on each page (30 per spread) depending upon the size of your book. A narrow grid concept makes it simple to isolate elements and to create multiple-column designs featuring copy of various widths. For example, you might have body copy the width of six grids, captions the width of two grids, and a sidebar the width of four grids. Grids also allow you to create a wide variety of photo sizes. If you have 28 grids, you can have photos as wide as one grid or as wide as 28 grids. It is likely, however, that one grid would be too wide and would not leave room for copy or captions.

If your grids are 4 picas wide, it is wise not to make copy wider than five grids. Five grids plus the space between columns would make your copy 24 picas wide. If your grids are 3 picas, you could carry your copy across six grids. Six grids, plus the 1-pica space between grids, would make your copy 23 picas wide. Five or six grids for the width of copy gives the copy an extra wide look. This works well if you want to add extra leading between lines.

Planned internal white space also works well with the grid. Single grid "rails" of three or four picas can go on either side of body copy, for example. The headline might extend into each of the side rails to give the appearance of a drop column.

Once you have decided on a column, freestyle, or grid structure for a section of the book, create a design concept sheet. This sheet will tell anyone looking at it all the details about the design. Include the following:

Typography: Body copy font and point size

Caption font and point size

Headline font and point size

Subheadline font and point size

Caption starters (initial letters, boldface, etc.)

Copy starters

Graphics: Rule lines (sizes, locations, shades)

Full color

Spot color (shades and locations)

Screens (percentages, color, locations)

Close registration (locations)

Special Items: Quote boxes (locations)

Sidebars (locations)

Information graphics (locations)

Silhouettes (cutout photographs—locations)

➢ *Cover*
Considerations
• *Be sure title and year appear on the front panel.*
• *Title, year, school name, school address, and volume number should appear on the spine.*
• *Select colors that complement end sheet colors.*
• *Some hint of the theme or concept should appear on the front panel.*
• *Avoid artwork that lacks a professional look.*
• *Have fellow students design the cover. Student work is always preferred to company-designed covers. Work by students gives them more ownership of the book.*

Indicate any special instructions about the preceding items. A design concept sheet should enable anyone working on the staff to understand a layout. This should help guarantee consistency.

Mosaic design. Most books use a variation of the mosaic design. Start by placing a dominant picture near the center. Use only one bleed to the external margin per spread—generally top or bottom and somewhere near the middle. Be sure that the horizontal internal margin does not split the page in half, but is interrupted by at least a one-inch drop or jump. This design has a pinwheel effect, with all elements revolving around the dominant. All copy is kept to the outside of the cluster of photographs.

Mondrian design. In this design, subdivide the area both horizontally and vertically anywhere except the gutter. Further subdivide subsequent areas anywhere except the middle. Internal margins intersect at one point, forming a cross or right angle. The vertical internal margin of the cross must run from top to bottom, and the horizontal internal margin from side to side. Place the largest photo at the intersecting lines. All picture elements must bleed off the edge of the page. This is the only layout in which it is permissible for one picture to bleed in the corners (top and left, for example).

This design style is not used much. Because all photos must bleed, there is little room for white space; also it is difficult to place captions next to photos and keep caption widths consistent. The style is named after the Dutch painter Piet Mondrian.

Modified design. Like the Mondrian, subdivide this style both horizontally and vertically anywhere except the middle. Further subdivide the subsequent areas anywhere except the middle. Place the dominant picture at the intersection of the vertical and horizontal lines. Like the Mondrian, the vertical internal margin should run from top to bottom. Like the mosaic, the horizontal internal margin should not split the page in half but should be stopped by a vertical element to form a T. As a weighted compromise between Mondrian (heavy) and mosaic (light), bleed one picture per external margin. In Mondrian design all pictures bleed; in mosaic only one picture bleeds, but in modified design four pictures bleed—one to each side, one to the top, and one to the bottom.

Modular design. This design may be either horizontal or vertical. In horizontal modular, establish a new top and bottom margin at least six inches deep. This becomes the master mod. The master mod should be above or below the center of the layout sheet; it runs from side margin to side margin, with all external elements bleeding off the margins. Subdivide the master mod into smaller mods or elements. Fill the master mod with a majority of vertical elements. One element should violate the established boundaries of the master mod by extending at least two inches into the larger area of white space; the violation becomes dominant.

In vertical modular design, establish a new left and right margin at least eight inches wide. Place this master mod to the

> ➤ *End Sheet Considerations*
>
> • *Table of contents could be placed on the front end sheets.*
>
> • *If back and front end sheets are of different content, and if you print on both, the cost will probably be more.*
>
> • *Cover pictures could be captioned on the front end sheets.*
>
> • *If cover contains a logo for design continuity, it should be repeated on the end sheets.*
>
> • *End sheet graphics should reflect graphics used on the cover and in the opening.*
>
> • *If photographs are used on end sheets, be sure each one is captioned.*
>
> • *End sheets may be plain, both front and back.*

➢ **Italic Type**

Using italic type for small copy areas, such as the Mustang staff at Andrews High School, Andrews, TX, did for its captions can work. Long copy blocks of italic type can become hard on the reader's eyes.

EIGHT THINGS to LOVE

love; (luv)

1. ROCK SOLID

Creativity was far from stifled in Applied Arts II. Senior Lisa Veillette said, "For our final project, we were given a rock, and told to make a part of the human body. I decided to chisel a hand. This project was both intimidating and interesting." Unusual materials were often used in this class.

2. HAPPY HOMEMAKERS

Making boxer shorts, wreaths, and decorating an apartment are just a few things that the students in Mrs. Hughes' Independent Living class learn to do. Senior Jeff Alexander said, "We had to pull some vines from behind the freshmen football field to make the wreaths. It was an interesting experience. I never thought that I would make a wreath and then give it to my mom." From this class, students take with them many lifelong skills.

4. LOOK HERE

Most students would agree that school is no playground, but occasionally amusing incidents occur. In the ninth period Spanish IV class, junior Jennifer Cudney, junior Andrew Gash, and senior Liz Humpage gave a presentation on Spanish Life-Styles. Andy said, "My group never prepared for our project, so we faked the entire thing. We didn't feel bad though, because [junior] Chad Brickley went before us, and accidently did his presentation in German." When Brickley organized his project the previous evening, he accidently used a German-English dictionary. It's fair to say that his presentation got a lot of laughs.

3. FLY BALL

In Mr. Shroeder's NSM Physics class, senior Luc Ward participates in a group lab. The objective was to send a baseball into projectile motion. After the distance of the hit was determined, the students used this information for a lab write-up. Luc said, "I found Physics labs enjoyable because of the laid-back atmosphere and interesting topics. For my favorite lab, my group used autocad to build a gazebo. It was a fun and interesting way to learn how buildings are supported." Many students looked forward to lab days because they created a nice break in the monotony of a week

5. CHEAP THRILLS

In A.P. Physics C, a class normally reserved for seniors, junior Andy Warren laughs as his partner, Scott Stroud, makes a funny face. In order for the class to be bearable, students had to find ways to amuse eachother. Andy said, "The best thing about this class is that an "A" is 68%." Most A.P. Physics C students agreed that the course is challenging, but well worth the struggle.

The yearbook staff at Bay High School in Bay Village, OH, found a unique way to present its academic section by using eight pictures and eight short copy blocks on each spread. The above is on Eight Things to Love. Other topics covered things like Eight Ways to Cram, Eight Stresses, Eight Truths, and Eight Things to Burn. Each spread covered activities in several departments, and each one also had a quote that showed the opposite viewpoint, such as unburn, unlove, and untruth.

left or right of center. The master mod runs from top to bottom of the page, with all external elements bleeding off the top and bottom. Because the mod is vertical, fill the master mod with a majority of horizontal elements. One element

7. MEASURE UP

In Mr. Sadonick's Environmental Science class, students participated in various self-study projects. Senior Steve Blados said, "I, along with eight others, conducted a forest study in Huntington Reservation. We established a 900 square meter area, and studied tree diameter, height, canopy density and wild life. The data that we collected was later used for calculations and experiments." One of Steve's partners, senior Brett Johnston, said, "I'm glad we chose the project that we did because I love spending time in the woods and being outdoors." Because of the laid-back atmosphere in Sadonick's class, students saw it as a relaxed, pressure-free course.

-C. Dyke

8. HANDS ON

During Ms. Widmar's fourth period Applied Arts Class, sophomore Grace Lanning helps with a banner for the K-12 Art Show. Grace said, "We drew outlines of hands and feet, and colored groovy designs within them. The hands and feet varied in size and shape to represent different ages of the Art Show participants." The K-12 Art Show was on display October 23rd through the 26th. Applied Arts was one of the most preferred art classes, because of its wide variety of projects and mediums.

unlove   *ways to avoid doing things you hate.*

Doing Homework: "Whenever I attempt to do homework with my friends, it never gets done. Subconsciously I think that is how I avoid doing my work." -Sophomore Laura Jerina ¶ "When it is time to do my homework I avoid it by practicing my cello." -Junior Sarah Byrnes ¶ Getting Up Early: "Because I hate to wake up for school, I don't go to sleep at night. That way I'm already awake in the mornings."

-Junior T.J. Putnam ¶ "Since most of the time I go to sleep really late, I'm always on the verge of dropping dead in class. I try to catch up on my rest in study halls or boring classes." -Junior Karyn Ott

A. Kohn

-C. Ferro

6. WHAT'S SO FUNNY?

While teaching the novel, *The Crossing*, to their A.P. English class, seniors Lyndsay Boggess and Jenny Miles laugh uncontrollably. Jenny said, "This novel was very difficult to teach because it was partly in Spanish. Mr. Billman always mispronounced one word and our class died laughing because he sounded so funny. We had the help of Mr. Cabassa when trying to decipher some passages." Even tough classes can be lightened up by silly incidents.

---

most valuable

Susan Brower

Leighanne Robnett

volleyball pride

Susan Brower

most improved

Fran Meyer

Amy Moeller

2nd team all-conference

Leighanne Robnett

honorable mention all-conference

Karen Duffner

> ➢ **Use of Grids**
> *The Mascot,*
> *Mexico High School,*
> *Mexico, MO,* high-
> lighted recognition for
> athletes in the above
> seven-pica grid.

---

should violate the established boundaries of the master mod by extending at least two inches to the right of the mod; again, the violation makes that element dominant.

Isolated element design. Begin with any of the other styles, and follow all rules and principles of that style. Violate, in one instance only, the rule of consistent internal margins by at least two inches by placing one or more elements in a pool of white space that far (two inches) from the rest of the elements. The isolated element(s) gains a secondary degree of dominance because of its separation. Maintain consistent internal margins at all points except the isolated element(s).

For best results use columnar or mosaic design, since they allow for effective use of white space and prevent overcrowding. The other designs may be used, however, for a specific purpose.

When you have decided on a layout style, it is time to consider what graphic effects you might use to make the style even more appealing. Do not overuse graphics.

1. Tool lines. Keep them simple. Lines should be 3-point or less in size. Don't make them so large that they dominate the copy. Most schools create their own lines on computers or they put down their own tool lines on artboard and submit them to the printer as art; that saves money and guarantees that the tool lines are in the proper places. Some schools close-register (no space between line and other element) tool lines to photographs. Be aware that close registration is usually an additional cost. Don't zigzag tool lines; like photographs, they look best if they form a rectangular shape. Rounded corners are permissible. If you use tool lines, consider stopping them at some point rather than boxing in an element completely. For example, a headline could be centered in the top tool line of a box around copy. Or if you have a tool line going completely around a spread, a photo could break out of the box at some point.

2. Careful use of type can add graphic appeal to a spread. Use of initial letters (large-type letters to begin headlines, copy blocks, or even captions) can add eye appeal to a spread. For example, a 36-point letter might begin a copy block of 10-point body type. Some books use initial letters to begin and end a headline. Initial letters might also be used to start several paragraphs of copy. This can be especially

➢ *Critiquing Your Design*

• *Are grids or columns established?*

• *Does every element start and stop at a grid or column?*

• *Is white space planned?*

• *Is the dominant element near the middle of the spread?*

• *Is there a caption for every photo?*

• *Are captions touching their individual photos?*

• *Does the copy block have a headline? Is it placed above or to the left of the copy? If not, is there an initial letter to get the reader back to the copy lead?*

• *Are graphics used effectively?*

• *Are external margins established on all four sides?*

• *Have internal margins been followed consistently?*

• *On disk to the yearbook company, are all elements coded to fit company specifications?*

effective to break up gray areas in long copy blocks. An initial letter can be raised above the line of type it goes with to add white space, or it may be dropped into the copy to align evenly with the top of the first line.

3. Boldface type can be effective to break up long columns of type. Boldfacing the first few words of a caption can draw the reader's eye. Again, be consistent. If you boldface one caption lead, you should boldface all caption leads within a section.

4. Tilting photographs can be attractive, but be careful not to tilt too much (normally no more than 30%). It is also permissible to tilt copy, headlines, and captions. When it is obvious that tilts have been done to create eye appeal, the internal margin violations do not offend.

5. Full cutout or partial cutout photographs can be effective if done well. In this device, all or part of the background is dropped out of a photograph. Partial cutouts are usually done at the top of a photograph. Cutouts, full or partial, can draw more attention to the center of interest. Staffs may do their own cutouts with a sharp Exacto knife; however, it takes a steady hand to assure that the picture subject is not mutilated.

6. Shadow boxes give copy or photographs a three-dimensional appearance as if they were jumping out of the page at the reader. The width of shadows may vary, but most do not exceed 6 picas. Most shadows are done on only two sides of an element. Some go the full width and height of the element, but many stop 1 pica short. The shadows are created by using tool lines.

7. Skillful use of gray can add eye appeal to a design. Many books contrast gray with solid

➢ *More Design Terminology*

• *Border: Plain or ornamental element around any element.*

• *Boston box: A quote set in the text copy with the text wrapped around; usually 14-point or larger.*

• *Butt: To join without overlapping or without space between elements.*

• *Camera-ready: Material ready to be photographed.*

• *Close register: Any element set closer than one-half pica. The elements may be butted with no white space between them.*

• *Color separation: Separating the four primary printing colors into their various components.*

• *Column rule: Lines used to separate columns of type.*

• *Continuous tone: An image with a wide range of tones.*

• *Cropping: Editing a photo to take out unnecessary parts.*

➤ *Sideways Type*

Running type sideways can work, especially when you run it from left to right. Avoid vertical type where you stack one letter on top of the other. That is not a natural way for someone to read. The above example is from the Pioneer, Kirkwood High School, Kirkwood, MO.

Quick read copy blocks, which accompany the main copy block on Prom, make this an appealing spread from the Excalibur, Francis Howell North High School, St. Charles, MO. Use of creative typography makes this an outstanding spread.

type or use gray backgrounds to highlight one element or an entire spread. For example, a gray background behind a scorebox can make the scorebox stand out.

8. Quote blurbs can attract the reader. Quote

346

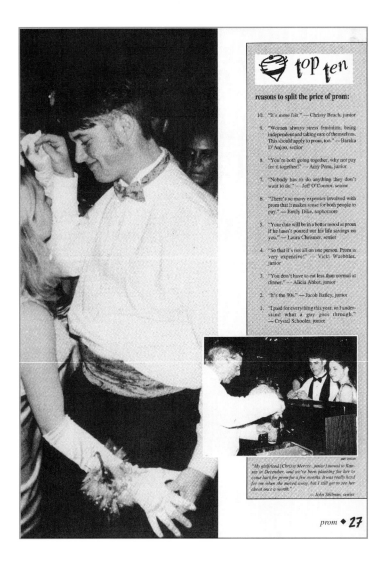

top ten

reasons to split the price of prom:

10. "It's more fair." — Chrissy Beach, junior

9. "Women always stress feminism, being independent and taking care of themselves. This should apply to prom, too." — Baraka D'Anjou, senior

8. "You're both going together, why not pay for it together!" — Amy Penn, junior

7. "Nobody has to do anything they don't want to do." — Jeff O'Connor, senior

6. "There's so many expenses involved with prom that it makes sense for both people to pay." — Emily Dike, sophomore

5. "Your date will be in a better mood at prom if he hasn't poured out his life savings on you." — Laura Chrismer, senior

4. "So that it's not all on one person. Prom is very expensive!" — Vicki Wuebbles, junior

3. "You don't have to eat less than normal at dinner." — Alicia Abbot, junior

2. "It's the 90s." — Jacob Bailey, junior

1. "I paid for everything this year, so I understand what a guy goes through." — Crystal Schooler, junior

"My girlfriend [Chrissy Mercer, junior] moved to Kansas in December, and we've been planning for her to come back for prom for a few months. It was really hard for me when she moved away, but I still get to see her about once a month." — John Stillman, senior

prom ◆ *27*

➢ *Special Effects*
By using software programs such as PhotoShop, staffs can create various special effects like this letter formed from a photograph in the Red & White, *City High School, Iowa City, IA.*

blurbs (also known as sandwich or Boston boxes, liftout quotes, or pulled quotes) are quotes or statements from the copy set in larger type. Sometimes quote blurbs are put in the middle of the copy with the type wrapped around them. Sometimes they are used as a separate element. Generally blurbs are set off by a thin tool line above and below. Sometimes the quote marks themselves are in an even larg-

347

> **Use of Color**

• Spot color adds impact to the page. If using four-color photos on a spread, choosing a spot color that is evident in the dominant photo creates a vivid effect.

• Don't overuse spot color. Headlines, dropped caps, caption bullets, logos, and ruled lines are good places to use color.

• Using a spot color mixed from the four-process colors (cyan, magenta, yellow, black) usually costs less than creating special colors.

• Using a percentage of any of the spot colors is cost-effective if used on a spread with four-color photos.

• Colorization of one area of a black-and-white photo can also be effective, but if not used carefully, it can look artificial.

• Graduated screens of color, with one color fading to a lighter color, can also be effective when used in small areas.

er point size than the blurb. It is also possible to use a shadow box around a blurb. For example, the left and top of a blurb might be enclosed with a 1-point line, and the right and bottom enclosed with a 4-point line.

9. Special effects may add eye appeal, but often they destroy a good photograph rather than enhance it. The most common special effect is the combination of black ink and a specially patterned photographic screen. The screen may create various patterns (pebble grain, mezzotint, etchtone, straight line, wavy line, cross lines, bull's-eye, sunburst). Screens distort the photographic image and therefore should be used sparingly.

Another special effect is the direct line shot. Such a photograph eliminates all shades of gray from the original photograph, leaving everything black or white. This effect causes a stark, uncompromising silhouette, with white whites and black blacks butted directly next to each other.

Posterization is a softer photo silhouette. The shadow areas of the photograph are reinserted and printed in one shade of dark gray, which becomes the second tone. The gradation of shades is from white whites to dark grays to black blacks. Posterization may also be done in color.

Ghosting is another special effect used in some books. With ghosting, a photograph is overexposed, reducing contrast. Black tones become dark gray; dark gray becomes light gray; light gray and white tend to blend together. Ghosted photographs appear to dissolve into the page. Be careful when you ghost; it can ruin an otherwise great photo.

Many books overprint type on a ghosted photograph. Sometimes this type is hard to read, just as white print over a dark background is hard to read. You must have the perfect photograph to do either reverse printing or overprinting (also called overburning).

10. Color (full or spot) is probably the most appealing of graphic elements. Colored inks may be printed in their maximum density or in lighter shades of 30, 50, or 70 percent. The lighter shades work best unless you want a brighter color to shock the reader. Spot colors work best as backgrounds rather than as tints for everything on a page, because people look best in their natural colors.

11. Avoid reversing a lot of copy out of dark backgrounds. Reversed copy is hard to read, especially if it is small. If reversing copy fits your design concept, be sure the type is at least 12-point or larger to make it readable. Overprinting type on a gray screen is acceptable, but again the type should probably be at least 10-point to make it readable. Type may be overburned on 10 or 20 percent tints. Darker tints than that will make the type hard to read. Avoid putting body copy on gray screens produced on the desktop and printed on a laser printer. At about 300 dots per inch (DPI), laser printer screens are too coarse behind copy. It is best to submit pages on disk to the yearbook company. That way, the company can use a Linotronic printer to produce your pages. Such a printer will eliminate the dot pattern laser printers create. A Linotronic will produce a solid gray.

12. Experiment with drop columns to make copy presentations more attractive. Drop columns can set off headlines or other copy elements as isolated elements. The empty column allows

"I do not really know what I would change about soccer, but it would be pretty nice if when you missed a shot, you would get a re-kick. I know that the games would have much higher scores then."
• Alicia Butler

➤ *Content Rules*
The old maxim that content dictates design still holds true. Note the shape of the headline in the Heritage, *Horizon High School, Scottsdale, AZ. The headline bends to go along with the content of the quote.*

➢ **Still More Design Terminology**

- *Downstyle:* A style of headline with only the first word and proper nouns capitalized.
- *Folio:* Page number and page identification information.
- *Hairline:* Very thin rule line. Approximately 1/4 point wide.
- *Halftone:* Photo screened for printing resulting in graduation of tones formed by dots of varying size.
- *Jump head:* A headline continued from one page to another page.
- *Line shot:* A photograph achieved by shooting a picture without a screen, which causes the light tone of a picture to drop out and only the black areas to appear.

options for copy starters or quote blurbs.

13. Experiment with oversized copy with excessive leading—especially for theme and divider pages. This technique might also be used for the lead of a story. Fourteen-point text with 24-point leading would give a double-spaced appearance to the copy.

14. Ragged-right copy can be effective in some instances. Do not overuse, however. It usually works well with narrow columns to help the designer avoid large gaps between words. It is most effective when used on a few pages such as opening spreads and dividers.

15. Spot color can be effective for pulled quotes and for headlines. Avoid putting entire copy blocks in any color but black. Black type, when it is small, is generally easier to read.

16. Use sidebar features to help set off a section visually. These sidebar presentations could be quote boxes, short stories related to the main copy block, or infographics. Sidebars help expand coverage, but they also enhance design. They allow the designer to experiment with screens, fonts, lines, and point sizes.

17. Experiment with a variety of typefaces—serif and sans serif, italic and roman, light and heavy. Know the message you are trying to convey in a section, and select a typeface that will help convey it.

18. Try various types of graphics with captions. An overline is a miniheadline placed above the caption. A catch-line also serves as a mini-headline, but it is set at the beginning of the caption, and it is a headline—not part of the caption. A lead-in could be used to start a caption. A lead-in sets the first three or four words in a different size or in a different style than the rest of the caption.

19. Keep design simple, but attractive. Have a reason for everything you do. Don't throw in a rule, for example, unless it somehow helps to unify the spread. Make sure all design elements complement each other.

20. Graphics can add appeal to folios (page numbers and page content). However, keep the folio design simple.

21. Graphics can add appeal to the advertising section of the book. Advertising pages should be graphically appealing. Avoid placing all ads on a spread. Add a feature story with an exciting candid photo. Select a unifying concept for the ad section that will give the section character and tone. Design ad pages as you would any spread in the book. Every spread should have a center of interest. Design ads to include headlines and copy. Illustrations (photos and/or artwork) should be planned as a unit with the copy. Incorporate graphics into each ad to give it a distinctive look. Avoid the traditional 1/16, 1/8, 1/4, 1/2 page approach for ad divisions. Opt instead for a columnar concept. When placing ads on a spread, begin with the largest ad and place it toward the center. Then work from the middle out in placing the rest of the ads. Avoid placing the same size ads side by side. All good ads should include a headline (14-point or larger), text copy (14-point or smaller), pictures (with captions), or artwork. Essential information for all ads includes the name of the business, the telephone number, and a complete address. Always try to sell a product or service. Avoid business-card type ads.

22. Browse through a variety of magazines, brochures, and newsletters to search for graphic ideas.

➢ *Logos*

Use of a repeating logo can be eye-catching. The Paragon *staff at Munster High School in Munster, IN, used a clock to illustrate a timeline. It ran a brief story about a particular time of the day. The staff changed the hands on the clock to indicate the time. The clock above points to 6 a.m. to show the time the student arose.*

➤ *Tilts and Shadow Boxes*

Although tilted elements and shadow boxes disappeared in the 1980s, they returned prior to the end of the 1990s. Note how the Heritage *staff at Horizon High School, Scottsdale, AZ, stopped the gray shadow 1/2 pica short on the bottom left and the top right.*

23. Remember that the elements of a layout include white space, body copy, captions, headlines, folios and folio tabs, and graphics. Use graphics to help tie all the other elements together.

24. Infographics can add to a page's appeal. Infographics are discussed in Chapter 8. Be creative. You might use a line graph that shows time spans, which works best for highlighting news events. You might use a bar graph or a pie graph to show the relationship between two or more items.

25. Another way to add appeal to a spread is through colorization. This means that certain elements of a photograph have spot color added. For example, a boy's sweater might be colorized blue; a girl's scarf might be colorized red. Be careful, however; sometimes colorization does not look natural. Choose appropriate items to colorize.

26. Be sure your cover design makes a good impression. Usually the impression the cover gives the reader is the impression he will have of the book. Some graphic element used on the cover should be repeated on the end sheets, the theme pages, and the divider pages for continuity. A graphic element used on the cover might also be used in the folios. The cover must introduce the theme and contain the year and name of the book. The spine must include the name of the school, the yearbook's name, the year, and the volume number. Avoid using stock covers provided by the yearbook company. If you do so, you remove any opportunity to be creative and unique in design.

27. The colophon needs to have a graphic appeal to bring the reader to it. The colophon includes information about the production of the

book, including fonts used, type sizes used, number of rolls of film used, and awards won. It also gives information about special effects used.

28. Graphics add to the appeal of an index. A staff might use a catch phrase and design for this section that is linked to the theme. Each letter of the alphabet provides a place for a logo, a quote, or a photo.

After considering these examples of what schools are doing to add graphic appeal to design, pay some attention to what magazines are doing. Adapt, but do not copy, their designs for your own purposes. All it takes is a keen imagination. Don't be afraid to be creative, but don't overdo. The key to all design is consistency and simplicity. Keep it simple, make it appealing, and the reader will find it exciting.

Magazine and yearbook designers also must create a dummy, just as newspaper designers do. Since designs are created as two-page spreads for a yearbook, it is necessary to use a dummy sheet that encompasses two pages. Only the first and last pages of a magazine or yearbook are designed as one-page layouts.

Rectangular shapes work well for showing all elements to be included on a spread. The designer should draw an X through each photo or piece of artwork and should key each copy to its appropriate place. Mark copy blocks with letters, and pictures with numbers. Mark the corresponding letters or numbers on the copy blocks and photographs before submitting them to the printer.

Some staffs do their own paste-ups. They may simply transfer their dummy design to a permanent layout sheet and paste the copy and pictures in their appropriate places. Pictures must be printed to size if a staff does all of its own pasteups.

In the illustrated dummy on p. 357 the staff pasted up its own headline (IN THE SPIRIT). It has keyed all other elements by letter or number and written special instructions in the

➢ *Bullets*
Circles, squares, triangles, and other objects can be used as bullets to highlight individual items within a list. The Red & White, *City High School, Iowa City, IA, used arrows for bullets. The staff also used a gradation of gray to white as a background for the copy going from left to right.*

Days of parades

Band, 'pommies' march around town

Sweat rolled down marching band members' faces, and the mercury in the thermometer rose above 90°. The band played the familiar "Varsity Valor" while marching along the hot pavement of downtown Kirkwood during the Greentree Parade, Sept. 10.

At the corner of Essex and Kirkwood Road, the parade stalled to take care of an injured participant. Mrs. Maxine Gilner, parent, filled milk cartons with water from a hose at a nearby house.

"It was so hot!" said Janet Enboden, drum majorette. "We decided to sit under a shade tree."

As the band marched by playing "Fame" in the Great Forest Park Balloon Race Parade, Sept. 16, the pom pon squad came into view.

Both organizations missed school for that parade. The pom pon girls missed another day of school to rehearse with the renown St. Louis Symphony Orchestra at Powell Hall, Jan 6.

The squad performed as part of the pops concerts, Jan. 6 and Jan. 8. They sang and danced to "The Ballad of Tank O'Hara."

The squad also performed at Busch Stadium with 23 other squads in conjunction with the Metro Area Pom Pon Association, Sept. 11.

"I performed with Normandy because I was an alternate," said Ashley Hall, junior, "but it was still a lot of fun."

A graphic effect on a portrait page design was achieved by use of a grid pattern screened on a 20% gray background and artwork to create the notebook effect.

margins. Note the use of outline lettering and boldface lettering for the headline to create contrast. The staff has used an initial letter to begin the copy on p. 169 and has ordered the 6-point tool line printed in 100% tempo 185 fire engine red. Note that the dominant photo that bleeds across the gutter is marked as a DPS (double-page spread) but that it is numbered on the side that has the largest portion of the photo. Do not key a DPS photo twice.

Disk submission has changed the way some staffs key elements now. Yearbook companies still require staffs submitting disks to print out a hard copy of each page. Photographs still need to be keyed, but copy, heads, and captions are already placed on a page, so it is not necessary to key those elements. Some schools are also scanning in artwork, photographs, and advertisements. Desktop publishing and disk submission have changed design.

Desktop publishing has given staffs more control over the final product, but at the same time it has created headaches. In some instances, it has meant more hours are needed to complete the work. An effective infographic cannot be created in a matter of minutes, for example. At the same time, disk submission has reduced the time needed to complete pasteups. Pasteups have virtually disappeared for staffs who submit final pages on disks.

One problem that desktop publishing has produced for staffs is keeping up with the software and hardware. Computer companies are constantly producing new versions of computers and software programs. A staff no sooner gets used to one version when a new one appears on the market. That means more variations to the programs, which are usually an asset to producing creative designs, but it means learning new things.

Most staffs today use Macintosh computers. PageMaker is still probably the most popular software program for creating finished pages, but Quark Express and Ready, Set, Go are also used a lot. Aldus Freehand and Adobe Illustrator are two popular graphics programs. MacDraw, Typestyler, and Cricket Draw are also in widespread use.

Staffs need to be careful with grammar and spelling checkers. Programs do not recognize a wrong word that is spelled correctly. For example, if a staff wants "their" and they have used "there," the computer will not question it. That's why manual copyediting is still important.

Be careful when working with a computer. It is easy to make your book look like a computer-designed book. Be

➢ *Layering*

Placing one element on top of another works for this scoreboard in the Pioneer, *Kirkwood High School, Kirkwood, MO. The black background is the first layer, the gray screen is the second layer, and the white boxes with the scores serves as a third layer.*

creative, but be simple. Don't let your book look like every other book in the country.

EXERCISES

1. Design a two-page spread using a three-column layout. Use no more than seven pictures.

2. To that same two-page spread, add some graphic elements to give the design more pizzazz.

3. Design a two-page spread using a two-plus columnar layout. Use no more than seven pictures.

4. Select a theme for your book, then design a cover and an opening section. Make the opening section seven pages in length (pages 1, 2-3, 4-5, 6-7). Keep your design style for all seven pages consistent. Then design a division spread (pages 8-9) to introduce the Student Life section of the book. The division page should carry over some continuity device begun on the cover. Design the end sheets, using the table of contents and continuing some continuity device that you started on the cover to help convey the theme.

5. Find examples of good layouts in exchange yearbooks or your school's yearbooks. Explain why they are effective.

6. Compile a notebook of graphic devices used in magazines. Label each one according to type. Find at least five examples of each type of graphic discussed in this chapter and/or in the previous chapter. Include initial letters, silhouettes (cut-out photos), partial silhouettes, quote blurbs, shadows, screens, rule lines, and type with extra leading. Also, include examples of all types of headlines from tripods to wickets to kickers.

7. Using the examples you collected in exercise 6, create three spreads. Make one spread 5 columns in width, the second 7 columns, and the third 6 columns

"I was the anchor in the relay at HERO Team Day. I put my shirt on backwards and dove at the finish line!" - Valerie VanDyke

➢ *Out of the Ordinary*

Staffs should break out of the box when coming up with graphic ideas. The Heritage staff at Horizon High School, Scottsdale, AZ, chose to do a ragged edge instead of straight lines around the photo and caption.

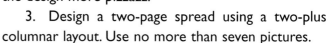

One way to get more photos on a page is to use a roving reporter question, as the staff at Bay Village High School in Bay Village, OH did. Responses let the readers find out something they did not know about the individuals.

in width, with one plus column. Use layout sheets your teacher provides.

    8.   In magazines and other yearbooks, find at least 10 design techniques to begin captions. Paste your

examples in a notebook.

9. By using six pictures, create a 6-columnar spread with one dropped column of a narrower width than the regular six columns. Use layout sheets your teacher provides.

10. Create a design concept for the Student Life section of your yearbook. Select a column format and sketch two spreads. Clearly label all design elements and graphics. For variety, use a horizontal dominant photo on one spread and a vertical dominant on the other spread. On your design concept sheet, include body copy type style and size, caption type style and size, main headline type style and size, secondary headline type style and size, and any specifications for copy starters and caption starters such as initial letters. Also, include any special content items to be used such as quote boxes, sidebars, or infographics. In addition, include any graphics to be used such as rule lines, screens, close registration, spot color, or full color.

11. Create a design concept for the Academic, Sports, and Club sections of your yearbook following directions in number 10.

12. Design 10 headlines for a story on Pet Day at your school. Over 1,000 students brought their pets to class first period as part of an organized day to have every student give a three-minute oral presentation. Students who did no have pets spoke for three minutes on their favorite animal. This school-wide effort was part of a project to improve students' abilities to make oral presentations. Look through magazines for possible design ideas. Make each headline 36 picas wide. You may vary number of lines and number of decks. You may also use different fonts. Be creative. Make your typographical choices stand out. Include artwork with the heads, if you wish.

CHAPTER
thirteen

Caption Writing

To caption or not to caption should never be the question. All photographs in yearbooks and newspapers should be captioned.

Reporters should give as much attention to writing a caption as they do to writing a story. Captions are necessary to help tell the complete story of an event. It is not necessary to keep captions to one sentence. Good captions often are two or three sentences in length. The first sentence should be written in the present tense and should describe the action taking place in the picture. The second sentence may add more to that description and stay in present tense, or it may give more information about a person or some item in the picture and be written in past tense. This sentence usually tells what happened before or after the picture was taken. A third sentence is usually a quote from someone in the picture. It is possible for captions to be longer than three sentences, but it is not advisable to go longer than five. Caption content varies depending on the type of photograph and its placement in the book. The following is an example of a five-sentence caption.

Six points go on the scoreboard as William Ennis-Inge intercepts a pass on Webster's 14-yard line and returns it for a touchdown in the Turkey Day game, Nov. 28. Ennis-Inge intercepted 15 passes during the season, and he returned four of those for touchdowns. "I couldn't believe it when I caught the ball on the 14," he said. "It was the first score of the game, and it was a turning point for us. I thought I would wind up with some broken ribs since my teammates mobbed me."

Like other types of journalistic writing, caption-writing also has rules:

➤ **Telling the Story Behind a Photograph**
• *Write in complete sentences; avoid sentence fragments.*
• *Write the first sentence in present tense. Every time a reader looks at the photo, the action will still be occurring. Change to past tense to describe anything that happened before or after the photographer took the picture.*
• *Tell how the photo relates to the school year or to the theme of the book.*
• *Choose candid photos that have good facial expressions, that show emotion, and that show action.*
• *Double-check the spelling of all names and double-check the identity of each person. There's nothing worse than calling a senior a freshman in caption or copy.*
• *Vary writing style from caption to caption.*

1. Avoid stating the obvious. Tell more than what the photograph shows. For example, if a principal is talking on the telephone, the caption should not read: "Principal Hattie Morris talks on the telephone." A complete caption would tell whom she is talking to, what she is talking about, and when she is talking.

2. Answer as many of the 5 W's (who, what, when, where, and why) and the H (how) as possible. As in news writing, it is best to leave *when* and *where* for the end. If all the pictures on a page or spread were taken at the same place and on the same date, it is not necessary to repeat when and where in all the captions. In fact, it is not necessary to include any information in a caption that is part of the copy.

3. Vary openings. Starting all captions with names becomes monotonous, especially in yearbooks where there are several pictures on a two-page spread. If there are six pictures on a spread, try to begin the caption in six different ways. Be careful of starting with participial phrases, as discussed in Chapter 3, and avoid beginning with *a, an*, and *the*. Avoid beginning with prepositions, especially with words, such as "before," "after," "on," "during," "as," and "while." Also avoid beginning with *ing* words, which are usually participial phrases or gerunds. All of these tend to be overused and therefore become monotonous.

4. Don't be dishonest. A yearbook at a Midwest school did a spread on getting ready to go to school in the morning. One picture was of a

JARRED YOUNG, SOPHOMORE, spends his free time rollerblading. (Photo Andy Gribble)

All-capital lead-ins draw attention to the captions in the Northwest Passage, *Northwest High School, Shawnee Mission, KS.*

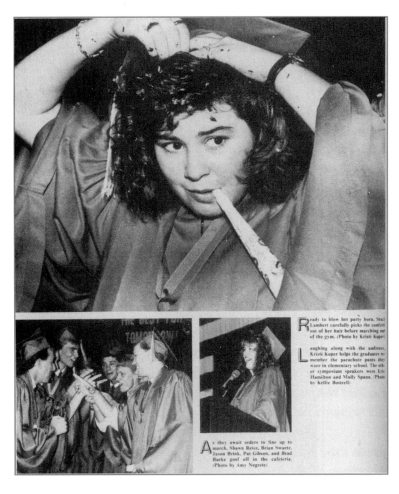

Outlined initial letters serve as an attention-getter for captions in the Student Life section of the Crimson and Blue, Abraham Lincoln High School, Council Bluffs, IA.

student waking up and stretching before getting out of bed. The caption said the picture had been taken at 7 a.m.; actually it was taken at 4 p.m. School newspapers and yearbooks must deal with facts; it is not their place to alter history.

The writer must do research to write a caption, just as a reporter does research to write a story. Photographers can help by supplying information, perhaps writing the 5 W's and the

H on the back of each photo. That is not always practical for a photographer who is snapping several pictures at once, but she can at least tell when and where she took the photograph. Photographers can help caption writers a lot if they remember to shoot the scoreboard at the end of every period in a sports event. That way they tell the caption writer in which period the action occurred. (Be careful when writing on the back of photographs. Regular pencil can make an impression that shows on the front of the photograph. Grease pencil works best. Ink tends to smear and may come off on another photo.)

5. Don't editorialize. Several words used in high school publications border on editorializing: they include *enjoy, intensely,* and *diligently.* Avoid any kind of editorial comment.
6. Normally write captions in present tense, active voice. It is permissible, however, to make a second sentence past tense. The following caption shows the switch in tenses:

Following school, Oct. 4, David Fischer and Philip Oakley, freshmen, discuss the completed B-team soccer season while preparing to leave from the Arts Building bike rack. Although Oakley lived far enough from school to take the bus, he preferred the 15-minute bike ride.

7. Use first and last name or first name and initial with last name when identifying subjects.
8. Do not use *left to right* in captioning group pictures. The reader normally goes from left to right when looking at a photo.
9. For group pictures of more than one row, indicate the rows by: Front Row, Second Row, Back Row. Put such directions in boldface or caps so that they stand out:
FRESHMAN CHEERLEADERS: FRONT ROW: Ann Rudolph, Karen Zuroweste, Kristi Eagle, Jennifer

➢ *Working Together to Write In-Depth Captions*
• *Photographers should write down information about the picture after they shoot it—time, date, place, significance, names of people involved. A pencil and a notepad should be part of all photographer's equipment. Only the photographer can capture the immediate emotions behind a picture.*
• *Designers must leave enough space on layout for three-sentence captions.*
• *Caption writers must go beyond the obvious in finding background information concerning the photograph—information that the reader could not know for himself or herself by just looking at the picture.*

➤ Writing In-
Depth Captions

• Have photogra-
phers write down
necessary informa-
tion (the 5 W's and
the H) when taking
the photo.

• Have designers
leave enough space
on layout for longer
captions.

• Have caption
writer go beyond
the obvious and tell
the readers details
they could not figure
out on their own.

• Have a caption
editor on staff
(sometimes called
an ID editor) to
assure staff mem-
bers write quality
captions.

ABOVE THE RIM

Perspiration drips down senior Steve Burgett and freshman Chris Ward's faces as they play a game of four-on-four during contact at open gym, Jan. 5. Burgett said players picked teams on a first-come, first-serve basis, so there were no permanent teams. The players started with a free throw contest, and the two top shooters became captains (photo by Lindsey Bilhorn).

FOUL PLAY

Mistakes in previous games spark Bruce Burgett and Andre Maclin, freshmen, and Randy Kriewall, math teacher, to get together at contact, Jan. 5, to discuss new strategies. "We made a lot of mistakes throughout our games," Burgett said. "We were going over some of the plays of our most recent ones. I'm not saying that our whole game consisted of mistakes, but since there were so many, people were bound to notice" (photo by Summer School).

PLAYING WITH FROSTY

Oddly-shaped snow angels amuse Emily Umbright, Margeaux Heaton and Courtney Osterholt, sophomores, as Mark Miller, senior, creates them, Dec. 19, outside the Walker Commons. "We couldn't throw snowballs, so we watched Mark make snow angels," Osterholt said. "I wasn't about to make an angel, so the rest of us made a snowman. When we were done, it was a little short and fat, but it was awesome. We got a carrot from the Foods I lab and used it for a nose. It was kind of gross because we put mud and grass on it for hair." Osterholt said they were somewhat worried Principal Franklin McCallie would catch them and be upset that they were playing in the snow. "We were afraid Mr. McCallie would come out because we were all kicking snow around" (photo by Andrew Wind).

Adam Dicus
Katrina Dillon-Fish
George Dobson
Alicia Dockett
Jenny Dolan
Kat Dreuel
Susan Dryden

Andy Duane
Katie Echelard
Jonathan Edwards
Beverly Ennis
Tami Evans
John Fakes
Tamara Farrington

Mandy Faser
Niki Femmer
B.J. Fendler
Christina Fernandez
Tif Filley
Ben Fillo
Liz Fischer

Captions make up most of the textual presentation on this spread from the Pioneer, *Kirkwood High School, Kirkwood, MO. Readership surveys have shown that captions are the most read copy on the spread, so the* Pioneer *staff decided to make each caption tell a full story since each one is several sentences in length.*

Van Asdale. BACK ROW: Ashley Hall, Kim Hill

(captain), Marie McMiller (co-captain), Lisa Browman.

Note that positions held in an organization are in parentheses after the person's name. It is also best in yearbook

spreads to identify group officers in the picture caption rather than in the copy.

10. Name and identify all people in a photograph except in the case of large crowds. Each staff may determine for itself what constitutes a large crowd; most, however, identify everyone in a photograph if there are six or fewer people.

11. Use colorful, lively verbs. To be verbs—*is, was,*

365

➢ Captions as
Design Elements
  • Leave six or more
picas on the design in
order to have in-depth
captions.
  • Consider head-
lines, screens, initial letters, bullets, and other
graphic devices to
draw attention to each
caption.
  • Consider putting
captions in boldface
type.

were—show little life. Describe what the people in the picture are doing. Be careful not to overuse such verbs as *provides, gives, helps, aids, enables, offers,* and *creates.* Use descriptive verbs: Say *slouches* rather than *sits,* for example.

12. Don't use phrases such as *it seems* or *it appears.* It either is or it isn't. Be specific.

13. Don't try to be cute. Captions must be factual. The following captions have actually appeared in yearbooks:

> Look at the birdie!
> What would you do if she said
> yes, George?
> Gee whiz, Scott!

14. Name opposing players in sports photographs, if possible. If the player's number is visible on his uniform, it is possible to get his name either from a program or from someone at his school. If the sport is an individual sport, such as tennis or wrestling, it is always possible to get the name of the opposing player. A coach will know the names of each opponent. Sometimes scorebooks do not include first names of opposing players. Therefore, it may be necessary for the caption writer to call the opposing school's coach. If it is impossible to find out the opposing player's name, at least include the name of the opposing school. Be as professional as possible with your captions. A professional publication would not fail to give the names of all the players.

15. Consider using quote captions for some photographs. It is a good way to add variety, and it also creates an atmosphere about an event that would not be captured in a regular caption. Compare the following two captions:

Regular: Jim Edmunds, senior, paints the Samaritan House in Las Vegas, NM, during the Presbyterian Youth group's summer work trip.

Quote: "Hanging from the bell tower, 60 feet in the air, I could see about 50 miles. My crew painted the Samaritan House in Las Vegas, NM."

—Jim Edmunds, senior.

Quote captions must be handled with care. Sometimes the person giving the quote does not name all the people in the picture; then a second sentence becomes necessary. For example:

"I liked meeting exchange students. The picnic was fun even though I didn't know anyone else."
—Sandra Rotramel, senior. Alicia Velasco from Colombia eats with Rotramel at the Fall AFS picnic.

Be aware also that the person giving the quote does not always give full names and identifications of other people. The writer can do that by using parentheses around the nonquoted information. Parentheses can also be used to add additional information to make the quote more complete. Parentheses indicate that the material within has been added by the writer. For example:

"It was so gross. Ned (Williams, senior) and I dissected this frog (Dec. 2) in biology. He thought it was a lot of fun, but I thought it was totally disgusting."

—Ken Blythe, junior.

It would probably be impossible to use quote captions for every picture in a newspaper or yearbook. It takes time to get a picture to a subject so that he can comment on the actions in the photograph. Even if it were possible, it would become monotonous. However, a few quote captions scattered throughout a publication can be effective. Consistency is important, however. For example, in a design that places copy

> **The Caption Writer's Job**
> • Interview. Interview. Interview. Just like the copy writer, the caption writer needs to talk to the subjects in the picture to get additional information.
> • Eliminate embarrassing comments. Don't try to make the reader laugh when the only thing to laugh at is at the subject's expense.
> • Find out more than the obvious. It is obvious that someone is laughing. Find out what made them laugh and why.
> • Find out the importance of a play in a sports picture. Did the score change? How many yards were gained? What was the opponent's name?
> • Don't put words in a subject's mouth. Don't speculate about what a person might be saying. Find out what he was saying. Never make up quotes.

in a U-shape around one photograph, a quote caption might be used for that photograph but regular captions for the rest of the photographs on the spread.

16. Do not pad captions to fill space. If necessary, revise a layout to prevent padding.

17. Make caption lead-ins catch the reader's attention. The first three words are important. Consider boldfacing them or putting them in all caps. Use other graphic devices, including bullets and initial letters, to draw the reader's attention to the captions. Headlines for captions are another way to attract the reader.

18. Remember that sarcastic captions could damage someone's reputation. Be aware that a publication can be sued for false or malicious statements in captions as well as in copy.

19. Bury dates at a logical thought break in the middle of a caption or place them at the end of a caption. Vary placement to avoid monotony. Remember, do not use dates in the captions if all pictures on the spread are from the same date and that date is mentioned in body copy.

20. Avoid repeating copy block or scoreboard information in captions.

EXERCISES

1. Analyze the following captions, and list problems based on the rules for caption writing. In parentheses after each caption is a description of the subject of the picture.

    A.   Senior Jean Cochran beams during floor exercise. (Gymnastics)

    B.   A promising junior, Donna Osborne,

warms up before the meet. (Gymnastics)

C.   Robert Pickett maneuvers a takedown. (Wrestling)

D.   George Bucken ties up an opponent. (Wrestling)

E.   Stuart Jones enjoys activities as well as school work. (Student Council)

F.   Steve Hall enjoys assembly antics. (Pep Assembly)

G.   A business student utilizes the typing lab during his free time. (Business)

H.   Mrs. Conklin helps a clothing student find an outfit in a pattern book. (Home Ec.)

I.   Quarterback Bruce Lauren fades back, looking for a would-be receiver. (Football)

J.   Halfback David Sweetman picks up some yards. (Football)

K.   The bench outside the cafeteria seems to be a popular place for students with unscheduled time. (Hallways)

L.   After a long day students get together with their friends to go home. (Hallways)

M.   This skier attempts a jump and is successful. (Skiing)

N.   Students decorate their lockers according to their own taste. (Hallways)

O.   After getting off the lift, two skiers start down the run. (Skiing)

P.   Accompanying the choir is an additional responsibility and pleasure for Pat Eden. (Music)

Q.   Lab write-ups are very important in all science experiments. (Science)

R.   Grading test papers is a joy for Mr. Meyer. (Teachers)

S.   A student listens intently to Mr. Bush's advice. (Math)

T.   Sipping Cokes and girl-watching are

some of the many things accomplished during lunch. (Cafeteria)

U.   A serious scholar is found studying under a tree during lunch. (Lunch)

V.   The talent of modern dance is skillfully performed by Janet Johnson. (Physical Education)

W.   In deep thought, Teresa Billins ponders the answers to the chemistry exam. (Tests)

2.   Rewrite the above captions so that they include the necessary 5 W's and H. Add facts to make them complete. Use the copy counting guide of your yearbook or newspaper, or make each caption three lines in length, 50 characters per line.

3.   Using pictures from your files, select five on the same topic (e.g., basketball, choir, social studies) and write a caption for each. Be sure to vary your openers. Use the copy counting guide of your yearbook or newspaper, or make each caption three sentences in length, 16 picas wide in eight-point type.

4.   Following are several sets of caption leads. Each lead in each set appeared on the same yearbook spread. Analyze each set by making lists of weaknesses.

Set I (Basketball)
1.   Exhibiting good defense ...
2.   Displaying good shooting techniques ...
3.   Getting good height ...
4.   Showing great concentration ...
5.   With great form ...
6.   Determination is evident ...

Set II (Music)
1.   Collecting all the music at the end of the year is a tedious job ...
2.   Choir members enjoy participation in ...

3. Accompanying the choir is an additional responsibility and pleasure ...
4. Adding the finishing touches, Joyce Martin prepares ...
5. At the spring concert, Debra Wilson begins ...

Set III (French Club)
1. Listening intently, Loretta Weeks doesn't miss a word ...
2. Giving a humorous speech ...
3. Reciting the pledge ...
4. Linda searches for ...
5. Finding a new use ...

Set IV (Sophomores)
1. Sophomore Anne Berlin ...
2. Sophomore Bill Tatum prepares ...
3. Sophomore Kay Chapman starts ...
4. Sophomore Doug Mitts prepares ...
5. Sophomore David Martin snickers at an unknown joke with Doug at the end ...

5. Select a spread from last year's yearbook and rewrite the captions so they're all three sentences in length. Make the first sentence present tense, describing the action in the picture. The second sentence may be present tense if it's still describing the action. If it adds information that does not describe the action, put the second sentence in past tense. The third sentence should be a quote from someone in the picture.

6. Select two spreads from last year's yearbook and analyze each caption. Answer the following questions for each caption. If you answer no to any question, rewrite the caption to include the necessary information. Does the caption avoid telling the obvious? Does the caption supplement the copy with details without being wordy? Does the caption name

everyone recognizable in the photograph with complete first and last names and identifications? Does the caption name people from left to right without using the words left to right? Is the caption written in the proper tense?

Picture 1   *Picture 2*

7. Using the two photos pictured above, write three-sentence captions for each. Use the following information for your captions.

Picture 1: Who: Kameron Hall, forward, makes a five-foot jump shot against the Ritenour Huskies. Tyler Hale, Ritenour forward, awaits a possible rebound. When: February 28 in the third quarter with 4:20 left on the clock. Result: Your team takes a 37-35 lead after Hall's shot and goes on to win the game 65-61. Hall scored 32 points. What: Varsity basketball game against Ritenour. Where: At home. Why: To determine conference champion. Quote: "We had a really good season this year, and I had a lot of fun," Hall said. "It was so cool since we were able to get farther than the other varsity basketball teams. I was really pumped that we got all that attention, like all the announcements and the pep rally."

Picture 2: Who: Cody Hale, center, connects on a lay-up even though Kylie Weaver, Pattonville guard, tries to stop him. When: Dec. 15 in the second quarter with :03 left on the clock. Result: Your team ties the game at 27-27 and goes on to win 55-54. What: freshman game against Pattonville. Where: Away. Why: To complete the final game of the Pattonville tournament. Quote: "I broke with the ball and drove the entire length of the court," Hale said, "and then I just shot."

CHAPTER
fourteen

Advertising

Few school publications could survive financially without advertising revenue. Many staff members, however, do not design ads with the same fervor with which they write stories. Far too many ads in high school yearbooks and newspapers are simply complimentary ads that give the name, address, and phone number of the business.

The trend, however, is to use ads that help a business sell a product or service. All publications should use a design artist to create ads. Salespeople could then take the ad to the merchant and show how it would help sell the service or product.

To design an ad, the layout artist should arrange all the elements—illustrations, copy (headline, subhead, copy, price), and standing details (trademark, firm name and address, reply coupons)—in an attractive and interesting format.

Basic rules of advertising design are the following:

1. Decide how much space is to be allotted to each part of the ad.
2. Be sure the ad has balance. Ads, however, are not divided at the mathematical center. They are divided at the optical center—a point about five eighths of the way up the ad, which the eye normally chooses as the center of a printed surface. Put the major part of the ad near the optical center and build around that.
3. Arrange elements to create eye movement. Guide the reader from one part of the ad to the next.

Coupons are always effective ways to draw the reader into an ad. The word "free" is another way to get a reader to read an ad. The above ad from the Echo, Webster Groves High School, Webster Groves, MO, is effectively designed.

4. Make each ad distinctive. Do not design two fast-food establishment ads to look alike.
5. Keep ads simple and uncrowded. Some white space is pleasing.

6. Illustrations—either photographs or artwork—add to the appeal of an ad.

7. Vary type size for headlines, subheads, and body copy. Make sure type fits the allotted space.

8. Write copy that appeals to the reader. If possible, say that the sale is for a limited time, that the price is special, that the supply is limited, or that it's "in" to own the product. The main function of copy is to get the reader to take action.

9. Determine the 5 W's and H to be answered. Who will buy the product or service? What will cause him to buy it? Why should he buy? When, where, and how can he get it?

10. Ad design has six essential parts: the sales pitch (body copy), a major headline, minor headlines, statistics (address, phone number, name of business), artwork or photograph, and white space. All parts should be included to sell a product or service. A reader will visit a place of business if its ad promises to satisfy a need. That is why the sales pitch is so important to stress what need will be satisfied. Keep the copy brief and in sentence format. If a merchant advertises in more than one issue, try to change the sales pitch in each issue. The major headline—like any headline—should catch the reader's attention. It usually works best if it is a phrase. The minor headline may be a sentence. Sometimes it is the slogan of the business. It is permissible to use a different font than the one used in the main headline; however, be sure they complement each other. White space is important to make an ad appealing. Do not cramp copy and other elements inside a border. Give all elements breathing room. Keep the statistics near the bottom of the ad, and vary the size and typeface of each

➢ *Adding Features to Yearbook Ad Pages*

• *Bring the reader onto the advertising spreads in yearbooks by adding features about local hangouts, shopping malls, real landmarks, or possible places of employment.*

• *Make the features different in appearance each year. For example, they could be help wanted ads, they could be bio boxes about favorite hangouts, or they could be bio boxes about student employees. Stretch your mind and develop a different presentation for the features each year.*

• *Other possible feature topics might be how students spend their weekends—concerts attended, movies viewed, fast-food restaurants, video rentals, and professional sporting events attended.*

Full-page ads are appealing if well designed, as is the above ad in the Canary, William Allen High School, Allenton, PA. The gymnast's foot helps bring the reader into the copy.

statistic. The name of the business should be larger and bolder than other statistics.

Before designing an ad, the staff should conduct a survey to find out how much money students have to spend and what items they normally buy. It helps to find out the grade level of each person surveyed and whether the respondent is male or female. An example of a spending survey follows:

Grade level:_____ Circle: Male or Female

Circle the appropriate answers or fill in the blanks:

1. Do you have a job? Yes No
2. If yes, how much do you earn per week? _____
3. Do you get an allowance? Yes No
4. If yes, how much is your allowance per week? _____
5. Do you have a personal charge account? Yes No
6. Do you use your parents' charge account? Yes No
7. Do you have a checking account? Yes No
8. Do you have a savings account? Yes No
9. What is your total weekly income from all sources? _____
10. On the average, how much of that do you save? _____
11. Do you assist in making decisions on family purchases? Yes No
12. List three things that you regularly purchase (products or services).
    A. _____ B. _____ C. _____

> *Designing an Ad*
>
> • *All ads should be graphic and individualized.*
>
> • *Photos and artwork add to the appeal of an ad.*
>
> • *Avoid ads that do not sell a product or a service.*
>
> • *Avoid business-card type ads. Ads should be more than the name, address, and phone number of a business.*
>
> • *Spot color can increase an ad's appeal. Perhaps a merchant would pay for spot color in an ad, which would allow for additional spot color in the publication for no more cost.*

Questions may be much more inclusive than those in the preceding survey. You may want to know how much students spend per week on particular products such as records. The more information you have, the better able you will be to persuade a prospective advertising client to buy space.

Selling advertising is not easy, but it is easier if a designed ad shows the merchant how it will increase his business. If an ad salesperson goes to a merchant with nothing in hand, it is likely that she will sell nothing but a complimentary ad, and perhaps not even that. It is easy for most merchants to answer "No" when asked, "Do you want to buy some advertising?" Even if the salesperson goes prepared with details from a spending survey and with a predesigned ad, it is still likely that some merchants will say "No." The Bureau of Advertising of the American Newspaper Publishers Association has prepared a booklet that covers 20 basic objections that merchants have to purchasing advertising space and suggested answers that a salesperson might use to overcome resistance. Some of them follow:

1. I don't have any money to advertise.
    A. A smart merchant invests money in order to make money.
    B. The secret of successful advertising is consistency, not size.
2. You don't have a large enough circulation.
    Our circulation is concentrated in the trading area, and each reader is a potential customer for you.
3. Our neighborhood store doesn't need all that waste circulation.
    A. About one fifth of the population moves every year.
    B. Ads in newspapers have more local impact than ads in any other medium.
4. I didn't get any results from my last ad.
    A. Advertise items people want, at the time they want them, and in the price range they are willing to pay.
    B. Lack of results is not necessarily the fault of the medium. Consider the ad. Is it attractive?
5. It isn't the right time of year.
    A. Do you mean you are not selling anything now? I thought you were open every week of the year and wanted customers every day.

> **Creating an Effective Ad**
> • Create a catch-phrase that will grab the reader's attention.
> • Use display type of 24-point or larger for headlines.
> • Write a paragraph of copy to explain the product or service in 12-14-point size.
> • If possible, use a photograph with a caption to gain attention.
> • Include the essential information of name of business, address, telephone number, and any other information, such as e-mail address or fax number, that might be important.
> • Use graphics to draw the reader into the ad.

B.   There are people all year round.
6. People don't read ads.
    A.   Feature a benefit for your customers, and people will read it.
    B.   Readership studies prove ads are read if they contain something of interest to the readers.
7. I can't afford to use big space.
    A.   The importance of an ad is what is said and how it is said.
    B.   Many big businesses started years ago with small-space ads and increased the size of the ads as the business volume increased.

Regardless of the argument a merchant might use, it can be countered if the salesperson has done his or her legwork. The salesperson should know the facts: what products the store sells that would interest teenagers, what ads the store has placed in other area newspapers, how large an ad is necessary to display the product or service to be sold.

Be persistent. It may take more than one call on a merchant to sell the ad. A good salesperson goes back each time with a different pitch.

If possible, avoid ads as small as one-column inch. Even two-column-inch ads are too small to be effective. Larger ads benefit both the merchant and the publication. When pre-designing an ad, design two or three sizes to show the merchant how much more can be said in a larger ad. Small ads are generally name, address, and phone number ads. Larger ads can use more copy, illustrations, and headlines. Publications that use photographs of students in ads should obtain signed releases from the students and from parents if the students are minors.

Be aware of special promotions. Dances, Christmas, Mother's Day, graduation, and other special days or events attract advertisers such as florists, gift shops, restaurants, and formal wear stores. Plan issues of the newspaper around such

> **Tips for Selling an Ad**
> • Do not call on the phone. Make contact in person. It's more difficult for a store's manager to say no in person.
> • Go back again if the manager is not available the first time.
> • Create an ad before you go to the business and try to sell the manager on your idea.
> • Dress neatly and always be courteous in your approach. A smile and a handshake will probably be helpful.
> • Take all materials you need with you, including an ad rate sheet, a contract, a copy of your publication, sample ads, and any ads that the merchant has run previously.
> • Be positive. Don't approach a merchant and say something like "I don't suppose you want to buy an ad, do you?"

Advertising spreads in yearbooks can be enhanced by feature stories, as shown in the Paragon, Munster High School, Munster, IN. Note also that the staff uses three sizes of ads on the spread and that the lines separating the ads do not totally fill the space.

special events. Since yearbooks usually are delivered in the spring or late summer, they can seek ads concerning graduation (spring books) or back to school (late summer books)

Coupons are a good way to help merchants gain customers. They immediately tell the reader that he/she can save money. Staffs should urge merchants to run coupon ads, especially to introduce a new store or a new product/service.

All publications should obtain an advertising contract signed by the merchant that specifies the size and content of the ad the merchant desires. A contract obligates the merchant to pay the bill.

Each publication should develop its own contract. Many

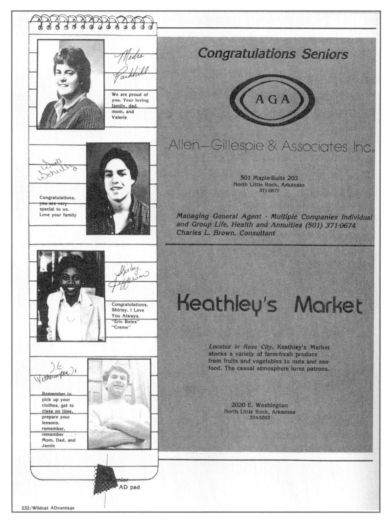

Personal ads by families of seniors bring additional income for the Wildcat, *Ole Main High School, North Little Rock, AR.*

have sliding rates based on the size of the ad and number of insertions. Others have standard rates regardless of size or frequency.

The business staff should mail bills to merchants immediately following publication of an ad. The billing form should show the date the ad ran and the total amount due. Either a copy of the paper or a tear sheet should be mailed with the ad. Some yearbook staffs give advertisers a copy of the book.

It is also a good idea to write to each advertiser at the end of the year, thanking him for his business and telling him that someone will be contacting him during the summer for the next school year.

Start a card file of advertisers, listing business name, address, phone number, contact person, and best time to contact. Keep a record of all contacts made during the year and of the merchants' responses. Some will say come back at a later date; a card can remind staff members to follow up.

A card file can also help reporters make price comparison studies. For example, a card file might list which stores in the area sold Levi jeans. From it the reporter could get the names, addresses, and telephone numbers and then visit all the stores on the same date to make a price comparison study. The date of the study should be noted in the report, and the reporter should be certain that all prices are regular prices. It would be unfair to use sale prices or discount offerings.

Just as the reporter can benefit from the advertising staff's card file to do a consumer report, the advertising staff can benefit from the consumer report. When the reporter has located the store with the best price, the advertising staff can contact that store's manager and suggest that she run an ad indicating the low price of the product.

Besides display advertising, many school publications also rely on patron ads. As the name implies, patrons buy space to indicate that they are supporters of the publication. Most patron ads run under a general heading, such as: "Good Luck, Yearbook Staff." Under the heading is a list of patrons who have donated money to support the publication. The list is generally names only, but sometimes addresses and phone numbers are included with a merchant's name. Many patron ads are sold to parents, but they usually want only their name listed in the ad. At $5 to $10 each, patron ads can mean a fair amount of additional revenue for staffs. Patron ads generally work best for special occasions, such as graduation. Many parents like to say "Best Wishes" to the graduates.

Some publications also run classified advertising and charge a certain price per line. Be careful of personalized ads. Hidden messages in them can sometimes be damaging to a person's reputation. Like April Fool's issues and gossip

➢ *Including Personal Ads in the Yearbook*

• *Personal ads— ads that feature greetings from relatives to students— are usually good moneymakers for yearbook staffs. These ads may include photographs of the student ranging from baby pictures to up-to-date pictures.*

• *Most personal ad spreads have greater reader appeal when the ads are mixed with other content, such as the index or feature stories.*

• *All ads must be attractively designed— even the ones with baby pictures. Vary the size and shape of each one, and vary the content to avoid monotony.*

columns, personalized classified ads should probably be avoided.

Regardless of the role advertising plays in their paper or yearbook, staff members of school publications need to realize the importance of advertising in society today.

Advertisers spend more than $130 billion annually in the United States. School publications can garner a share of the advertising market by working with local merchants and advertising agencies. A trend is for companies to turn their advertising over to an agency, which then designs and places the ads. The agency, of course, receives a commission.

Most companies use a logo or a phrase to identify their product. The phrase is often set to music to be used in commercials on radio or TV. Because of constant repetition, the consumer becomes so familiar with the phrase that he immediately knows the company being advertised without ever hearing its name. Most consumers today would readily identify "You deserve a break today" with the McDonald's fast-food chain and "It's the real thing" for Coca-Cola.

Obviously, the purpose of the advertisement is to sell a product. The buyer should not believe every claim an ad makes. Be aware of such generalized phrases as "best," "better," "a real bargain," and "it's right for you."

Buyers should also be alert to products advertised by a well-known person. The manufacturer is obviously using the "transfer" device, hoping to get the consumer to transfer her admiration for the personality to an admiration for the product.

Remember that advertising is a method of delivering a message from a business. Advertising can be expensive for some businesses. For example, an advertiser on television paid $1 million for a 30-second commercial during the sitcom *Seinfeld*. All publications need to have their own rate sheet to show a merchant. That way the merchant knows immediately how much an ad of any size will cost.

Be sure when accepting an ad from a merchant that all information in the ad is correct. Congress has passed laws requiring truth in labeling of all products, which helps to prevent false claims. The Federal Trade Commission and the U.S.

➤ *Planning an Ad Campaign*

• *Set ad prices, and create an ad rate sheet for every staff member.*

• *Train staff in proper sales techniques.*

• *Teach staff members how to fill out an ad contract.*

• *Have staff members sign up for the business or businesses they wish to contact.*

• *Pair staffers into teams if there are staff members who are shy about contacting businesses.*

• *Develop a sales packet that includes information on the number of readers, the student body's buying power, and where students spend their money.*

Food and Drug Administration help to regulate business, and in turn their regulation protects consumers.

Many publications include as part of their editorial policy what kinds of advertising they will or will not accept.

EXERCISES

1. Make a detailed study of two stores in your area. List all products that each store sells that would be of interest to teenagers. Design an ad for each store, pushing one product. Find out the manager's name for each store and attempt to sell your ad to him for either your yearbook or newspaper. If the manager of either store says that he does not advertise in school newspapers or yearbooks, ask why not?

2. Interview an employee of a local advertising agency. Ask him details of how to design and sell an ad. Ask for career information about advertising.

3. Clip, mount, and label 10 ads from daily newspapers. Analyze the effectiveness of each one.

4. Clip, mount, and label 10 ads from school newspapers. Analyze the effectiveness of each one.

5. Write a 200-word paper describing a product you have bought recently. Discuss your reasons for buying the product. Were you influenced by advertising of any kind?

6. Select a newspaper ad from a place of business and compare it with an ad for a similar product or business on television.

7. Conduct a market survey of your student body. Prepare a list of questions that will help you determine the needs of your student body.

8. Select one store in your community and design a 2-inch ad, a 4-inch ad, an 8-inch ad, and a 16-inch ad that will help sell the store's products.

➢ **The Advertising Contract**
• Complete two copies—one for the merchant and one for the staff.
• Include all information that should go in the ad, or attach camera-ready artwork.
• Indicate all costs.
• Include the name of the business, the billing address, and the phone number.
• Have both the salesperson and the merchant sign the ad.
• Indicate billing dates and any penalty for late payment.
• Include the staff's advertising policy on the contract.

9. Find five ads in past issues of your school newspaper and redesign them. Be sure that all essential parts are included in your new design, including statistics, a main headline, a secondary headline, artwork or photograph, and white space.

10. Create new business forms for your staff. Include a contract, stationery, business cards for salespeople, rate sheets, and billing statements. If you have computers, use a computer to create your forms. Create a logo for your newspaper or yearbook that can be used on all the forms.

➤ **The Rate Card**
• *Create one that is attractive in appearance. Consider putting the rate card on a card stock for durability.*
• *Be sure the rate card includes the distribution date(s) of your publication.*
• *Be sure the rate card includes the circulation figures for your publication.*
• *On the rate card, list awards the publication has received. This might help sell ads.*
• *Include all ad sizes and rates for all sizes.*
• *Include charges for any special services, such as reverse print, photographs, and color.*
• *Include information about camera-ready artwork.*
• *Payment information should also be part of the rate card. Do you accept a discount for ads paid in advance?*

Advertising Rates and Publication Dates 2002-2003
The Kirkwood Call

The Call is published 16 times a year at Kirkwood High School. Dates of publication are:

September 18
October 2
October 16
October 30
November 17
December 9
December 22
January 12
February 5
February 23
March 5
March 23
April 13
April 27
May 11
May 27

Dates are subject to change depending on school holidays or snow days.

Address all correspondence to:

THE KIRKWOOD CALL
801 W. ESSEX
KIRKWOOD, MO 63122

TELEPHONE: 314-213-6100
ext. 1415
FAX: 314-984-4412
E-Mail:
hallhom@gw.kirkwood.k12.mo.us

ADVERTISING RATES

Minimum advertising size: one column by 2 inches (1 x 2), or two columns by one inch (2 x 1)

OPEN RATE: $5.00 PER COLUMN INCH PER ISSUE (1-7 ISSUES)
PERIODICAL RATE: $4.50 PER COLUMN INCH PER ISSUE (8-12 ISSUES)
CONTRACT RATE: $4.00 PER COLUMN INCH PER ISSUE (13-16 ISSUES)

Sample Rates (price per issue)

	OPEN	PERIODICAL	CONTRACT
2 x 1	$10.00	$9.00	$8.00
2 x 2	20.00	18.00	16.00
2 x 3	30.00	27.00	24.00
2 x 4	40.00	36.00	32.00
3 x 3	45.00	40.50	36.00
3 x 4	60.00	54.00	48.00
4 x 4	80.00	72.00	64.00

DISCOUNT & TERMS

Five percent discount if ad is paid in advance of publication date. Credit customer terms are net 10 days after publication date. All accounts past due by the 10th of the following month will be assessed a 1 percent per month finance charge, which is 12 percent per year.

SERVICES

Artwork, typesetting and design are all included in the price of the advertisement. Excessive charges, special effects or photos are $10 each and reverses are $10 each. Advertisers may provide camera-ready slicks, or we can help you create your own advertisements. We have Macintosh computers and a Xanté printer. All copy much be received ten days prior to publication date.

ADVERTISING POLICY

The Call has the right to accept, reject, edit, or cancel any advertisement at any time. If a business pays for the advertising in advance of publication and the staff decides to cancel the ad, money will be refunded for remaining ads. Advertising shall be free of statements, illustrations, or implications that are offensive to good taste or public decency based on the opinion of the staff. Advertising shall offer merchandise or service on its merits, and refrain from attacking competitors unfairly or disparaging their products, services or methods of doing business. The staff may run political advertisements. The staff will not accept advertising that is racist, sexist, illegal for high school students, or violates other standard journalistic principles (libel, obscenity, invasion of privacy, disruption). Ads which the staff accepts are not an endorsement from the staff, the adviser, the administration, or the Kirkwood R-7 board of education.

---

11. Analyze the above ad rate schedule and create one of your own. Do not merely copy the one above.

CHAPTER

fifteen

Photography

It is a fun world, but not as simple as it looks. "It" is the world of photography, which begins with the selection of equipment. Many types of cameras are available.

Basically, a camera is made up of a lens, a shutter, and a film carrier. The lens focuses the image on the film while the shutter opens and closes, regulating the time during which exposure takes place, whether it is 1/500 of a second or 10 minutes.

The type of camera used most often for newspapers and yearbooks at the high school level is the 35mm single lens reflex (SLR) camera. One of the greatest advantages of the 35mm SLR is being able to see exactly what images will go on the negative, because it has a mirror that snaps out of the way during exposure.

Other advantages of the 35mm SLR are good negative size, easy handling, and the ability to use interchangeable lenses (wide-angle to telephoto).

The exposure of an image is controlled by the shutter, along with the aperture, which regulates the amount of light entering.

The shutter speed refers to how long the film is exposed to light. The most common shutter speeds on cameras today are $\frac{1}{1000}$, $\frac{1}{500}$, $\frac{1}{250}$, $\frac{1}{125}$, $\frac{1}{60}$, $\frac{1}{30}$, $\frac{1}{15}$, $\frac{1}{8}$, $\frac{1}{4}$, $\frac{1}{2}$, and 1 second. One second admits the most light, and $\frac{1}{1000}$ the least light. Note that the shutter speeds are multiples of approximately $\frac{1}{2}$ of each other; thus, $\frac{1}{30}$ lets in half as much light as $\frac{1}{15}$ or twice as much light as $\frac{1}{60}$. Some manual cameras also have a B (bulb) setting, which lets the user open the shutter for any length of time.

Page 12

SPORTS

TAKING THEIR BEST SHOT

*The photographer for the Hi-Spots, Tigard High School, Tigard, OR, cap-
tured the action at its peak in this soccer game. Great facial expressions
add to the photo's appeal.*

The f/stop, or aperture, refers to the amount of light that
enters the lens to strike the film. The lens has an iris
diaphragm to control the size of the opening in the lens. The
most common f/stops on today's cameras are f22, f16, f11, f8,
f5.6, f4, f2.8, and f1.8. The f22 admits the least light and f1.8 the
most. The "multiple of two" principle also applies to f/stops; f8
admits twice as much light as f11 and half as much light as f5.6.

Combinations of aperture and shutter speed give the correct exposure for the situation. When the shutter speed is
changed in one direction (up or down the scale), the aperture
must be changed in the opposite direction, and vice versa.
Suppose a light meter dictates a setting of f8 at $\frac{1}{60}$ of a second.
If the subject required a faster shutter speed, say $\frac{1}{500}$, the shutter
speed would be moved down two stops to f4 to have the same
exposure as f8 at $\frac{1}{60}$. In the same example, an increase in the
aperture to f22 would call for a three-speed decrease to $\frac{1}{8}$.

Obviously fast-action shots, such as in many sports, require a shutter speed of $\frac{1}{250}$ or more in order to freeze the action. Speeds from $\frac{1}{60}$ to $\frac{1}{125}$ are basically for normal motion, such as a person walking or eating.

Speeds of $\frac{1}{15}$ and below are rarely used in everyday situations. They are used for still photos and low-light conditions and require the use of a tripod. Generally a tripod should be used when the shutter speed is less than the length of the lens. A shutter speed of $\frac{1}{125}$ with a 200mm lens would require a tripod.

Several lenses are available for 35mm SLR cameras.

Normal lens. Ranging from 45 to 55mm, the normal lens has no magnitude according to human eyesight. This is the basic lens; it can be used for almost any subject and is limited only by the photographer's imagination.

Wide-angle lens. Wide-angle lenses from 24 to 35mm are as versatile as the normal lens. They are invaluable in tight spaces and are perfect when the photographer wants to get close to the subject. These lenses tend to distort the subject out of proportion. Lenses from 4 to 18mm are generally used for special effects. Some wide-angle lenses are good for group shots.

Telephoto lens. These magnifying lenses range from 75mm to telescopic and are used to cut down the distance between the subject and the photographer. Telephotos are useful to get closer to the action in sports.

Zoom lens. These lenses cover a range of magnification such as 35—75mm zoom or 100—200mm zoom. The zoom is great for composing a picture without moving around a lot, but it lacks the sharpness that can be achieved with a standard length lens.

Besides the shutter speed and the f/stop opening, two other variables affect exposure: film speed and available light.

Most users of 35mm cameras use Tri-X or T-Max film. Both are fast films that can be used in low light conditions. Plus-X, a medium film, works better in brighter light. Panatomic-X is a slow film and needs sunlight for greatest effectiveness.

➢ *Choosing a Photograph*

• Readers will choose color photos over black-and-white ones.

• Readers will choose photos of people in motion over ones where people are motionless.

• Readers will choose light photos as opposed to dark ones.

• Readers will choose photos with sharp contrast over ones with little contrast.

➢ **Photo Illustrations**

• By using a software program like PhotoShop, you can create a photo illustration.

• Be sure to label the photo as an illustration. The reader has the right to know if any photo has been altered for content.

• It is best to stick with simple subjects and easily recognized objects.

• Illustrations can be effective in color or black and white.

• It is possible to use an imperfect photo and create sharper detail. As long as the illustration retains the essential shapes, the designer can apply countless textures and patterns.

• Have a concept in mind before beginning the illustration.

Feature Photo

JAY HASTY, SENIOR, was crowned as the NW Homecoming Queen during the October 4 Homecoming game. Jill Scherzer and Traci Wilson, seniors, were the runners up. (Photo by Vince LaVergne)

Facial expressions grab the reader's attention. This photo from the Northwest Passage, *Northwest High School, Shawnee Mission, KS, captures the reaction at the moment of the announcement.*

Even with fast film, low-lighting situations indoors require use of a flash. If just a little extra light is needed, it is wise to bounce the flash off the ceiling or to the left or right to avoid the harsh shadows that flash units can create. It is even possible, if the photographer is wearing a white shirt, to bounce the flash off his shirt (not too close). That will provide enough light without creating the shadow effect.

When available light does not permit normal exposure, satisfactory results can still be obtained by pushing the film. To do this, underexpose by one stop and then push-process the film by using a film speed number that is twice the ASA speed of the film. For example, expose Tri-X film at a speed of 800 instead of its rated speed of 400. To push-process the film, increase the recommended development time by 50 percent. The instruction sheet that comes with each roll of film specifies which chemicals to use and proper times. Be aware that film underexposed one stop and push-processed for 50 percent more than the recommended time gives negatives with increased contrast and graininess. To get acceptable contrast in the prints, use printing paper of a lower contrast grade than is normally used.

T-Max film has made it possible to avoid pushing. It is possible to shoot pictures in dimly lit gymnasiums or on dark football fields. Because this film has a 3,200 ASA, it should not be necessary to push it. There is also a T-Max developer created for use with the film. The film should be processed promptly because of its high speed and sensitivity to environmental radiation. The film should also be loaded in subdued light.

Other changes in photography techniques are occurring because of desktop publishing. For example, a photographer can shoot a picture with a Xapshot camera, connect the Xapshot to a computer with a digitizer board, and view the photo image on the monitor. This image can be saved or transferred to other formats for later use. A Xapshot camera can completely eliminate the hassles of dealing with a photo lab. It records up to 50 images on a reusable floppy disk and offers precision point-and-shoot operation with a built-in flash and automatic exposure.

Scanners have also made it possible to scan a photographic image from any source into a computer for repro-

➢ *Keeping It Simple*
 • *Avoid cluttered backgrounds.*
 • *Avoid including objects that compete for the reader's attention, such as banners or sports equipment in group shots.*
 • *Eliminate clutter by using a narrow depth of field. This puts only the main center of interest in focus.*
 • *Focus on a single, dominant subject by moving in close.*

duction. The world of computers is changing photography just as it is changing design.

Regardless of the technology used, the key to a good photo is still composition.

Composition is an art. One of the first things a photographer must master is the ability to hold the camera steady. Some photographers grip their elbows to their sides to avoid camera movement that creates a blurred or out-of-focus image. Other rules of composition a photographer must learn include the following:

1. Move in close. This is especially important if you are not using a telephoto or zoom lens. How close is close? That, of course, depends on the subject, but you need to move in close enough to get the largest possible image in the viewfinder. Exclude everything that is not essential to the photograph. That often means moving in to four or five feet or even closer. Zero in on five people or fewer in ordinary situations. With more than five people it is difficult to get close. Again, it depends on the subject and the story that is being told.

2. Create a center of interest. Crowd shots seldom have a center of interest—just a sea of faces. Sometimes one person in the crowd is doing something to create a center of interest; for instance, one person cheering while everyone else is quiet. If there are two or more persons in a photo, be sure that they are close together, so that the viewer's eyes do not have to wander from one to the other. Also, be sure to keep the center of interest in the photograph. For example, if someone is putting a license plate on a car, don't leave the license plate out of the viewfinder.

3. Concentrate on faces when shooting pictures of people. Strong facial expressions can make a

➤ **Cropping Photographs**

• Crop closely to the center of interest, but don't crop so close that the reader can't tell where a moving subject is headed.

• Normally crop within two to three picas of the center of interest, unless the subject is moving.

• Remember the rule of thirds in cropping. Divide the photograph visually into thirds vertically and horizontally, and let the main action fall on the axis points. The main axis should never be in the middle of the photo.

• Vertical photos should be cropped to fit a vertical space, and horizontal photos should be cropped to fit a horizontal space.

> **Digital Photography**

By the turn of the century, the digital camera was rapidly changing photography techniques. Schools throughout the country were closing their darkrooms and capturing photographic images on smartcards with their digital cameras and then downloading the images directly into their computers. These digital cameras automatically recorded all the information about a picture, including such things as f/stops, time, and date. Once downloaded, the user could add additional information such as the names of people in the picture. This quickly gave the caption writer the needed information.

The photographer caught the action at a peak moment in the above photograph from the Eugenean, *South Eugene High School, Eugene, OR. Great facial expressions add to the photo's appeal.*

➢ Shooting
Basketball

➢ *Shooting
Basketball*

• *Poor light condi-
tions in some gyms
may make it neces-
sary for you to use a
high speed film
(3200).*

• *Shoot crowd
shots and player
reactions on the
bench from near
midcourt.*

• *Shoot rebound-
ing shots, shooting
shots, and defensive
shots from a side
corner using a
50/105 mm lens.*

• *Shoot under the
basket with a 24/35
mm lens for lower
angles.*

*The photographer gets the soccer players off the ground and still manages
to keep the ball in the picture in this effective shot from the* Kirkwood
Call, *Kirkwood High School, Kirkwood, MO.*

photograph come alive. Someone screaming,
laughing, or crying can create a visual mood
that is transmitted to the viewer.

4. Get people in action. Motion pictures are more
exciting than posed photographs.

5. Be aware of the various angles from which photographs may be shot. Instead of staying at eye
level, the photographer may achieve a much
stronger photograph by being above or below
the subject. A simple movement to the left or
the right may bring the subjects closer together.

6. Be aware of backgrounds. Shooting toward windows almost always creates a glare; get on the other side of the subject. Be careful of poles or trees seeming to grow out of heads.

7. Be aware of the rule of thirds. Divide the picture area into three roughly equal vertical and horizontal segments and position the subject at one of the four points of intersection. Never place the center of interest directly in the middle.

8. Use leading lines if possible. Fences, sidewalks, highways, railroads, paths, rivers, and other features can sometimes serve as leading lines to guide the viewer's eyes toward the center of interest. The angle at which the photograph is shot can make leading lines more effective.

9. Control the depth of field. Depth of field is the zone from the point closest to the camera to the point farthest from the camera that is acceptably in focus. The photographer focuses on one point, and an area in front and in back of that point is also in focus. Depth of field functions so that the zone of focus is in a ratio of about one to two. For example, if the area in focus in front of the point is three feet, the area in focus in back will be six feet. Shallow depth of field or great depth of field can have dramatic effects. With shallow depth of field, only a small portion of the picture will be in sharp focus and the photographer can eliminate unwanted detail—such as distracting background or foreground. A large lens opening gives shallow depth of field. For example, an f/4 aperture gives less depth of field than f/22. Use a small lens opening for greater depth of field.

10. Look for possible frames. Trees or other features can frame the subject to help draw the

> *Taking Group Shots*
> • *Focus on the faces—not on paraphernalia or formations. Leave musical instruments and sports equipment out of the group shots.*
> • *Arrange in even rows. If that's not possible, the shortest row should be in the back and the longest row in the front because the front row should be cropped at the waists.*
> • *Avoid arranging groups in odd shapes, such as in the shape of letters or standing on ladders.*
> • *If groups are so large that it is difficult to see all faces well, consider dividing the group in half and taking two group shots.*
> • *Individuals in the second row should be between those in the front row so all faces can be seen.*
> • *Be careful of background mergers, such as poles growing out of heads.*

➢ *Portrait Photography*

• In yearbooks, it is best to have all portraits consistent—consistent in head size and consistent in background.

• Choose backgrounds carefully. A pale blue or a pale gray tends to work best. Avoid outdoor backgrounds, which include trees and other nature settings. These only detract from the faces.

• Keep sizes small but large enough to see faces well. It is satisfactory to make senior portraits in a yearbook larger than undergrad portraits. However, don't make them so large that there is a noticeable difference.

• Keep the attire simple. For senior portraits in a yearbook, it is a good idea to have students dressed similarly, but this is not mandatory.

viewer's eyes. A picture is a two-dimensional copy of a three-dimensional world. The framing technique can help create a sense of depth.

11. Be aware of eye flow. The action should lead the viewer into and out of the photo at various points. Contrast may help a viewer go from a light area to a dark area. Contrast may also help separate the center of interest from the other areas.

12. Be sure secondary items in the photo do not distract from the center of interest. They should be subordinate to it.

13. Be sure to capture sharp images. The texture of a photo should mean that the subject is detailed and the images are sharp.

14. Look for the unusual. Look for student reactions to the action. Look for the mood of the people, but don't ask people to smile.

15. Limit the number of people in the picture. For best results, one to four is suggested. Avoid crowd shots.

16. Put people in your picture. Avoid scenic shots for yearbooks and newspapers.

17. Don't forget to turn the camera vertical for a vertical shot.

18. Use available light when possible. Flash often creates harsh shadows and reflections.

19. Crop effectively. Normally crop within one to three picas of the center of interest unless the center of interest is moving. If it is, then you need more foreground to show the direction of movement.

A good photographer must master darkroom techniques. All schools should have a darkroom with the following equipment for developing film: tank and reel, thermometer, scissors, can opener, clothespins, storage bottles, graduates, funnel, photo sponge, timer, stirring rod and container, and chemicals:

film developer (D-76, Microdol-X, HC-110, Acufine), stop bath, fixer, clearing bath, and wetting agent (Photo-flo).

Following are suggested steps for developing film:

1. Load film on reel. The film is sensitive to all colors of light, which necessitates loading it in total darkness. Secure the lid of the developing tank before turning on the lights.

2. Obtain chemicals. Be sure there is enough solution to fill the developing tank; otherwise, part of the negative may be underdeveloped. It takes about 10 ounces for one roll of film. Have beakers with all the necessary chemicals ready before starting. A minimum amount of time should be lost in changing from one solution to another.

3. Check the temperature of the chemicals. The normal range is 68° to 75°F. Warm or cool the solution as necessary. Consult the developer time-temperature chart that comes with the film.

4. Pour in the developer. Agitate for the first 30 seconds and every 30 seconds thereafter for the remaining time to assure even development.

5. Drain the developer. Developer should not be reused. Its purpose is to react with the film to make the latent image visible. It is the most important of the chemicals in the developing process. Some developers produce a fine-grained negative; others produce moderate-grained results. Some produce high-contrast negatives; others produce low-contrast ones.

6. Use water rinse or stop bath. The temperature range is 68° to 75°F. Fill the developing tank with running water, agitate it, and then empty it. Repeat this twice. If a stop bath is used, fill the tank, agitate it for 10 seconds, and then empty it. The purpose of a stop bath is to stop

➢ *Shooting Football*

• *Shoot from both sides of the field. All of the action does not happen on the side of the field where the home team's bench is.*

• *A motor drive could be useful, as could two cameras— one with a zoom lens (80 mm to 200 mm) and one with a longer zoom (300 mm to 400 mm).*

• *Use a wide-angle lens for a shot of a field goal kicker.*

• *Shoot sideline pictures. Capture the facial expressions of the players.*

• *Stay within 10 feet of the line of scrimmage and wait for sideline shots to come your way.*

Photography Terminology

- Aperture: The opening in the camera lens through which light passes.
- Depth of field: This is the distance range between the closest and farthest objects that are in focus in the camera lens. Photographers determine depth of field by the size of the aperture opening, the focal length of the lens, and the distance between the lens and subject. You can increase the depth of field by closing the aperture down (increasing the f-stop). To blur a distracting background, use a small f-stop number.
- F-stop: The size of the aperture, which controls the amount of light hitting the film. A large opening has a small number and a small opening has a large number.
- ISO: Stands for International Standards Organization to classify film speed.
- Push-processing: Used to increase film speed and contrast. Film is usually pushed to stop action in low light situations.

the development of the film and to clean it before using a hardening agent. Water may be used if a stop bath is not available.

7. Pour in hypo (fixer). The temperature range is 68° to 75°. Agitate about every 30 seconds. After 3 minutes the lid may be removed. The total time in the fixer depends on the brand used, usually about 10 minutes. The fixer hardens the film, makes it light-resistant, protects it from scratches, and clears the unexposed silver off the emulsion.

8. Drain the fixer. Fixer is reusable if it's not too old; pour it back into its container.

9. Start the final rinse. The temperature range is 68° to 75°F. Rinse for 30 minutes, with rapid changes of water. The time can be cut to 10 minutes if hypo clearing agent is poured on the film and allowed to remain for three minutes before the final rinse.

10. Soak the film in a wetting agent. The temperature range is 68° to 75°F. Soak the film for no longer than 30 seconds. A prepared solution may be used for many films.

11. Remove film from developing reel. Attach the film to a hanging negative clip (clothespins work well). Wipe both sides with a clean, wet sponge or wet your fingers in the wetting agent and lightly squeeze off excess liquid from the negative. Be careful not to scratch it.

12. Dry the film in a dust-free area. Attach a negative clip to the bottom of the film to prevent it from curling. Let negatives dry, cut the negatives into six-frame strips and put into glassine negative sleeves. Paper envelopes can scratch them. Handle the negatives by the edges at all times. A thumb print or a scratch will ruin a perfect picture.

When the film is dry, the next step in the photographic process is making the print. The photographer first makes a contact print of all the negatives on a roll of film. This provides a negative-size print of each photograph so that she can determine which she wants to enlarge.

To make a print, four liquids should be used: developer, stop bath, fixer, and water. The time needed in each liquid varies, but on the average a print is left in the developer for 1½ minutes, the stop bath for 10 seconds, and the fixer for two minutes if resin-coated paper is used. It takes five to ten minutes in the fixer if a fiber-based paper is used. Wash time

> **National Press Photographers Association**

Photo Ethics Policy
"As journalists we believe the guiding principle of our profession is accuracy; therefore we believe it is wrong to alter the content of a photograph in any way that deceives the public.

"As photojournalists, we have the responsibility to document society and preserve its images as a matter of historical record. It is clear that the emerging electronic technologies provide new challenges to the integration of photographic images. This technology enables the manipulation of the content of an image in such a way that the change is virtually undetectable. In light of this, we, the National Press Photographers Association, respect

(Continued)

in water is about four minutes for resin-coated paper and 30 minutes for fiber-based paper.

Before a print can be placed in the developer, it must be exposed, using an enlarger. The enlarger is a key element in obtaining good photographs. The lens of the enlarger has a diaphragm aperture control, like that on a camera lens, to regulate the amount of light. A very dark negative requires a large amount of light. Otherwise, the aperture opening is usually kept small to give the lens enough depth of field to offset any manual errors in focusing.

The best way to determine how long to expose an enlargement is to make a test print. Cover four fifths of an 8" x 10" sheet of paper, thus exposing only ⅕ of the paper. Expose each of the other ⅕'s for additional five-second periods until five different exposure times show on the sheet of paper. The first ⅕ will have a 25-second exposure, and the last ⅕ a five-second exposure. Select the one that looks the best and make a full print using that amount of time. Making contact prints and test strips can save both time and money.

To focus the print on the enlarger, it is probably easiest to open the f/stop to its widest opening, then close down as necessary. Be careful when using paper in the darkroom. It should be taken out of the box only when the lights are off, and the lights should stay off until the print is in the fixer. Printmaking is carried out in the illumination of a "safelight," which emits light of a color that does not affect the photographic paper. Even a safelight, however, cannot be used when loading film onto a reel; total darkness is required for that procedure. Lights may go on only after the film is enclosed tightly in the developing tank.

There are many tricks a photographer can learn to produce better prints, such as dodging (holding back printing light in selected areas where less density is desired) and burning in (increasing the exposure in selected areas where greater detail or density is desired). After a photographer makes his first print, he should analyze it to determine areas that need to be burned or dodged and then print it again. The determination of how much time and exposure to burn in is experi-

the basis of ethics: Accurate representation is the benchmark of our profession.

"We believe photojournalistic guidelines for fair and accurate reporting should be the criteria for judging what may be done electronically to a photograph. Altering the editorial content of a photograph, in any degree, is a breach of the ethical standards recognized by NPPA."

The mud-spattered game is over, and the photographer captures the fatigue of a football player in this photo from the Kirkwood Call, *Kirkwood High School, Kirkwood, MO.*

> ➢ *Taking the Sports Shot*
>
> • *Getting good action shots in sports takes time. Photographers must stay for the entire game.*
>
> • *Use high-speed film, such as T-Max 3200 or Neopan 1600. These films at least triple the speed, and if the photographer pushes these films, an even sharper image will be created.*
>
> • *Observe the event before beginning to shoot. This will let the photographer know who the key players are and where the action will be.*
>
> • *Know the rules of the game.*
>
> • *Work in three-person teams. One photographer can shoot sideline reactions, another can focus on where play begins, and a third can focus on where play ends.*
>
> • *Shoot a lot a film. It takes more than one shot to get that perfect picture.*

mental. Burning in allows the photographer to control the subject matter in a photo. He can emphasize what is important and eliminate what is not. Sometimes it is necessary to burn in the corners and edges of photographs when the backgrounds are light and distract from the center of interest. Most burning in can be accomplished by the photographer moving his hands under the enlarger lens.

After a print has been correctly exposed once, the photographer should form an opening with his hands that will

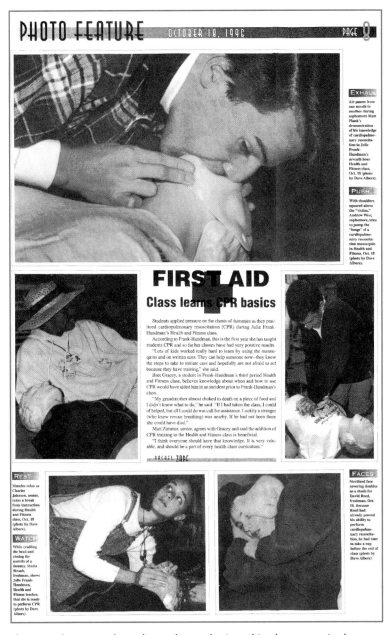

A strong dominant photo draws the reader into this photo story in the Kirkwood Call, *Kirkwood High School, Kirkwood, MO. Note the caption headings, which serve as entry points into each caption.*

allow additional exposure to reach the light areas. The photographer should keep his hands moving slowly so the burned-in area blends into the rest of the print area. It is also

94   sPorTs

Freestyle biking is an unusual topic to cover in most yearbooks. The photographer from the Lair, Shawnee Mission Northwest High School, Shawnee, KS, makes the sport look dangerous and exciting for the reader as he captures the action at this height.

possible to use an opaque board with small holes cut in it. Keep the board moving while you give some areas of the print additional exposure time.

The photographer can also use her hands for dodging, but it is also possible to make a dodging tool with thin wire and mounting board. Several of these are necessary in order to have different sizes. Attach the wire to the end of the board with masking tape. Move the board slowly as you dodge the area desired. If you don't, the board's shadow image will be burned into the photo. Dodging should be done during the initial exposure. Burning is a step after the initial exposure. Photographers need to practice and experiment until they know how many seconds of exposure will result in a correct dodge.

Once a photo has been dodged or burned, the photographer may still improve print quality by spot toning. By using spot-tone dyes and a fine camel hair brush, a photographer can remove lint and dust spots from a photograph. Spot-tone dyes come in various shades, including black, gray, warm black, brown-black, and blue-black. Use these dyes carefully. Too much of a dye in one spot can ruin a photograph.

These and other tricks are best learned through experimentation.

Using filters can also help improve prints. Filters with a good multicontrast paper can make a lot of difference in the quality of a print. Both Kodak and Ilford have multicontrast papers and filter sets. Kodak's filters come in holders that are easily attachable beneath the lens of any enlarger. Kodak I is a set of five filters, ranging from 1 to 4 in half increments. This set is not speed-rated, which means that the addition of each filter requires a new exposure test to determine the change in exposure. Kodak II, an 11-filter set, is speed-rated. If a photographer uses filters 0 to 3, no change in exposure is needed. The 4 to 6 filters require one stop more in exposure. In both sets, the low-numbered filters lessen contrast, and the high-numbered-filters increase contrast. Learning to use filters requires experimentation with the enlarger's f-stops and timer. Filters must be kept clean if they are to be effective. A photo editor should devise a method of checking out the filters to be sure that each photographer using them keeps them clean.

All aspiring photojournalists should keep the following pointers in mind:

> **Taking Care of Problems**
> • Eliminate blurry photos by using faster shutter speeds to stop action, by cleaning the lens regularly, and by holding your breath while shooting.
> • Eliminate streaks, scratches, and dust on negatives by keeping the darkroom clean.
> • Eliminate out-of-focus photos by holding your breath when shooting, by working with manual and auto focus to decide which works best for different situations, and by carefully focusing the enlarger.
> • Develop film correctly by being sure you have the right times and temperature for your film and the right chemicals.
> • Make test strips. Change the f-stop and the time when printing to determine which time and f-stop gives you the best print.
> • Reshoot when necessary.

1. Good photographic coverage demands planning.
2. Photographic schedules should be set up with the editors as far in advance as possible.
3. Group pictures are best shot against a plain background.
4. Carry your camera at all times. You never know when that once-in-a-lifetime shot will occur.
5. Pictures must communicate. Every shot must tell a story.
6. Good portraits depend on posing, lighting, printing, and cropping.
7. Photographers must not be afraid of people. Shy photographers usually lack the aggressiveness necessary to get close to the subject(s).
8. The principal parts of a picture are subject, foreground, and background. If the principal subject is far away, introduce elements of interest into the foreground to keep the picture from being dull.
9. Moving objects should be moving into, not out of, the picture.
10. To make a figure look tall, place it high in the picture composition; to make it look small, place it low. Never crowd a stout figure into a tight setting.
11. Strive for a full range of tones in the final print, from clear white to deep black.
12. Have the urge to experiment. Continually practice with a camera until it becomes a natural extension of the eye.
13. When staging pictures, always take several shots so you will have several to choose from. Then you can weed out those shots in which people yawned or shut their eyes.

Those are the basics. Through experimentation, the basics can be fine-tuned. Photography is a fun world. Picture ideas are everywhere. Make those ideas come to life through print photography. If you want to be a photojournalist, you need to know the difference between a photographer and a photojournalist. A photographer is one who takes pictures. A photojournalist is one who records events with the camera as well as with words. A good photojournalist writes down information about each picture she takes. That way the caption writer can help record history as it happens. A good photograph is enhanced by a good caption. A photojournalist gets the names of the people she photographs at the time she takes the picture. She also jots down notes about the event—when and where it took place. She gives the caption writer more than the obvious.

EXERCISES

1. Analyze the last issue of your newspaper. Point out the strengths and weaknesses of each photograph.

2. Analyze the last issue of your high school yearbook. Select 10 photographs that you think need improving and tell how you would improve them. Select 10 photographs that you think are outstanding and tell why they are outstanding.

3. Select 10 photographs from your school's morgue (a file of clippings and photographs of past issues) and crop them to emphasize the center of interest.

4. Select a topic for a photo essay, such as high school life before the first bell of the day or during the lunch hour. Shoot a roll of film for the topic. Develop and print the photographs. Design a layout using at least five of the photographs, and write copy to further develop the topic. When you are finished, you will have a photo essay. Use the design techniques discussed in Chapter 12 for your essay. A yearbook spread is essentially a photo essay on one topic.

5. List the important elements of photo composition.

6. Explain the term depth of field.

7. There are constant changes in the field of photography. Visit your local photo store and talk to the manager about the latest developments in photo technology from types of film to types of developer to types of paper. Write a paper on your findings.

8. Obtain an issue of one of the following magazines: *American Photographer, Photographic, Popular Photography, Life, Time, Newsweek, National Geographic, Sports Illustrated.* Clip 10 photographs from the magazine and write a paper explaining what composition techniques the photographer used to make it a good photograph.

9. What is the difference between a photographer and a photojournalist?

10. Cut examples of dynamic photos from other sources and create a bulletin board display. Add your own photos to this display by selecting a photo of the week.

CHAPTER
s i x t e e n

Broadcast Journalism

It's a different world from print journalism, but in many ways it's the same. Broadcasters must be responsible for what they put on the air, they must possess a sense of ethics, and they must write clearly.

One of the major differences is that broadcasters must also be able to speak clearly. Some poor speakers have become successful in broadcasting, but either they have a fantastic personality or they have already established themselves in another field. The latter is particularly true among sports announcers, many of whom played the sport before becoming broadcasters. Their knowledge has qualified them to be broadcasters even though they may not have great speaking voices.

The key to broadcasting is to be able to communicate with the listener, just as the writer must communicate with the reader. Successful broadcasters usually show great warmth and poise, have an expert knowledge of their subject, possess a bit of wit, and have the ability to ad-lib. Along with those qualities, they must be enthusiastic about their work, and they must have writing ability. Although some announcers allow others to write for them, most broadcasters will tell you that a combination of written and verbal skills generally brings more success.

As in newspaper and magazine writing, the most important part of a broadcast news story is the lead. The lead in broadcast news is much like a headline in a newspaper: It tells the audience what the story is going to be about.

The single-feature lead, in which the writer emphasizes the most important part of the story at the beginning, is one of the most common. The most important part is usually the *what* element. Be straight and to the point. Next in importance is generally the *who*; if the story centers around the *who* element, it will be the first mentioned. The *when* element must be as current as possible. For instance, if the story happened at 7 a.m. and you are broadcasting at 11 a.m., it would probably be better to say *this morning* rather than *7 a.m.* Don't forget to include the *where* of an event if it is not clear to the listener. The *why* is usually left for last because it takes time to explain why something happened.

Another type of lead is the several-feature lead, sometimes called the umbrella lead or the blanket lead. It is like a several-feature lead in a newspaper story, covering more than one item.

> The school board ruled on three major issues last night.

The listener has been made aware that he will be hearing about three issues rather than one.

The third type of lead is the chronological approach, which tells a story in chronological order.

> The varsity football squad defeated Lindbergh last night, 21-0. The team scored its first touchdown on a pass play from quarterback Bill Johnson to right end Courtenay Smith. The second score came in the third quarter on a 21-yard scamper by tailback Bob Bright, and the third score came two minutes later when Joe Blank intercepted a pass and returned it 75 yards.

Avoid question leads. Save them for commercials. It is also best to avoid beginning with a name, unless the person is well known. Many listeners do not listen carefully, so if you start with a name the listener may miss it. Start with a person's title or tell why he/she is in the news.

➤ *Fundamentals of Good Reporting*
• *Good broadcast reporters must learn to work within a time frame. Newscasts cannot run overtime, nor can they run too short.*
• *Good broadcast reporters will learn to ad-lib to add to a newscast, if necessary, without making it look as if they are just trying to fill time.*
• *Good broadcast reporters will establish a regular beat for obtaining news, just as the print journalists do.*
• *Good broadcast reporters will develop good interviewing techniques to get the information without stumbling or searching for words.*

A 17-year-old boy from Mehlville died last night when his car crashed into a tree. Henry Tudor was on his way home from the Prom.

Once you have your lead, the rest of the story should flow smoothly. Keep in mind these general guidelines:

1. Be sure to attribute comments. The best attribution is *says*. Note that you use the present tense to make the story seem current.

2. It is difficult to use direct quotes in broadcast newswriting because the listener cannot hear the quote marks. Avoid using the *quote, unquote* method. Rather, use such expressions as *Those were his exact words*, or *That's the way she said it*, or *Quoting her exactly*. Be sure not to take quotes out of context.

3. Paraphrases or indirect quotes probably work better than direct quotes. You should attribute paraphrases. It is generally possible to give the essence of what a person said without quoting exactly.

4. Write the story in your own words. Don't copy it from another source, such as the daily newspaper.

5. Keep sentences short. Be as brief and concise as you can.

6. Eliminate most adjectives and adverbs. Time is of the essence in delivering a news story.

7. Write the way you talk. Your writing should have a natural, conversational flow.

8. Don't be afraid to repeat words two, three, or more times, if necessary. In newspapers and magazines it is helpful to use synonyms, as the reader has a chance to go back and reread a story, but in broadcasting the listener does not have the opportunity to hear the story again. Repeat the most significant facts of the story

> Types of Broadcasts
> • A live broadcast occurs as the event happens. This requires the reporter to ad-lib the information he or she presents.
> • A delayed broadcast means a tape is made as the action occurs, and then the tape is incorporated into the broadcast at a later time.
> • A good interview should be part of both types of broadcasts. Eyewitness accounts are usually more interesting than an account from a third party who did not view the action occurring.

Growth of the Electronic Media

• Alexander Graham Bell discovered in 1876 that human speech could be carried by wires through the air.

• In 1896, Guglielmo Marconi discovered that sound could be transmitted without the aid of wires. His discovery led to the invention of the radio.

• The country's first radio station was established as KDKA in Pittsburgh in 1920.

• The first network, the National Broadcasting System, was established in 1926.

• Regular scheduling of television programs began as early as 1939.

• The first political conventions to be covered live by television were in 1948.

• The first successful communications satellite, Echo I, was launched in 1960. This successful launch created a spurt in cable television throughout the 1970s and 1980s.

• By the mid-1990s, the Internet had become an important part of American businesses and schools as schools used telephones, modems, and computers to send electronic mail and to do research.

toward the end, so listeners who missed them at the beginning can hear them again.

9. Avoid using the words *former* and *latter*. The listener can't necessarily recall which was the former and which was the latter.

10. It is acceptable to begin stories with *a, an*, or *the*, but try to add variety to your openers.

11. Although newspapers and magazines do not use contractions except in quotes, contrac-

➢ Interviewing Techniques

• Live interviews must move along rapidly without hesitations by the reporter. Avoid ums, ohs, *and* ahs.

• If it is not a live interview at the time of an event, research your topic before conducting the interview. Think about possible questions before the interview begins.

• Never ask questions that can be answered yes *or* no.

• Address the subject by name frequently.

• Do not allow the interviewee to digress from the topic.

• Introduce the person being interviewed at the outset, and conclude the interview by giving the name of the individual again.

tions are acceptable for broadcast stories. People talk in contractions, and broadcasting should sound as if you are carrying on a normal conversation.

12. It is permissible to use *us* and *our* in stories. The announcer is part of the community, so it is better to say, *Our school taxes are going up* than to say, *Your school taxes are going up.*

13. Like printed news stories, broadcast news is written in active voice, not passive. *The pie hit the principal* rather than *The principal was hit by the pie.*

14. It is possible to mix verb tenses in broadcast writing as long as the sentences make sense. Also, write in the present tense whenever possible. Use such phrases as *moments ago, just before noon,* or *this afternoon.*

15. Avoid using abbreviations in broadcast newswriting, except for such abbreviations as Mrs., Mr., and Dr., which the announcer would read as full words. If you do use abbreviations, use hyphens between letters and numbers that you want pronounced separately.

U-S, U-N, C-B-S, F-B-I, N-double-A-C-P.
The telephone number is 2-4-7-8-1-9-7.
The Pioneers won 14-to-6.
She lives at 8-0-1 West Essex.
By 1999 there will be a housing boom.

16. Numbers pose special problems for the announcer. Write numbers so that the announcer can read them easily. Write out as words the numbers one through nine and the number eleven. For 10 and 12 through 999, use arabic numerals.

one, three, eleven
10, 220, 651, 999

For all other numbers, use word-numeral combinations.

> one-thousand-10, 26-hundred-37, 123-thousand-nine,
> 338-billion-999-thousand-eleven

17. Help your listeners understand numbers by relating them to things with which they can identify. For example, 310 yards is about the length of three football fields.
18. Spell out symbols.

    149-dollars, nine dollars—not $149, $9
    12 cents—not 12¢
    99 percent—not 99%

19. Spell out words that deal with measurements or amounts.

    eleven inches, nine feet, 73 yards

20. Except for the word *first*, it is acceptable to use *st, nd, rd*, and *th* after numbers used in addresses and wherever else an ordinal number might be used.

    23rd Congressional District
    29 29th Street
    17th place

21. Round off numbers to make them easier to understand. It is okay to say *about 1,000* if the number is 1,002, or you can use words like *just under, nearly, close to,* or *around.* Then the listener knows that you are not using exact amounts.
22. When reporting times, avoid using *a.m.* and *p.m. This morning* or *yesterday afternoon* sounds more current. Write times as you do numbers when you use specific times.

10-30, or nine-30.

23. Sports times follow the same rules as other times.

Mike ran the mile in four-minutes-13-seconds.

24. Punctuation in broadcast newswriting is limited to the period, the dash, the question mark, and the comma. Use three periods to indicate a pause. A double hyphen is often used instead of parentheses. Many writers use three periods instead of a comma to help the announcer see that he is supposed to pause.

H. L. Hall ... journalism teacher ... was fired this morning.
Although they scored 79 points ... the Pioneers still lost last night.

Note that the first example uses the passive voice. It would have been better to say:

The school board fired H. L. Hall ... journalism teacher ... last night.

25. It is not possible to use copyediting or proofreading symbols in correcting broadcast writing. To correct a typographical error, strike out the word or sentence completely and type it over correctly.
26. Use phonetic spelling for difficult-to-pronounce words. Example: isentropic (I-sen-trop-ik)
27. Write for the ear. Avoid long, complex sentences that will confuse the listener. Keep in mind the Easy Listening Formula: Avoid more than 12 two-syllable or more words in a sentence.

28. Make sure the script flows wells from one point to the next. You must use transitions that guide the listener along the way. If you are offering examples, use: *for example, for instance, to show this, as an illustration.* If you are showing conclusions use: *therefore, thus, we find, to sum up.* If you are showing an argument continuing, use *furthermore, in addition, to continue, moreover.* To show contrasting ideas, use: *but, on the other hand, in contrast, nevertheless.* To show sequence, use: *first, next, furthermore, to begin with.* To show time relation, use: *before, after, meanwhile, at the same time.* To show effects, use: *therefore, as a result, accordingly, the consequence is.* To show causes, use: *because, this leads to, since.* To show meaning, use: *this means, we find, this suggests, this implies.*

29. Inject an appropriate amount of personality and spirit into your script. Do this by writing in active voice and by using the right adjectives and adverbs. Be serious if your subject matter is serious, but be light and lively if your subject matter is light and lively. You do this also by sounding natural. That is why contractions are acceptable. Say "I'm trying" instead of "I am trying."

30. Avoid causing sibilance. A series of words that begin with or contain the letter "S" often causes a hissing sound.

31. Always read scripts out loud after writing them; you will frequently hear problems that you didn't see as you read silently.

Once you know the style for your scriptwriting, you need to establish a format. A suggested format is to divide your page into two columns. Put instructions (video and/or audio) in the left column and the dialogue in the right column. Include names of announcers, directions for music, sound and/or visual effects in the left column, double-spaced and written in all

> ➢ *The Five W's and the Four C's*
> • *Just like print journalists, broadcast reporters must answer who, what, where, when, how and why in all stories. However, when and where are more often the lead in broadcast stories than they are in print ones.*
> • *Broadcast reporters, as well as print journalists, should also be concerned with correctness, clarity, conciseness, and color. Being correct the first time is important in any type of journalism, but it is especially important in broadcasting. Making a correction of an error in a later broadcast is not like making a correction in a print medium. Some studies have shown that 90% of all corrections on the airwaves are for a different audience—not the same listeners who heard the mistake in the first place.*

caps. Underline directions for music and sound and/or visual effects. Everything but the dialogue should be written in all caps. Write the dialogue in caps and lower case.

News should be written in a conversational style. Writers also need to learn the proper terms, including the following:

> *Actuality*—field recording made by audiotape or videotape of events or interviews.
>
> *Slug*—word used to identify a news story. The slug goes at the top of the page with the reporter's name and date of broadcast.
>
> *Bite*—portion of an interview used in a news program.
>
> *Sound bites*—portions of a videotaped interview used in a news program. These are like quotes in a printed story.
>
> *Package*—story videotaped in the field and put together with the reporter's narration. A package includes sound bites and narration.
>
> *Track*—portion of narrated field report usually written out and recorded in the newsroom.
>
> *Bridge*—brief transition between one element of a story and something else. Bridges are used to create continuity, and they are often tracks.
>
> *Lead*—the beginning of a story meant to catch the viewer's or listener's attention. Leads are like the headline of a newspaper story. They are usually no more than 10 to 12 words in length.
>
> *Standup*—a videotaped or an audiotaped section of a package made by a reporter on location.
>
> *Closer*—the way a reporter ends a package. It serves as a wrapup to the story.

You should also be familiar with the following commonly used terms in radio and television production:

on mike	performer speaks at microphone
off mike	performer speaks away from microphone

> ➢ *Qualities of a Good Announcer*
>
> • *Must have a good speaking voice. It may be high or deep, but it should not be breathy or adenoidal.*
>
> • *Must have good enunciation. Clear articulation is important.*
>
> • *Avoid stressing the last syllable of a word or the last word of a sentence.*
>
> • *Create "melody" when reading a story. "Melody" is created by the proper stress on words and by proper pronunciation of words.*
>
> • *Keep a moderate voice level. Avoid emotion unless you are reporting live at an emotional scene. Even then, try to avoid an excited, high-pitched voice. Let the impact of the news, rather than the pitch of the voice, determine the importance of a story.*

A Few Broadcast Style Rules

• Avoid starting a lead sentence with a name. Most listeners are half-listening ones. They will probably miss the name at the beginning.

• Use pronouns sparingly. It's hard for the listener to refer back to he or she, especially if the story is about more than one person.

• The best attribution is said. Avoid words like insists, admits, and charges. They border on being the broadcaster's opinion.

• Avoid saying a thousand because it sounds like eight thousand.

• Use only familiar abbreviations like U-N for United Nations or U-S for United States. Do put the hyphen between each letter as shown so the broadcaster will pronounce the abbreviation correctly.

• Spell unusual words phonetically so the broadcaster will pronounce them right on the air.

• Signal the listener that a quote is coming up. Quotes tend to slow a newscast, but they still add color to a story, so they should be used.

• Use informal time references. Today, Tomorrow, and Yesterday, are better than Tuesday, Wednesday, or Monday.

fading on	performer moves toward microphone
fading off	performer moves away from microphone
filter mike	performer sounds as if he is on the telephone
blend	more than one sound heard at same time
fade in/fade out	making sound volume greater or smaller, or in television the picture

➤ *Electronic News Gathering*

• *Domestic satellites, cable, fiber-optic communications, and laser beams became part of broadcast terminology beginning in the 1970s, and by the 1990s cyberspace and the Internet also had become part of the terminology.*

• *The Federal Communications Commission allowed satellite transmission beginning in 1972.*

• *Pay television via cable began in 1976 by Time Inc.'s Home Box Office subsidiary. Cable TV developed rapidly in the late 1970s and continued its growth throughout the 1980s and 1990s.*

	slowly forms from a blank screen or slowly disappears to a blank screen
up and out	volume rises and then fades out
cut or switch	rapid alternation from one sound to another, or in television a transition from one picture to another
sound effects (SFX)	types of sound effects to be used with story
carts	cartridges with actualities or interviews to be used in a radio news broadcast

The following terms are also part of television production:

dissolve	as one picture fades, another is created
superimposition	one picture imposed on another for brief period
wipe	picture is eliminated from a particular direction (vertical, horizontal, diagonal)
split screen	separate images on each half of the screen
film and slides	film clips or slides keyed to a script
key	one image inserted over another—words over a picture
voice over (VO)	announcer's voice heard as film is being shown
O/C or live	on camera; the copy is being read live in the studio
Full CG	use of a caption (character generator)
SOT (sound on tape)	both sound and video come from the tape
remote	a broadcast directly from the field. Live remote refers to a live broadcast from the field
TRT (total running time)	total time a tape runs

418

The following terms are kinds of camera shots. On scripts, the initials for the types of shots are usually used in the directions column on the lefthand side.

extreme close-up (ECU)	face fills screen
close-up (CU)	shot of face and neck
medium close-up (MCU)	shot of face and upper part of body
medium shot (MS)	shot of an individual or small group
full shot (FS)	full view of announcer
extreme long shot (ELS)	setting and general area shown
2 shot, 3 shot	either two or three people shown
over the shoulder (OTS)	shot from behind, above the performer's head
surveying pan (SP)	camera passes (pans) across scene
cut in (CI)	camera moves in for close-up detail
cut away (CA)	camera moves to a different scene
zoom in (ZI)	camera lens moves in close
zoom out (ZO)	camera lens moves away from a person or object
reaction shot (RS)	camera shows reaction of someone to some event or another person

All of the preceding terms are important to commercial writers as well as scriptwriters.

When writing a commercial, you must remember to include something to attract the attention of the viewer or the listener so he will not walk away during the commercial. You must also stimulate a desire to take action and buy the product. There are several techniques a commercial writer should use. First, she needs to create a scenario, a scene in which one character participates or in which various characters interact with each other. Sound effects and music may be used. Second, she needs to create a direct pitch. Body language and facial expressions can help create the sales pitch in television commercials. Third, she should add a jingle or a slogan to help sell the product. Jingles use music and rhymes. They should be catchy so they are memorable. A successful commercial speaks to the audience in three ways: It shows them, it talks to them, and it sings to them. The showing is done in the scenario, the talking is done in the direct pitch, and the singing is done in the jingle.

The average television commercial costs $200,000 to $250,000 to make, and it costs even more to air depending on the program, the time it airs, and the program's popularity. Super Bowl commercials cost nearly $1 million for 30-second spots.

> *Creating the Television Story*
> • *Use graphic devices to add interest to the announcer's reading of a story.*
> • *Headlines can create interest.*
> • *Showing live footage can create interest.*
> • *Using split screens that show two or more scenes, using rear projection, and changing camera angles can create interest.*
> • *Use still photos of news personalities or use logos to help illustrate a story.*
> • *Maps, charts, graphs, and diagrams can also add extra dimension to a story.*
> • *Zooming in and out on the announcer can also add interest as long as it is not overdone.*

EXERCISES

1. From the last issue of your school newspaper, select three stories and rewrite them in broadcast style.

2. Write a paper comparing and contrasting newspaper style with broadcast style.

3. Rewrite the following story in broadcast style in 150 words or less.

SNAGOV ISLAND, ROMANIA—Hopes have been raised that the headless skeleton of Dracula, long missing from his tomb here, may turn up next year in a fresh excavation beneath the floor of Snagov Chapel.

Such development would be at least as interesting to lovers of vampire fiction as to archeologists and historians. Perhaps the greatest beneficiary would be the Romanian government, for which Dracula, thanks to his attraction of foreign

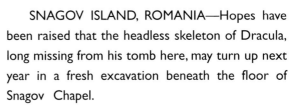

tourists, has become an important national asset. Touristic parallels have been drawn between Dracula and the Loch Ness monster.

The location of Dracula's bones would at least settle an old controversy among concerned scholars regarding a somewhat obscure period of Romanian history during the Byzantine period.

Prince Vlad of Wallachia, who lived 1431-76, sometimes used the nickname "Dracula," and the name stuck. His father's name was "Dracul," meaning dragon or devil, and "Dracula" means son of a dragon or devil.

But Dracula was also given a nickname by which he is much better known in Romania today—"Vlad Tepes," meaning "Vlad the Impaler." The 16th-century accounts describe him as having had thousands of people slaughtered, most by slow impalement on upright stakes.

Dracula is supposed to have died at the age of 45 in one of his many battles with the Turks, who carried off his head on a pike for public display in Constantinople. The rest of his body is believed to have been taken by Romanian orthodox monks to their monastery here at Snagov, a wooded island about one mile long in a large lake 15 miles north of Bucharest.

He is believed to have been buried under a heavy stone slab set in the floor directly in front of the chapel altar, possibly to facilitate prayers for his exceptionally troubled spirit.

In 1931 Snagov Island was extensively excavated and many skeletons were found (some buried upright where they had been impaled) but in the grave supposedly belonging to Dracula, only ox bones and some very old Romanian artifacts were found.

Another unmarked grave near the door of the chapel contained human bones, some scraps of red

➢ Skills of
Producers
• Be a good com-
municator and an
active listener.
• Be enthusiastic.
• Know your
audience.
• Know how to
write.
• Resist the ten-
dency to do every-
thing yourself.
• Write teasers
that will capture the
viewer's attention.
• Set the tone by
determining style and
shaping content.
• Seek the truth.

silk clothing, and some jewelry bearing the emblem of Dracula, all of which were taken to Bucharest Historical Museum, from which they mysteriously disappeared. One theory is that the body was disturbed by Dracula's enemies at one time and moved away from the altar to the second grave. The disappearance of the bones and the ornaments from the museum has not been explained. The latest theory was described by Sebastian Buchiu, a 27-year-old theological student, who lives with two monks on Snagov Island.

"The new thinking," he said, "is that Vlad Tepes is really still down there, but deeper than they dug before. The grave at the top with the animal bones may have been intended to divert and discourage grave robbers from the real grave, which perhaps lies just under it. That principle was used to conceal some of the tombs in Egypt, too.

"We understand that the government intends to initiate a major archeological search there next year, and then perhaps we shall know."

Some Romanians take supernatural phenomena seriously and even believe in dangerous vampires. But the association of Dracula with vampirism is a wholly foreign idea, having originated with the 1897 novel about Dracula by the Irish-born writer Bram Stoker.

Romanian interest in the real Dracula has been enhanced in recent years not only by the tourist attraction that the memory of the "Undead Prince" is generating, but through the painstaking research of two American historians, Raymond T. McNally and Radu Florescu.

The Dracula studies of these two scholars are regarded as definitive by at least one cabinet minister of the Communist government of Romania.

4. Select a news story from the front page of your local paper and rewrite it as a 50-word radio or television news story. Now take that same story and rewrite it as a 100-word radio or television news story.

5. Use VCRs to tape three network broadcasts that occur at the same time each day (e.g., 5:30 p.m.). Show the three broadcasts in class and compare the news selection and order of stories presented. Did all three newscasts cover the same stories in the same order? Which of the newscasts do you think placed the stories in the proper order? Did any network fail to include an important story?

6. Write a 30-second radio commercial and a 30-second TV commercial for some brand of jeans. For the TV commercial, draw storyboards to show how the video will progress from segment to segment. A storyboard shows the most important images (frames) from a commercial as envisioned by the writers and artists. It is not essential that your artwork be outstanding, but it is important to get the message across.

CHAPTER
seventeen

Careers in Journalism

High school journalism can be a stepping-stone to becoming a professional journalist. Skills learned at the high school level are the same skills that professional journalists use daily. Professionals go through the same process that high school journalists do in selecting stories. They base their decisions on the importance of the story to their audience, the timeliness of the story, and the human interest factors involved.

Professionals also use the same guidelines in deciding placement of articles, realizing that front-page stories and stories placed at the top of a page are more likely to be read than those buried at the bottom of a page or on inside pages.

Being responsible is also a concern of professionals. They, like high school journalists, strive for accuracy, balance, and objectivity. It is the role of media at all levels to give their audience all the facts necessary for a complete understanding of an issue and to report those facts in an unbiased manner.

It is also the responsibility of the professional media to identify opinion, or editorial comment. Professional broadcasters introduce editorial comment by saying, "This is the opinion of this station," and they usually conclude such a broadcast by saying, "This has been an editorial comment based on the opinion of this station."

Print media clearly label editorials. Most editorial pages of professional papers run a partial masthead (staff box) and include in it a brief summary of editorial policy.

USA Today, for example, says in its masthead that "it hopes to serve as a forum for better understanding and unity to help make the USA truly one nation."

Most editorial pages are distinctive by their consistency. A larger type size and wider columns than in the rest of the paper are generally used. Standing columns help to identify editorial pages. High school papers also try to make the design of editorial pages distinctive, as discussed in Chapter 11.

High school journalists who are contemplating a career in journalism would be wise to learn the rules of writing as presented in this book, as they are basically the same rules used by all journalists. Copyreading and proofreading symbols are international, and the symbols are printed in dictionaries and stylebooks.

Style rules are usually similar in nature, although each publication has its own style. Rules of grammar, spelling, and punctuation, however, are universal.

Job possibilities in journalism-related careers are international in scope. With the growing use of word processors and computers, knowledge of typing and use of the word processor are becoming even more important. Some jobs may require only a high school education; others require some college training. A special talent, interest, or skill, coupled with journalism training, can be an additional asset. Examples are knowledge of a foreign language or medical science or expertise in carpentry or outdoor living.

Advertising

There are more than 5,000 advertising agencies in the United States, and the number is growing. Competition for the advertising dollar is intense among the media. Advertising agencies employ copywriters, account managers, media directors, production managers, and research directors.

Magazines, newspapers, radio, and television also employ copywriters, managers, and salespeople. Some retail stores have their own advertising staffs, which include copywriters and managers.

These jobs require some proficiency in writing and speaking. Good oral and written communication skills are mandatory. A general background in business is also desirable.

> ➢ *Journalism Career Perks*
> • *Travel opportunities abound for many reporters.*
> • *Opportunities to meet and interview personalities.*
> • *Satisfaction in knowing you are influencing others.*
> • *Satisfaction of knowing you're recording history.*
> • *Great way to improve one's writing and editing abilities.*

425

High School Journalism

➢ Web Site
Designer

High school is a
good place to learn
how to be a Web site
designer by develop-
ing a Web site for the
high school yearbook
or newspaper. Good
Web site designers
will:

• Learn how to
market a product.

• Create a well-
designed home page.

• Provide a number
of different links, each
with a different pur-
pose. One link could
be a promotional one.

• Include appeal-
ing graphics.

• Provide an
e-mail address to give
those who access the
site a chance to
react.

• Include a list of
staff members.

• Be aware of
various software pro-
grams available for
building Web sites.
These include
PageMill, Netscape
Gold, and Microsoft
Publisher. PageMaker
6.5 also includes Web
software.

• Know how to
scan photos and use
digital cameras.

• Know how to
maintain the site.

Agricultural Journalism

Some agricultural publications are in print today. These publications employ advertising copywriters, managers, and salespeople as well as circulation managers, editors, and reporters. A general knowledge of agricultural terminology and the latest advances in farming would be helpful for some-one desiring a career in this area.

Book Publishing

Jobs available in this area include advertising and promo-tion managers, designers, production managers, editors, copy-editors, readers, sales managers, and salespeople. Book editors and copyeditors need solid skills in English usage.

Business

The world of business, from corporations to small firms, is finding its need for clear communication as great as ever and competent, well-trained people harder than ever to find.

Commercial Artist

Commercial artists create visual images for advertise-ments, instructional materials, and other communications media, such as newspapers, magazines, and books. The main employers of commercial artists are advertising agencies and large corporations. Commercial artists at a managerial level with an advertising agency usually work side by wide with copywriters to formulate advertising campaigns. Most publish-ers of magazines, newspapers, and books also need commer-cial artists who can create layouts and produce pages. Commercial artists who work with desktop publishing must have a knowledge of graphics design. They must also be famil-iar with computer software programs, typography, illustra-tions, and page makeup.

Possible Newspaper Positions

- *General assignment reporters: Must have a "nose for news" and be willing to be persistent in getting information for a story.*
- *Wire reporters: Scan stories coming over the wire to see which ones might be reprinted or localized through additional reporting.*
- *Copyeditors or rewrite persons: Check all copy for accuracy, libel, and grammatical correctness. Add information as necessary to make story complete.*
- *Specialized writers: These reporters cover specific areas, such as travel, entertainment, education, medicine, and sports.*
- *Editors: These individuals assign stories for a particular section of the paper and oversee the production of that section. The editor-in-chief oversees the production of the entire paper.*
- *Managing editor: Ultimately responsible for production of the paper. Usually oversees the various department editors and reports directly to the editor-in-chief.*
- *Circulation or business manager: The circulation manager is in charge of distribution of the paper. The business manager oversees advertising sales and sets up advertising campaigns.*

Copywriters

Copywriters create the scripts—the copy—for advertising and marketing campaigns. Copywriting is often the entry point into the advertising profession. For others it is an introduction to a writing career. Copywriters must have the ability to sell a product through the written word. That product may be a car, a box of cereal, or even a story.

Desktop Publishing

Because most publications today are using computers, careers in word processing and computer design have become plentiful in the world of journalism. Knowledge of various types of computers and software programs is essential for a career in desktop publishing. A college education is not necessary. However, a college education might be necessary to become a computer engineer or a computer programmer. Computer engineers work primarily to integrate hardware components with software, and computer programmers manage or maintain computer systems. A degree in computer science might be desirable, but degrees in information science and electronics technology are also worthwhile. Some computer programmers receive degrees in electrical engineering. The Institute for Certification of Computer Professionals predicts that the growth market in computer programming will increase remarkably in the next few years.

Magazines

Writers, promotion managers, production managers, layout designers, editors, business and circulation managers, and advertising managers and salespersons are among the positions available with magazines. There are more than 17,000 periodicals in the United States, covering a myriad subjects, so the jobs available are varied in scope. A strong liberal arts background paralleled with journalism training would be beneficial to someone interested in a career in this area.

News Agencies

Wire services such as the Associated Press, United Press International, and Reuters have positions for copyreaders, editors, picture editors, writers, and photographers. Many reporters working for news agencies serve as correspondents, working in large metropolitan areas or in foreign countries.

> **Career Areas**
> • Public relations.
> • Advertising—sales, design, copywriter, market researcher.
> • Television broadcasting.
> • Radio broadcasting.
> • Art Design.
> • Photography.
> • Business management.
> • TV camera operator.
> • Sound technician.
> • Video technician.
> • Graphic design.

Newspapers

Newspaper careers are as varied as those with magazines, since there are so many types of newspapers, ranging from the large metropolitan daily to the weekly suburban paper to the small-town monthly. Jobs available include advertising copywriters and salespeople, business and circulation managers, cartoonists, critics (art, books, drama, movies, music), columnists, copyreaders, copyeditors, editorial writers, editors (book section, city, feature, financial, picture, religious, society, sports, Sunday, wire, women's page, travel), feature writers, foreign correspondents, reporters, rewrite people, Washington correspondents, and promotion managers.

A liberal arts background with courses in history, literature, political science, economics, sociology, psychology, philosophy, science, speech, and foreign languages can be beneficial to the newspaper journalist. Such a background coupled with journalistic training would be wise.

Photography

Jobs for photographers in journalism are numerous, as all areas of journalism use pictures. Besides being a photojournalist for a publication, however, photographers with a strong knowledge of photo equipment and some business know-how would have the option of operating a photo store.

Public Relations

Most large companies and corporations have public relations offices. So do large newspapers, magazines, and radio and television stations. Even school districts have public relations directors. Many of the companies and corporations produce their own public relations magazine. Jobs for writers, counselors, editors, and photographers are among those available. Public relations firms provide services for various organizations.

Radio and Television

To be an announcer on radio or television requires some different skills than being a reporter for the print media, but a need for strong writing skills still exists. Announcers must have solid speech skills and the ability to ad-lib. Several jobs exist in radio and television that do not require on-the-air performance, including copywriter, news writer, editor, program director, station manager, promotion manager, and advertising salesperson.

Research

Market researchers, research analysts, and reader-interest surveyors are all special-interest positions available in today's job market. Many major businesses employ researchers to study the consumer and why he or she buys or does not buy a product.

Syndicates

Syndicates provide lucrative jobs for some people, including cartoonists and columnists. Syndicated work appears in several publications. Most syndicated columnists and cartoonists begin work for one publication and when their work becomes well known go into syndication.

Teaching

Although most secondary schools in the United States have only one journalism teacher, good ones are still hard to find. Strong writing skills and a love of journalism are essential if one is to be successful in teaching the subject.

Jobs are also available for teaching at the college level, and many colleges have positions for directors of publications. Employment possibilities in journalism are numerous. Those desiring a career in journalism must examine the choices and make a choice based on individual needs, talents, and resources.

Online Communications

Technology has opened doors to jobs that were not available a few years ago. Video photographers are in demand now. Writers are needed--some for copy and some for audio. Audio writing is different than copy writing. Saying words is different from writing them. A good speaking voice is a plus. Computer whizzes who are artists are also in demand, as are individuals who are Web savvy. Knowing how to design a visually attractive Web page is a plus. Knowing how to use PhotoShop is a plus. Marketers are also in demand by Internet companies. Although Internet companies need people who know the technology, they also need those who know how to sell the products.

EXERCISES

1. Visit a local newspaper, magazine, radio station, television station, advertising agency, public relations firm, or book publisher and write a report on your observations.

2. Interview a professional journalist and write a report on his/her experiences.

3. Invite a professional journalist to speak to your class to point out the thrills and the frustrations of his or her profession.

4. Invite a Web designing expert to your class to talk to you about how to design a Web page and to talk to you about possible careers with online companies.

G
L
O
S
S
A
R
Y

Glossary

ad   Abbreviation for advertising.

add   Additional copy to be added to the end of a story.

advance story   Story about an event to occur in the future.

agate   5½ point type.

airbrush   Small pressure gun shaped like a pencil that sprays watercolor pigments by means of compressed air; used to correct or alter photographs or artwork.

all caps   Words typed or printed entirely in capital letters.

AP   Abbreviation for Associated Press, a news-gathering organization.

applied color   One or more silkscreen lacquers or lithographic inks applied to a cover to decorate or distinguish the design.

art board   Durable, protective paperbase board on which artwork is mounted or drawn to prevent damage in shipping and handling. Used to put down own headlines, rule lines, and photographs.

artwork   Any hand-produced illustrative or decorative material submitted for printing; e.g., drawings, paintings, collages, and ornamental, typographic, or lined borders.

backbone   The bound side of a book; also called spine.

bank   Section of a headline; also called deck.

banner   Headline that extends across the top of a page; also called streamer.

beat   Source of news that a reporter covers regularly.

bleed   Picture that runs to the edge of the page or across the gutter of a two-page spread.

body copy   Main text of a page, section, or book, as distinguished from headlines or captions.

boldface   Type that is heavier and blacker than standard type.

box   Materials enclosed by a border line, either completely or partially.

byline   Name of the writer, usually placed between the headline and the story.

candids   Generally unposed pictures taken without the subject's knowledge or consent.

caption   Identifying copy for a picture; also called legend or cutline.

caricature Humorous exaggeration of the outstanding features of a person or thing.

center of interest The focal point of a picture, page, or spread.

close register The printing of two or more colors within six points of each other, partially or completely overlapped, resulting in increased printing precision.

collage Work of art composed by pasting on a single artboard various materials such as photos, newspaper clippings, etc.

column The width of one line of type in a newspaper or yearbook.

condensed type Narrow or slender typeface.

contrast Degree of difference between dark and light parts of a picture. In black-and-white prints, contrast is obtained by having an appropriate amount of blacks and whites mixed in with grays.

copy Typed material sent to the printer.

copy-fitting Determining the amount of copy that can fit into a given area in a specified size and style of type.

copyreading Checking typed copy to make sure it is accurate and properly styled.

credit line Line of type stating the source of the material.

crop marks Black ballpoint marks on the white margin of photographic prints, or masking tape overlays on transparencies, or grease-pencil marks, that indicate where the print is to be cropped.

cropping Eliminating unwanted portions of a picture.

crossline Headline made up of a single line of type running across two or more columns.

cut Engraved plate of a photograph or artwork to be printed.

cutout background (COB) Elimination of background of a photo, leaving only the center of interest.

deadline Time by which all materials must be ready.

deck Section of a headline; also called a bank.

display type Type that is larger than body type, used for headlines and advertising.

division page Page that introduces a section of a yearbook.

downstyle Headline style in which capitalization is limited, usually to the first letter and proper nouns.

drop-line Headline having two or more lines of the same length with each succeeding line indented.

dummy Layout of a newspaper page or a yearbook spread, showing the position of each story and picture.

duotone   Photograph printed in two colors.

ears   Boxes on either side of a newspaper's name on page one.

editing   Checking reporter's copy; see copyreading.

edition   One issue of a newspaper or yearbook.

editorial   Article of opinion or interpretation.

editorial policy   Rules for publishing a newspaper or yearbook.

elements   Items that comprise a page (photographs, headlines, artwork, copy, white space).

em   The square of any given size of type.

en   One-half the width of an em.

enlargement   Increase in the size of a photo or artwork.

external margins   White space between the printed or written matter and the edge of the page.

eye flow   Natural eye movement from left to right.

family   One particular design or style of type in all its sizes, weights, widths, and variants.

feature   The most interesting fact in a story.

feature story   Article designed to entertain as well as to inform.

filler   Extra material used to fill space.

flag   The name of a newspaper as printed on the front page; also called nameplate.

flush left   Copy set so that the left margin forms a straight vertical line.

flush right   Copy set so that the right margin forms a straight vertical line.

folio   Page number and identifying information.

follow-up story   Story written after an event has occurred.

font   The complete set of a given size and style of type.

full color   Reproduction of a photograph in natural color (four colors).

graphics   Combinations of type (heads, text/body copy, captions/cuts, folios), art (illustrations, photos), and white space in a special way for effect.

guideline   Key to the printer to identify a story; also called slug.

gutter   The space between columns on a printed page of a newspaper or between facing pages in a yearbook.

halftone   Reproduction of a black-and-white continuous tone original with a pattern of tiny dots that vary in size.

hanging indent   Headline with at least three lines; the first line fills the column and each succeeding line is indented one em.

headline   Type, usually 18-point or larger, used to introduce a story or a yearbook spread.

headline schedule Set of headline patterns to be used in a newspaper.

initial letter Letter in a larger size of type used to begin paragraphs.

internal margin The distance between elements on a page or spread.

interview story Type of story in which the facts are gathered primarily by interviewing another person or persons.

inverted pyramid Type of headline consisting of three or more lines; the first line fills the column and succeeding lines are decreased by the same number of units on each side and centered. It is also a method of writing a story using facts in the order of importance.

isolated element Layout style in which one element is separated from all others by at least 2 picas.

italic Style of letters that slant forward, in distinction from upright, or roman letters.

justified Copy set so that left and right margins are flush, forming a perfect column.

kicker Phrase used above headline to identify page or to introduce the main headline.

layout design Arrangement of the elements of a spread.

lead Introduction of a story.

leading Space between lines of type.

letterpress Method of printing in which the impression is made directly by type and engravings.

libel False material that damages a person's reputation.

loose register Printing of colored inks so that the colors are printed at least one pica from each other.

lowercase Small letters of a typeface.

masthead Statement of ownership, principles, and other facts pertaining to a publication.

modified layout Layout style in which one element bleeds to each of the four sides of a yearbook spread.

modular layout Horizontal or vertical layout of a page.

Mondrian layout Layout style in which all external elements bleed.

morgue Newspaper library in which stories, clippings, and cuts are filed.

mortice Window or clear space in a photograph or artwork that is photomechanically dropped out so that type or a photo may be inserted.

mosaic layout　Layout style that bleeds only one picture to the external margin.

mug shot　Portrait showing head and shoulders of a subject.

multiple　One side of a signature (pages 1, 4, 5, 8–9, 12–13, 16); also called flat.

natural spread　Two-page spread that falls naturally in the center of a folded signature or section (pages 8–9 of the first 16-page signature).

offset printing　Method of printing that involves photographic processes.

overline　Type set over a cut.

overprint　Printing of one color over another color. Also, the printing of one color over another application of the same color, such as printing solid black type over a black-and-white halftone.

paneling　Series of photographs printed directly next to each other or separated only by a thin tool line.

paste-up　Pasting up type, line art, and photo blocks on a layout sheet.

pica　Unit of measurement one-sixth of an inch in length.

point　Unit used for indicating the size of type; 1/72 of an inch equals one point.

popouts　Partial cutouts.

portrait　Photograph of a person usually emphasizing head and shoulders; also called mug shot.

posterization　Special effect adapted from a direct line, in which a shade of dark gray is photomechanically inserted along with pure black-and-white values.

process color　Printing of yellow, magenta, cyan, and black in various intensities, values, and screens to reproduce full-color photographs or art.

proof　Impression of type ready to be proofread.

proofreader　Person who reads printed material for errors.

proportion　Comparative relation between the width and height of photographs, artwork, and copy.

reverse　Type, a geometric shape, or art illustration inside a halftone or tint background that is not printed, allowing the color of the paper to show through—thought of as white print on a dark background.

rewrite　Altering a story for purposes of improvement.

roman type　Style of type that does not slant; it is characterized by serifs.

running head   Headline that extends across both pages of a double-page spread.

sans serif   Type without serifs (hooks on ends of letters).

scaleograph   Cropping and proportioning tool.

screen   Device for printing a color or black in a lighter shade than its maximum density, usually 30, 50, or 70 percent.

scoop   News that has not been published before.

second color   Color other than black.

serifs   Hooks at the ends of the main stems of letters.

sideways type   Words set sideways.

signature   Folded section of a book, usually 16 pages.

special effect   Photographic distortion making a picture appear as artwork.

spread   Facing pages.

streamer   Headline that extends across the top of a page; also called a banner.

subhead   Minor headline or title, usually set in a point size larger than body copy.

tip-in   Insert, usually of a different paper stock, glued to a bound page of a publication.

tombstones   Headlines similar in type style and size, placed side by side.

trapped white space   Area of white space more than 2 picas by 2 picas, separating photographs or copy and giving an appearance of disunity to the design.

tripod head   Three-part headline, with the line at left at least twice the size of two lines at the right.

UPI   United Press International, a news-gathering organization.

widow   Line of type less than column width occurring at the top of a column.

For Further Reading

Bragg, Rick. *Somebody Told Me: The Newspaper Stories off Rick Bragg.* New York: Vintage Books, 2001.

Brooks, Charles (editor). *Best Editorial Cartoons of the Year.* Gretna, LA: Pelican, 2000.

Epstein, Robert. *The Big Book of Creativity Games: Quick, Fun Activities for Jumpstarting Innovation.* New York: McGraw-Hill, 2000.

Gilman, Mary Louise. *One Word, Two Words, Hyphenated?* Vienna, VA: NCRA Press, 1998.

Greenberg, Steven. *Idiot's Guide to Digital Photography.* New York: Prentice Hall, 1999.

Hall, Homer L. and Puntney, Martin. *Observe, React, Think, Write: A Novel Approach to Copy Writing.* Marceline, MO: Walsworth Publishing Company, 1998.

Hall, Homer L. *High School Journalism.* New York: The Rosen Publishing Group, 2003.

Hall, Homer L. and Vahl, Rod. *Effective Editorial Writing.* Fourth Edition. Iowa City, IA: Quill & Scroll, 2000.

Hart, Christopher. *Everything You Ever Wanted to Know About Cartooning But Were Afraid to Draw.* Toronto: Watson-Guptill, 1994.

Hawthorne, Bobby. *The Coverage of Interscholastic Sports.* Austin, TX: Interscholastic League Press Conference, 2001.

Hawthorne, Bobby. *The Radical Write: A Fresh Approach to Journalistic Writing for Students.* Second Edition. Minneapolis, MN: Josten's, Inc., 2003.

Heedgecoe (spelled Hedgecoe), John. *The Photographer's Handbook.* Third Edition. New York: Knopf, 1999.

Horton, Brian. *Associated Press Guide To Photojournalism.* New York: McGraw Hill, 2001.

Levin, Mark. *The Reporter's Notebook: Writing Tools for Student Journalists.* Columbus: NC: Mind-Stretch Publishing 2000.

McClelland, Deke and Eismann, Katrin. *Real World Digital*

Photography. Berkley, CA: Peachpit Press, 1999.

Price-Groff. *Extraordinary Women Journalists*. Danbury, CT: Children's Press, 1997.

Raskin, James B. *We the Students: Supreme Court Decisions for and About Students*. Washington, D.C.: Congressional Quarterly Books, 2000.

Reilly, Rick. *The Life of Reilly: The Best of Sports Illustrated's Rick Reilly*. New York: Total/Sports Illustrated, 2000.

Ryan, Buck and O'Donnell, Michael. *The Editor's Toolbox*. Ames, IA: Iowa State University Press, 2001.

Shrunk, William Jr., and White, E.B. *Elements of Style*. Fourth Edition. Boston, MA: Allyn & Bacon, 2000.

Savant, Marilyn vos. *The Art of Spelling: The Madness and the Method*. New York: W.W. Norton, 2000.

Titelman, Gregory. *Random House Dictionary of American Popular Proverbs and Sayings*. New York: Random House, 2000.

West, Edie. *Icebreakers: Group Mixers, Warm-Ups, Energizers, and Playful Activities*. New York: McGraw-Hill, 1997.

Index

INDEX

INDEX

I
N
D
E
X

I
N
D
E
X

INDEX

I
N
D
E
X